Language Change

How and why do languages change? This new introduction offers a guide to the types of change at all levels of linguistic structure, as well as the mechanisms behind each type. Based on data from a variety of methods and a huge array of language families, it examines general patterns of change, bringing together recent findings on sound change, analogical change, grammaticalization, the creation and change of constructions, as well as lexical change. Emphasizing crosslinguistic patterns and going well beyond traditional methods in historical linguistics, this book sees change as grounded in cognitive processes and usage factors that are rarely mentioned in other textbooks. Complete with questions for discussion, suggested readings, and a useful glossary of terms, this book helps students to gain a general understanding of language as an ever-changing system.

JOAN BYBEE is Distinguished Professor Emerita of Linguistics at the University of New Mexico.

CAMBRIDGE TEXTBOOKS IN LINGUISTICS

General editors: P. AUSTIN, J. BRESNAN, B. COMRIE, S. CRAIN, W. DRESSLER,
C. EWEN, R. LASS, D. LIGHTFOOT, K. RICE, I. ROBERTS, S. ROMAINE,
N.V. SMITH

Language Change

Language Change

JOAN BYBEE

University of New Mexico

CAMBRIDGE
UNIVERSITY PRESS

University Printing House, Cambridge CB2 8BS, United Kingdom

Cambridge University Press is part of the University of Cambridge.

It furthers the University's mission by disseminating knowledge in the pursuit of
education, learning and research at the highest international levels of excellence.

www.cambridge.org
Information on this title: www.cambridge.org/9781107655829

First published 2015
Reprinted 2016

Printed in the United Kingdom by Clays Ltd, St Ives plc

A catalogue record for this publication is available from the British Library

Library of Congress Cataloging-in-Publication Data
Bybee, Joan L.
Language change / Joan Bybee, University of New Mexico.
    pages cm
Includes bibliographical references.
ISBN 978-1-107-02016-0 (Hardback: alk. paper) – ISBN 978-1-107-65582-9 (Paperback: alk. paper)
1. Linguistic change.   2. Historical linguistics.   I. Title.
P142.B93 2015
417'.7–dc23   2014037873

ISBN 978-1-107-02016-0 Hardback
ISBN 978-1-107-65582-9 Paperback

Contents

Figures

Tables

Preface

Language change is endlessly fascinating, whether it involves change in sounds, morphology, words, syntax, or meaning. When language changes we see that language users are not just passive recipients of the language of their culture, but are active participants in the very dynamic system that is communication with spoken language. Change reveals the nature of the cognitive processes and patterns used in speaking and listening, and shows us what ordinary language users can make out of the material they are given to work with. In fact, I believe that no approach to language is complete unless it deals as much with language change as with language states. Because I find change so revealing, it is no surprise that of all the courses I have taught, Language Change at the introductory level has always been my favorite. In that course I can lay out what is revealed by particular changes and demonstrate how the main patterns of change produce the general phenomena of language.

This emphasis on the dynamic aspects of language has also guided my research, so that the topics that go into a course on language change are many of the same topics I have focused on in my research, such as sound change, the morphologization of sound change, analogical change, and grammaticalization.

This book reflects my approach to teaching and understanding language change that has developed over many years of teaching and doing research. I have chosen to call the book *Language Change* because the perspective I have developed is more integrated with cognitive and usage factors than the perspective found in more traditional historical linguistics textbooks. I seek to suggest a certain coherence in the nature of change and thus, rather than cataloging and labeling the many types of change that have been identified over the centuries of study of how languages change, I hope to give students an idea of the major trends in change by accessing examples now available on change in many different languages and language families and reporting what is known about which changes are common and which are not. While I try to avoid polemical discussions in the book, I do have a certain perspective that drives the presentation; it is the view that language change takes place during language use, and the mechanisms that drive change are the psycholinguistic or cognitive processes operating in everyday conversation and language use.

The motivation for writing the book was to fill in certain gaps that occur in the excellent historical linguistics textbooks that were available when I regularly taught Language Change. I have tried to follow the lead of the excellent books written by Campbell 1999, Crowley 1997, Hock 1986, and Trask 1995 (many of which exist in more recent editions than I am citing here). My decision to produce a book on language change rather than on historical linguistics follows from a desire to produce a more up-to-date treatment and one more integrated with new findings in cognitive and functional linguistics.

In particular, I feel that the topic of grammaticalization, which has recently generated so much research with stunning results, deserves a focused presentation in a book on language change, and this is absent from all other general surveys. So in this book two chapters examine the general mechanisms of change and survey the common paths of grammaticalization discovered in the languages of the world. I also feel that what we know about the traditional topic of analogical change has benefitted greatly from an examination of the processing and usage factors involved in change and, just as important, resistance to change. Analogical change can now be approached as the interaction of a number of cognitive factors, rather than by the traditional list of "principles". The other great pillar of historical linguistics – sound change – can also be presented in a more coherent way as we learn more about sound change in the languages of the world. Rather than a disjointed laundry list of named types, we now know what types of change are more common and can begin to formulate some general hypotheses about the directionality and causes of sound change. We also have a clearer understanding of how sound changes diffuse through the lexicon. Finally, our understanding of syntactic change has made great strides due to the view that syntactic constructions develop from looser discourse structures using some of the same mechanisms we see in grammaticalization. In addition, viewing morphosyntax as expressed by constructions, we are able to examine the questions of where constructions come from, how they compete with pre-existing constructions, and what happens to old constructions. In addition, we can address the question of how constructionalization and grammaticalization interact with word-order change. In all these areas, we now have valuable studies of change in progress, which are essential to the identification of the mechanisms and processes involved in change.

The inclusion of these topics and particular approaches taken to the factors involved make this book a good companion to any synchronic approach that recognizes cognitive and usage factors in understanding language. The book is directed towards anyone who has a basic grounding in linguistics and would like to know more about how languages change, whether they are approaching this goal with a professor in a class on language change or reading on their own. If it contributes to the understanding of the linguistic phenomena that interest the reader, it will have succeeded in its goals.

Acknowledgements

It was on the suggestion of Andrew Winnard, editor at Cambridge University Press, that I considered writing a book, as he put it, to help students learning about language change. I had originally intended just to write up my class notes from the many times I have taught Language Change. However, once embarked on the project, I felt compelled to write a more inclusive account with examples that I would never have had time to present in class. This was partly for myself, to see for myself how the different areas of historical linguistics were each internally coherent, to argue for directionality in change, and to identify outstanding theoretical problems for our understanding of language change.

The perspective presented here has evolved in my own mind over several decades, starting with the influence of my first teachers, notably Theo Vennemann at UCLA and colleagues such as Tom Givon, whose class I attended at the 1976 Linguistic Institute, where I was also teaching. Joseph Greenberg's methods of diachronic typology, and his use of grammaticalization were imparted via Givon's lectures. The many colleagues whose interest in grammaticalization blossomed along with mine were very helpful in clarifying the phenomenon and my views about it. I thank Elizabeth Traugott, Bernd Heine, Paul Hopper, and William Pagliuca. I have also been influenced by the many brilliant students in Language Change classes as well as Grammaticalization classes over the years. Among them are William Pagliuca, Richard Mowrey, Scott Schwenter, K. Aaron Smith, Rena Torres Cacoullos, Damian Wilson, Esther Brown, Jessi Aaron, and Matt Alba, just to mention a few.

In preparing the manuscript I was fortunate to be able to call on colleagues with expertise in areas I have not researched myself. In particular, Larry Hyman and Jeff Stebbins helped me with material on tone change and reviewed my interpretations of it. Rena Torres Cacoullos and Shana Poplack discussed language contact with me and helped with comments on these sections. Carol Lord reviewed parts of the manuscript on serialization and grammaticalization. Also, I appreciate the folks I called on to help with specific examples or topics: Christopher Adams and Peter Petré. I am also grateful to my friends who were willing to just talk generally about the book with me and to offer support: Sandy Thompson, Bill Croft, and Carol Lynn Moder. Of course, any remaining errors of fact or interpretation are completely my own responsibility.

Series editor Bernard Comrie went far beyond the call of duty with a careful reading of the entire manuscript resulting in numerous valuable suggestions, most of which I was able to implement. For reading specific chapters and offering comments, I owe a debt to Carol Lynn Moder and Damián Wilson. For reading the whole manuscript to check for errors and incongruities of all kinds and for constructing the Language Index, I am grateful to Shelece Easterday. Again, any remaining flaws are entirely my responsibility.

A major "thank you" also goes to Rena Torres Cacoullos and her 2014 students who read Chapters 1 through 9 together in their History of Spanish class at Pennsylvania State University and sent me comments and questions. That was a tremendous help!

1   The study of language change

1.1.   Introduction

This book examines the topic of how and why languages change. This field of study has traditionally been called "historical linguistics" and under that label the history of particular languages has been studied, and methods for the comparison of languages and reconstruction of their family relations have been developed. While this book covers many of the traditional topics in historical linguistics, I have chosen to focus on the topic of how and why languages change because linguistic researchers see now more than ever before that language change is not a phenomenon of the distant past, but is just as evident currently in ongoing changes as it is when we look back into documents that show older stages of languages. Moreover, it has become clear that language change helps us explain the features of language structure because it provides a window onto how those structures come into being and evolve. Thus we identify explanations for the characteristics that language has by examining how language changes.

What we will see as we progress through the types of language change is that change is built into the way language is used. The mental processes that are in play when speakers and listeners communicate are the main causes of change. This helps us explain another very important fact: all languages change in the same ways. Since language users the world over have the same mental processes to work with and they use communication for the same or very similar ends, the changes that come about in languages from Alaska to Zambia fit into the same categories as changes found in English and French.

1.2.   Languages change all the time and in all aspects

The changes in our language that are the most obvious to language users are changes in words. Most languages acquire new words fairly easily in ways that you are probably already familiar with. These include borrowing from other languages, derivation by adding prefixes or suffixes to existing words, compounding, and other types of word-formation. Here are some examples:

Borrowing. Most languages borrow words from other languages, especially when new items or concepts are introduced from another culture. Some recently borrowed words in English are *karaoke* (from Japanese) and *ski* (from Norwegian), and some words borrowed long ago into English from French are *elite, poultry,* and *beef.*

Derivation. Most languages have affixes that can be applied to current words to form new ones: English *hyperactiveness, ethnicness.* Also English easily changes nouns into verbs: for example, when the name of a tool is used for the action of using the tool, as in *He was **hammering** a cedar plank.*

Compounding. Not all languages allow compounding, but Germanic languages use it quite a bit to form new words. *Text-message, text-messaging, YouTube, MySpace.* English compounds can be identified because they are two-word sequences that are stressed more heavily on the first word than on the second one.

Also, changes in spelling and punctuation (or the lack of it) have been cropping up since people started using a lot of e-mail and text-messaging. Examples are *LOL* ('laugh out loud') or *OMG* ('oh my god'). These are changes in the written form of language and do not have much effect on spoken language, except to the extent that we use these abbreviations in speaking.

However, most changes in language occur slowly and gradually, and sometimes we do not notice that these changes are going on right under our noses. This applies to changes in the sounds of a language and also to changes in morphological and syntactic constructions. A very distinguished American linguist, Leonard Bloomfield, wrote in his book *Language,* originally published in 1933, "The process of linguistic change has never been directly observed" (Bloomfield 1933: 347). We can see what he means if we consider how complex language change can be. One speaker can make a change, say by regularizing a verb such as *slept* saying *sleeped* instead, or by pronouncing *I don't think* without a real [d] sound in *don't* or extending a construction by saying *that drove me out the window* to mean 'that drove me crazy', but until the change is taken up by other members of the community, we do not regard an innovation as a change. Thus it *is* difficult to observe change since it requires knowledge of the mental processes that lead to the innovations as well as the social processes that allow them to spread.

Yet Bloomfield was probably being too pessimistic. Now it is possible to search large corpora of spoken and written language from different periods of time and different geographic regions and to observe how an innovation or a variant spreads and gains acceptability. Now we also know more about the mental processes within the speaker and hearer that make innovation and spread of change possible.

Even though changes in words are the most obvious sorts of changes, they are not usually very systematic nor do they have much impact on the general structure of languages. So in this book we will be more concerned with changes in the phonology and structure of languages and in semantic changes that correspond to structural changes. We will see that change can affect all aspects of language from the sounds to the morphology and syntax all the way to the meaning of words and constructions. Here are a few examples.

We have just read about some examples of how new words come into a language. Established words can also change their meaning. It is often the case that when a word has two or more meanings, one of them is the older meaning and the others were derived from it by usage in context. For example, the English noun *field* refers both to a piece of ground and an area of study or investigation. The more concrete meaning of 'piece of ground' came earlier, and the more abstract metaphorical meaning came later.

A different sort of example concerns the Spanish verb *quedar* in a construction with an adjective, such as *quieto* 'still' or *sorprendido* 'surprised'. Earlier *quedar(se)* meant 'stay', but now in this construction it can also mean 'become' as in *se quedó quieto* 's/he became still'.

In the West African language Yoruba, the verb *fi* 'take' can be used in a serial construction with other verbs, as in (1) (Stahlke 1970):

(1)   mo   fi   àdé   gé igi
        I   took machete cut tree
        'I cut the tree with the machete'

In (1) the verb *fi* can either mean 'take' or 'with', but in (2) it can only mean 'with':

(2)   mo   fi   ọgbọ̀n   gé   igi
        I   took   cleverness cut tree
        'I cut the tree cleverly'

So this verb with the more concrete meaning of 'take' has also taken on the more abstract meaning of instrumental or manner.

The meanings of constructions can change, too. A resultative construction of the form

(3)   SUBJECT   + *have/has*   +   OBJECT   + PAST PARTICIPLE

as in *I have the letter written* occurred in Old English and in fact still occurs in English. This construction gave rise to our present perfect construction, as in *I have written the letter*, which does not signal resultative but rather anterior or perfect, with the meaning 'a past action has been completed and it has current relevance'.

Also the outward form of a word can change, especially if it is made up of more than one morpheme. Thus the English verb *work* formerly had *wrought* as its past participle (the form used in the passive and present perfect, as in *he has wrought*), but now the past participle is regular, as in *he has worked*. In Latin the verb meaning 'to be able' had stem forms based on *poss-* (first person present indicative as well as present and imperfect subjunctive) and also *pot-* (for most other forms). For instance, *possum* was the first person singular present indicative. This root became *pod- /pued-* in Spanish and the first person singular present indicative is *puedo* which replaced the irregular forms with the medial *ss*.

Pronunciations also change quite commonly, and such changes usually affect all the words that have a particular sound; we can see that by comparing American and British English. Since much of North America was colonized by people from Britain, in the seventeenth and eighteenth centuries the same varieties of English were spoken on both sides of the Atlantic. But since then, changes have taken place in both American and British English that now make them different in the way they are pronounced. For instance, American English speakers pronounce a /t/ or /d/ in the middle of a word before an unstressed syllable as a flap [ɾ] as in *butter* or *rider*, but most British English speakers still use a /t/ or /d/ in this position or substitute a glottal stop. Thus we can say that the sound change of flapping of /t/ and /d/ has occurred in American English.

Syntactic structure also changes over time. In English before the middle of the sixteenth century, in a question the verb was placed before the subject. These syntactic structures remained in some of Shakespeare's plays, as in the following:

(4)   *What say you of this gentlewoman? (All's Well that Ends Well, 1.3)*

In Present Day English, however, with most verbs, we use *do* in questions, as in (5), and it occurs before the subject rather than the main verb.

(5)   *What do you say about this lady?*

This change, among others in English, resulted in a special class of verbs designated as 'auxiliaries'.

A structural change took place in French when the construction for the negative *ne ... pas* developed. In Old French (ninth to fourteenth centuries) the marker of negation for a clause was *ne* and it appeared before the verb and also before any object pronouns, as in the fourteenth-century example in (6) from Jehan Froissart (*Chroniques, Livre Premier, Bataille de Cocherel*).

(6)   mais on <u>ne</u>   lui   avoit voulu ouvrir   les portes
       but   one <u>NEG</u>   them have   wanted open-INF the doors
       'but one had not wanted to open the doors for them'

Even at this period it was common to reinforce the negation by adding a noun after the verb such as *pas* 'step', *point* 'dot, point', *mie* 'crumb', or *gote* 'drop'. In Modern French negation is ordinarily made by putting *ne* before the verb and *pas* after it. Now *pas* no longer means 'step' but is just part of the negative construction, as in (7):

(7)   *avant c'était une institution, qui comme toutes les administrations,* <u>*ne*</u>
       communiquait <u>*pas*</u>*...*
       'before it was an institution, like all administrations, it did not communicate ...'

Now while one can leave out the *ne* (see discussion below), the *pas* is essential to expressing negation.

All the languages that have ever been studied diachronically show changes in all these aspects. But it is not just the fact of change that attracts our attention, but also the nature of change. There are certain common patterns and directions of change that occur over and over again in the same language or in different languages. We will be examining these patterns in the chapters of this book. We will see that change itself is inherent in language and can tell us something about the nature of language and its structures. Thus, studying how languages change is just another way to do linguistics, that is, to try to understand how language works.

1.3. Languages also keep old features around a long time

The previous section mentioned the importance of the social dimension in language change. Language is conventional. What this means is that it has to be used in pretty much the same way by speakers and listeners in order to be effective as communication. In addition, language is specific to communities of people and helps to define these communities. For this reason, each speaker tends to use language in a way that is very, very similar, if not identical, to the way it is used by other members of the same community. Here 'community' refers to social or geographic groups, usually both together. That is, you might speak very similarly to your parents and siblings and/or the people you went to school with or the people you hang out with now. Actually, we all have the ability to adapt to current situations by modifying our choice of sounds, words, and structures to fit in better if we choose.

The conventionality of language holds back change to a certain extent. Since speakers have to use established words, sounds, and patterns to be understood, these established patterns are reinforced and that contributes to their stability. Today we use many expressions, words, sounds, and constructions that have been used continuously for centuries and even millennia. Because of this, languages contain within them nuggets of information about their histories. The following are some examples.

Modern European languages contain many words that can be traced back thousands of years to the reconstructed language Proto-Indo-European. For instance, when you refer to your nose with the English word *nose* or the French word *nez*, Russian *nos*, or Swedish *näsa* you are continuing a tradition that started more than 6000 years ago! The similarity among these words is part of the evidence that the words for 'nose' in these languages are of very ancient origin.

Another place we find ancient patterns is in irregular morphology. The vowel changes we find in English verbs such as *take/took, choose/chose, fight/fought* are similar to vowel changes found in other Germanic languages, such as Dutch, German, Icelandic, and other Scandinavian languages. The fact that they are shared by these sister languages shows that they originated more than 2000 years ago. Yet we still use them today to signal past tense.

Relics of older forms can also be found in idiomatic expressions, though they are rarely as old as the preceding examples. For instance, the phrase *far be it from me* contains the subjunctive form *be* as a finite form; while the subjunctive was quite alive in Old English, it is all but lost in Present Day English. Also, this expression has the verb inverted with the subject after the adverb, *far*. This is also an older pattern that is not used as often today.

Compounds, idioms, and derived words also sometimes preserve old words that have been lost elsewhere. For instance, the English compound *werewolf* contains the old word for 'man', which was *were, wera*. The phrase *the quick and the dead* uses the word *quick* in its old meaning of 'alive'.

Older syntactic structures can be preserved in particular contexts. In the last section we saw that in sixteenth-century English, main verbs came before the subject in questions, such as *What say you of this gentlewoman?* In current English, this verb does not appear before the subject, but the auxiliaries still do:

(8)   *What can you say about this lady?*

(9)   *What should I do to help you?*

The auxiliaries were verbs at an earlier stage, but because they are of relatively high frequency in this type of construction, they maintained the older inverted position when other verbs came to form questions with *do*.

Languages such as Latin, which used suffixes to mark nominative, accusative, and other cases, have case forms for both nouns and pronouns. Today many European languages, such as English, Spanish, French, Italian, and Portuguese, no longer distinguish different cases for nouns. However, all of these languages maintain different forms for nominative vs. accusative in pronouns, and some also distinguish a dative case, too. Thus Spanish has nominative singular forms *yo* 'I', *tú* 'you (familiar), *él* 'he', and *ella* 'she', and these contrast with accusative forms *me* 'me', *te* 'you (familiar)', *lo* 'him', and *la* 'her'. These accusative forms also behave differently from nouns that are functioning as objects, because the pronouns come before the verb, while noun objects come after. This difference in position is probably a retention of an older characteristic as well.

So we see from these examples that, despite the many changes that languages undergo across time periods, many aspects of languages can also stay the same for long periods of time. Although we know that some changes occur more readily than others – for instance, that changes in vowels and consonants occur more rapidly and more often than changes in the basic order of subject, object, and verb in a language (Perkins 1989) – we are still a long way from predicting what is going to change in a language and what is going to stay the same.

1.4.   Evidence for language change

There are many sources of evidence for language change which we will be relying on for examples in this book. Traditionally, the most typical source of evidence comes from the comparison of two stages or different periods of the same language, as, for instance, the comparison of Middle English and Present Day English, or the comparison of Latin and Romance languages, Old Norse and modern Norwegian, Chinese from the Han dynasty with twenty-first-century Mandarin Chinese. Of course, such comparisons require that the earlier stages have a written record, so this type of evidence is not available for all languages. For languages for which earlier written records are available, we can easily spot changes that have occurred.

For instance, we can look back at earlier stages of English and find that the second person singular pronoun for subjects was *thou*, for objects *thee*, and for possessives *thy/thine*. Today, of course, these pronouns are not in use except in very special circumstances (usually religious), and instead for second person singular we use *you* for subjects and objects and *your* for possessives. Consider this passage from the work of William Shakespeare, from the end of the sixteenth century (*As you Like it*, 1.3):

(10)   CELIA
         O my poor Rosalind, whither wilt <u>thou</u> go?
         wilt <u>thou</u> change fathers? I will give <u>thee</u> mine.
         I charge <u>thee</u>, be not <u>thou</u> more grieved than I am.

In the 400 years since Shakespeare wrote this, these second person singular pronouns have disappeared from ordinary conversational speech. In their place we use the forms of *you*, which earlier indicated second person plural.

Changes in sounds also can be tracked in historical documents. For instance, words that are spelled with a *t* between two vowels in Latin are spelled with a *d* in Spanish (which descended from Latin, as did all the Romance languages). Examples are given in (11). (As is traditional in Romance linguistics, the Latin nouns are cited without their case endings to represent what is called Vulgar Latin.)

(11) | Latin | Spanish | Gloss |
         |-----------|---------|---------|
         | *vita* | *vida* | 'life' |
         | *metu* | *miedo* | 'fear' |
         | *rota* | *rueda* | 'wheel' |
         | *civitate*| *ciudad*| 'city' |

When using written documents, we must have evidence about the value of the symbols used. How do we know that Latin *t* stood for [t], a voiceless dental or alveolar stop? In this case, we have the writings of Roman grammarians, who described the sounds of their language and report that *t* stands for a voiceless dental stop. In the case of Modern Spanish, we also need to question the value of the written symbol. While *d* usually stands for a voiced stop at the same point of articulation as [t], indicating that between Latin and Spanish, this stop became voiced, if we listen carefully to the Spanish of today, we find that now between vowels the letter *d* is pronounced as a voiced interdental fricative.

Just as in this example, another source of evidence about sound change is in differences between the written representation and the current pronunciation.

If we have good evidence that the spelling in a language once represented the pronunciation more or less accurately, then cases where the pronunciation no longer matches the spelling indicate a change has occurred. In the Spanish example above, we can be pretty certain that at one time the letter *d* represented a stop. The fact that now it is a fricative means a sound change has occurred. Another example is the post-vocalic *r* in English dialects. Though it is there in the spelling, speakers of British, Australian, and some American dialects of English do not produce an [ɹ] in words such as *car*, *here*, and *bird*. They produce a long vowel or a schwa-like vowel rather than the retroflex [ɹ].

For languages that do not have documented earlier stages and whose writing systems have been so recently developed that they do not show much difference from pronunciation, there are other sources of evidence for changes that have taken place. Changes are revealed when we compare related dialects and languages. Because languages are changing all the time, when speakers of the same language become separated geographically by one group migrating away from the other group, the language of the two groups may change in different ways. Over time the accumulation of many changes will result in the two groups speaking different languages and no longer being able to understand one another. But when we compare the two resulting languages, we will see similarities and differences. The differences will represent changes, so from these differences we can reconstruct what changes must have occurred. For example, among the varieties of Quechua (the language of the Incas now spoken across a wide area in South America), one variety, Ancash Quechua, has an initial /h/ in words such as *hara* 'corn' where the other languages have an initial /s/. Given certain other considerations, we can tentatively conclude that initial /s/ in the parent language changed to /h/ in the Ancash variety some time in the past.

Another such case appears in the Austronesian language To'aba'ita, where Lichtenberk 1991 found that some prepositions behave somewhat like verbs. For example, the ablative preposition *fasi* (meaning 'away from') takes a suffix much as verbs do to indicate the object. Yet *fasi* is never used as a verb in this language. However, in the related language Kware'ae, there is a verb *fa'asi* which means 'leave, forsake, depart from'. This provides evidence for the hypothesis that *fasi* was once a verb in To'aba'ita.

In languages with and without written histories, ongoing changes create variation, and the study of this variation can also provide excellent evidence about how change occurs. For instance, there is a lot of variation in Spanish dialects about how /s/ is pronounced, especially at the ends of syllables. It is common for the /s/ to sound more like an /h/ or to be left out entirely. Many Caribbean dialects and some South American dialects have this variation. For instance, *estas casas* 'these houses' can be pronounced as [ehtahkasah] in these dialects or even [etakasa]. Such pronunciations represent a change that has occurred in these dialects.

Another case of variation that appears to represent a change in progress is the loss of French *ne*, part of the negative construction we discussed earlier in the chapter.

As we saw in Section 1.2, the usual way to negate a clause in French has two parts – *ne* goes before the verb and *pas* goes after it. The *ne* is a very small syllable with a reduced vowel that can be deleted, as in *n'est* 'is not'. Now it is common for the consonant as well as the vowel to be deleted leaving *pas* to indicate negation. This is a change in progress as indicated by the fact that younger speakers delete the *ne* more often than older speakers (Ashby 1981).

Of all these sources of evidence, the best and most reliable are the most direct – the study of variation due to ongoing change. In these cases we can see change as it is going on and we can identify the factors that affect its origin and spread. The other sources of evidence are more or less reliable depending upon the time-depth – stages of a language separated by a few hundred years provide better evidence than stages represented by a thousand years; dialects separated by a few hundred years provide better evidence than languages separated by a few thousand years. But because the same types of change occur in different languages and at different times, we can use a broad range of evidence to help us understand the how-and-why of change. In this book I will be using all these types of evidence to help us understand the nature of change.

1.5.   Why do languages change?

So far we have seen examples of changes that have taken place in different languages and I have commented on the fact that much also stays the same in a language across time. It is convention, that is, the tendency to speak like those around us, that keeps features of language the same across many generations of language users. But what makes it change? A very general answer is that the words and constructions of our language change as they cycle through our minds and bodies and are passed through usage from one speaker to another. This process is the topic we will study in this book. Right now I will list three tendencies in language change that seem to occur very commonly.

Because language is an activity that involves both cognitive access (recalling words and constructions from memory) and the motor routines of production (articulation), and because we use the same words and constructions many times over the course of a day, week, or year, these words and constructions are subject to the kinds of processes that repeated actions undergo. When you learn a new activity, such as driving a car, which has many different parts, practice or repetition allows you to become more fluent as you learn to anticipate and overlap one action with another and to reduce non-essential movements. A similar process occurs when you repeat words and phrases many times. Such a process is evident in many aspects of change in the sounds of a language, as we will see in Chapter 2. We also see the effect of repetition when words and constructions undergo a kind of reduction in the amount of meaning they carry, as when phrases that are repeated often, such as *how are you?* or *what's up?*, become just greetings and do not really require a literal answer.

Another pervasive process in the human approach to the world is the formation of patterns from our experience and application of these patterns to new experiences or ideas. Languages are full of patterns that are repeated, such as for English "add /s/, /z/ or /ɨz/ to a noun to make it plural" or "put the auxiliary before the subject to make a question" or more specific patterns, such as conventional word combinations like *good friends* to describe a close personal relationship rather than *nice friends*. When we use language we are constantly doing pattern-matching, and in so doing we reinforce certain patterns. Also, we apply patterns in novel ways. These acts during language use can change the language. Change occurs when new patterns arise, when patterns change their distribution, or when they are lost. Many of the chapters of this book will be concerned with how linguistic patterns change over time and what factors influence their change in a particular direction.

The other major factor in language change is the way words or patterns of language are used in context. Very often the meaning supplied by frequently occurring contexts can lead to change. Words and constructions that are used in certain contexts become associated with those contexts. If *what's up?* occurs frequently as the first utterance when people meet one another, it becomes a greeting and no longer requires a literal answer. Listeners make inferences from the context in which constructions occur, and these inferences can become part of the meaning of the construction. The construction *be going to* + VERB is often used where an expression of intention can be inferred, as in *I'm going to visit my sister today*, so eventually the construction comes to express intention even where no motion is involved, as in *I'm going to tell him the truth*.

Because the processes that speakers and listeners use when they communicate are the same for all languages and their users, language change is very similar across languages. What I mean by this is that, for instance, for all the examples I have given so far in this chapter, we can find a different, unrelated language that has undergone or is undergoing a similar change. The details might be different in some respects, but there is an uncanny similarity in changes across languages and across time. It is this similarity that makes language change interesting and worthy of study.

1.6.   Is language change good or bad?

Linguistic researchers view language change as an integral part of language and an inevitable outcome of language use. Changes are natural to language and they are neither good nor bad. This view contrasts with the view sometimes expressed in the popular press, that ongoing changes diminish or degrade the language. Because language exists by social convention, many people feel that it should stay the same as it was when they arrived on the scene. For instance, the dialect I grew up speaking used the English second person plural form *you* or *you all*. Now a growing number of American English speakers (especially those who are younger) use *you guys*. I don't particularly like *you guys* because it seems very informal and also because it seems inappropriate for female addressees. However, I end up using it anyway, just because so many other people use it. It is very difficult to resist a speech pattern that is being used all around you. So once a change gains momentum, it is unlikely that it can be stopped.

The fact that *you guys* used to refer to men and now can refer to anyone is a very natural change of the type just mentioned above – the meaning of 'male' has been lost. Is the change to *you guys* good or bad? It doesn't really matter because, if it is going to take over second person plural, there is nothing anyone can do about it. But in a way it is good, because it solves the problem of the ambiguity of *you*.

1.7.   Why study language change?

Understanding language change helps us to understand synchronic states, their structure, and the variation that is found in them. As an example, consider the status of *you guys* in American English today. Why is this form being introduced and gaining in usage? How does its development relate to what happens in other languages? At an earlier stage of English, there was a distinction between second person singular pronouns *thou, thee, thy* and second person plural *ye, you, your*. Then the practice developed of using the plural form to be polite even when the addressee was a single person. This changed the relation between the *thou* forms (which were used only in familiar situations) and the *you* forms (which were used in formal situations and for the plural). You might recognize this pattern from other European languages, such as Spanish, where familiar *tú* contrasts with formal *usted*, French where *tu* contrasts with *vous*, or German where *du* contrasts with *Sie*.

English was once at this stage, but what has happened is that the *you* forms have taken on uses in more and more situations until the *thou* forms have become vanishingly rare. The result is that English has been using the same set of forms for singular and plural for quite some time. Now, if one wants to make it quite clear that second person **plural** is intended, one adds something to *you*. Thus we find *you all > y'all, you folks, you lot, you people, youse, you guys*, and possibly many other variants. At the moment in American English, the form *you guys* is gaining in usage. It has lost its meaning of referring only to masculine addressees and now is free to expand to more and more geographic areas and social groups and may end up as the normal way to indicate second person plural in American English. This example shows how the current situation is best understood in the context of past developments as well as developments in other languages.

On the typological level, understanding language change is also important for explaining why we find both similarities and differences among languages around the world. Even languages that are unrelated genealogically or areally often undergo very similar changes. For instance, languages that have phonemic nasalized vowels always also have phonemic oral (non-nasalized) vowels and nasal consonants. In such languages, nasal vowels are less common than oral vowels; also in the languages of the world, phonemic nasal vowels are less common than oral ones. As Greenberg 1978a argues, all of these facts can be explained with reference to the way nasal vowels develop diachronically. In typical cases, nasal vowels develop by assimilation to a neighboring nasal consonant. If that consonant then deletes, a nasal vowel phoneme remains. This process has occurred in French, Portuguese, and other languages around the globe. Because nasal vowels develop only in certain environments – next to a nasal consonant – they will be less common in words than oral vowels. Because they derive from oral vowels, all languages that have nasal vowels will also have oral vowels. In this way, patterns of language change contribute to our understanding of crosslinguistic patterns.

Viewing language as a dynamic and ever-changing social instrument helps us to understand why linguistic structure is the way it is. As mentioned in the first section, change is inherent in language; indeed, change creates language in the present and also in the past. Thus, if studying change helps us identify the factors that create language, it will also help us understand how language evolved in the first place.

In addition, there are some other collateral advantages or applications of knowledge of language change. An important focus of historical linguistics has been the comparison of languages to discover their family affiliations. The languages of Europe and those in Asia have been compared in this way to establish families such as Indo-European, Semitic, Finno-Ugric, and Sino-Tibetan, to name just a few. In Chapter 10 we will discuss how the comparative method works. There are still many languages spoken in the world today whose relations to other languages and language families are yet to be determined, for instance the many languages spoken in Papua New Guinea and some of the remaining native languages of the Americas. These relations may eventually be established based on what we know about language change.

Knowing how languages in a geographic area relate to one another sometimes provides evidence about the migrations of peoples in prehistoric times. For example, the Native American languages Apache and Navajo are spoken in the American Southwest, but it turns out that all the other languages of their family (Athapaskan) are spoken much farther north, mostly in northwestern Canada and Alaska. From this fact, and others, we conclude that the group or groups that speak Athapaskan languages in the Southwest migrated from the North, leaving behind their relatives. Similar observations can be made about the movements of people in other parts of the world, such as Africa.

Other information about prehistoric cultures is available from linguistic reconstruction. For example, we noted above that many Indo-European languages have similar words for 'nose'. This is not surprising since all cultures need some way to refer to this feature of the human face. More interesting is that comparison of many Indo-European languages reveals that there was also a common word for 'wheel', 'horse', and verbs for 'ride' and 'drive'. What a culture has words for provides important information about how the culture is organized and how it sustains itself. Scholars are thus certain that the early Indo-Europeans had carts and horses. Studies of the words that go back that far allows us to reconstruct aspects of family and political organization as well as agriculture and religion (Beekes 1995).

As the present book is focused on language change rather than language history, we will explore the comparative method, but not all of its applications. Rather we will focus here on how and why languages change their words, phonology, morphology, syntactic constructions, and semantic structure.

Notes on notation

Many different notational systems are used in works on language change. The following are recommended for students to use in their own writing. These conventions are followed in this book to the extent possible. However, when an author whose work is cited uses different conventions, the current book usually follows those conventions.

Sounds intended to be understood as roughly phonemic should appear between slash lines, English /pæn/ 'pan'.

When a more precise phonetic rendering of the sound is intended, it appears between square brackets, English [pʰæn] 'pan'.

The orthographic or spelled form of a word no matter what language should be in italics, English *sand*, Spanish *arena*.

The translation or gloss for a word, phrase, or sentence will be in single quotes, Spanish *arena* 'sand'.

Sounds or words that are reconstructed appear with an asterisk before them, Proto-Indo-European *nokt(i) 'night'; they are often italicized.

Useful references for historical linguistics

A standard dictionary with very good etymologies and a listing of Indo-European roots is *The American Heritage Dictionary*, Houghton Mifflin.

The *Oxford English Dictionary* has very complete histories for English words, including many examples from texts dating from the earliest documented period (about 800 CE) to the twentieth century. It is available online.

A book giving examples of common words in thirty or more Indo-European languages:

Buck, Carl Darling. 1949. *A dictionary of selected synonyms in the principal Indo-European languages*, Chicago and London: University of Chicago Press. Available in paperback.

Questions for discussion

1. Rephrase the quote in (10) from Shakespeare in Present Day English. What other changes are found here besides the use of *thou*, *thee*, and *thy*?

2. What are some other words in the languages that you know that have both a concrete meaning and an abstract one? Check an etymological dictionary to find out which meaning came first. What would you expect about the word *shrimp* used to refer to a small person? Check the Oxford English Dictionary to see if you are correct.

3. Go to the COHA website http://corpus.byu.edu/coha/ and ask for a count of *you guys*. This corpus spans American English from 1810 to 2000. What do you see there about the frequency of use of *you guys*? You might compare this to other second person plural expressions such as *you all*.

4. Identify a feature of speech in your community that bothers you when you hear it, like the previously mentioned *you guys* example. What bothers you about the feature? How does it differ from what you would say in the same context? Can you think of ways this element serves a useful or distinct function in the language or why speakers might prefer to use it?

2   Sound change

2.1.   What is sound change?

The sounds of a language can change in various ways over time. What we refer to as "sound change" is a particular type of change in the sounds of a language. We are especially interested in this one type of change because it is very common, it is quite systematic within a language, and it is very similar across languages. This chapter and the next will be concerned with sound change, as defined in the next paragraph.

Sound change is a change in the pronunciation of a segment within a word (or occasionally more than one segment) conditioned by the phonetic environment, that is, the surrounding sounds. Sound change is typically regular, by which we mean that it affects all the words of the lexicon that have that sound in the required phonetic environment. The segment in question can be changed in a variety of ways that we will examine in detail below, or it can even be lost entirely. Here are two examples of well-studied sound changes:

1. Since 1970 it has been noted that in some dialects of Brazilian Portuguese (especially in Rio de Janeiro and other major cities) the dental stops /t/ and /d/ are palatalizing before the high front vowel /i/ and the high front glide /j/. Consider the words in Table 2.1 with data from Cristófaro-Silva and Oliveira Guimarães 2006.

The examples in Table 2.1 show that both the voiceless and voiced dental stops change to postalveolars before the high front vowel or glide whether it is stressed or not and whether or not it is nasalized. Even though the change is very recent, it is quite regular in certain dialects. In this case we know that a change has taken place because there are direct reports from the 1970s and there are dialects that have not changed. This change is considered an *assimilation* because the dental stops become more like the palatal vowel and glide that they precede. We will discuss assimilations in detail in the next section.

2. A second example of a sound change occurred in the sixteenth and seventeenth centuries in English. Up to that time, the initial /k/ and /g/ before an /n/ in words like *knee, know* and *gnaw, gnat* were pronounced. By the end of the seventeenth century, these consonants were no longer pronounced in any English words (Görlach 1991). We know that they were once pronounced because of reports of grammarians at the time. Also, in related languages, these clusters are still pronounced. For example, in two sister languages of English, in

Table 2.1: *Words affected by palatalization in Brazilian Portuguese*

Palatalizing varieties	Non-palatalizing varieties	Orthography	Gloss
'tʃipʊ	'tipʊ	*tipo*	'type'
'tʃĩtə	'tĩtə	*tinta*	'paint'
'ahtʃɪ	'ahtɪ	*arte*	'art'
'patʃu	'patju	*pátio*	'yard'
tʃi'atrʊ	ti'atrʊ	*teatro*	'theater'
'dʒitʊ	'ditʊ	*dito*	'said'
'dʒĩdə	'dĩdə	*Dinda*	'woman's name'
'ahdʒɪ	'ahdɪ	*arde*	'sting'
'ĩdʃʊ	'ĩdʊ	*índio*	'Indian'
dʒi'baiʃʊ	di'baiʃʊ	*debaixo*	'under'

the German word *Knie* 'knee' and Dutch word *knie* 'knee' the /k/ is pronounced. This change is a reductive change because a consonant is lost. This occurs at the beginning of the word only. Word-internally, the /k/ and /g/ remain in English, as in *acknowledge* and *signal*, because they are at the end of a syllable in these words.

These two changes illustrate the two most common types of change: assimilation and reduction. In Sections 2.2 and 2.3 we will examine each of these types in some detail, exploring the variety of changes that fall into these two categories and trying to understand their phonetic causes. To this end, we will consider carefully how the articulation of sounds changes in assimilation, reduction, and other types of change and what their acoustic consequences are.

Before continuing, however, two properties of sound change need to be emphasized:

1. As mentioned above, sound changes are **regular** in the sense that once they are complete, they will have affected all the words of the language that have the affected sounds in the conditioning environment. That does not mean, however, that all words are affected simultaneously as the change is going on. Note that all the examples given in this chapter, unless otherwise noted, are regular across all the words of the language.

2. Sound changes are also **gradual** rather than abrupt. There are various ways in which we can think of sound change as being gradual rather than abrupt. First, most sound change appears to be phonetically gradual, progressing by very small incremental steps, accompanied by variation. The gradual loss of /k/ would progress as weaker and shorter articulations of /k/ occur until no /k/ is heard at all. The assimilation of /t/ and /d/ to /i/ and /j/ can also occur gradually, as in early stages the /t/ and /d/ take on a slightly more palatal offset, and then assimilate more fully to a postalveolar articulation. This would be in contrast to an abrupt change, where for example, the /k/ in *knee* is either present or absent with

nothing in between, or the postalveolars abruptly replace /t/ and /d/ in Brazilian Portuguese.

Another sense in which sound changes can be gradual is in their spread through a community. When alveolars started to palatalize in Brazilian Portuguese dialects, some individuals led the way and others retained their old pronunciation longer. The dialects in certain cities such as Rio de Janeiro changed first and then gradually other dialects have adopted the change.

Finally, there could be gradualness in the way the change affects words – rather than all words changing at once, some words may change earlier than others. This phenomenon will be treated in Section 2.8 under the heading of "lexical diffusion".

In the following I will emphasize phonetic explanations for the sound changes we discuss, referring to the changes in articulation and the resulting changes in acoustic properties. Because an important property of sound change is that it takes place in particular phonetic environments, we search for the causes in phonetics. Because sound change has phonetic motivation, the same sorts of sound changes occur in different languages at different time periods, whether or not those languages are related. In the following discussion, this point will be emphasized by providing examples of similar changes from different languages.

This chapter deals with assimilation, lenition, and fortition. Other types of sound change, such as vowel shifts, are presented in Chapter 3. In addition, Chapter 3 deals with tonogenesis (how tones arise in a language), prosodic changes, and changes motivated by factors such as the phonotactic patterns of a language.

2.2.   Assimilation

Assimilation is common in the rules of synchronic phonology as well as in sound change. In fact, the rules of phonology arise through sound change, so it follows that the two are very similar. One way to identify assimilation is to say that it is a change by which one sound becomes more like another adjacent sound. In understanding exactly why certain sound changes occur, it is useful to consider in detail how the sequence of sounds in question is articulated. For assimilation it is particularly important to consider the movements of the articulators and the temporal dimension. As a word is produced, the articulators move in certain sequences. Our alphabetic writing system (including that of the International Phonetic Alphabet) is sometimes misleading in the way it represents the sounds of a word as discrete units. Instead we know that movement towards and away from certain targets (such as stop consonants) is really what is important in producing and identifying sounds and that the gestures that produce certain sounds overlap and influence one another. For these reasons we will examine the changes that take place in the sequences of articulatory gestures for each of the types of sound change that we consider.

2.2.1.   Assimilation as gestural retiming

Assimilation as defined above comes about because the gestures used to produce the sounds in question change their timing: they can be anticipated, that is, started earlier, in which case they may overlap preceding gestures, or they can be extended, that is, not stopped so soon, and in that case they may overlap or persevere into following gestures. These two types of assimilation are traditionally distinguished as anticipatory assimilation and perseverative assimilation. Other terms sometimes used are "regressive assimilation" for anticipatory and "progressive assimilation" for perseverative. I prefer the terms "anticipatory" and "perseverative" because they describe better what is going on in terms of articulation. In the phonetic literature, synchronic assimilation that is perseverative is also called "carry over", a term that is both pronounceable and descriptive.

2.2.2   Anticipatory assimilation

Anticipatory assimilation occurs when an upcoming gesture in the sequence of gestures commences early and therefore overlaps other gestures. Sometimes that overlap obscures the existing gesture and other times it modifies it. As an example, consider the palatalization of /t/ and /d/ in Brazilian Portuguese discussed in Section 2.1. Here we see that the palatal tongue position is anticipated and overlaps with the articulation of the dental with the tongue tip. This pulls the tongue body forward towards the alveo-palate and produces the strident sound of the affricate. A similar assimilation occurs in American English between two words that occur together frequently, such as *did you*, *would you*, and *last year*, where anticipation of the palatal glide makes it occur simultaneously with the alveolar stop, producing a postalveolar affricate, [tʃ] or [dʒ]. Similar changes to coronal stops before high front vowels and glides occur in Japanese as well. In Romance, sequences of coronal stops and the high front glide also produced a postalveolar affricate (see Section 2.2.5).

2.2.3.   Palatalization of velars

Another very common palatalization sound change affects velar stops before front vowels, usually high front vowels. It is common for velar stops to be fronted to a palatal position before front vowels; thus one can discern the difference in the initial stops in English words such as *key* and *car*. In some languages this assimilation is taken even further and the consonant before the front vowel becomes a postalveolar affricate. This happened in Old English to produce words such as *chin*, *church*, *choose*, and *chest* (compare these to Dutch *kin*, *kerk*, *kiezen*, and *kist*). Similar changes took place in languages and language families as widely separated as Slavic, Indo-Iranian, Salishan, Chinese, and Bantu. Here are some examples from the Bantu language

Table 2.2: *Palatalization of root-initial velars in Ci-Bemba*

a.	*-kít-	>	-cít-a	'do'
	*-kínd-	>	-cínd-a	'dance'
	*-kèk-	>	-cèk-a	'cut'
	*-kè-	>	-c-á	'dawn'
b.	*-kuuc-	>	-kuus-a	'rub'
	*-kum-	>	-kum-	'come to an end'
	*-kóm-	>	-kom-a	'hit'
	*-kòc-	>	-kòs-a	'be strong'
c.	*-kám-	>	-kam-a	'squeeze, milk'

Ci-Bemba (Hyman and Moxley 1996). The forms in the left-hand column are reconstructed forms of Proto-Bantu. The letter *c* stands for [tʃ]; the accents are tone marks.

The examples in (a) show the velar before a front vowel, where it palatalizes, while the (b) and (c) examples show that the velar does not change before a back vowel.

As the postalveolar affricate is even farther to the front than the palatal (as in *key*) and uses a different part of the tongue, Guion 1998 argues that this part of the change is not just a further articulatory fronting, but a change based on the acoustic similarity of the palatal to a postalveolar affricate. The palatal in *key* is more similar to a postalveolar than it is to a velar. Also, the change appears more frequently with the voiceless velar/palatal and might be aided by the appearance of friction in the offset of the voiceless sound that is more noticeable than in the voiced one.

In the next few sections we continue on the topic of palatalization, because there are many important changes due to palatalization in European language families, such as Germanic, Slavic, and Romance languages.

2.2.4.   I-umlaut as palatalization

Also within the realm of palatalization, there was a set of vowel changes that took place in early Germanic. A stressed vowel was affected if there was a high front vowel or glide in the next syllable. Low vowels were raised and back vowels became fronted. This change occurred before Old English (Anglo-Saxon) was first written down around 800 CE. While this change, called "i-umlaut", also occurred in other West and North Germanic languages (Dutch, German, and Frisian), the examples in Table 2.3 illustrate the outcome for Old English. The words with asterisks are reconstructed words – that is, they were not documented in writing, but were arrived at by comparison of the different Germanic languages.

In addition, the diphthongs underwent comparable changes. Note that the mid front rounded vowels were attested in some written documents, but they became

Table 2.3: *I-umlaut changes in Old English*

Low vowels become high

æ > e	*sættjan > *settan* 'set'	*æġi > *eġe* 'fear'
æ + consonant group usually remained æ:		*fæstjan > *fæstan* 'to fasten'
a > e	*manni > *mænni > *menn* 'men'	*sandjan > *sendan* 'send'
ā > ǣ	*hāli > *hǣl* 'health'	*hāljan > *hǣlan* 'to heal'

Back vowels become front

o > œ > e	*dohtri > *dœhtri > *dehter* 'daughter', dat. sg.
ō > œ̄ > ē	*dōmjan > *dœ̄man > *dēman* 'to judge'
u > y	*fulljan > *fyllan* 'to fill'
ū > ȳ	*tūnjan > *tȳnan* 'to enclose'

unrounded fairly early – by 900 in West Saxon, one of the dialects of Old English (Moore and Knott 1968). The high front rounded vowel was retained in some dialects until the Middle English period.

As the examples suggest, i-umlaut is the source of some vowel alternations that survive into Present Day English. The singular/plural pair, *man/men* has a vowel change because of i-umlaut. The plural marker for this and many other nouns was –*i*, so we now have some singular/plural pairs that change their vowel from back to front, as in *foot/feet*, *tooth/teeth*, and some derivationally related words, such as *full/fill* and *food/feed*. In German, where a comparable umlaut sound change occurred, the front rounded vowels have remained and the alternations between back and front vowels provide the marking for some morphological categories, such as noun plurals, as shown in the following examples. (Orthography is used; all the vowels with the umlaut mark are front vowels.)

(12)	German	Singular	Gloss	Plural
		der Garten	'the garden'	*die Gärten*
		der Bruder	'the brother'	*die Brüder*
		der Boden	'the ground, floor'	*die Böden*

I-umlaut was an anticipatory assimilation by which the palatal (high front) tongue gesture was retimed to occur earlier in the word; in fact, it moved across the consonant or consonant cluster to affect the stressed vowel of the word, raising low vowels and fronting back vowels. The effect on the intervening consonant is not always evident, but velar consonants were palatalized and there is some evidence that other consonants were affected as well (A. Campbell 1959). In support of the retiming account, note that the palatal glide is lost – as if it moved forward in the word – or, if the conditioning was a high front vowel, it lost its high articulation.

As with other sound changes, this type of change is not restricted to Germanic languages, but has been documented in Yele (Papua New Guinea, Henderson

1996), where a following high vowel causes raising in the preceding vowel, and Atchin (Oceanic, New Hebrides, Capell and Layard 1980).

2.2.5.   Palatalization in early Romance

The palatal glide in Latin also had a major impact on the phonological development of the Romance languages from spoken Latin. This glide (called the 'yod' in Romance studies) could develop from an unstressed /i/ or /e/ that occurred before another vowel or from a consonant; it affected the consonant that preceded it as well as the vowel of the preceding syllable in most cases. The series of changes outlined in Table 2.4 began in Vulgar Latin and continued into the period in which the Romance languages began to develop. The final forms in the table are Spanish forms. (It is customary when citing developments from Latin to Romance languages to cite nouns in the case form that survived into Romance [usually the accusative] and to omit the final consonant, as that consonant was lost in Romance.)

What Table 2.4 shows is a long chain of developments caused by the anticipatory retiming of the palatal glide. Almost every consonant and vowel in the language is affected in some way over the course of several centuries. As we know a good bit about the relative chronology of these changes, the order in which consonants and vowels were affected provide us with evidence about the susceptibility of certain sounds to change under the pressure of a strong palatal articulation. Here are some points to note about these changes:

The palatal glide itself often derived from an unstressed front vowel before another vowel, as in *cŭnea* or *fīliu*. The Latin grammarians make it clear that this sound was earlier a vowel, then became a glide, which means it could be even higher and more fronted than the comparable vowel (Kent 1945). The first consonants to be affected were the dental and velar voiceless stops, /t/ and /k/. As mentioned above, voiceless stops are more prone to becoming postalveolar affricates than voiced stops are. If the assimilation were just a matter of the consonant becoming more like the glide, the glide would remain. In the case of /t/ and /k/, Table 2.4 gives a long string of developments leading up to Modern Spanish. The /tʃ/ that developed in the initial palatalization underwent further changes, becoming more fronted to /ts/ and then reducing to a fricative (/θ/ in Castilian Spanish and /s/ in Latin American Spanish). The voiceless velar stop before front vowels also palatalized and underwent the same developments as when /k/ preceded /j/. Thus Latin *circa* becomes Spanish *cerca* 'near' and *dīcit* becomes *dice* '3rd sg. say' (in Latin the *c* was pronounced as /k/ and in Spanish as either /s/ or /θ/).

The other coronals, /n/ and /l/, are affected next, but in this case the yod may be either before or after the /n/ or /l/. In both cases the two sounds come to be articulated simultaneously with the dental sonorant. Note that the yod disappeared, which is evidence for the retiming. The palatal lateral later lost its lateral

Table 2.4: *Effects of palatalization in Vulgar Latin and Romance in chronological order*

In each case the first form cited is Latin and the last form Spanish (Menéndez-Pidal 1968; Penny 2002). In some cases intermediate stages are reconstructed based on the descriptions just cited (marked with *); in other cases intermediate stages are attested in dialects or in Portuguese. The Latin spelling is phonemic, and Spanish spelling is used where it corresponds to the phonemic representation.

1. Voiceless alveolar and velar stops palatalize before /j/[1]
    (Vowels are not yet affected)
    fŏrtia > *[fortʃa] > *[fwertsa] > [fwerθa] or [fwersa] *fuerza* 'force'
    minacia > *[minatʃa] > *[minatsa] > [amenaθa] or [amenasa] *amenaza* 'threat'

2. Short mid vowels (which are lax and lower than long vowels and would ordinarily diphthongize) are raised
    fŏlia becomes *hoja* [oxa]   'leaf' rather than non-occurring *hueja*
    nĕrviu becomes *nervio* [nerβjo] 'nerve' rather than non-occurring *niervio*

    a. A palatal glide either before or after /l/ coalesces to /ʎ/. The glide preceding /l/ came from a velar consonant; /ʎ/ later became a postalveolar fricative and finally a velar fricative:
    fīliu   > *[filju]   >[fiʎu]   > [fiʒo]   > [ixo]   *hijo*   'son'
    vĕrmĭcŭlu > *[vermijlu] > [vermeʎu] > [vermeʒo] > [bermexo] *bermejo* 'bright red'

    b. /n/ followed or preceded by a palatal glide coalesces to /ñ/
    signa   > *[sejna] > *seña* 'mark, sign'
    cŭnea   > *[kunja] > *cuña* 'wedge'
    arānea > *[aranja] > *araña* 'spider'

3. Short high vowels and long mid vowels merged in Vulgar Latin in stressed position
    ŏ   and   ŭ   become   o
    ĕ   and   ĭ   become   e
    Although not usually influenced by the yod formed by the preceding changes, when a palatal glide formed later occurs in the next syllable, these vowels become high, *i* and *u*.
    fŭgio   becomes   [ujo]   *huyo*   'flee' 1st sg. pres.
    vindĕmia becomes   [bendimja] *vendimia* 'vintage'

4. The voiced dental and velar stops /d/ and /g/ delete before /j/
    radia   >   *raya*   'stripe'
    exagio >   *ensayo* 'attempt'
    Labials plus palatal glide are unaffected, except that sporadically /b/ or /v/ delete.

5. Syllable final /k/ becomes /j/, which merges with /t/ to produce /tʃ/:
    nocte >   [nojte] >   [notʃe] *noche* 'night'
    lacte >   [lejte] >   [letʃe] *leche* 'milk'

6. /rj/, /pj/, and /sj/ metathesize. Palatalization retimes to the stressed syllable.
    riparia > *[ribaira] > [ribeira] > [riβera] *ribera* 'bank, shore'
    casium > *[kaisu]   > [keiso]   > [keso]   *queso* 'cheese'
    /aj/ > /ej/ > /e/ (/a/ is not affected by previous palatalizations)

1. One step is left out of the sequences illustrating the change: the affricate voiced in intervocalic position and later devoiced.

articulation (so that both sides of the tongue were down rather than only one) and became a palatal fricative, which later became a velar fricative.

After a syllable-final /k/ became a palatal glide, as in (5) in Table 2.4, it then fused with the following /t/ to produce a /tʃ/, but this affricate did not undergo the same fronting as the ones produced earlier. This palatal glide, which developed later, had an effect on the low vowel /a/, raising and fronting it to /e/, and finally disappearing in Spanish.

The labial consonants and coronals, /r/ and /s/, were generally unaffected. However, a very interesting development that gives strong evidence for anticipatory retiming is a metathesis, or change in position, of the yod with the preceding /p/, /r/, or /s/, as shown in (6) in Table 2.4. (For more about metathesis, see Section 3.7.2.) As with the Germanic i-umlaut, we can observe the palatal gesture passing through the consonant (leaving no permanent effect) towards the vowel of the stressed syllable, raising it. While it is not surprising that the /p/ and /r/ were unaffected by the anticipation of the yod, the fact that /s/ remains non-palatal seems surprising, given that /t/, /n/, and /l/ are affected. I do not know what the explanation is for this.

This set of changes conditioned by a palatal glide spans the centuries between Vulgar Latin and Western Romance, demonstrating how a group of related changes might take a long period of time to be fully manifested. It also shows how assimilation can affect both consonants and vowels, and that a gesture that is being retimed may move over several segment positions.

2.2.6.   Assimilation of point of articulation

Another common type of anticipatory assimilation is the assimilation to the point of articulation of nasals and obstruents before other consonants. For example, Latin labial and velar voiceless stops at the end of a syllable assimilate to the point of articulation of the following voiceless stop in Italian:

(13)   Latin   Italian   Gloss
          nocte-   *notte*   'night'
          factu-   *fatto*   'fact'
          septem   *sette*   'seven'
          scriptu- *scritto* 'writing'

Note that it is the consonant in syllable-final position that assimilates to the one in syllable-initial position. The burst of energy in a syllable occurs at the beginning and decreases at the end, so syllable-final position makes a consonant more vulnerable to change than other positions. (This is also the case for lenition, as discussed in Section 2.5.8.) In this case, the syllable-initial gesture is anticipated and thus overlaps the syllable-final gesture, masking it. That is, the original gesture might be present at first, but its perception is masked by the overlapping gesture. As the gradual change progresses, the original syllable-final gesture is lost.

A common sort of change is the assimilation of a nasal consonant to the point of articulation of the following consonant. In the following examples from Latin, we can see that an /n/ at the end of the prefix *in-* assimilates in point of articulation to a following obstruent and assimilates completely to initial /r/ and /l/. We know that the prefix originally ended in /n/ because that is the consonant that appears when the stem begins with a vowel. (The /n/ before *c* was a velar.)

(14)   Latin   Gloss
         immōbilis   'immovable'
         indignus   'unworthy'
         inōrnātus   'unadorned'
         incommodus   'inconvenient'
         inhūmānus   'inhuman'
         irreparābiliter 'irreparably'
         irresolūtus   'unloosed'
         illegitimus   'unlawful'
         illimitātus   'unlimited'

This was not a change that occurred only in this prefix. The prefix *com-* also assimilated in like fashion. Before a vowel it was *com-* as in *comitium* 'a place of assembly', but it had other assimilated forms: *corrīdeo* 'to laugh together', *collabōro* 'to work with', *condesertor* 'a fellow deserter'. You have probably recognized this assimilation as occurring in English and other languages in words such as *illegal, irregular, important, incompetent, collaborate, correspond, conduct,* and so on. These words were borrowed from Latin with the prefix already on them and already assimilated.

As mentioned above, it is most common for syllable-final consonants to assimilate to the syllable-initial consonant. Occasionally the opposite occurs: the syllable-initial consonant assimilates to the preceding, syllable-final one. This would be a perseverative assimilation and it will be treated in the next section.

2.3.   Perseverative or carry-over assimilation

The pattern of assimilation that is the opposite of anticipatory is one in which a gesture of an earlier sound is extended into the following sound. This is a type of retiming of a gesture in the sense that the end point of the gesture is carried over to co-occur with the next set of gestures. This direction for assimilation is much less common both diachronically and synchronically than anticipatory assimilation.

One type of carry over that occurs in Indo-European languages involves cases where an /n/ assimilates to a preceding liquid, as in the case of Proto-Germanic (PGmc) *wulna > *wullō> OE *wull* 'wool', PGmc *fulnaz > *fullaz > OE *full* 'full', and PGmc *hulnis > OE *hyll* 'hill' (Hock 1986). Similar examples are Proto-Indo-European (PIE) *kolnis > Latin *collis* 'hill' and OE myln > PDE *mill*.

L. Campbell 1999 also supplies a similar example from alternations in Finnish: *kuul-nut* > *kuullut* 'heard', *pur-nut* > *purrut* 'bitten', and *nous-nut* > *noussut* 'risen'. A similar assimilation is found in Kanakuru, a Chadic language of Nigeria (Newman 1974) and in Kanuri, a Nilo-Saharan language (Cyffer 1998). In these examples, both consonants are coronal, and a notable feature is that nasality is lost. From a gestural perspective, a nasal assimilating to a non-nasal must be viewed as the loss of the gesture that opens the velum. Thus two things are going on in these examples: the two coronal gestures blend, with the [l], [r], and [s], none of which involve complete closure, affecting the closure of the nasal and the loss of velum opening, perhaps in response to the loss of closure.

Another suggested perseverative assimilation is the voicing of stops after nasal consonants. For example, in Zoque, this takes place when morphemes are combined and the two consonants are homorganic, as in *k'im* + *pa* 'rise 3rd sg.' which becomes *k'imba* (Zendejas 1995). Voicing of stops after nasals is also found historically in Kannaḍa, where Proto-Dravidian (PD) *onṭu 'one' becomes Kannaḍa *ondu* and PD *kaṇ-ṭV 'warrior' becomes Kannaḍa *gaṇḍu* 'brave person' (Krishnamurti 2003). From a gestural perspective, the voicelessness of the obstruent is created by a gesture which opens the glottis. The voicing of this obstruent is not so much an assimilation, as the loss of the glottal-opening gesture. In this case what appears to be a perseverative assimilation is better described as the loss of a gesture.

In our discussion of anticipatory assimilation, we saw examples of a consonant assimilating in place of articulation to a following consonant, as when Latin *nocte* 'night' becomes Italian *notte*. This is the usual pattern for two contiguous consonants. However, when both consonants are coronal, carry-over assimilation is possible (Blevins 2004). This is the general pattern in Australian languages, for example, but it also occurs in Norwegian between words, as when /væt/ 'been' with a final retroflex precedes /dæːr/ 'there' to give /væʈæːr / 'been there'. Of course this variation occurs between words, so we do not know if it will result in a sound change.

It is not common, but palatalization can also be perseverative rather than anticipatory. For instance, syllable-final Latin /k/ before /t/ became a palatal glide, as in Latin *lacte* > Portuguese *leite* 'milk', and then in Spanish the glide and the /t/ merged to become the postalveolar /tʃ/ in *leche*. See the discussion above.

There are also some assimilations in which the conditioning environment can be either before or after the changed segment. The languages that constitute Quechua are thought to originate from a language with only three vowels: *i, *u, and *a. High vowels both before and after uvular consonants were lowered, as when Proto-Quechua *quʎ'qi 'money' is pronounced [qɔlʸqe] and *suqta 'six' is pronounced [sɔqta] in Cuzco Quechua. Even if a sonorant intervenes, the uvular still lowers the vowel: *sunqu 'heart' is [sɔnqo] and *pirqa is [perqa] in Cuzco Quechua (Adelaar 2004). A uvular stop is made by pulling the tongue back to come in contact with the uvula, and this pulls the tongue away from the high position needed for the vowels [i] and [u].

2.4.   Conclusions regarding assimilation

In articulatory terms, assimilation comes about when the timing of gestures changes so that one gesture overlaps and affects an adjacent set of gestures. Anticipatory retiming is more common than perseverative or carry-over retiming. This difference is probably related to the fact that sequences of neuromotor activities become fluent through the anticipation of the next action in the sequence. In order for normal speech to be fluent, speakers must be able to anticipate the gestures in a sequence. This anticipation can lead to a gesture being produced early. It is less clear what the causes of carry-over retiming are; one suggestion is that bulkier articulators (such as the tongue body and lips) are not agile enough to terminate their gesture precisely at the segment boundary (Recasens 1999).

Given the understanding of assimilation as due to gestural retiming, it follows that most assimilations will involve sounds that are contiguous to one another. One example we have discussed here where this is not the case is umlaut, where a non-adjacent vowel or glide can affect an earlier vowel. In this case it is because the tongue position for vowel gestures can continue across consonants. In the case of Romance sound changes, the consonant and the vowel are affected, but in the case of umlaut, only the vowel is affected (vowel harmony). The other case is the lowering of high vowels in Quechua, where a sonorant can come between the uvular and the vowel. Hock 1986 also makes the point that features that do not represent gestures, such as vowel length, are never assimilated.

2.5.   Reduction or lenition

We will be using the term "reduction" for any change in which the magnitude or duration of a gesture is reduced. Lenition is a broad category within reduction that includes reduction in consonant articulation medially and some-times initially in a word. In this section we will discuss cases of lenition first and then move on to other types of reduction, including those affecting vowels. As lenition is a traditional term, it is defined differently by different researchers. There is no reason to make an issue of distinguishing lenition from reduction; the terms will be used here in a way that is consistent with most of the literature and convenient for exposition.

2.5.1.   Lenition

When it comes to reduction or lenition, there are two aspects of change to consider: one concerns the type of gestural changes involved and the other the positions in which change is most likely to occur. In discussing lenition, we will first consider the gestural changes, distinguishing two types: reduction to zero, in which the consonant articulation becomes weaker and eventually is lost, and sonorization, in which the consonant becomes more vowel-like.

2.5.2.   Reduction towards zero

In identifying reduction we will use a consistent articulatory definition and not refer to the acoustic or perceptual properties of the sound. A change will be considered a reduction if it constitutes a reduction in the magnitude or duration of an articulatory gesture. At times a gestural reduction might enhance acoustic or perceptual strength, but we will still consider it a reduction. The reason for stressing this point is that some researchers have proposed that a change from a stop to an affricate (which later changes to a fricative) is a strengthening, since an affricate with the friction of its offset is acoustically stronger than a stop (Foley 1977). For instance, as part of the Second Germanic Consonant Shift (also called Old High German Consonant Shift), voiceless stops become affricates, as in Modern German *Apfel* compared to English *apple*, *Zeit* [tsait] compared to *tide*. In some contexts, these stops have become fricatives: German *Schiff* [ʃɪf] vs. English *ship*, German *aus* vs. English *out* and German *machen* [maxən] vs. English *make*. In articulatory terms, such changes are reductions or lenitions because the duration of the stop closure is reduced. It is also significant that fricatives have resulted in some cases because the change from stop to fricative is uncontroversial as a reduction. A modern case of the change of voiceless stops to affricates and fricatives has been described for Liverpool English (Honeybone 2001). Further discussion of this type of change can be found in Section 2.10.

These changes are put in the category of "reduction towards zero" because we find there are many cases in which the resulting fricatives reduce further, as shown in the next section.

2.5.3.   Loss of oral articulation

The change of a stop to an affricate or fricative can be the first step in a longer lenition process, which leads eventually to the loss of the articulation in the oral cavity, sometimes called "debuccalization" (where -*bucca*- comes from the Latin word for mouth). For instance, the voiceless bilabial stop /p/ has a tendency to weaken and is sometimes deleted entirely. Thus many languages which have other voiceless stops lack a /p/ (Maddieson 1984). Such a change apparently happened in Japanese, which has geminate /pp/ but no non-geminate /p/ except in loan words. The result of the lenition of /p/ in Japanese is a voiceless fricative that occurs in the same place of articulation as the following vowel: [ɸ] before [ɯ], [ç] before [i], and [h] before other vowels. A similar change is evident on the other side of the world: the Bantu language, Lumasaaba, spoken in Uganda, has alternations that show a change of /p/ to /h/ before /a/, /j/ before front vowels, and /w/ before back vowels if no nasal consonant precedes. In the examples, the forms with /p/ have the prefix /iː-/, which formerly was /in-/. The /p/ in these words has remained after the nasal consonant was deleted.

(15)   Lumasaaba, Luhugu dialect (G. Brown 1972)
            iːpaya   'a male goat'   *kahaya*   'a small male goat'
            iːpamba   'I catch'   *kuhamba*   'to catch'
            iːpiso   'a needle'   *kuyiso*   'a small needle'
            iːpeːla   'I pant'   *kupeːla*   'to pant'
            iːpola   'I rest'   *kuwola*   'to rest'
            iːpuna   'I stab'   *kuwuna*   'to stab'

Besides illustrating the reduction of /p/ and its assimilation to the following vowel, these examples also illustrate the result of sound changes occurring in a certain order. The reduction of /p/ did not occur after the nasal stop, which was /m/ before /p/ because the stop closure of the nasal reinforced the stop closure of the /p/. Later, the nasal deleted before voiceless stops, putting the /p/ back in position for lenition. However, apparently the sound change that weakened /p/ was no longer in operation, so this /p/ has remained.

Other well-attested changes that result in the loss of the oral constriction involve the reduction of fricatives such as /s/ and /f/ to /h/. A widespread change in varieties of Spanish is the aspiration and loss of syllable-final /s/. When /s/ occurs before a consonant, in these dialects (particularly Spanish of the Caribbean and some parts of Latin America and Andalusia), the alveolar articulation is lost and the result is a glottal fricative or period of voicelessness, often transcribed as [h]: *estilo* [ehtilo] 'style', *felizmente* [felihmente] 'happily'. This also happens at the end of the word, particularly when a consonant follows: *animales finos* [animalehfinos] (Terrell 1977). In some dialects /s/ is also reduced between vowels, especially if a mid or low vowel precedes, even if it is in word-initial position: *pasar* [pahar] 'to happen', *la señora* [laheñora] 'the lady' (Raymond and Brown 2012).

Other fricatives can also undergo debuccalization, or loss of the oral constriction. Old Spanish /f/ has been reduced to /h/ and then deleted completely in most words. Old Spanish *fecho* > Modern Spanish *hecho* 'done'; also *fablar* > *hablar* 'to speak'; *fumo* > *humo* 'smoke'. This is a sound change that did not turn out to be completely regular. Besides the phonetic environment before /w/ which reinforced the labial gesture, giving Modern Spanish *fuerte* 'strong', *fuego* 'fire', proper names sometimes kept the /f/, giving doublets such as *Fernando* and *Hernando*, and some other words retained /f/. See Brown and Raymond, 2012 for further discussion of why certain words retained /f/.

A velar fricative can undergo a very similar change. The Indo-European velar stop *k, as found in the following Latin stems or words *cent-* '100', *capere* 'take, seize', *cornū* 'horn', *-clinare* 'to lean', and *canis* 'dog' became a velar fricative in Old English, as shown in the words *hund* '100', *habban* 'have', *horn* 'horn', *hlæn* 'lean', and *hund* 'dog'. In Old English, the letter *h* before a consonant just indicated a period of voicelessness, which has now mostly disappeared. In some

Table 2.5: *Paths of lenition for voiceless stops*

Voiceless stop	>	Affricate	>	Fricative	>	Voicelessness	>	Zero
p	>	pf	>	f	>	h	>	ø
t	>	ts/tθ	>	s/θ	>	h	>	ø
k	>	kx	>	x	>	h	>	ø

dialects, initial /h/ before a vowel is also deleted. Also in Uralic languages, an original /k/ becomes /h/ in Hungarian.

These lenition changes can be arranged in terms of paths of change – certain sequences that occur in the languages of the world, whether they are related or not. These paths are unidirectional; that is, the changes always proceed from stop to affricate to fricative to /h/ to zero, and not in the other direction. The paths are laid out in Table 2.5. In the foregoing discussion, most of the steps on these paths have been documented in more than one language. There is also some variation in how the paths are manifested in a language. We noted above that the reduction of /p/ can lead to an /h/ that assimilates to the following vowel. It may also happen that the affricate stage is not observed and other variants are also possible. However, Table 2.5 represents general trends.

Our examples so far have involved voiceless stops becoming fricatives, but voiced stops can also become fricatives, especially in intervocalic position. This lenition occurs in Spanish, both Peninsular and Latin American. The voiced stops, /b/, /d/, and /g/ become fricatives between two vowels, both word-internally and between words. Thus *lobo* 'wolf' is pronounced [loβo], *lado* 'side' [laðo], and *lago* 'lake' is [laɣo]. It is also common for the dental fricative to further weaken and delete in high frequency words.

2.5.4.   Voicing

Voiceless stops and fricatives can become voiced, especially in a position between two vowels or in other voiced environments. Latin voiceless stops, /p/, /t/, /k/, and /kʷ/ became voiced between vowels beginning in Vulgar Latin and thus end up as voiced in most Romance languages. The examples shown here are in Latin orthography and Spanish orthography. There are also other changes shown between the Latin and Spanish, especially in the vowels. Ignore these for the moment. As I just mentioned, these voiced stops in Spanish are now pronounced as fricatives or at times deleted entirely.

(16)

	Latin	Spanish	Gloss
	lupu	*lobo*	'wolf'
	ad-ripa	*arriba*	'above, up'
	vita	*vida*	'life'
	rota	*rueda*	'wheel'
	secure	*seguro*	'safe'
	aqua	*agua*	'water'

As this voicing change takes place between vowels, it is sometimes described as assimilation – the voicing of the vowels spreads to the consonant. However, in articulatory terms, what is really happening is that the glottal gesture that causes the vocal cords to open for the voicelessness of the stop shortens, decreases in magnitude, and is eventually lost, leaving continuous voicing through the vowels and the stop. In this interpretation, it is the weakening of the glottal opening gesture that causes the change and appropriately classifies it as a lenition.

Voiceless fricatives commonly voice between vowels as well. Old English had the voiceless fricative phonemes /f/, /θ/, and /s/, which were voiced between vowels.

(17)   Old English   Present Day English
         seofon   *seven*
         hefiġ   *heavy*
         ofer   *over*
         broþor   *brother* [ð]
         hwæþer   *whether* [ð]
         risan   *rise* [z]
         dysiġ 'foolish' *dizzy*

This is also considered lenition because the gesture opening the glottis is reduced and eventually lost.

2.5.5. Degemination

Geminate consonants are consonants whose constriction is held longer than non-geminates. Many languages have a contrast between geminate and non-geminate consonants, e.g. Old English, Finnish, Latin, Italian, and Tamil. When a geminate consonant shortens to become a simple consonant, that is also considered lenition because the duration of the closure or partial closure gesture is reduced. Latin had voiceless geminate stop consonants, and in many Romance languages these have reduced to simple stops, remaining voiceless, as in the following examples (*c* in Latin is /k/):

(18)   Latin   Spanish   Gloss
         cŭppa   *copa*   'cup'
         gutta   *gota*   'drop'
         mittere   *meter*   'to put'
         bucca   *boca*   'mouth'

2.5.6. Chain shifts: degemination, voicing, spirantization

Several of the lenition processes just discussed are linked together in the history of Romance languages. Table 2.6 shows the three changes that form a chain shift.

Notice that the degemination just discussed in the evolution of Latin into Spanish did not cause a merger with the existing non-geminate (simple) voiceless

Table 2.6: *Chain shift of Latin stop consonants*

			Latin	Spanish	Gloss
pp	>	p	*cŭppa>*	*copa*	'cup'
p	>	b	*lupus>*	*lobo*	'wolf'
b	>	β	*probare >*	*probar*	'to try, test'
tt	>	t	*gutta>*	*gota*	'drop'
t	>	d	*vita>*	*vida*	'life'
d	>	ð \ ø	*sŭcidu >*	*sucio*	'dirty'
kk	>	k	*bucca>*	*boca*	'mouth'
k	>	g	*sacratu>*	*sagrado*	'holy'
g	>	ɣ \ ø	*regale >*	*real*	'royal'

stops in intervocalic position because the existing simple stops had already become voiced in intervocalic position. This means that words that were phonemically distinct before the degemination are still distinct; for instance, /pp/ did not merge with /p/, rather the distinction between /pp/ and /p/ is now a distinction between /p/ and /b/. When it comes to the voiceless stops becoming voiced, there was eventually some merger, but the voiced stops had become fricatives or deleted, so there was still a distinction between these series of stops. In parallel fashion, the voicing of these simple stops did not cause them to merge with existing voiced stops (at least not right away) because these had become fricatives or had deleted.

This set of changes is called a chain shift since the three changes seem to be related, not just because they are all lenition changes, but because the three series of consonant phonemes remain distinct. In order for that to happen, the voiced stops must first become fricatives, then the voiceless stops become voiced, and finally the geminates become simple. This is the order of events that would preserve the phonemic contrasts. If the geminates simplified first, they would be indistinguishable from the existing voiceless stops, and so they would acquire voice along with them. Another possibility is that all three changes were occurring simultaneously, and as each series of consonants changed gradually, they all remained phonemically distinct. As this change took place very long ago, we do not know whether the changes were simultaneous or sequential. In the next chapter we will see examples of vowel shifts that are also chain shifts.

2.5.7.   Lenition as sonorization

Another type of lenition, overlapping with the process of voicing discussed as lenition in the preceding sections, is sonorization, by which a consonant becomes more sonorant or more vowel-like. These changes often occur in syllable-final position. Such changes took place in the Chadic language

Table 2.7: *Hausa lenition*

Syllable-final velars are weakened to /u/

Reconstructed form	Hausa form	Related form
*talak- cì	*talaucì* 'poverty'	*talàkà* 'common man'
*hagni	*hauni* 'left'	*hagu(n)* 'left'
*wàtàk	*wàtàu* 'that is to say'	*wàtàkà* western Hausa

Syllable-final coronals are weakened to /r̃/

	far̃kà 'wake up'	*fàɗàkà* 'wake up'
	ɓàr̃nā 'damage (n.)'	*ɓāta* 'to damage'

Syllable-final labials are weakened to /u/ in Standard Hausa only

		Western Hausa
	Audù proper name	*Abdù*
	kaurì 'thickness'	*kabri*

of Africa, Hausa, as described in Klingenheben's Law. Syllable-final labial and velar consonants become the glide /w/ and dental consonants become /r/ as shown in Table 2.7. This is a reconstructed change, but the evidence for it can be found in the way morphemes change in context and in dialect differences (Newman 2000).

Similar changes have taken place in various Romance languages. For example, Latin *debitus* 'debt' becomes Old Spanish *debdo* and Middle Spanish *deudo*; Latin *captivus* 'captive' becomes Spanish *cautivo*.

These changes occur in syllable-final position, but sonorization can also occur between two vowels, as in Kanuri (a Nilo-Saharan language of Africa), where the phonemes /k/ and /g/ have allophones that are glides /w/ and /y/ between vowels. The palatal glide occurs before front vowels and the labio-velar glide occurs before back vowels (Cyffer 1998). Also /b/ becomes /w/ before back vowels.

(19)   Kanuri /k/, /g/, and /b/ sonorize between vowels
   lekáda   >   *leyáda*   'they went'
   fukáda   >   *fuwáda*   'they blew'
   zábúna   >   *záwúna*   'they have eaten'

Another form of sonorization is rhotacism, a change by which an [s] or [z] becomes an [r]. Such a change occurred in Latin as exemplified by the alternation *corpus*, *corpora* 'body, nom./acc. sg. and pl.', *opus*, *opera* 'work, nom./acc. sg. and pl.' and in Germanic where Old English infinitive *cēosan* 'to choose' has a past participle *coren*, and *wæs* 'was' alternates with *wære/wæron* 'were'. This change involves voicing and loss of fricative closure; it takes place intervocalically.

Within one language, lenition may be manifested as both debuccalization and sonorization. For example, in the Lusoba dialect of the Bantu language

Lumasaaba /p/ sonorizes to [y] or [w] depending upon the following vowel and /t/ sonorizes to [r] but /k/ spirantizes to [x] (G. Brown 1972).

2.5.8.   Consonant cluster reduction

Consonant deletions from consonant clusters also qualify as reductions, as they involve the reduction in magnitude of a gesture. Shortening leading to eventual loss is probably the cause of the deletion of initial /k/ and /g/ before /n/ in English, the sound change mentioned at the beginning of this chapter. However, some deletions around other consonants may be caused by overlapping of adjacent gestures, which masks the acoustic properties of a consonant. Browman and Goldstein 1986 studied the movements of the articulators while a subject produced the phrase *perfect memory*. They found that even when no /t/ was perceived at the end of *perfect*, the tongue was still making the gesture at the alveolar ridge. But because the labial gesture for the /m/ was anticipated it completely overlapped the /t/ gesture and hid it acoustically. Final t/d deletion is a common process in American English, and the contexts in which it is most found are consonantal ones, following and preceding another consonant. Thus while studies show that the /t/ and /d/ become shorter in certain contexts, the loss of these final consonants is also due to the overlap of other gestures.

Word-initial clusters can be simplified by the loss of the second consonant. In the Middle Indic language Pāli which developed from Sanskrit, initial clusters were reduced to just one consonant, as in these examples (Murray 1982).

(20) | Sanskrit | Pāli | Gloss |
        | prajnā | paññā | 'knowledge' |
        | krayavikraya | kayavikkaya | 'commerce' |
        | srotas | sota | 'stream' |
        | svapna | soppa | 'sleep' |

In some of these examples, internal consonant clusters are simplified by perseverative assimilation.

2.5.9.   Contexts in which reduction occurs

The examples of lenition or reduction that we have examined in the preceding sections show a strong tendency for these processes to occur in certain contexts. Researchers who have noticed these trends have suggested a division between strong positions and weak positions, as shown in Table 2.8 (Ségéral and Scheer 2008).

You might have noticed that most of the lenition sound changes presented above occurred in intervocalic position. The examples cited did not distinguish between consonants at the beginning of stressed and unstressed syllables, but one can observe this difference in the American English pronunciation of *pretend* vs. *pretty*, where the flapping of /t/ (a lenition process, since it results from the

Table 2.8: *Positions favoring (weak positions) and disfavoring (strong positions) lenition*

Strong positions	English examples
Word-initial position	*tend*
Syllable-initial after a C	*after*
Weak positions (from strongest to weakest)	
Intervocalic before a stressed vowel	*pretend*
Intervocalic before an unstressed vowel	*pretty*
Syllable-final before a consonant	*atmosphere*
Word-final	*hat*

shortening of the tongue tip and glottal gestures) usually occurs before an unstressed vowel. The sonorization examples we discussed occurred in syllable-final position as well as intervocalically. Word and syllable-initial position do not usually accommodate lenition processes unless the lenition is very general, or the syllable-initial consonants are often preceded by vowels. Phonetic studies have shown that word- and syllable-initial consonants are produced with more force and are longer than syllable-final consonants (Keating et al. 2003).

2.5.10.   Vowel reduction and deletion

Vowels can also reduce and delete but, of course, under different conditions than consonants do. When two vowels are next to one another they can fuse into one vowel, preserving some features from both vowels. The diphthong /ɑi/ can give rise to a simple front vowel, either the low front vowel /a/, as in the dialects of the southeastern USA, where *I* is pronounced /aː/, or a mid vowel as found in the Romance outcome for Latin *ai*. For instance, the Latin perfect 1st sg. suffix *–avi* lost the medial consonant, giving *–ai* which became *–ei* in Portuguese *falei* 'I spoke' and *–e* in Spanish, *hablé* 'I spoke'.

When vowels reduce between consonants, the main determinant is the lack of stress. Vowel reduction is most prominent in languages that have a strong stress, particularly if stress is realized as an increase in duration along with loudness and pitch. That is, if the rhythm of the language is such that stressed syllables are longer and unstressed ones are shorter, then the vowels in the unstressed syllables are likely to reduce (Bybee et al. 1998). Usually reduction constitutes a change from a more peripheral vowel (high, back, front) to a more central and/or mid vowel, such as schwa. For instance, English reduced vowels are [ə] as in the last vowel of *Rosa* or [ɨ] as in the last vowel of *roses*. However, there are languages in which reduced vowels are raised. Thus in Brazilian Portuguese, final unstressed [o] and [e] raise to [u] and [i] respectively while a final [a] centralizes to schwa. Examples can be found in Table 2.1.

In languages that do not have a strong stress, reduction of vowels can be by coalescence or by devoicing. Devoicing of vowels occurs in a voiceless environment – between two voiceless consonants or between a voiceless consonant and the end of the word, as seen in high vowels in Japanese. For instance, the first vowel in *kishitsu* 'temperament' is devoiced, as is the last vowel in *desu* 'be' when it is before a pause.

Devoicing, shortening, and centralization can all lead eventually to deletion of vowels. This is quite common in final unstressed syllables. For example, Old English nouns had vowels that marked number and case, but by Middle English these had all reduced to schwa, and by Early Modern English most of these schwas had deleted. (The final /m/ of the dative plural became /n/ and then deleted, too.)

(21)   Old English *scip* 'ship'

	Singular	Plural
nominative/accusative	*scip*	*scipu*
genitive	*scipes*	*scipa*
dative	*scipe*	*scipum*

In the next chapter we will discuss in more detail the consequences of different types of rhythm on sound change.

2.6.   Reduction and retiming acting together

In this section we consider a common sequence of sound changes that involves both retiming and reduction. It is common across languages for vowels to be nasalized when adjacent to a nasal consonant. Vowel nasalization before a syllable-final nasal occurs as a regular synchronic process in many languages. For example, the vowels in English *can*, *canned*, and *can't* are heavily nasalized, which means that the velum is open during their articulation, allowing air to flow through the nasal passages. The reason for this is of course the anticipation of the opening of the velum for the nasal consonant. The nasalization appears to be more extreme when the following nasal is in the same syllable, as in the examples above, than when it is intervocalic and begins the next syllable as in words such as *banana*. This difference is due to the way gestures are organized into syllables. In English it has been found that the syllable-initial gestures making up a consonant are timed to be simultaneous, while syllable-final gestures are more spread out and more sequential (Browman and Goldstein 1995).

In some languages, vowel nasalization is accompanied by the weakening of the stop portion of the nasal consonant. As mentioned above, syllable-final position is a weak position for consonants, and in some languages the nasal consonant deletes after or in conjunction with the vowel becoming nasal. These two linked developments have the effect of creating new nasal vowel phonemes, as shown in the following examples from French in the tenth to thirteenth centuries:

(22)   *fin*   > [fĩn]   > [fẽn]   > [fɛ̃]   'end'
        bon   > [bõn]   > [bõ]   'good'
        chanter   > [ʃãnte]   > [ʃãte]   'to sing'
        enfant   > [ẽnfãnt] > [ãnfãn]   > [ãfã]   'child'

Unlike in some languages, Old French vowels nasalized before nasal consonants that were syllable-final and syllable-initial, but in Middle French the nasal vowels before intervocalic nasal consonants became oral again (Hajek 1997). You can also note in (22) that some of the nasal vowels became lower as well. Once the nasal consonant has deleted, the nasal vowels contrast with oral ones in minimal pairs such as *ange* [ãːʒ] 'angel' vs. *âge* [ɑːʒ] 'age'. A process of this type is the major source of nasal vowel phonemes in the languages of the world.

Several studies of the vowel nasalization and consonant deletion process across languages have revealed some general patterns of change. The first one, which I have already mentioned, is that the vowel is more likely to nasalize and nasal consonant to delete if they are in the same syllable. In French the nasal consonant only deleted if it was syllable final. However, Portuguese has taken this process somewhat further and also deleted intervocalic nasals, leaving behind a nasalized vowel or diphthong in word-final position, or an oral vowel or diphthong in non-final position (Mattoso Camara Jr. 1972):

(23)   Latin   Portuguese
        manus 'hand'   >   *mão* [mãw̃]
        pōnit 'put 3rd sg.'   >   *põe* [põj̃]
        tenēre 'to have'   >   *ter*
        pōnere 'to put'   >   *pôr*

A generalization that can be made about these facts is an implicational one: if a language has vowel nasalization and nasal deletion between vowels, it also has it when the nasal consonant is syllable-final (Hajek 1997; Ruhlen 1978).

Second, there are certain syllable-final contexts in which the nasal consonant is more likely to delete, in particular when the nasal precedes a fricative rather than a stop. In spoken Latin, /n/ was deleted before /s/ as in these examples with their Spanish outcome: *mensa* > *mesa* 'table' and *mansione* > *mesón* 'inn'. In Pre-Old English, there is a similar loss of /n/ before a fricative. Compare English *goose* to German *Gans*, English *tooth* to German *Zahn*, English *five* to German *fünf*. By an earlier change the nasal was lost before /x/, leaving English with related forms such as *think*, *thought* and *bring*, *brought*, where the spelling *gh* represented the velar fricative (A. Campbell 1959). The greater likelihood of the nasal deleting before a fricative than before a stop is due to the fact that the following stop reinforces the closure of the nasal, while the fricative has the effect of weakening the closure of the nasal consonant. In these examples, the nasalization on the vowel is not preserved.

Third, in cases where there is vowel nasalization and consonant deletion in unstressed syllables, the nasalization is prone to loss, probably because of the lesser perceptibility of vowel nasalization on unstressed vowels.

The example of vowel nasalization illustrates the way that retiming and reduction can work together. It also shows that by comparing similar phenomena in different languages, both related and unrelated, we can discover certain recurrent patterns of change that can help us find explanations for sound change.

2.7.   Ease of articulation and cross-linguistic similarities in sound changes

As we have seen in many of the examples given in this chapter, very similar sound changes can occur in languages that are unrelated and quite distant in time and space. This means that at least some of the forces that cause sound change are not specific to particular languages, but rather reside in characteristics that all humans have in common. One obvious source of cross-linguistic similarities in sound change is the human vocal apparatus – including the glottis, oral cavity, nasal cavity, velum, tongue, and lips. The different active articulators that must move through space and time to create linguistic sounds also have their characteristic ways of moving, based on the size and shape of the muscles that comprise them. The line-up of articulations in sequence as well as their organization into syllables has an effect on individual articulations. All of these factors are sure to be similar across languages. In addition, the acoustic effect of the positions and movements of articulators will be similar across languages. For these reasons, explanations for sound change are most commonly based on phonetic factors.

Our discussion so far has focused on assimilation and reduction, which most researchers agree are the most common types. Given these two types of change, it is not surprising that terms such as 'ease of articulation' are often invoked to explain sound change. Hockett 1958 proposes that the directionality of sound change is caused by 'the tendency to speak sloppily' (p. 456) or more specifically the fact that 'the speaker (is) quite sloppy in his aim (at an articulatory target) most of the time' (1958: 440). Hock 1986 also cites 'relaxation' or 'weakening' of articulatory effort, and even 'the lazy tongue phenomenon' as the cause of lenition. Such statements are common in popular textbooks, and indeed reflect the popular conception of phonetic variation as being degeneration away from correct pronunciation.

While it is easy to understand the intuition behind such statements, there are many reasons to be dissatisfied with the characterization of sound change as due to laziness or sloppiness, or even the pursuit of ease. Lehmann (1992: 207) makes the valid observation that what seems easy in one language is difficult in another; indeed, it is practice or the lack of it that makes one articulation seem easier or more difficult than another. Certainly the outcome of a reducing sound change can also be quite complex and difficult on some level, as when Old Irish lenition produced a bilabial nasal fricative (Thurneysen 1956: 85).

Also the proposal that speakers are lazy or sloppy would suggest that speakers of the same language might each reduce articulation in an individual way: given an intervocalic /t/, some speakers might voice it, some might make it a fricative, and others a glottal stop. However, within a speech community, reduction is quite regular across speakers. There may be differences in the degree of reduction, but the paths that reduction and assimilation follow are conventional within the dialect. In fact, given the extent to which speakers within a dialect produce utterances that are so alike in phonetic detail that one can recognize the dialect of a speaker, it seems implausible to claim that speakers are lazy or sloppy.

Despite these facts, one need not totally reject the idea that sound change is largely reductive, but rather than invoking a lack of effort on the part of speakers, it is more reasonable to view speech as just one of many finely tuned neuromotor activities that can be automated with the effect of becoming more efficient. With repetition, sequences of neuromotor acts become chunked into units, and within these units the sequences become more integrated, with transitions between actions becoming smoother, and parts of the actions overlapping. Thus, producing a word or a phrase containing a sequence of articulatory gestures can be seen as analogous to other repeated behaviors, such as starting your car or tying your shoes. Assimilation and lenition can be viewed, then, as a consequence of articulation as a highly practiced neuromotor activity.

One way organisms respond to experience is by learning what to expect next, or what to do next. Even non-humans can plan an upcoming action while executing a current action. Experiments with both humans and monkeys have shown that when sequences of button-presses are learned, with practice they become chunked as whole units (just as words and phrases do when they are repeated) (Rand, Hikosaka, Miyachi, Lu, and Miyashita 1998; for a review of such research see Rhodes, Bullock, Verwey, Averbeck, and Page 2004). These experiments also showed that the processes needed to execute an upcoming element overlap with the execution of the preceding element. In order for speech to be fluent, such overlap in planning must also occur: while a speaker is executing a series of syllables or a word, the next one is in the planning stages. Chunking of production movements in articulation and anticipation of the next movement have an impact on the transitions between articulatory gestures (or segments) as well as on the gestures themselves.

While articulation of the sounds of language is a motor activity and subject to the same influences as other motor activities, speech is different from more isolated activities such as tying your shoes because the same neuromotor activities are repeated across distinct words and phrases. Thus a change in one word or phrase may also occur in other words and phrases. In addition, this particular neuromotor activity is embedded in a conventionalized communicative system and as such is constrained by the goal of communicating. Thus reduction and overlap cannot be carried too far. The other effect of community is social identification. Speakers like to behave like other members of the community.

For this reason, a group of speakers all change their pronunciations in the same direction. They do this because they begin with similar pronunciations and then they track one another's small gradual changes and make similar changes themselves. I like to think about the way a sound change progresses within a speech community as similar to flocking behavior that occurs when birds fly together in a group. Each individual is unconsciously tracking the pronunciations of other members of the group and, with each of his or her pronunciations, trying to stay within a range, both for the purposes of being understood and towards the goal of sounding like a member of the group. Over repeated instances of use of a sound, it may very slowly and gradually change in the usage of the individuals.

The tendency towards automation and efficiency that produces sound change also explains why sound change usually occurs earliest in casual speech as opposed to formal speech. If there is a tension between making articulation more efficient and maintaining communicative effectiveness, then it will be in the most familiar and casual situations (as among close friends or family members) that the constraints that keep change from happening are the most relaxed. In such situations, communication is easier because of shared background, and conservative social constraints are the least applicable, so the articulatory patterns that are the most efficient are allowed to emerge.

2.8.   Lexical diffusion

The discussion so far has emphasized the fact that most sound changes eventually affect all the words of the language that have the sound in question in the required phonetic environment. Occasionally we find changes that leave some words unaffected, as in the case of Old Spanish /f/ which weakened to /h/ in many, but not all, words, as mentioned above. Such cases are sometimes referred to as "lexical diffusion" changes, meaning that the change has failed to diffuse through the whole lexicon. They suggest that not all words are affected at the same time when a change is in progress. Thus an important dimension to consider in understanding sound change is the way the change spreads among the words of the lexicon, or its lexical diffusion. This dimension of sound change has been ignored in many studies, or assumed to be uninteresting. The view taken here and in more recent studies is that all sound changes have to diffuse through the lexicon in some way or another, gradually or abruptly, reaching completion or not, even if all the words of the language are eventually affected, and the sound change turns out to be regular.

William Labov has suggested a distinction between "regular" sound changes and "lexical diffusion" changes (Labov 1981). What his distinction implies is that when a regular sound change is taking place all the words with the requisite phonetic environment are affected at the same time and the same rate, and any variation depends more on social factors than on lexical ones. More in-depth studies of phonetically conditioned sound change that turns out to be regular show that not all words are affected simultaneously; rather, some words undergo change earlier and at a faster rate than other words. A common pattern that is found is that words that are frequently used, or used frequently in the environment that conditions the change, are affected earlier than words that are less frequently used (Bybee 2000b; Phillips 2006).

It is impossible to study lexical diffusion of a change that turns out to be regular in the end unless there are records showing how the words were affected as the change was in progress. Our best information on lexical diffusion comes from changes that can be studied currently while they are in progress. Ongoing sound changes such as the deletion of final /t/ and /d/ in English, the deletion of intervocalic /ð/ in Spanish, reduction of unstressed vowels in English and Dutch, and lenition of final /s/ in Spanish all show systematic lexical diffusion effects, in that words that are more frequent undergo the change earlier than words that are less frequent. In all of the examples, the phonetic conditioning environment is the most important factor in predicting the change, but in the class of words that have the conditioning environment, the high-frequency words are more likely to be affected.

In the case of English final /t/ and /d/ deletion, the phonetic conditioning that favors the change is a preceding consonant (in the same word) and a following consonant (in the next word). All studies of this phenomenon mention that the words *just*, *went*, and *and* have very high rates of deletion and they are often excluded from the study. These are three very frequent words, and this factor could likely explain their higher rates of deletion. Indeed, when all words are considered, with and without favoring conditioning environments, a strong frequency effect can be observed, as shown in Table 2.9 (Bybee 2000b).

The results in Table 2.9 rely on a fairly arbitrary cut-off between high and low frequency because it is not currently known exactly how to determine what is low and what is high. Also, if a change is advanced further, more low-frequency words will be affected, so the cut-off point may change over time.

Vowel reduction and deletion also show robust word-frequency effects. In a very early study of the effects of word frequency, Fidelholz 1975 demonstrates that the essential difference between American English words that reduce a

Table 2.9: *Rate of t/d-deletion in American English for entire corpus by word frequency*

	High frequency	%	Low Frequency	%
Retention	752	45.6%	262	65.7%
Deletion	898	54.4%	137	34.3%

Chi-squared: 41.67, p < .001, df = 1

prestress vowel, such as *astronomy, mistake*, and *abstain*, and phonetically similar words that do not, such as *gastronomy, mistook*, and *abstemious*, is word frequency. Van Bergem 1995 finds that reduction of a prestress vowel in Dutch also is highly conditioned by frequency. The high-frequency words *minuut* 'minute', *vakantie* 'vacation', and *patat* 'chips' are more likely to have a schwa in the first syllable than the phonetically similar low-frequency words *miniem* 'marginal', *vakante* 'vacant', and *patent* 'patent'.

It is important to bear in mind that word frequency is only one of several factors that are operating when a sound change occurs. The most important factor is the phonetic environment, which determines what change occurs. The role of frequency or repetition is to move the change forward. As mentioned in the previous section, many sound changes seem to be the result of the increased automation that occurs in highly practiced behaviors, such as driving a car. Since repetition is important to increases in automation, it follows that words (and phrases) that are repeated often will have had a chance to undergo more extensive automation than those that are repeated less often. Thus high-frequency words will undergo a sound change that automates production earlier than low-frequency words. Also, words that are predictable in context can reduce more because it is easier for the listener to identify a predictable word.

As we have noted, most sound changes end up as regular – affecting all the words of the lexicon, even low-frequency words. The explanation for this is that as more and more words have the changed sound, the general pronunciation patterns of the language are changed, with the older pattern being replaced by a newer one that applies to all words.

Some sound changes we have discussed here apply at the ends or beginnings of words. That means that part of the conditioning environment is in another word. Since we use words in a productive way, the same word will occur in lots of different combinations with other words. That means that the conditioning environment might differ from one use of a word to another. For example, the English word *perfect* has a final /t/ following a consonant, making it a candidate for /t/ deletion; this deletion is more likely if the following word begins with a consonant, as in *perfect memory*, than if it begins in a vowel, as in *perfect accent*. The few detailed studies that have been done of such changes in progress show that it is the frequency with which the word occurs in the environment that is conducive to the change that determines how rapidly the word will undergo that change (Bybee 2002; Brown and Raymond 2012).

Lexical diffusion does not always proceed from the most frequent to the least frequent words; sometimes classes of words are affected, and sometimes the least frequent words are more susceptible to change. Lexical diffusion operates differently on changes whose motivation is not automation of production. In the next chapter these other types of changes will be discussed, and we will also discuss the role that lexical diffusion patterns can play in helping to determine the motivation for sound change and other types of phonological change.

2.9.   Special reduction

In addition to sound changes that are highly systematic and lexically regular, one also finds in all languages cases of special reduction, reduction that occurs in particularly high-frequency items such as greetings, discourse markers, or grammatical sequences. There are many familiar examples, such as *goodbye* from *God be with ye* or *hi* from *how are you*. The very popular word *ciao*, which is used in many European languages for 'goodbye' and in some for both 'hello' and 'goodbye', comes from the Venetian expression *s-ciao* /ˈstʃao/ from *s-chiavo vostro* 'I am your servant, slave', from Medieval Latin *sclavus* 'Slav, slave'. Such forms shorten by the omission of words, such as *vostro* 'your' in the expression just mentioned, and also by phonological reduction, such as loss of /v/ in *schiavo* and the fusion of /skj/ to /tʃ/ in the same word.

Terms of address also tend to undergo special reduction. Spanish *usted* 2nd person singular developed out of the longer and more elegant phrase *vuestra merced* 'your grace'. Old English *hlafweard* which contains the roots *hlaf* 'loaf' and *weard* 'keeper' is reduced to *hlaford* and eventually *lord*. Both Mrs. [mɪsɨz] or [mɪzɨz] and Miss [mɪs] are reduced forms of *mistress*.

Such extreme reductions are not aberrations, but usually follow the same patterns as regular sound changes: gestures are both retimed and reduced. For example, American English *don't* reduces in phrases such as *I don't know*: the /d/ becomes a flap and then further shortens or deletes, the final /t/ deletes, and vowel reduces by becoming more central: [ɑjɾə̃no] or [ajə̃no]. All of these changes occur regularly in other words, but not usually to this extent. The extreme reduction in phrases such as this is in part due to their high frequency of use and also the contexts in which they are used. They sometimes undergo semantic change or change in usage patterns at the same time as they reduce phonetically.

Sometimes special reduction is a harbinger of later regular changes. A change in a particular morpheme or word of high frequency can later on be observed to apply more regularly to all words. For example, the 2nd person plural inflection in Latin *–tis* became *–des* in Old Spanish by the voicing change we discussed earlier. That /d/ was subject to spirantization and weakening. In the fifteenth century, the 2nd person plural morpheme lost its /d/ in all verb forms except the imperfective indicative and subjunctive. For example, *amádes* > *amáes* 'love, 2nd pl. pres.'. Later, in the seventeenth century, the /d/ in the other forms was lost as well: *amábades* > *amábais* 'love, 2nd pl. imperfective' (Menéndez-Pidal 1968). This change comes long before the more general loss of /d/ that is ongoing today, yet the change itself and conditioning are the same as that occurring today.

Grammatical elements that are often used together also contract. Here are a few examples: Prepositions contract with articles, as in French *à + le > au* 'to the (masc.)', auxiliaries contract with subject pronouns, as in English *I'll, you'll* etc., negatives contract with frequent verbs or auxiliaries as in Latin *nōn + volō* 'neg. + I want' > *nōlo* or English *do* + *not* > *don't*. This phenomenon will be discussed more in connection with grammaticalization in Chapter 6.

2.10.   Fortition and insertion

As we have seen in this chapter, sound change follows a partly predictable direction even in different languages, and rarely do we find changes that go in the opposite direction. The vast majority of documented sound changes fit into one of the categories discussed above, or into the category of vowel shifts, which we will discuss in the next chapter. However, there are certain changes that appear to be neither assimilations nor reductions; in fact, there are some changes that have to be viewed as strengthening or fortition. We discuss these changes in this section after clarifying the definition of fortition.

Just as lenition was defined as the reduction in magnitude or duration of a gesture, fortition, its opposite, must be defined as the increase in the magnitude or duration of a gesture. In the types of sound changes we have discussed so far, gestures have either been retimed or reduced, and no new gestures have been introduced. These assimilations and reductions are by far the most common types of sound change. One might be tempted then to propose that sound change never increases the magnitude of a gesture and never introduces new gestures. In fact, some researchers have made this proposal (Mowrey and Pagliuca 1995). There are, however, some well-documented cases that do not quite fit this hypothesis. We will examine such cases of fortition after discussing some cases that seem like they might exhibit fortition, but, in fact, do not by the definition we are using here.

First, there are the cases we have already mentioned in which stops (especially voiceless ones) become affricates on their way to becoming fricatives. While some researchers have viewed the creation of affricates in this way as fortition because they are acoustically stronger than plain stops, they fit our definition of fortition only if the gestures involved gain in magnitude or duration. For example, in one well-studied case, Liverpool English, the stop that becomes affricated loses some of the duration of the stop closure, probably because the whole stop gesture has decreased in magnitude, so the change is, as we classified it above, lenition (Honeybone 2001). If there are cases of affrication in which the consonant lengthens, they would be described as exhibiting fortition.

Second, there are cases where a new segment appears where it did not occur before. Common cases are those in which an obstruent appears in a consonant cluster. These are called *excrescent consonants*. Some systematic examples occur in Spanish future and conditional verb forms. These forms arose when forms of an auxiliary suffixed to the infinitive forming a new future. In some verbs, the vowel in the syllable before the stressed suffix deleted, leaving a cluster of nasal plus liquid. Then a consonant /d/ arose in these clusters.

(24)   Spanish

Suffixation	Vowel deletion	Excrescent consonant	Gloss
venir + á	*venrá*	*vendrá*	'come, 3rd sg. fut.'
poner + á	*ponrá*	*pondrá*	'put, 3rd sg. fut.'
salir + á	*salrá*	*saldrá*	'leave, 3rd sg. fut.'
valer + á	*valrá*	*valdrá*	'be worth, 3rd sg. fut.'

Similar examples involve the /t/ found in a word such as English *prince*, which in many dialects is pronounced just like *prints*, and in the historical change of English *brœmle* to *bramble*, Latin *hominem* to Old Spanish *homne*, *homre* to Modern Spanish *hombre* 'man', or Latin *nomine* to Old Spanish *nomne*, *nomre* to current *nombre* 'name'.

In understanding such cases, it is important to note that the new consonant /d/ or /b/ is at the same point of articulation as the consonant preceding the liquid. Nothing new was added in terms of gestures for the point of articulation. Rather, what has happened is best described as a retiming. If the velum-opening gesture for the nasal ends before the liquid articulation begins, a voiced obstruent will arise. In the case of *prince*, the glottal opening gesture for the voiceless /s/ is anticipated, turning the end of the /n/ gesture into a /t/. In the case of a preceding /l/, as in *salrá* to *saldrá*, an important factor is the fact that the /r/ after an /l/ in Spanish is trilled, so the /d/ develops in the transition from the /l/ to the trilled /r/. These excrescent consonants are not instances of fortition, but rather of adjustments in timing, mostly anticipatory.

Though somewhat less clear, it is possible to view vowel insertions as also growing out of the surrounding contexts, which usually involve sonorant consonants (and occasionally fricatives) that may be extended into syllabic elements. The vowel inserted is a minimal vowel for the language (usually the same one as would result from vowel reduction) or one that has the same features as the surrounding consonants. In Dutch a short schwa develops between an /l/ and an obstruent or obstruent cluster at the end of a word. Thus *melk* 'milk' is pronounced [mɛlək] and Delft 'proper name of a city' is pronounced [dɛləft]. In Irish Gaelic, a vowel is inserted in similar clusters, between an /r/ and a following consonant. If the consonant is palatalized, the vowel is a high front vowel [i], and if it is not palatalized, the vowel is a schwa (O Siadhail 1980: 226).

(25)   Irish Gaelic orthography and pronunciation

fearg	[fʲarəg]	'anger'	*feirm*	[fʲerʲimʲ]	'farm'
dorn	[dorən]	'fist'	*stoirm*	[sterʲimʲ]	'storm'
dearg	[dʲarəg]	'red'	*tairbhe*	[tarʲifʲi]	'good, benefit'
seomra	[soːmərə]	'room'	*airgim*	[arʲigʲimʲ]	'I offer'

Thus the inserted or epenthetic vowel "grows" out of the gestural environment, the way the excrescent consonants do. That is why the "inserted" vowel is a high front vowel in a palatal environment but a schwa in non-palatal environments.

As with consonants, retiming is involved as well. The gestures for the /r/ or /l/ are not continued through the whole duration of the sequence, but are suspended, leaving the minimal vowel. (Inserted vowels also occur commonly in borrowed words, but changes that make a borrowed word fit the phonological patterns of the language are not considered sound changes.)

Glides between vowels, also "grow" out of the surrounding vowels, as they are the transitions between vowels. Since glides themselves have more extreme articulations than vowels, this is a case of an increase in the magnitude of a gesture.

The clearest cases of fortition are gemination and glide strengthening. Geminates can be created by retiming as we saw in examples from Latin to Italian as in example (13), but when a simple consonant becomes a long consonant, then by our definition this is fortition. Let us consider now under what conditions this happens. We find examples in the history of West Germanic and also in the history of Italian. Current accounts argue that this type of gemination is related to the stress accent and to other changes in syllable structure (Murray and Vennemann 1983). The following examples show the evidence for gemination in West Germanic represented here by Old English and Old Saxon. Gothic represents something closer to the pre-gemination stage (examples from Murray and Vennemann).

(26)

	Gothic	Old Saxon	Old English	Gloss
	satjan	*settian*	*settan*	'to set'
	-skapjan	*skeppian*	*scieppan*	'to create'
	kunjis	*kunnies*	*cynnes*	'race, gen.'
	halja	*hellia*	*hell(e)-*	'hell'
	akrs	*akkar*		'acre'

Murray and Vennemann propose that this gemination occurs because stressed syllables, such as the initial syllable in these examples, tend to be long (or to have two morae). Thus the consonant before the /j/ is attracted into the first syllable, leaving the /j/ or /r/ to initiate the second syllable. Since the glide, and also the /r/, are very sonorous segments, they do not provide an optimal onset for a syllable. The gemination, which allows a less sonorous segment to begin the syllable, creates a better syllable onset. Murray and Vennemann apply a similar analysis to Italian gemination by which Latin *sapiat* becomes Italian *sappia* 'know, 3rd sg. pres. subj.' and *cufia* > *cuffia* 'bonnet'. Cases of gemination of this sort clearly require more research before we completely understand their causes. It does appear, however, that changes in prosody (the nature of the accentual system), which were occurring in both Germanic and Romance at the time, are related to gemination. In the next chapter we discuss these changes in prosodic type.

The other common consonant strengthening or fortition reported in many languages can be called glide strengthening or glide hardening. In such a change, the glides /j/ and /w/ in syllable-initial position strengthen into the fricatives

/ʒ/ and /ɣw/. A familiar example is the fricative pronunciation of /j/ and /w/ in Argentinian Spanish, where *yo* 'I' is often heard as [ʒo]. This is a regular change in this dialect, with all words being affected, at least to some extent.

A comparable change took place in the Germanic languages Gothic and Old Norse (Page 1999). A glide after a short vowel geminated and then strengthened. In the examples below, Old High German (OHG) shows only the gemination while Gothic and Old Norse show the hardening.

(27)   Proto-Indo European   OHG   Gothic   Old Norse   Gloss
        *dwoj-   *zweiio* *twaddjē* *tveggja*   'two, gen.'
        *drew-   *triuwi* *triggwa* *tryggva*   'true'

As French developed from Latin, palatal glides strengthened in a different position – after labials. As in the Spanish examples shown in Table 2.4, the palatal glide had affected coronal and velar consonants already, and it only remained after labials. In that position it strengthened and the labial consonant was lost, giving the French forms shown here:

(28)   Latin   French   Gloss
        rŭbĕus   *rouge* [ʁuʒ]   'red'
        răbĭes   *rage* [ʁaʒ]   'rabid'
        căvĕa   *cage* [kaʒ]   'cave'

One might be tempted to think that the palatalized labial developed directly into a palatal consonant, but intermediate stages where *apje* for *ache* 'celery' and *salvje* for *salge* or *sauge* 'sage' are found attest to hardening of the glide followed by loss of the labial (Nyrop 1914; Bateman 2010).

Finally, vowel-length changes, which often occur in open syllables and/or in stressed syllables, are fortitions or strengthening in the sense that they increase the duration of gestures. Such changes are also related to prosodic changes, for example, in which an accent that is primarily signaled by a high pitch or increased intensity changes to also be signaled by an increase in duration, as we will see in the next chapter. When duration becomes associated with stress, then stressed syllables tend to be long or heavy, while unstressed syllables tend to become reduced.

Our discussion of fortition has shown that although it is less common than lenition, there are cases where the duration or magnitude of a gesture can increase. Note, however, that there are no cases where a completely new gesture appears where it did not occur before. For this reason, it is important to examine carefully the gestures involved in the change to look for explanations.

2.11.   Causes of sound change

Some researchers believe that phonetic variation itself is not sound change, but rather sound change is a change in phonological structure or inventory. John Ohala, in a series of papers (see Ohala 2003), suggests that sound change occurs when the listener misperceives the sounds in the speaker's utterance. For instance, in the case of vowel nasalization before a nasal consonant, as discussed in Section 2.4, a mini-sound change occurs if the listener takes the nasalization to be inherent to the vowel rather than a result of the presence of a nasal consonant. If many listeners did this it would result in a type of reanalysis or phonologization of vowel nasality. For Ohala, the sound change is not the spread of nasalization to the vowel, but rather the reinterpretation that follows from it. Blevins 2004 agrees with this point and also proposes that sound change occurs when children acquire a different phonological structure than adults have. This can happen in three ways according to Blevins: first, the way suggested by Ohala, second, by simply misperceiving the sounds or sequences of sounds, and third by changing the frequency with which a variant is used.

As for the role of young children in creating sound change, the actual evidence from children learning their phonology in situations where change is ongoing does not support the idea that children initiate change. Rather, a careful study of the child's variants and those of the surrounding adults shows that children mirror rather successfully the distribution and frequency of the variants that adults use (Patterson 1992; Díaz-Campos 2004; Foulkes and Docherty 2006). These studies indicate that while children might help to extend a change, they probably are not the source of the change itself.

What I have assumed in the preceding in introducing sound change to the reader is that variation itself is the beginning of sound change, and that variation arises primarily for articulatory reasons. Increases in efficiency involve increased overlap of gestures or reduction of their magnitude. Such automation occurs gradually as language is used. Changes in articulation are paralleled by changes in perception as speakers keep track of their own variants and those of others, so change on both dimensions occurs gradually. Changes are constrained by the need to communicate clearly and by the conventions established in the community. For these reasons, I have assumed that all aspects of sound change are gradual and there are no major leaps from one phonological structure to another.

Further reading

Blevins, J., 2004. *Evolutionary phonology: the emergence of sound patterns*, Cambridge: Cambridge University Press. A large-scale survey of phonological patterns with many examples of the sound changes that create these patterns.

Lass, R. and Anderson, J.M., 1975. *Old English phonology*, Cambridge: Cambridge University Press.

Labov, W., 1994. *Principles of linguistic change*, Vol. 1 *Internal factors*, Oxford: Basil Blackwell.

Questions for discussion

1. In the following Italian examples, the /l/ or /n/ of the verbal stem assimilates to the /r/ of the future suffix:

val + rà	>	*varrà*	'will be worth, 3rd sg.'
dol + rà	>	*dorrà*	'will be hurt, 3rd sg.'
ten + rà	>	*terrà*	'will hold, 3rd sg.'
ven + rà	>	*verrà*	'will come, 3rd sg.'
pon + rà	>	*porrà*	'will put, 3rd sg.'

    What type of assimilation is this? In what position is the affected segment?
    Compare the Italian development to a similar situation in Spanish as presented in (24). How do the two cases differ?

2. How can "ease of articulation" be applied to non-linguistic activities? How does practice lead to increased anticipation in non-linguistic activities in humans and non-humans?

3. In what ways are assimilation and reduction similar?

3 Sound change and phonological change in a wider perspective

3.1. Introduction

The last chapter discussed a large of set of common sound changes, and in this chapter we take up some of the consequences of sound change, some other kinds of common sound changes, and also some phonological changes that do not exactly fit the definition of sound change. We begin by examining the consequences of the sound changes discussed in the last chapter for phonemic systems, considering splits that create new phonemes and mergers that spell the demise of some old phonemes. Then we consider how phonemic contrast operates in chain shifts, taking up vowel shifts which can operate in a chain-like manner, just as the consonant shifts can, as discussed in the last chapter. We also consider how contrastive tone arises in a language and how, in languages with a stress accent, prosodic change is associated with a cluster of other changes. Then we consider certain types of dissimilation, metathesis, and change motivated by phonotactic patterns. Finally, we consider once again the causes of sound change and what factors can be considered to discover the causes of sound change.

3.2. Phonologization

As we discussed particular types of sound changes in the last chapter we noted that each type occurs independently in unrelated languages and further that the changes have a phonetic motivation, usually in articulation. Many linguists have observed that sound changes arise from the universal tendencies that are present in many if not all languages (Hyman 1975; Ohala 2003), but for such a universal tendency to become a sound change, it must take on language-specific properties. The process by which a universal phonetic tendency becomes a sound change and is incorporated into a language-specific phonological system is called phonologization (Hyman 1975). The first step in phonologization is for the phonetic tendency to extend beyond the normal range predicted by universal co-articulation effects. For example, while it is normal for a vowel before a nasal consonant in the same syllable to have some nasalization on it, when this nasalization comes to involve full velum opening for all or most of the duration of the vowel we would say that vowel nasalization is phonologized. It is important to note, however, that since this process is quite gradual, it may be impossible to determine the exact moment at which a phonetic tendency crosses over into the phonology of a language.

One important effect of phonologization (and therefore sound change) in some cases is to make a phonetic feature that was previously redundant into a contrastive feature. This occurs as the conditioning environment weakens and the previously redundant feature extends beyond its normal range. In our example of the nasalized vowels, if the syllable-final nasal consonant is weakening as the vowel becomes more nasal, the nasality on the vowel will become more important for discriminating the word than the consonant is. Another example is the lengthening of vowels before voiced consonants. This is a universal tendency, but in English this tendency is quite exaggerated. English vowels in words such as *bed*, *pig*, and *tab* are nearly twice as long as their counterparts in the words *bet*, *pick*, and *tap*. Experimental studies have shown that English speakers use the vowel-length difference to discriminate words with final voiced vs. voiceless consonants. Indeed, even if the final consonant is deleted, speakers are able to correctly identify words. We would thus say that the vowel-length distinction in English is phonologized. However, since it is still based on the voicing of the final consonant, it is not phonemic in the traditional sense; still, sound changes can affect the phoneme inventory of a language, as we shall see in the next section.

3.3. Changes in phoneme inventories

Many of the sound changes discussed in the last chapter have an effect on the phoneme inventory of a language. There are three possible outcomes of sound change with respect to the phonemes of a language: (1) no effect – all phonemes stay intact; (2) the creation of a new phoneme, and (3) the loss of old phonemes. Each of these outcomes will be illustrated in the following paragraphs.

3.3.1. No change in phonemes

No change in the overall phoneme inventory occurs when a new allophone is created through sound change. When English voiceless stops are affricated in Liverpool English, the dialect still maintains all the phonemes it had before; only their phonetic realization is changed. Even when Spanish intervocalic /d/ becomes /ð/ and deletes in some words, the phoneme inventory is not changed, as /d/ still exists as a phoneme in initial position and after a nasal or /l/.

3.3.2. Creation of a new phoneme

The creation of new phonemes is somewhat more interesting and involves several factors that act together. One important factor is the loss of the conditioning environment. Consider the development of phonemic nasal vowels discussed just above and in the last chapter. The vowel is nasalized when followed by a syllable-final nasal consonant and that nasal consonant also weakens and is eventually lost, as shown in the French examples in (29). At the point at which the nasal consonant is no longer present, a new set of phonemes must be recognized, as there are then minimal pairs such as *âge* [ɑːʒ] 'age' and *ange* [ɑ̃ːʒ] 'angel'.

(29)   *fin*   >   [fĩn]   >   [fɛ̃n]   >   [fɛ̃]   'end'
         bon   >   [bɔ̃n]   >   [bɔ̃]   'good'
         chanter   >   [ʃɑ̃nte]   >   [ʃɑ̃te]   'to sing'
         enfant   >   [ɛ̃nfɑ̃nt] >   [ɑ̃nfɑ̃n]   >   [ɑ̃fɑ̃]   'child'

Some might view this as an abrupt process, as nasal vowels are either phonemes or they are not. But it could also happen gradually, as the vowel becomes more nasalized and the nasal consonant becomes shorter. At some point, even though the nasal consonant might still be present, the language users take the nasalization on the vowel to be the main cue to the identity of the word.

Thus, in addition to the loss of the conditioning environment, another factor in the creation of new phonemes is the extent of the phonetic difference between the erstwhile allophones of the phoneme. The nasalization needs to grow strong enough for it to be taken as the marker of a contrast. Evidence for this is the fact that when an unaccented VN syllable undergoes vowel nasalization and nasal consonant loss, the nasality on the vowel is usually lost too (Hajek 1997). Apparently, in an unaccented syllable, the nasalization is not acoustically strong enough to qualify for phonemic contrast.

A surefire diagnostic for the establishment of a new phoneme is its occurrence outside of the environment that once conditioned its appearance. This happens, as we just saw, when the environment is lost. It can also happen when the phoneme appears in new words, such as those borrowed from another language (see Sections 9.2.3 and 11.2.1). For example, the German velar fricative [x] developed a palatal variant after front vowels, giving *ach* 'oh!' [ax] vs. *ich* 'I' [iç]. But now the [ç] appears also at the beginning of the word in certain loan words from French, such as *Chemie* 'chemistry'. In order for this consonant to occur in initial position, it must have become established as a sound distinct from [x] in the minds of the speakers. One factor that might have helped is that the palatal fricative has continued to move toward the postalveolar region, giving [ʃ] in some dialects which increases the phonetic difference with [x]. In addition, a few near minimal pairs of words have appeared because the palatal fricative occurs in the diminutive suffix *–chen* even when a back vowel precedes, as in the word *Kuhchen* [kuːçən] 'cow + dim.' vs. *Kuchen* [kuxən] 'cake'.

3.3.3.   Loss of a phoneme

The most obvious way for a phoneme to be lost is for it to be deleted in all environments. Latin had a phoneme /h/, which occurred only in syllable-initial position, but it was already being lost in the Latin period. Words with Latin /h/ appear in French with no /h/: Latin *habere* > French *avoir* 'to have'; Spanish lost Latin /h/ as well as the /h/ which originally derived from /f/ in initial position: Latin *habere* > Spanish [aber] 'to have', Latin *facere* > Spanish [aθer] or [aser] 'to make, do'.

Another way for a phoneme to be lost is through the merger of two phonemes. An ongoing merger in American English results when earlier [ɔ] is pronounced [ɑ], so that the contrast of [ɔ] and [ɑ] as found in words such as *caught* and *cot* no longer exists for some speakers. These speakers have the phoneme [ɑ] in words such as *hawk, bought, fought* where other more conservative speakers have [ɔ] in these words. As this change progresses, the phoneme [ɔ] will be lost in these dialects and may eventually disappear from American English.

Loss of phonemes by merger leads to fewer contrasts in a language, and some researchers have wondered whether there might be forces that prevent merger and preserve contrast even while change is ongoing. In Section 2.5.5 we discussed a chain shift in consonants that occurred in Romance languages. There we saw that, between vowels, Latin voiced stops became fricatives, voiceless stops became voiced, and voiceless geminate stops became simple voiceless stops. Despite these shifts in phonetic realization, the phonemic distinctions remained intact, at least at first. In such a chain shift, then, boundaries between phonemic categories do play a role in sound change, perhaps constraining it, perhaps also triggering it. We will discuss this issue more in the following sections, where we examine chain shifts in vowel systems.

3.4.   Vowel shifts

3.4.1.   The Great Vowel Shift

One of the most famous sound changes in the history of the English language is called the Great Vowel Shift. It took place in the Early Modern Period, primarily in the sixteenth century, though some parts of the change started earlier, and the change is not completed even now, at least in some dialects. This change affected the "tense" vowels of English – the vowels that had previously been long vowels. Each one of these vowels shifted its position, as shown in Figure 3.1, with the high vowels becoming diphthongized and all the other vowels becoming higher.

The Great Vowel Shift had extreme consequences for the spelling-to-sound correspondence in English (basically wrecking it!) because English spelling was never completely reformed after the shift took place. As you will see, this is the reason why one letter, such as *i* can be pronounced as [aɪ] or [ɪ].

At the end of the Middle English period, there were seven long vowels, as shown in (30) with their phonemic form and a Middle English example translated into Present Day English (some of these vowel phonemes had more than one spelling).

(30)　　　Front vowels　　　　　　　　　Back vowels
　　　　　/iː/　　*bide* 'wait'　　　　　　/uː/　　*hūs* 'house'
　　　　　/eː/　　*gees* 'geese'　　　　　/oː/　　*goos* 'goose'
　　　　　/ɛː/　　*meat* 'meat'　　　　　/ɔː/　　*gote* 'goat'
　　　　　　　　/aː/　　*name* 'name'

In the Great Vowel Shift (see Figure 3.1), each of these vowels changed its articulation or its position in the vowel triangle. The long high vowels began to diphthongize, as the beginning of the vowel was not produced in the high position, but rather in a lowered and more central position, giving [ɪi] > [ïi] > [əj] for the front vowel and [ʊu] > [ʉu] > [əw] for the back vowel. Later, in many dialects the high vowels became the diphthongs [aj] and [aw], as in the present day pronunciation of *bide* as [bajd] and *house* as [haws].

The mid vowels /eː/ and /oː/ were raised and became the high vowels /iː/ and /uː/ respectively, as seen in the current pronunciation of *geese* and *goose*. The lower mid vowels, /ɛː/ and /ɔː/ also were raised one notch to become /eː/ and /oː/. Later the front mid vowel was further raised. The low vowel /aː/ was fronted to /æː/ and then raised to /ɛː/ only later ending up as /eː/. Figure 3.1 shows these changes in a diagram.

There are several interesting points to note about this vowel shift. First, the front and back vowels underwent parallel changes, with the high vowels diphthongizing and the other vowels being raised. Whatever forces caused and propelled this change, they applied equally to front and back vowels. Second, the mid and low vowels each moved up one height position. Clearly, this change was phonetically gradual; the vowels did not skip around the space jumping over positions. Reports from observers at the time (from about 1500 to 1700) indicate that there was a lot of variation, and the changes moved very gradually (Dobson 1957). Third, most of the phonemic contrasts remained in place, even though the phonetic quality of the distinctions changed. The only mergers were among the

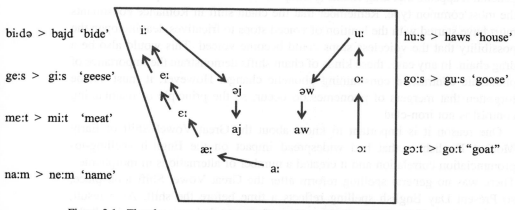

bi:də > bajd 'bide'

ge:s > gi:s 'geese'

me:t > mi:t 'meat'

na:m > ne:m 'name'

hu:s > haws 'house'

go:s > gu:s 'goose'

go:t > go:t "goat"

Figure 3.1. *The changes comprising the Great Vowel Shift of Early Modern English (1400–1600)*

front vowels, where /eː/ and /ɛː/ both become /iː/ (making *meat* and *meet* homophones). Because most of the phonemic contrasts are maintained, this set of changes is considered a chain shift.

Observing vowel shifts and other kinds of chain shifts, André Martinet proposed that phonemes tend to maintain a maximal perceptual distance from one another (Martinet 1952). Liljencrants and Lindblom 1972 propose that vowel systems are organized to maximize perceptual contrast among the vowel phonemes. That is why most vowel systems include the vowels /i/, /u/, and /ɑ/, which are at the extremes of the vowel space in terms of articulation and perception. This maximization of contrast could be operative when vowel shifts are occurring, with the vowels shifting their position to maintain or enhance perceptual contrast. Martinet proposed that in a chain shift there is a causal connection among the various linked changes; in other words, one change triggers another change. There are theoretically two ways this could proceed: First, a change could occur by which the phonetic territory of one phoneme begins to crowd a neighboring phoneme. In this case, for instance, if /aː/ is fronted and then begins to raise, it will encroach on /ɛː/, possibly causing this vowel to raise as well. This type of change is called a *push chain*. The second alternative is that a phoneme changes, leaving a gap which allows a neighboring phoneme to expand its variants in the direction of the gap and possibly change its center of gravity. Thus, if the high vowels diphthongize first, vacating the high positions, the mid vowels are free to become higher. This type of change is called a *drag chain*.

In the case of the Great Vowel Shift, we do not know the exact chronological sequence of the changes, though it does seem that the diphthongization and raising of the higher mid vowels took place earlier than the other changes (Dobson 1957), making this change a drag chain. Of course, there are other alternatives involving a mixture of push and drag chains. Perhaps the mid vowels were becoming higher and the high vowels diphthongizing at the same time. In general, it appears that drag chains (perhaps in combination with push chains) are the most common type. Remember that the chain shift in Romance consonants must have started with the lenition of voiced stops to fricatives, leaving open the possibility that the voiceless stops could become voiced. This would also be a drag chain. In any case, these kinds of chain shifts demonstrate the importance of phonemic contrast in constraining phonetic change. However, it must not be forgotten that mergers of phonemes do occur, so the principle of maintaining contrast is not iron-clad.

One reason it is important to know about the Great Vowel Shift of Early Modern English is that had widespread impact on the English spelling-to-pronunciation correlation and it created a number of alternations in morphemes. There was no general spelling reform after the Great Vowel Shift took place, so Present Day English spelling reflects a time before the shift. As a result, one vowel grapheme can have a number of pronunciations, as seen in all the ways *a* can be pronounced: *same* [ej], *Sam* [æ], *spa* [ɑ]. Similarly, most vowels have at least two major pronunciations. This is because what were earlier long vowels all shifted, while the short vowels did not. In teaching English spelling, the long vowels are still differentiated from the short vowels, even though there is no longer a vowel duration contrast in English. Linguists use the terms "tense" and "lax", though the major distinction between the two types of vowels is distributional: the class of vowels designated as "lax" cannot occur in open syllables.

The two (or more) pronunciations of each English vowel sometimes show up in alternations within morphemes (a topic to be discussed more in Chapter 4). In verbs we have stem changes such as *bite/bit*, *speed/sped*, and *sweep/swept* that once corresponded to vowel length differences, but today involve vowel quality as well. Similar alternations can be found in derivational morphology, where *decide* with [aj] alternates with *decision* with [ɪ], *nation* with [ej] alternates with *national* with [æ], and *serene* with [ij] alternates with *serenity* with [ɛ]. All of these alternations and many more like them go back to a long/short alternation before the Great Vowel Shift. Like many other sound changes that we will discuss in Chapter 4, this one had a major impact on morphologically related words.

3.4.2. The Northern Cities Vowel Shift

As noted above, the Great Vowel Shift took place within the system of long vowels. The short vowels were not affected at that time. Currently in American English there is a series of rather salient vowel changes occurring among the short or lax vowels.

The lax vowels of American English are those that cannot occur in open syllables; rather they have to be followed by a consonant. They are /ɪ ɛ æ ɑ ɔ ʌ/. These vowels are participating in a chain shift that has been dubbed the "Northern Cities Vowel Shift" because it has been noticed and studied in Syracuse, Rochester, Buffalo, Cleveland, Detroit, and Chicago. As it is an ongoing change, there is variation in the extent to which the shift has progressed among speakers depending upon age, gender, education, and other factors. Also, some parts of the shift have spread to other geographic regions. Figure 3.2 shows this shift using phonemic symbols and lexical items to indicate the vowels affected. The numbers in the figure indicate the proposed order in which the changes have occurred and the order in which we will discuss them.

Since this change began fairly recently and has been continuing to affect more vowels and more speakers, researchers have been able to study it in some detail. One way to establish the order in which the changes have occurred is to study the vowels of speakers of different ages. The older speakers will have vowels that are less advanced in the change than the younger speakers. Thus we can see the change occurring in what is called *apparent time*. In addition, since this change has been studied since the 1970s, we also have data from real time. The following summary is based on Labov 1994.

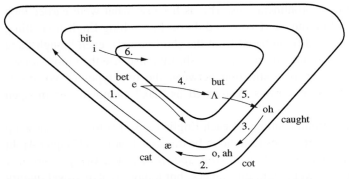

Figure 3.2. *The Northern Cities Vowel Shift (source: Figure 14.1 in Labov, Ash, and Boberg 2006)*

1. The first shift was the raising of /æ/, as in *cat*. This raising is more extreme before a nasal, as in *sandal*, and after a palatal, as in *Jackie*. Figure 3.2 shows this vowel moving from a low front position up past the mid vowel position. As there is still much variation, different speakers may have a more or less raised vowel. This vowel can even be phonetically realized as a diphthong with a high nucleus and a centralized offglide [iᵊ]. Labov characterizes this part of the change as near completion.

2. The second phase is also present in the oldest speakers studied. It involves the fronting of [ɑ] as in *cot* or *Don* to [a] (a low front vowel) or even [æ]. In the figure, the phonemic symbols /o/ and /ah/ are used for this vowel.

3. The third phase is the centralization and fronting of /ɔ/ (phonemically represented in the figure as /oh/) to [ɑ] or [a] as in *caught* or *bought*.

4. Fourth, the [ɛ] vowel in *bet* (represented as /e/) has been traveling towards the central region of the vowel space, giving pronunciations such as [drʌs] for *dress*, and [rʌst] for *rest*. As shown in the figure, for some speakers the vowel is even lower (Labov 2001: 473). This shift and the next two are described by Labov 1994 as "new and vigorous" changes.

5. The central vowel /ʌ/, as in *but* or *strut*, is moving towards the back, where the vowel of *caught* /ɔ/ used to be.

6. The lax high vowel /ɪ/ (represented in the figure as /i/) is becoming lower, approaching the position of where /ɛ/ used to be.

Now it should be clear that this set of changes constitutes a chain shift, and that furthermore at least parts of it make up a drag chain. The raising of /æ/ opened up a space in the lower front region and /ɑ/ has moved towards that space. Then the back vowel /ɔ/ moved into the space vacated by /ɑ/.

Shifts such as these – in which phonemes encroach on or take the space formerly occupied by a different phoneme – can cause misunderstandings across dialects. My personal experience as a speaker from the American Southwest moving to Buffalo, NY, in the 1970s was full of such experiences. When I first moved to Buffalo I attended a party where I was introduced to a man whose name was given as [dan], with a low, but very fronted vowel. I didn't know if his name was *Dan* or *Don*! It sounded more like *Dan* to me, but once one understands the Northern Cities Vowel Shift, one can see that his name was *Don*.

3.4.3.   General principles of vowel shifts

As with other sound changes we have discussed, vowel shifts show general cross-linguistic patterns, that is, similar shifts occur independently in different languages. Based on examples of vowel shifts in a number of languages (many of them Indo-European, but some from other families), Labov (1994: 16ff.) proposes the following three principles of vowel shifting:

(31)   Principle I: In chain shifts, long vowels rise.
        Principle II: In chain shifts, short vowels fall.
        Principle IIa: In chain shifts, the nuclei of upgliding diphthongs fall.
        Principle III: In chain shifts, back vowels move to the front.

The Great Vowel Shift, which affects only long vowels, illustrates Principle I, as we see that all of the vowels – except those that were already maximally high – shift higher by one or more positions. Quite a number of languages have vowel shifts that follow this pattern. Principle II is less well supported. For instance, in the Northern Cities Vowel Shift, the vowel in *cat* rises, but the vowels in *bit* and *caught* fall. Principle IIa refers to diphthongs with an initial nucleus and a high (upgliding) glide following, such as /ij/ or /ej/. The tendency is for the nucleus to become lower, as in the Great Vowel Shift when /ij/ and /uw/ became /aj/ and /aw/. This is grouped into Principle II, because the nucleus is a short vowel. This part of Principle II is quite well attested across languages, as shown in Labov's work (1994). Principle III accounts for some of the changes in the Northern Cities Vowel Shift, that is, the fronting of /ɑ/ to /a/ or /æ/, but the centralization of the front vowel /ɛ/ seems to go against this principle.

So far, there has not been a proposed explanation for vowel shifts that covers all cases. There are, however, some specific factors that have been singled out for discussion. According to Labov 1994, the difference in behavior of long and short vowels has long been noted and attributed to the amount of articulatory effort that goes into producing long versus short vowels. The theory is that the greater amplitude and duration of long vowels leads to their articulation being extended, not just in terms of tongue height, but also in lip rounding. In contrast, short vowels may be more affected by the tongue position for surrounding consonants, and thus tend to lower. An important factor to consider in applying this theory to the Northern Cities Vowel Shift is that English vowels no longer have a true long/short distinction. Because all English vowels are longer in stressed syllables and in monosyllables, the so-called lax vowels may not really qualify as short vowels in the sense of Principle II. Studies of the Northern Cities Vowel Shift show that vowels with primary stress are more advanced in their shifting than vowels with secondary stress (Labov 1994: 192), suggesting that length is a factor. Another approach to understanding the Northern Cities Vowel Shift is to distinguish between more peripheral vowels (those that are at the extremes of height, frontness, and backness) and the less peripheral vowels (those that are slightly more central). Proposing this distinction, Labov finds that peripheral vowels rise and non-peripheral vowels fall. In Figure 3.2 the peripheral vowels are in the outer triangle and the more central vowels fall in the inner two triangles.

Another factor to consider is the influence of the consonantal environments, which may serve as the trigger to begin a vowel shift. For instance, the raising of /æ/, which seems to have started the Northern Cities Vowel Shift, is most advanced before a nasal consonant, as in *hand*, *can*, or *sandal*. It is possible that it started in this context and then spread to other contexts (Labov 2010). Another example can be found in the fronting of /uw/ in the southern United States, as well as in standard southern British English, where words such as *tooth* or *shoe* are pronounced with a fronted vowel while preserving the original rounding of the glide, giving [ɨw] or [iw] in these words. This change is most advanced after a palatal consonant or glide, suggesting that it might have started as assimilation to the front tongue gesture and then spread to other contexts. A following /l/ inhibits the change, probably because the English /l/ is velarized, meaning the back of the tongue is raised in its production. Thus the following /l/ would keep the tongue positioned to the back.

An alternate explanation for the fronting of /uw/ could be the general tendency, proposed by Martinet (1952), that back vowels tend to move to the front. The reason for this is that the vowel space is not a symmetrical triangle, but instead, there is less space for making vowel distinctions among back vowels than among vowels at the front. Given the need to maintain a perceptual "margin of security" between distinct phonemes, Martinet suggests that if there are too many back vowels, one or more of them might move towards the front.

In the last chapter we identified a large number of changes that were the result of the automation of production, and these involved the reduction in magnitude of a gesture or the increased overlap of gestures. We also discussed a smaller number of changes that appear to be instances of fortition, that is, they increase the magnitude of the gesture. A question to briefly consider here is whether vowel shifts fit into any of these categories of change or whether they have a different kind of motivation. Because the causes of vowel shifts are still not completely understood, this discussion must be somewhat speculative; however, we can say the following:

1.   To the extent that vowel shifts are motivated by the consonants surrounding the vowels, assimilation, or the retiming of gestures, would be implicated. Note that in the Northern Cities Vowel Shift the surrounding consonants have been shown to be a strong factor in the advance of the shift.

2.   Given that low vowels require the jaw to be opened more and the tongue to be lowered, and that high vowels require the jaw as well as the tongue to be raised, the raising of low vowels and the lowering of high vowels would both be gestural reductions.

3.   Diphthongization, such as that found in the Great Vowel Shift, e.g. [ɪi] > [ɨi] > [əj] > [aj], shows a lowering of the onset of the vowel, which can also be viewed as a reduction in the magnitude of the tongue-raising gesture.

4.   Fronting and backing to a central or neutral position is also analyzable as the reduction in magnitude of the gesture, but fronting and backing beyond the central position must have another motivation, perhaps assimilation to surrounding consonants or fortition.

5.   Raising or lowering beyond the mid-vowel position would also be considered a form of assimilation or fortition.

We await further investigations of vowel shifts to understand their nature better.

There is some evidence for lexical diffusion in vowel shifts. The Great Vowel Shift ended up affecting the whole lexicon in British Received Pronunciation and Standard American English, but Ogura et al. (1991) find that the pronunciation of what was /iː/ in Middle English still varies across English dialects, and this variation has a lexical factor: some words have changed more in these dialects than have others. Studies of the raising of /æ/ in Philadelphia show that, even with similar phonetic environments, some words have changed while others have not. Thus *bad*, *mad*, and *glad* consistently have a raised vowel, but *sad* and *dad* generally do not (Labov 1994). In contrast, for the other vowel shifts that Labov has studied, the phonetic conditions supplied by surrounding consonants seem to be much more important than any lexical effects.

3.5.   The origins and evolution of stress accent

The prosodic type of a language is based on the way the language uses pitch, intensity (loudness), and duration (which produces rhythmic properties). Many European languages (e.g. English, German, Greek) are considered to have a stress accent because each word has a prominent syllable that is manifested as having a higher pitch, greater intensity, and longer duration than other syllables of the word. Another possibility is pitch accent, in which the prominent syllable can have a contrast in pitch level or contour, but not all words or syllables have an assigned pitch (e.g. Japanese). Contrasting with these types are tone languages, in which each syllable of a word can have a characteristic level or contour pitch. As with most typologies, there are also intermediate cases which are difficult to classify, such as tone languages with highly restricted tone patterns for words, or overlapping cases, such as a tone language that also has a prominent syllable that is longer than the other syllables (some Bantu languages, e.g. Mwera and Setswana). In this section and the next we will discuss the sources of prosodic properties on words, common patterns of change in prosodic systems, and the interaction of prosodic patterns with change in consonants and vowels. Bear in mind that much less is known about how tone and accent change than is known about how consonants and vowels change.

Languages that have a stressed syllable in each word can also be of different types. In many languages word stress is quite regular and falls on a particular syllable of the word counting from the beginning or end of the word. Such a pattern is called *demarcative stress*. For instance, Finnish and Czech have very regular stress patterns by which stress falls on the first syllable of the word. French and Turkish have stress on the final syllable of the word. Such patterns have the benefit of marking off the boundaries between words. Another common pattern of this type is penultimate stress, or stress on the next to the last syllable. This pattern is found in Quechua and Swahili. In addition to these types in which stress is quite predictable, there are also languages in which different words have different stress patterns, e.g. some words have initial stress, some final, or the morphological structure of the word might determine its stress placement. This would be called lexical or morphological stress.

3.5.1.   Where does stress accent come from?

One possible source of word stress is intonation on phrases (Hyman 1977). Intonation refers to the pattern of pitch changes that occurs across an utterance independently of the particular words or morphemes contained in the utterance. Very often intonation is different in statements versus questions. Bolinger 1978 found that intonation across languages generally includes a high–low sequence at the end of statements, and in many languages there is also a high pitch at the beginning of utterances. Hyman proposes that high pitch at the beginning of utterances can be reanalyzed as an initial high pitch or stress on the first syllable of words. The high falling pitch at the end of utterances can be reanalyzed as final stress, or, if the high–low pattern is distributed over the last two syllables of a word, the result would be penultimate stress. If a language does not have any particular stress pattern for words (as in Mapudungun, an isolate spoken in Chile and Argentina), the production of words in isolation or at the beginnings or ends of utterances would yield a certain pitch pattern that speakers could associate with the word as its stress pattern. Even if a language already has a stress or pitch accent pattern, it could be replaced by one motivated by the intonation, as has apparently happened in Czech, where initial stress has replaced the inherited pitch-accent system. Some Bantu tone languages have a lengthened penultimate syllable, which could be reanalyzed as a stressed syllable and possibly replace the tone system. Thus, one possible source for a stress-accent system could be the intonational patterns – the initial high pitch or the final falling pitch – that can become associated with the individual words.

Languages that have recently developed stress accent in this way would have regular demarcative stress. A further change that often occurs is that the demarcative stress loses its strict predictability because of other changes, especially vowel deletions, and becomes lexical stress or morphological stress. We will discuss morphological stress in the next chapter, so let us concentrate for a moment on lexical stress, using the example of Latin stress.

The regular pattern for stress in Classical Latin was that stress fell on the penultimate syllable (of words with two or more syllables) unless that syllable was weak, i.e. contained a short vowel in an open syllable, in which case it fell on the antepenultimate syllable (the one before the penultimate). This system depended upon the contrast between long and short vowels. Thus in words such as *amāre* 'to love' or *civitātis* 'city' the stress was on the penultimate syllable, but in *popŭlus* 'people', the stress is on the antepenultimate syllable. Later, as spoken Latin developed into Spanish, Portuguese, and French, the short *u* in *popŭlus* deleted, as did the final syllables of *amāre* and *civitātis*. Since the stress remained on the syllable where it had resided before, the placement of stress was no longer predictable by the same rules. Thus in (32) we see the development from Latin into Spanish:

(32)

	Latin	Spanish	Gloss
	pópŭlus	*puéblo*	people
	amā́re	*amár*	to love
	civitā́tis	*ciudád*	city

As you can see from the Spanish words, the stress is no longer predictable by the Latin rule. So the vowel deletion, along with the breakdown of the distinction between long and short vowels, has changed the nature of the stress system in the Romance languages. In the next section we consider how and why this has happened.

3.5.2.   Typical changes in stress-accent systems ▰▰▰▰▰▰▰

When stress accent develops out of intonational patterns, the initial expression of stress is high pitch. We noted earlier, however, that intensity (loudness) and duration can also distinguish stressed syllables from unstressed ones. The hypothesis put forward in Bybee et al. 1998 is that when stress is mainly expressed by high pitch, the stress can switch to different syllables when conditions change, but when duration is added as a correlate of stress, changes in consonants and vowels occur that anchor the stress in its historical place. Consider Turkish, where stress is a matter of high pitch. The regular pattern is to stress the final syllable of a word. Because Turkish has many suffixes, the final syllable can be a different morpheme in different inflections of the same stem, as shown in (33).

(33)

	odá	'room'
	odadá	'in the room'
	odadakí	'that which is in the room'
	odadakilér	'those who are in the room'

Compare this situation to English, where stress is expressed through duration as well as high pitch. The lengthening of stressed syllables and the shortening of unstressed ones makes the consonants and vowels of stressed and unstressed syllables phonetically very different. For instance, compare the words *attic* (with initial stress) and *attack* (with final stress). Not only are the initial vowels very different, but the medial consonants are also different. If one were to change the stress of *attack*, the listener might not know what word was meant.

When duration becomes a correlate of stress accent, many changes in the consonants and vowels occur: vowels are reduced in unstressed syllables, vowels are lengthened and diphthongize in stressed syllables, and consonants reduce at the beginnings of unstressed syllables (e.g. the medial /t/ in *attic*). Because of such changes, stress can cease to be demarcative and become instead lexical and unpredictable. Such changes have occurred in Romance and Germanic languages in the last 2000 years. In the examples in (32) we see that some unstressed vowels have deleted, in particular final vowels and vowels following the stress, which were short to start with. Short mid vowels diphthongized in Spanish, as seen in *pueblo*. As the phonemic distinction between long and short vowels was lost, all stressed vowels become slightly longer than unstressed ones.

Germanic languages also had a phonemic distinction between long and short vowels which developed in English into the tense/lax system discussed in Section 3.3. At the same time other changes suggest that duration had become a correlate of stress. Between Old and Middle English, vowels in unstressed syllables were reduced and deleted. While Old English distinguished *a*, *e*, *u*, and *o* in final syllables, these merged to *e*, which came to be pronounced as schwa and then in some cases disappeared. Consider these words from Old and Middle English showing the change in final vowels (Mossé 1952):

(34)	Old English	Middle English	Gloss
	sōna	*sōne*	'at once, soon'
	dogga	*dogge*	'dog'
	sceadu	*schāde*	'shade'
	talu	*tale*	'story, tale'
	mōdor	*mōder*	'mother'
	macod	*māked*	'made'

As we know from the way the PDE glosses are pronounced, the final unstressed vowel deleted.

Thus a suite of changes accompanied the change of the stress accent expressed mainly by high pitch to stress expressed also by lengthening the stressed syllables and shortening the unstressed ones. As mentioned above, another consequence of vowel reduction and deletion is the development of lexical or unpredictable stress. See the examples in (32) again. When unstressed vowels delete, the stress does not shift, but rather stays on the syllable where it had been diachronically. Because these changes all relate to duration as a correlate of stress, rather than just pitch, Bybee et al. 1998 hypothesized that languages that have lexical stress are highly likely to also have processes conditioned by stress, such as vowel reduction. Their study tested this hypothesis on forty-two stress languages that were selected to be maximally unrelated genetically. The results were consistent with the hypothesis: vowel reduction was the process found most frequently in the survey and it occurred in languages with lexical stress significantly more often than in languages with predictable stress. Vowel lengthening and consonant changes conditioned by stress were not as frequent, but they were also more common in languages with lexical or unpredictable stress. Thus the crosslinguistic data supports the proposed diachronic hypothesis – that the development of duration as a correlate of stress leads to vowel and consonant changes, and these in turn anchor the stress on the syllable so that it is not likely to move if conditions in the word change.

3.6. Development of tone and tone changes

As we have seen, in languages with a stress accent, there is one syllable per word that has special prominence expressed by some combination of pitch, intensity, and duration. In contrast, in a tone language, each syllable has a characteristic pitch level (such as high or low) or contour (such as rising or falling). Two words with the same segmental structure can have different tone patterns that keep them distinct. These pitch patterns are usually not accompanied by differences in intensity or duration, though there are some languages that use both tone and accentual prominence. In many tone languages we can find words that are distinguished only by differences in their tone patterns. The Nigerian language Igala (Volta-Niger) has three tones, a high (H´), mid (M‾), and low (L`) which distinguish words such as the following (Welmers 1973).

(35) | áwó | 'guinea fowl' | àwó | 'a slap' |
      | áwō | 'an increase' | àwō | 'a comb' |
      | áwò | 'hole (in a tree)' | àwò | 'star' |

As in this example, many African languages have two or three level tones and some also have contour tones, in which there is a pitch change. Many Asian languages, such as Mandarin Chinese and her sisters, are tone languages and typically have contour tones as well as level tones.

3.6.1. Tonogenesis: how tones arise from consonants

In the last few decades, the question of how languages acquire tones has been a research topic that has yielded interesting results, so that now we understand much better how languages acquire tone. Much more than a hundred years ago, researchers observed that high and low tone corresponded diachronically to distinctions between voiceless and voiced consonants. That is, where one language has a voicing distinction in initial consonants, another related language has a distinction between high and low tone.

Further research into the related Mon Khmer languages has indicated that the tone distinctions do not always come directly from onset voicing distinctions, but often pass through a stage with distinctions in voice quality (Thurgood 2002). In fact, in many tone languages, differences in pitch are accompanied by differences in voice quality (sometimes called *register*). Because onset voicing of the consonant, pitch, and voice quality (e.g. modal or normal, breathy and creaky) are all controlled by the larynx, Thurgood offers a "laryngeal account" of tonogenesis among these languages (Thurgood 2007: 268–269). The most common pattern is for vowels after voiced onsets to have breathier voice quality and lower pitch, in contrast to vowels after unvoiced onsets, which have a modal (normal) voice quality and higher pitch. These voice quality differences are the key to understanding how consonant voicing gives rise to tones, because even though the onset of a vowel following a voiceless consonant has a higher pitch than the onset of a vowel following a voiced consonant, these differences alone are probably not salient enough to lead to the development of tone (Thurgood 2007: 268–269). When a relaxation of the muscles controlling the vocal cords occurs during a voiced stop, this creates a slightly increased opening of the vocal cords, which can have the effect of producing a breathier articulation of the onset. The pitch of the following vowel is lowered as well. The breathy consonant can go on to become voiceless and merge with the voiceless consonants in the system, while the breathy and low-tone vowel maintains the contrast between words with consonants that were formerly voiced and those that were voiceless. A common further development is the loss of the breathiness with only the lowered pitch remaining.

Strong support for this proposed sequence of events comes from studies of closely related dialects, such as the dialects of Khmu, a language related to Khmer and Vietnamese, studied by Suwilai Premsritat (2004). These dialects represent all the stages in the development of tone: an initial stage with an onset voicing contrast, [glaːŋ] 'stone' vs. [klaːŋ] 'eagle'; an intermediate stage with breathy voice where the voiced onset used to be, [kla̤ːŋ] vs. [klaːŋ]; and a final stage with no breathy voice but a tone contrast, [klàːŋ] vs. [klâːŋ].

There are also cases in which the loss of final consonants led to changes in pitch. The reduction of the oral articulation, or debuccalization, (see Section 2.5.3) of final consonants left only their laryngeal qualities, which, as with initial consonants, included breathiness, creaky voice, and pitch distinctions. For instance, when a fricative reduces to [h] and then the [h] deletes, it leaves a low pitch, which makes the preceding tone a falling tone. Thus the Vietnamese word for 'firewood' *củi* with a falling tone and no final consonant corresponds in the related language, Thavung, to *kuyh or kuuʃ* with the same meaning.

While the development of tones from consonants may seem to be a very exotic kind of change, all the mechanisms involved fall into two categories which are already very familiar to us – reduction and phonologization.

Table 3.1: *Vietnamese monosyllabization*

Ruc	Vietnamese	Gloss
kŭcit³	cɛt³ (*chết*)	'to die'
ĭcim¹	cim¹ (*chim*)	'bird'
rŏka¹	ɣa² (*gà*)	'chicken'
kăhɔy³	kʰɔi³ (*khói*)	'smoke'

Reduction: A lot of the work on tonogenesis has been done on Vietnamese and related Mon Khmer languages. It is clear from comparing the related languages that Vietnamese in particular has undergone extreme phonological reduction, from a language with mostly bisyllabic words to one with mostly monosyllabic words. This can be seen in Table 3.1 extracted from (Stebbins 2010) where cognate words in Ruc, a language closely related to Vietnamese, are compared to words in Vietnamese. What one can observe is that the two-syllable words in Ruc have only one syllable in Vietnamese, and that the syllable that is preserved is the final one. The reason for this is that the final syllable had the primary accent and the first, unstressed syllable was lost. (Vietnamese data from Stebbins 2010: 58 and Ruc data from Hayes 1992.)

Along with reduction leading to monosyllabic words, Vietnamese and related languages have undergone consonant loss in the remaining syllable. As mentioned above, the loss of the voicing contrast came about as the voiced consonants became breathy and then devoiced. This change can be characterized as the reduction in magnitude of the gesture (the tensing of the specific laryngeal muscle, the cricothyroid muscle) that brings the vocal cords together to produce voicing.

Vietnamese is now at a stage at which the creaky voice from the loss of final glottal stop is also being lost. This loss patterns with other reductions in affecting high-frequency words before low-frequency words (Stebbins 2010). Stebbins also points out that these changes are unidirectional. We do not know of any cases where tones are lost and consonants emerge. This fact also points to these changes as reductive.

Phonologization: The transfer of contrast from consonant voicing to voice quality (or register) to high and low tone is a classic case of phonologization. As one set of contrastive gestural configurations reduces, another set takes on the role of distinguishing words.

3.6.2.   Tone changes

As you might expect, when tones occur in sequence within words and across words, they can change because of surrounding tones or pauses. In some ways, these changes resemble the changes in consonants and vowels that we have examined in this chapter and the previous one, and in other ways they are quite different. In this section we review a few of the general tendencies that have been discovered in the ways tone can change.

One type of change in tones that is superficially similar to segmental changes is a change in pitch when a L–H sequence becomes either M–H or L–M. In other words, the L is raised before a H or the H is lowered after a L. Hyman and Tadadjeu (1976) compare more than twenty Eastern Grassfield Bantu languages to understand the changes they have undergone. One change that can be seen is this type of "vertical" assimilation. In the most conservative dialect, Mankon, the three syllable word for 'tooth' is *ǹsɔ̀ŋ́*, with the tone pattern L–L–H. In another dialect, Mbui, the cognate word has two syllables, *ǹsɔ̀ŋ*, with a surface tone pattern M–M. Hyman and Tadadjeu propose that the sequence of changes in Mbui was L–L–H > L–LH (where LH is a rising contour tone) > M–M with both tones adjusting. Hyman (2007) notes that changes of the sequence L–H to M–H or L–M are much more common than changes involving the sequence H–L. The stability of H–L sequences is underscored by another phenomenon by which the H in such a sequence actually becomes super high. Thus, in the Engenni word *únwónì* 'mouth' the second H is super high (Hyman 2007).

An even more common type of tone change is called *tone spreading*, or horizontal assimilation. This is a perseverative change by which the tone from one syllable spreads onto the next syllable. The evidence for this type of change comes from synchronic alternations, such as that found in the Batcham language (Bamileke, Eastern Grassfields Bantu), where the noun *ká̌* 'crab' which has a high tone in the singular, has a rising tone once the plural prefix with its low tone is added to it: *mɔ̀ká̌* 'crabs'. In this example, a rising tone is created as the low tone of the prefix spreads partially to the next syllable. In other cases, a tone can spread onto several successive syllables, as in example (36a) from Ndebele (Nguni, Bantu), in which the high tone of the prefix spreads up to the antepenultimate syllable, so as more suffixes are added, the H can spread further (Hyman 2011).

(36)   a. Ndebeleb.   b. Zulu
           ú-kú-hlek-a   *u-kú-hlek-a* 'to laugh'
           ú-kú-hlék-is-a   *u-ku-hlék-is-a* 'to amuse (make laugh)'
           ú-kú-hlék-ís-an-a   *u-ku-hlek-ís-an-a* 'to amuse each other'

Comparing the Ndebele forms to those of related Zulu, we see that the H appears to shift to the antepenultimate syllable. However, this shift occurred first through spreading and then through the change of all but the last two of the Hs to Ls (Hyman 2011). High tone spreading as in this case appears to be more common than cases where a L or M tone spreads. What is interesting is that it is also usually perseverative rather than anticipatory, making it different from segmental assimilation (Hyman 2007).

Another way that tone changes differ from segmental changes is that when the vowel or syllable upon which a tone resides is lost (through the ordinary type of lenition processes discussed in Section 2.5), the tone very well might remain, moving to an adjacent syllable. When this happens, if the tone of the adjacent syllable is the same, the tone will be absorbed and leave no traces. But if the tone is different, then a contour tone can be created, which may remain or undergo further simplification (Hyman and Tadadjeu 1976). Another possible outcome is what is known in synchronic phonology as a *floating tone* – a tone whose impact can be observed even though it does not have any segmental material associated exclusively with it.

Hyman and Tadadjeu 1976 study the associative construction in the Eastern Grassfields Bantu languages mentioned above. They are able to reconstruct grammatical markers of this construction (which differs according to the class of the noun) that have been deleted in most dialects, while the effect of the tone remains. For example, in Babete the word for 'strangers' when produced in isolation has two L tones, *pòγù*, but when it is in the associative construction with a word such as 'message' *ŋkù*, the phrase is *ŋkù póγù* 'the message of the strangers' with an H tone on the first syllable (the prefix) of 'strangers'. Where does this H come from? Hyman and Tadadjeu and other specialists in these languages have reconstructed a grammatical marker of this construction which had an H tone in this noun class. Though the segmental marker has been deleted, the H tone it once bore has relinked onto the first syllable of the second noun. By comparing a number of languages, researchers can reconstruct the associative markers for all the noun classes, including their tones, and can predict the behavior of each class of nouns in this construction.

3.6.3.   Intonation interacting with tone

In many African tone languages, pitch changes akin to intonation occur over a breath group of an utterance, that is, the string of words between pauses. The typical pattern is called "downdrift" because the pitches of the tones gradually drift downwards as the utterance proceeds and because a H that comes after a L is not as high in pitch as previous Hs. A L–L or H–H sequence does not go down, only the H after a L, giving a pattern such as (37):

(37)   H
                    H
            L   H
                  L
                        L

In a sequence such as this, if the syllable that bears a L tone is deleted, the next H does not raise up to the level of the preceding one, but rather stays at its lowered pitch. Such a lowered H tone is called a *downstep*. For instance, in Akan (a language of Ghana) when the possessive pronoun /mí/ 'my' is combined with the noun /ɔ̀-bó/ 'stone', the noun prefix /ɔ̀-/ is deleted. However, the H of the noun stays at its downstepped pitch, giving /mí ↓bó/ where the ↓ indicates a lowered H

(Schachter and Fromkin 1968). In effect, this process creates a new tone on the surface, and in some languages this may be the source of a new mid tone. This is another instance illustrating the stability of tones when changes occur in the vowels.

3.6.4.   Tone reduction

In Section 2.9 we discussed some cases of special reduction, in which a high-frequency word or phrase undergoes reduction that is not necessarily general in the language at the time. Such reduction can also occur with tones. For example, in Mandarin Chinese, where there are four contrastive tones – one high level tone and three contour tones – if a syllable has a weak stress or is unstressed, it loses its contrastive pitch and is said to have a neutral tone (Li and Thompson 1981). The negative marker *bu* 'not' which can have either a rising or falling tone is usually produced with a neutral tone at normal conversational speeds and where emphasis is not intended (Wiedenhof 1995). Another more complex example of a change that is currently ongoing in spoken Mandarin involves the numeral one, yi^{55} with a high level tone which often precedes the classifier ge^{51}, which has a high falling tone. In this combination, following the regular pattern, the numeral has a rising tone: yi^{35}. In a construction with a noun, where it means 'one N', the following change occurs (Tao 2006):

(38) $yi^{55} + ge^{51} + N > yi^{35}\ ge^{51} + N$

As this combination is frequently used in a function similar to the indefinite article *a(n)* in English, the second part, the classifier, reduces by losing its tone to have only the neutral tone and by reducing the vowel to schwa:

(39) $yi^{35} + ge^{51} + N > yi^{35}\ g\partial + N$

In further reduction the consonant /g/ can become a glide and delete, and the schwa may also delete, leaving only yi^{35}, which, rather than having its original tone 55, now has an unchanging tone 35, but just where it was earlier followed by ge^{51} and only where it is used in the new function of an indefinite article.

3.7.   Language-specific changes

The sound changes we have discussed to this point are changes that can be documented in different, unrelated languages and thus can be hypothesized to stem from universal phonetic principles, even if we have not in all cases confirmed the nature of those principles. The literature on sound change also includes other changes that are influenced by language-specific factors and may not proceed in the same direction across languages. Many of these changes are also not regular across the lexicon, that is, they only affect certain words. Even in these cases, however, we can identify certain conditions that lead to changes that are similar across languages.

3.7.1. Dissimilation ▀▀▀▀▀▀▀▀▀▀▀▀▀▀

In Section 2.2 we noted that assimilations are cases where one segment becomes more like an adjacent or nearby segment. Dissimilation is the opposite in one sense, since the term refers to cases where a segment becomes different from a nearby segment. However, dissimilation is not just the opposite of assimilation because it does not occur under the same conditions nor does it occur in the same way. For one thing, the conditioning environment is almost never contiguous to where the change occurs; rather, it is separated from the changing segment by one or more segments. For another, dissimilations are usually not lexically regular. In addition, the mechanism of retiming does not seem applicable to dissimilations; related to this point is the fact that the result of dissimilation always seems to be a segment that already existed in the language, unlike assimilation, which can create new segments. Finally, dissimilations are quite rare compared to assimilations. Let us start with some examples and then consider some possible explanations for dissimilations.

Dissimilations often involve words that have more than one liquid consonant. A famous example occurs in Latin, where the *–ālis* suffix as in *liberālis* becomes *–āris* when the stem ends in *–l*, as in *populāris* 'popular'. This alternation in the suffix was quite regular in Latin and survived when words with this suffix were borrowed into other languages, such as English, giving us words such as *national*, *dental*, and *chemical* vs. *regular*, *velar*, and *tubular*. Other examples of such a dissimilation occur as Latin developed into the Romance languages. Latin *peregrīnus* 'foreigner, alien' becomes Italian *pellegrino* 'foreigner, pilgrim, traveler'. A number of examples can be found in Latin developments in Spanish, as shown in (40), where we see that words with two instances of /r/ often change the second one to /l/, but there is also a case (the last example) where the second /l/ in a word changes to /r/.

(40)

	Latin	Spanish	Gloss
	arbor	*árbol*	'tree'
	robre	*roble*	'oak'
	marmore	*mármol*	'marble'
	carcere	*cárcel*	'prison'
	locale	*lugar*	'place'

One explanation offered for such dissimilations by John Ohala can be called perceptual hypercorrection (Ohala 2003). His hypothesis is based on the finding that listeners *normalize* the incoming speech stream by filtering out predictable features that are not part of the phonemic contrast. Ohala's hypothesis is that listeners sometimes normalize incorrectly. As the rhotic quality of /r/ can extend over more than one segment, the listener erroneously concludes that the second /r/ in the first four words above sounds like an /r/ because of features extended from the first /r/. By normalizing or analyzing the rhotic quality away from the second /r/, the listener concludes that the consonant should be /l/. Ohala's theory predicts that features that dissimilate are those that can spread over many segments such as the rhotic feature in these examples. This prediction remains to be tested. He also predicts that dissimilation occurs only within words, as normalization is a function of decoding particular words. This prediction appears to be correct, and we could further note that the misperception account would imply that the change would be made word-by-word and not turn out to be regular. Other predictions that appear to be correct are that a novel segment is not created, as is often the case in assimilation. The reason for this is that the listener is trying to identify which segments (of those existing in the language) s/he is hearing. Also, Ohala predicts that the conditioning environment does not disappear in the change, as often happens in assimilation.

Other features that appear to be affected by a type of dissimilation are the features of laryngeal states, such as aspiration or laryngealization of obstruents. A famous case affecting both Sanskrit and Greek is the de-aspiration of aspirated stops when there is a following aspirated stop in the same word. In Ancient Greek this dissimilation is apparent in inflected forms, such as those with reduplication. When a verb with an aspirated initial consonant is reduplicated, the reduplicated prefix has a plain voiceless stop, e.g. *tí-thē-mi* 'put' and *pé-phūka* 'converted'. In stems that have two aspirated stops, the second is unaspirated if a consonant such as /s/ follows so that the initial aspirated stop appears, but if the second remains aspirated, the first becomes unaspirated: thus *thrík-s* 'hair, nom. sg.' and *trikh-ós* 'hair, gen. sg.' (Beekes 1995). This pattern, however, is not completely regular (Buck 1933). Other languages also have constraints on the appearance of two consonants produced with certain laryngeal states in the same word or root. Hausa (Chadic, Newman 2000) and Yucatec Mayan cannot have two glottalized consonants in the same word unless they are otherwise identical. Quechua is also reported to have only one glottalized consonant per word. Note that, in all these cases, the result is always a "plain" consonant. Cases which do not occur would have two plain Cs dissimilating so that one becomes ejective or aspirated. Thus it appears that the dissimilation involving laryngeal features could be partially motivated by reduction in which a more complex laryngeal state or sequence becomes simple.

According to Ohala, other features that can be affected by dissimilation are palatalization, labialization, and pharyngealization. As dissimilation is rather rare and is often not regular across the lexicon, it is possible that there is not one single explanation that will account for all cases.

3.7.2.   Metathesis

Metathesis is evident in alphabetic notation when it appears that one segment has exchanged places with a contiguous segment. We saw a case of metathesis in Section 2.2.5, which we regarded as a retiming. In that case, in the transition of spoken Latin to Spanish, /rj/, /pj/, and /sj/ metathesize, as in these examples: *riparia* > *[ribaira] > *[ribeira] > *ribera* 'bank, shore'; *casium* > *[kaiso] > *queso* 'cheese'. We regarded this as a retiming because it seems to be a continuation of the anticipatory retiming of the palatal glide, which had such an impact on Romance phonology. Other cases, however, are not so obviously articulatory retimings, but rather, as some researchers have argued, come about because of perceptual difficulties.

Investigations of metathesis have shown that it can be lexically regular as well as sporadic, and it can go in different directions in different languages. It has also been observed that metathesis tends to occur in sequences with specific features such as glottals, liquids, and glides (Blevins and Garrett 1998; Hume 2004). One important question about metathesis is whether it is phonetically gradual, having intermediate stages, or phonetically abrupt, with one segment leaping, so to speak, over the other. Consonant-vowel metathesis appears to be gradual, as when English /rV/ metathesizes to /Vr/ in cases such as *pretty* being pronounced as [pəɹɪ]. Here the r-quality fuses with the vowel and there is only the illusion of the /ɹ/ following the vowel. This of course could be a type of reduction as it occurs mostly in high-frequency words.

Hume 2004 underscores the language-specific nature of metathesis by showing languages in which the direction of change is the opposite. In Hungarian, when the word *teher* 'load' takes the plural suffix *–ek*, the absence of the second vowel brings the sequence *–hr–* together, giving **tehrek*. However, this form has been affected by metathesis, giving *terhek* for the plural. This metathesis affects other forms that would have an /r/ or glide in contact with /h/. In contrast, a similar situation in Pawnee (Caddoan) shows an opposite direction of change. When the sequence /rh/ arises in morpheme combination, it has been changed to /hr/: *ti-ir-hisask-hus* > *tihrisasku* 'he is called'. Assuming in both cases that the synchronic analysis reflects a diachronic change, it appears that metathesis can go in both directions.

A metathesis involving strident coronal consonants occurs regularly in certain verb paradigms of Modern Hebrew. Certain forms of perfective verbs take a prefix which usually has the form /hit/, as shown in (41a), but when the stem begins with a strident coronal, that consonant changes places with the /t/ of the prefix, which agrees in voicing with the stem consonant, as shown in (41b).

(41)		Morpheme sequence	Surface form	Gloss
a.		hit-nakem	hitnakem	'he took revenge'
		hit-raxec	hitraxec	'he washed himself'
		hit-balet	hidbalet	'he became prominent'
		hit-darder	hiddarder	'he declined, rolled over'
b.		hit-sader	histader	'he got organized'
		hit-zaken	hizdaden	'he grew old'
		hit-calem	hictalem	'he took pictures of himself'
		hit-ʃamer	hiʃtamer	'he preserved himself'

Hume's hypothesis about the origin of metathesis has two parts. First, the features that are assigned a different order are features that can spread over more than one segment, making their assignment to a segment difficult. This factor is similar to what Ohala proposes for dissimilations – a difficulty in perception making it hard to know which feature belongs to which segment. Second, Hume proposes that listeners tend to interpret the ambiguous sequence in the order they are more familiar with – the sequence that is most common in their language. This would explain why metathesis can go in one direction for one language and in a different direction for another language; it would just depend upon which sequence is more common in the language. For instance, in the case of Modern Hebrew, the sequences with the strident coronal before the /t/ are much more common than the reverse order. We will see in the next section that there are other changes motivated by a tendency to replace a less common sequence with a more common one.

Thus Hume's hypothesis explains why there are certain features involved in metathesis (in many cases the same features as found in dissimilation) and why metathesis can go in opposite directions in different languages. Like dissimilation, metathesis usually occurs within words and it is often sporadic, only affecting certain words of the lexicon.

3.7.3.   Change with phonotactic motivation

Other changes that are difficult to explain on a crosslinguistic phonetic basis may be motivated by the familiarity speakers have with certain phonotactic sequences in their language. Rare sequences can be replaced by sequences that are more common, especially those that occur in more words, or have a higher type frequency. We will see in our discussion in later chapters that a high type frequency leads to productivity in morphology and syntax, and in the cases to be discussed here as well as in metathesis, which we just discussed, it appears to also affect changes in phonology.

Across Latin America there is a tendency in some dialects to use a syllable-final /k/ before /t/ or /s/ in words that are spelled with /p/, as in *concepto* 'concept' pronounced as *concec[k]to*. This tendency has attracted a lot of attention since the introduction of the soft drink Pepsi into these countries. So many speakers replace the second /p/ in Pepsi with a /k/, that in 2010, the official ads for this drink began to spell it as *Pecsi*. One Pepsi add reads: *Tomás Pecsi ahorrás* 'drink Pecsi, save', then below that it says *Tomás Pepsi también* 'drink Pepsi also'. (You can google "Pecsi" and see examples of the ad.) A change from a labial to a velar is not likely a phonetically conditioned gradual change, so what is the motivation for this pronunciation? E.L. Brown 2006 studied the token and type frequency of syllable-final /p/ and /k/ in the Corpus del Español and found that a syllable-final velar stop is seven times more frequent in text than a syllable-final labial stop. In addition, syllable-final velar stops occur in four times as many words as syllable-final labial stops. Thus a Spanish speaker's response to this rare cluster might well be to alter it to something more familiar. In the Spanish spoken in Spain, another response is found: the speakers simply omit the /p/ and say "Pesi". (You can find a YouTube video of a Pepsi commercial with the soccer great Fernando Torres, saying "Pesi" rather than "Pepsi" at http://www.youtube.com/watch?v=RWoLKc6udR0.)

A change based on common phonotactic patterns has in common with metathesis and dissimilation that it may be lexically sporadic, reuse segments already existing in the language, occur in a phonetically abrupt fashion, and not move in the same direction across languages. The language-specific nature of the change relates to the fact that the specific phonotactic patterns of the language are governing its outcome.

3.8.   Causes of sound change and phonological change

In this chapter and the preceding one, we have surveyed a large number of different types of sound change. In Chapter 2 we focused on assimilation (retiming) changes and lenition (reductive) changes. These changes tend to be lexically regular, phonetically gradual, and similar across languages. In this chapter further changes that are regular, gradual, and similar crosslinguistically were discussed: vowel shifts, changes related to stress accent, tonogenesis, and tone changes. Section 3.7 treated changes that seem more language-specific in their motivation – dissimilation, metathesis, and phonotactically motivated changes. To the extent that these types of change are different, we expect to find different causes for them.

As we proceeded through the discussion, I mentioned some other characteristics of sound change that might differ for different types of change. These characteristics can be used to help us understand the causes of change. I summarize them here:

1.   The phonetic path and conditioning of the change – that is, what phonetic features are affected and under what conditions.

2.   The gradualness or abruptness of the change in phonetic terms. For example, [d] can change gradually to [ð] but [p] cannot change gradually into [k].

3.   The presence of similar changes in many unrelated languages, versus changes going in opposite directions in different languages, as is the case with metathesis.

4.   Many sound changes create new segments or tones or new sequences of segments (assimilation, lenition), but for others, the result is an existing segment (dissimilation) or a rearrangement to get an existing and more common sequence of segments (metathesis).

5.   In some changes the conditioning environment is lost (this happens frequently in assimilation, tonogenesis), while in others the conditioning remains (lenition, dissimilation).

6.   Some changes take place only within words (dissimilation, metathesis, vowel shifts), while others can take place across word boundaries (assimilation and lenition), that is, between two words.

7.   Many changes exhibit patterns of lexical diffusion. Assimilation and lenition in particular affect high-frequency words first; other types of

changes may affect low-frequency items first (changes based on difficulties in perception).

8.   Most sound changes are lexically regular – that is, they end up affecting all the words of the language that have the relevant conditioning environment (assimilations and lenitions, vowel shifts, tonogenesis). Some changes are more sporadic – that is, they affect only some words and not others (dissimilation, metathesis, and some vowel shifts).

The study of sound change is one of the pillars of the field of historical linguistics and the basis for the comparison of languages that leads to the establishment of genealogical relations among languages (as explained in Chapter 10). As you might expect, sound change is not an isolated phenomenon, but rather affects other aspects of language. In the next two chapters we will see how the alternations created by sound changes come to affect the morphology of inflectional languages and the subsequent changes that ensue.

Questions for discussion

1. The well-known twentieth-century linguist Jim McCawley used to joke that you knew the Great Vowel Shift had started when a man went into a pub and ordered an ale, only to be told that the fish store was next door. How was the pub employee pronouncing *ale* and how was the customer pronouncing it? Which one demonstrated the beginning of the Great Vowel Shift?

2. Thinking back over the changes discussed in Chapters 2 and 3, apply the criteria gathered together in Section 3.7 to some of these changes. What further research questions are suggested by the answers you found or the gaps in the information available?

3. What are some of the ways that stress and tone interact with intonation?

4. What are some of the reasons that assimilation occurs more commonly than dissimilation?

5. Consider how consonants change and how vowels change. How are they similar and how are they different?

4 The interaction of sound change with grammar

4.1. How sound change affects morphology

Sounds are used in words, morphemes, and phrases; thus sound change has an impact on language beyond just changing pronunciations in some words. Because sound change is usually regular (affecting all words with the required phonetic conditions), it applies within morphological paradigms and syntactic constructions with the result that some instances of a morpheme may undergo the change, while other instances of the same morpheme (in a different context) may not. For example, in Old English voiceless fricatives became voiced between voiced sounds: /f, þ, s/ > /v, ð, z/.

(42)   Old English

seofon > *seven*	*oþer* > *o[ð]er*	*ceosan* > *choo[z]e*
hefig > *heavy*	*broþer* > *bro[ð]er*	*wæs* > *wa[z]*
giefan > *give*	*weorþig* > *wor[ð]y*	*rīsan* > *ri[z]e*
lufian > *love*		

In some morphologically related words this sound change created an alternation which is exemplified here with Present Day English, though not all speakers have all of these alternations:

(43)   Present Day English, singular/plural pairs

Singular	Plural	Singular	Plural
wife	*wives*	*house*	*hou[z]es*
thief	*thieves*	*bath*	*ba[ð]s*
knife	*knives*	*path*	*pa[ð]s*
calf	*calves*	*roof*	*roofs/rooves*
turf	*turves*	*hoof*	*hooves*

In these words the voicing is no longer due to the phonetic conditioning, since the fricative is not intervocalic in words such as *wives* and *thieves*. In fact, the voicing of fricatives is no longer a productive process or sound change in English, as shown by the fact that we now have many words with voiceless fricatives between vowels, e.g. *glasses*, *kissing*, *ether*, and *offer*. Despite the fact that the sound change is no longer applicable or productive, the voiced fricative remains in the words in (42) and also in most of the words in (43). This shows that when a sound change goes to completion and becomes obsolete, the words it has affected do not switch back to the way they were before. Rather, the sound change has a permanent effect on the words that were in the language at the time of the change.

Because some words have the phonetic conditioning for the sound change and some do not, alternations arise in morphologically related words. So in the singular-plural paradigm of PDE, some nouns have two forms, one for singular (with a voiceless fricative) and one for plural (with a voiced fricative). When paradigms (groups of inflectionally related words) show variants of morphemes (allomorphs), we say that an alternation exists in the paradigm. There can also be alternations in words that are derivationally affected, as for instance in *give/gift* or *thieve/thief*.

Alternations can either have phonetic conditioning, as they would while the sound change is alive and productive, say, in Old English, as in (42), or they can have morphological or lexical conditioning, as the forms in (43) demonstrate. The forms in (43) show a morphologically conditioned alternation because the variation in form occurs only in the plural. It does not occur, for instance, in the possessive, even though the possessive marker is the same as the plural marker. Thus we have *my wife's car*, not *my wive's* [waɪvz] *car*. The alternation also has lexical conditioning, because not all nouns have the alternation: words such as *grass*, *chief*, and *myth* do not have a voiced fricative in the plural. In fact, the words with the alternation are considered somewhat irregular; one just learns which nouns have this change and which do not. Lexical conditioning and morphological conditioning often go together, as they do in this case.

What we note in the case of the nouns in (43) is that the alternation is associated with the expression of the plural concept (thus the oddity of *my* [waɪvz] *car* in a culture that practices monogamy). Once alternations created by sound change become part of a paradigm they come to stand for the meanings expressed in the forms of the paradigm, and in so doing, they become *morphologized*, by which we mean that alternations created by a sound change have moved from being conditioned by phonetics to having an association with morphology. This direction of change from phonetic to morphological is the most common direction of change. Cases of change from morphological conditioning to phonetic are virtually unknown. Thus we have another case where there are clear trends in directionality of language change.

4.2.   Morphologization

Given the common trend for sound changes to take on morphological (and sometimes syntactic, as well as lexical) conditioning it is reasonable to ask why this direction of change? The answer is close at hand: sound changes start for phonetic reasons, as we have seen in Chapters 2 and 3, but the basic function of language is the expression of meaning, so differences in sounds that arise for phonetic reasons tend to become associated with meaning, if conditions are right (Bybee 2001; Dressler 2003). That is, if the variants occur in contexts where meaning is different, then the variants become part of the expression of the meaning. In this section we will discuss alternations that arise in morphological paradigms, and in the next section we will discuss alternations that have become part of morphosyntactic constructions.

The example of the previous section involved certain nouns that show an alternation between singular and plural forms. That is, a set of lexical items is affected. Another case, this time involving forms that are derivationally related, came about because of the shortening of certain long vowels in Middle English. Recall from the last chapter that Middle English had pairs of long and short vowels, and the long ones underwent the Great Vowel Shift in Early Modern English. Before that happened, long vowels that were in the third syllable from the end of the word shortened. Most words with three or more syllables were formed by adding suffixes, so this shortening has become associated with certain affixes. After the Great Vowel Shift, the long and short vowels differed in quality, too. Thus in PDE we have vowel alternations in words such as the following:

(44)

Original long vowel	Shortened vowel
vain	*vanity*
crime	*criminal*
sign	*signify*
clean	*cleanliness*
cone	*conical*
pronounce	*pronunciation*

We know that this alternation is morphologized because there are words with the same structure that do not have the shortened vowel in the third syllable from the end:

(45)

obese	*obesity*
pirate	*piracy*

As mentioned above, exceptions show that the earlier sound change has become unproductive. Also, there are words that vary according to the speaker's dialect, such as *plenary* which can be pronounced with [iː] or [ɛ] and *privacy*, which has [aɪ] in American English and [ɪ] in British English. Thus a sound change that was earlier regular has become associated just with certain words and certain derivational suffixes.

There are other more complex ways that a sound change can create morphologically and lexically conditioned alternations. Here is a case in which the alternation occurs just in a grammatical affix. The famous case of the Maori passives was brought to light by Hale 1973 after studying the morphological structure of Polynesian languages. In (46) we see Maori verb forms – first the base form of the verb (lacking in all affixes) and in the second column the passive form. If you examine the passives in comparison to the base forms, you see that the passive suffix consists of a C + *ia*, but the consonant varies according the verb.

(46)   Maori passives

Base form of verb	Passive	Gloss
awhi	*awhitia*	'embrace'
hopu	*hopukia*	'catch'
aru	*arumia*	'carry'
tohu	*tohuŋia*	'point out'
mau	*mauria*	'carry'
wero	*werohia*	'stab'

This situation arose because in a prehistoric stage of Polynesian, the verb bases themselves ended in consonants: **awhit*, **hopuk*, **arum*, **tohuŋ*, **maur*, and **weroh*. A regular sound change deleted all word-final consonants. This meant that all the base forms lost their final consonant, but the consonants remained when they occurred inside a word, as in the passive form. So today there are several allomorphs of the passive suffix, among them *–tia*, *–kia*, *–mia*, *–ŋia*, and *–hia*. We know that morphologization has taken place in this case because of changes that simplify the system by using the allomorph *–tia* in place of the others (Hale 1973; Harlow 2007). One example occurs when the causative prefix *whaka* is followed by the passive of a word that does not itself have a passive, such as a noun, as shown in (47) (Harlow 2007: 117).

(47)   *whaka-māori-tia*

        CAUS- Māori-PASSIVE 'translate into Māori'

Also, when polysyllabic loan words are passivized, as in (48) where the source word is English *broom*:

(48)   *puruma-tia* 'sweep'

Harlow (2007: 117) points out that *–tia* is used "increasingly on indigenous, simple polysyllabic stems", that is, non-derived stems such as:

(49)   *kōrero-tia* 'speak'
        waiata-tia 'sing'

These innovative forms show that the speakers no longer associate the consonant with the preceding stem, but rather take the consonant to be part of the passive suffix. This in turn sets up a situation with multiple allomorphs which may be difficult to learn and remember. One of these allomorphs is starting to replace the others. This replacement takes place by analogical leveling, which will be discussed more in the next chapter.

    As a final example of an alternation created by sound change, let us consider one which becomes an important part of the expression of a morphological category. In Section 2.2.4 we saw that in the history of German a sound change of i-umlaut occurred. It fronted a back vowel if there was a high front vowel or glide in the following syllable. Since the noun plural suffix in German for some nouns was *–i*, an alternation was created between singular and plurals, as in shown in (50a). Nouns with a different plural suffix *–a*, as in (50b), would not be expected to have a fronted vowel in the plural. However, because the fronted vowel comes to serve as a marker of plural, it was sometimes extended to paradigms where it was not originally there because of the sound change (Hock 2003). In the next chapter we discuss analogical extension in greater detail.

(50)   Old High German   New High German
            Singular   Plural   Singular   Plural
   a.   *gast*   *gasti*   *Gast*   *Gäste*   'guest'
   b.   *boum*   *bouma*   *Baum*   *Bäume*   'tree'

4.3.   Alternations in morphosyntactic constructions

Sometimes alternations that occur for phonetic reasons can become entrenched in constructions that encompass more than one word. An English example is the alternation in the indefinite article *a/an* in which the form with the final consonant occurs before words beginning with a vowel and the other form occurs before words beginning with consonants. This pattern arose when the indefinite article developed out of the unstressed form (OE *ān*) of the numeral one (OE *āne*) during the course of Middle English. The article developed within the noun phrase construction where it had a close coherence with the following word. In Middle English, final /n/ in unstressed syllables deleted in most cases. In this case, it deleted when the next word began with a consonant, but was retained when the next word began with a vowel. This pattern is still part of the construction today. Interesting evidence for the close coherence of the article with the following noun comes from cases in which the /n/ that occurred before a vowel has been reanalyzed as belonging to the noun. For instance, the word *nickname* goes back to an OE compound, *ekename* 'real' + 'name'. It apparently got its initial /n/ from the indefinite article, when *an ekename* was taken to be *a n-ekename*. Other similar examples of reanalysis are presented in the next chapter.

Similar more complex cases in which alternations occur between words within constructions can also be found. Such cases are often called *sandhi phenomena*, or *external sandhi*, using the Sanskrit word *sandhi* for such cases. The phenomenon called in French *liaison* also came about because of the deletion of final consonants, which occurred in French in the sixteenth and seventeenth centuries. The result of this sound change was that many words, notably nouns and some adjectives, lost their final consonants completely. For instance, nouns such as *haricot* 'kidney bean', *buffet* 'sideboard', *bois* 'forest', *goût* 'taste', *tabac* 'tobacco', and *sirop* 'syrup' are pronounced without a final consonant. However, words that occurred frequently in particular grammatical or idiomatic conditions that placed them before a vowel, tended to develop an alternation. Word-internally such conditions existed before the feminine suffix, which was vocalic and thus yielded alternations between masculine and feminine nouns and adjectives, such as found in *petit* [pəti] 'small, masc.' and *petite* [pətitə] 'small, fem.', which today, with the loss of final schwa, yields the alternation [pəti], [pətit].

At this time also there was a strong tendency, as there is today, for forward resyllabification when a final consonant was followed by a vowel (Encrevé 1983; Green and Hintze 1988). This process, known as *enchaînement*, makes a final consonant syllable-initial when a vowel follows within the same pause group. Words or morphemes that frequently occur in constructions that put them in prevocalic position are able to maintain their final consonant in those constructions. Here we will just look at a few contexts that have the alternation (based on Morin and Kaye 1982 and Tranel 1981: 233). For instance the cases in (51), which show determiner + noun constructions, have the consonant indicated when the following word begins with a vowel, but have no consonant when the following word begins with a consonant. The [z] and [n] in square brackets indicate that this consonant is pronounced as the syllable-initial consonant. The *(s)* or *(n)* in parentheses indicate that this consonant is not pronounced:

(51)   Determiners
   (a)   *vo[z] enfants*   'your children'   *vo(s) livres*   'your books'
   (b)   *le[z] autres*   'the others'   *le(s) personnes* 'the people'
   (c)   *u[n] ancien ami* 'an old friend'   *u(n) journal*   'a newspaper'

Similarly, in the examples in (52) with clitic pronouns and verbs, the pronouns end in consonants only if the next word begins with a vowel:

(52)   Clitic pronouns
   (a)   *nou[z] avons*   'we have'   *nou(s) voulons*   'we want'
   (b)   *il[z] ont*   'they have'   *il(s) veulent*   'they want'
   (c)   *allon[z]-y*   'let's go'
   (d)   *parle-t-il?*   'is he speaking?'

The example in (52d) is quite interesting because the *–t–* is written as though it belongs neither to the verb nor the pronoun. However, originally, this *–t–* was the 3rd person singular suffix on the verb, cf. Latin *amat* 'love, 3rd sg.'. This /t/ has been deleted in French in most cases, but in a 3rd person singular question, where the inverted pronoun begins with a vowel, it is always preserved.

There are many other cases where the appearance of a final consonant before a word beginning with a vowel is variable. In all cases the two words affected are used together frequently; for example, prepositional phrases such as *dans*[z] *un mois* [dɑ̃zɛ̃mwa] 'in a month'. In other cases, fixed phrases such as *États-Unis* 'United States' or *rien à faire* 'nothing to do' always have the final consonant pronounced. These cases suggest that phrases that are processed together are behaving more like a single word, and so the consonant is more like a medial consonant and thus pronounced. At the same time, however, in the optional cases the component words of the phrase are affected by the many cases where the word appears without a consonant. Thus the presence or absence of the consonant is variable.

Though not superficially similar, the tone pattern of the associative construction in Eastern Grassfields Bantu (discussed in Section 3.6.2), probably arose in much the same way. The associative construction consists of two noun phrases in sequence and has the very general meaning of 'NP$_1$ of NP$_2$', as in the example in (53) from Babete (spoken in Cameroon) (Hyman and Tadadjeu 1976):

(53)   ŋkù péyù   'the message of the strangers'

The interesting problem with the associative construction in many of the related languages of this group is that certain tone changes take place. In example (53), the high tone on the first vowel of the second noun only occurs in this construction. In other uses, the noun 'strangers' has a low tone. Since the preceding noun also has only low tones, it is particularly interesting that there is a change to a high tone. As I mentioned in Section 3.6.2, scholars comparing the different languages of this family have proposed a solution to this puzzle. It seems there was in earlier times a morpheme marking the associative relation and this marker was either a V or CV syllable, and in the case shown in (53) it had a high tone. The segmental representation of the morpheme has been reduced and lost, but the tone change it caused on the second noun has remained, and is now the sole grammatical marker of the construction. In synchronic analysis, a 'floating tone' is assumed to cause the alternation in this construction and it is designated as a 'grammatical floating' tone. Similar to the case in French liaison, where there are several consonants involved in the alternation (/z/, /n/, and /t/), the associative morpheme apparently at one time had several allomorphs, some of which had low tones in addition to the high tone just illustrated. Thus in certain noun classes the effects of a floating low tone can be observed.

In this section, we have seen that the effects of sound change can be fixed in certain grammatical constructions so that alternations occur just in these constructions. This result occurs when the sound change (or tone change) occurs across word boundaries and where the two words involved are in a close morphosyntactic relation or occur frequently together. Note that the English and French cases involved grammatical morphemes (articles, clitic pronouns) and that the Bantu case involved the loss of the segmental features of a grammatical morpheme.

4.4.   Rule inversion

In 1972 Theo Vennemann introduced the notion of "rule inversion" into the study of morphologization (Vennemann 1972). He noted that the directionality of a morphologically conditioned alternation is sometimes the opposite of the sound change that took place. We have already seen some examples. For instance, we think of the alternation between the indefinite article *a/an* in English as adding an /n/ before a word beginning with a vowel, but historically it was actually a deletion. The same is true for French liaison, though there is some disagreement about whether the best synchronic treatment involves deletion or addition of a consonant (Tranel 1981). In both cases, because there are more consonant-initial words than vowel-initial, the alternating form that lacks a consonant is dominant.

A case of inversion of a word-internal alternation of a grammatical morpheme is the plural, possessive, and past suffixes of English. The regular plural and possessive suffixes have three allomorphs /s/, /z/, and /ɨz/, and the past has three parallel allomorphs /t/, /d/, and /ɨd/. As is well known, the voiceless allomorph occurs after a stem ending in a voiceless consonant (*cats*, *cat's* and *walked*), the allomorph with the vowel occurs with stems ending in sibilants in the case of plural and possessive (*classes* and *class's*), and after stems ending in /t/ or /d/ for past (*added*). The simple voiced consonant occurs elsewhere. Most synchronic analyses view the vowel in /ɨz/ and /ɨd/ allophones as inserted, as these allomorphs occur in the most restricted environments, so it is simpler to state the conditioning for the appearance of the vowel than for its absence. Historically, however, the alternation arose because of the deletion of the unstressed vowel; the suffixes originally contained a pronounced vowel, as in the Middle English forms, *lovede* or *loved* 'loved' and *endes* 'ends'. Thus if we think of this vowel as inserted today, then a rule inversion has occurred.

In morphologization, as the morphological categories begin to take precedence over phonological ones, what was earlier a single sound change may divide according to morphological function and reverse its direction of change only in certain categories. For instance, the voicing of certain stems in the plural in Old English, as illustrated in (42) and (43) above created an alternation in which the singular is taken as basic and the voiced variant conditioned by plural marking. But other alternations resulted from the original intervocalic voicing. Intervocalic fricatives in verbs also voiced, setting up alternations between the infinitive or present stem and the past participle, as in *leave/left* or *lo[z]e/lost*. Earlier examples are Middle English *bilēven/bilefte* 'believe, believed', *bereave/bereft*, and *heaved/heft*. In these cases, the voiced fricative of the infinitive could be taken as basic, and the voiceless fricative of the participle derived from it by devoicing. In support of this analysis, we note that when the alternation is lost, it is the voiced fricative that remains, as in *believed*, *bereaved*, and *heaved*. Contrast this situation with the loss of the alternation in nouns, which is occurring among some speakers of American English, where the voiceless fricative of the singular survives in *hou[s]es* or *ba[θ]s*. Thus the alternation has become inverted under morphological pressure, but only in verbs and not in nouns. The noun alternation is morphologized, as noted earlier, but it is not inverted.

4.5.   Rule telescoping

As the results of sound change become more entrenched in the language, they also sometimes continue their phonetic trajectory so that the alternations that have been established sometimes involved sounds that are quite phonetically distinct. This is not so much the case with voicing or devoicing, as in the example just discussed, but in assimilation sometimes the resulting segment undergoes further change. For example, the palatalization processes discussed in Section 2.2.3 often start with the assimilation of a velar to a high front vowel or glide, producing a palatal stop or fricative, but in some cases, the palatal consonant may move further forward in articulation, giving a postalveolar [tʃ] or even a [ts] or [s]. This sequence of events occurred in Romance languages, giving in Spanish verbs forms such as *digo* 'I say' from Latin *dīcō* (with voicing of the velar) alternating with *dice* [dise] 's/he says' from Latin *dīcit* (in Latin American dialects; in most Peninsular dialects the *c* is pronounced as [θ]). The alternation is also seen in derivationally related forms such as *opa[k]o* 'opaque' and *opa[s]idad* 'opacity', *críti[k]o* 'critical' vs. *criti[s]ismo* 'criticism'. Similar alternations occur in French (from the same Romance sound changes): *opaque* [ɔpak], *opacité* [ɔpasite], *publi[k]ation, publi[s]ité* 'publication, publicity', and from French these alternations entered English, as the French words were borrowed with the alternations intact. So, after this long history, Spanish, French, and English have words showing alternations between [k] and [s]. All the intermediate stages have disappeared, so Hyman 1975 called this phenomenon "rule telescoping". Because of telescoping, it is often the case that morphologically conditioned alternations involve a much greater phonetic distance than alternations that are phonetically conditioned.

4.6.   The development of exceptions

As mentioned earlier, a strong indicator that the results of a sound change have morphologized and are no longer productive on a phonetic basis is the development of exceptions to the sound change. The sources of exceptions are various. Here we will discuss briefly the pronunciation of borrowed words and the outcome of subsequent sound changes.

When a phonetic process or ongoing sound change is productive, it will apply in the pronunciation of new items, such as borrowed words. When speakers of one language pronounce words from another language they do not know too well, they will use their native phonetic patterns and apply them as best they can to the foreign word. Thus when the voicing of fricatives shown in (42) and (43) was productive, loanwords would have been pronounced with an intervocalic fricative as voiced. Thus loanwords from Old Norse, borrowed in the Old English period, have undergone voicing: e.g. *geyser, give, raise,* and *scathe.* However, words borrowed later from other languages do not have the voicing: e.g. *ether* from Latin via Old French in the late fourteenth century; *fifer* 'one who plays the fife' from German or French, fifteenth century; *mathematics* from Greek via French, sixteenth century. These examples indicate that, by the late fourteenth century, the intervocalic voicing of fricatives was no longer productive.

Sometimes the phonetic conditions for a sound change are set up by subsequent sound changes; if the original sound change then applies, it is still productive and in progress; if it does not apply, then it has become unproductive, and alternations it created morphologize. An example concerns the palatalization of velars in Romance that was mentioned in Section 4.5. Plain velars palatalized before front vowels but rounded velars did not. However, the rounded velars tended to lose their rounding before all vowels except /a/. In some words the rounding was lost very early and the velars in these words went on to palatalize: Latin *coquer* > *co[k]er* > Spanish *co[s]er* 'to cook'; *coquina* > *co[k]ina* > *co[s]ina* 'kitchen'. In most words, however, the loss of rounding took place later, and the resulting velars were not palatalized: consider Spanish *que* [ke] 'that, what', *quince* [kinse] 'fifteen', *águila* [agila] 'eagle', where the spelling shows the earlier presence of the rounding and the modern pronunciation is velar, not palatal or [s].

Consider another example where exceptions have developed. In the Luhugu dialect of Lumasaaba (Bantu, Uganda) there is a consonant alternation that gives evidence for a lenition process by which a weakened voiceless bilabial stop assimilates to the following vowel (G. Brown 1972). The lenition is conditioned by a preceding vowel and does not occur when the /p/ is preceded by a nasal consonant, which reinforces the bilabial closure.

(54)   Luhugu

Noun	Gloss	Diminutive
impiso	'needle'	*kayiso*
impale	'pants'	*kahale*
impusu	'cat'	*kawuso*

In a closely related dialect, Lufumbo, the nasal of the noun class prefix has subsequently been deleted, leaving a lengthened vowel, giving the following forms:

(55)   Lufumbo

Noun	Gloss
i:piso	'needle'
i:pale	'pants'
i:pusu	'cat'

These forms now have the right conditions for the lenition of /p/, yet the /p/ remains unchanged, indicating that the lenition sound change has become unproductive. Thus the alternations shown in (54) can be considered morphologized. Further evidence for this are the diminutive forms in (56) that G. Brown 1972: 81 reports are produced commonly by children:

(56)   Children's forms

Diminutive	
kapiso	'a small needle'
kapale	'pants'
kapusu	'a little cat'

The children who produce these forms have not yet learned the morphologized alternation and are using the consonant found in the base noun in the diminutive without changing it. Such forms indicate that the children are perfectly comfortable with the /p/ in the leniting environment and that the sound change is no longer productive.

4.7. Can sound change be grammatically conditioned?

So far in this chapter we have discussed the ways that sound change impacts the morphology and syntax of a language. Now we consider the question of whether the morphology and syntax of the language can affect sound change. In Chapters 2 and 3 it was emphasized that sound change is phonetically conditioned, and we have seen examples in this chapter that show that sound change applies even if it creates alternations in paradigms or constructions. Thus it would be reasonable to hypothesize that sound change is blind to everything except phonetics. This is in fact a hypothesis formulated in the nineteenth century by German linguists which has come to be known as the Neogrammarian Hypothesis (Wilbur 1977). The Neogrammarian Hypothesis posits that sound change is always regular, applying to all lexical items that have the phonetic conditioning regardless of grammatical or lexical factors. This would mean that there cannot be a sound change that occurs just in nouns or verbs, or just in a particular morpheme. It also would mean that there should not be any exceptions to sound changes in morphological paradigms or grammatical constructions.

In our discussion of sound change in Chapters 2 and 3, we found that in general this hypothesis holds. However, we also noted that there is substantial variation while a change is in progress, and some of this variation involves lexical items. We noted that there is evidence, at least for some types of changes, that high-frequency words change before lower-frequency words. If the change ends up regular in the end, then the hypothesis is not violated. However, the period of variation where lexical and, as we shall see below, grammatical factors appear to play a role means that sometimes sound changes do not go to completion as predicted. In the following some such cases will be discussed, but it will be seen that in no case is it the grammatical factors *per se* that are causing the change or the exceptions to it, but rather phonetic conditions will be seen to be primary if we expand our understanding of the phonetic context to include the broader contexts in which words and morphemes are used.

4.7.1. Changes in morphological context

In Section 2.9 we discussed "special reduction", phonetic changes that occur only in certain high-frequency phrases. These are not usually considered sound changes in the sense the Neogrammarians meant, but, as pointed out there, in some cases the special reduction is a prelude to a more general change that will take place later. The case in point was the weakening and deletion of intervocalic /d/ in the 2nd person plural verbal suffix in fifteenth- to seventeenth-century Spanish. This change appeared to be restricted to a certain morpheme, yet it could have been the phonetic conditions of the morpheme as well as its frequency which caused the change to occur earlier there than elsewhere.

Another interesting case involves the ongoing deletion of final /t/ and /d/ in American English. The variation involved in this case has been studied intensely, and there has been some interest in the morphological conditions that appear to encourage the deletion and those that appear to retard it. First, it needs to be said that the strongest factor conditioning /t/, /d/ deletion is the phonetic environment. Deletion is favored before a consonant, especially an obstruent in the next word and after a consonant in the same word.

Since /t/ and /d/ are used to signal past tense in English, this case presents a situation where morphology and sound change interact. One early finding was that when the /t/ or /d/ was the past tense morpheme, deletion was less likely (Labov 1972; Guy 1980; Neu 1980). A ready explanation for this trend is that deletion is constrained if a meaningful morpheme would be lost. Further support for this hypothesis is that when the past tense suffix occurs on a verb that also has a stem change (*told*, *left*) which could signal past tense, deletion is more likely to occur, not less likely. However, further investigation into the contexts in which deletion occurs reveals an effect of word frequency. Bybee 2000b found that deletion was more likely in high-frequency words and, more importantly, that the deletion of the past tense suffix was more likely in high-frequency past tense words than in low-frequency past tense words. This finding casts doubt on the hypothesis that deletion is constrained to preserve morphological information. In addition, Bybee finds a very strong frequency effect among the verbs that have the suffix and also a stem change. Only the most frequent of these (*told*, *felt*, *left*, *kept*, and *sent*) have high levels of deletion. The lower-frequency words, such as *found*, *lost*, and *meant*, have lower levels of deletion. Again, this casts some doubt on the preservation of meaning hypothesis.

But what is the cause of the lower probability of deletion in the past tense? A closer look at the environments in which the words occur helps to answer this question. A word-final /t/ or /d/ is in an *alternating environment*. What this means is that, in running text, sometimes the word is in favorable conditions for deletion (before a consonant, *perfect memory*) and sometimes it is not (before a vowel, *perfect answer*). Now, if the phonetic conditions were all that was at work here, then we would have a perfect line-up of deletion with a following consonant. But clearly something else is at play, because there are cases where deletion occurs when a vowel follows and cases where deletion does not occur when a consonant follows. Bybee 2002 investigated this issue more thoroughly and found that words that tend to occur more before vowels had lower rates of deletion overall, even before a consonant, and words that tended to occur more

Table 4.1: *Occurrence of /t/ or /d/ in different contexts and their deletion in these contexts*

	Occurrence _#V	Occurrence _#C	Occurrence _pause	Deletion _#V	Deletion _#C
All words	21%	64%	15%	37%	59%
Past tense	40%	47%	13%	07%	47%
Neg. auxiliaries	10%	80%	10%	86%	84%

N = 1272

before consonants had higher rates of deletion overall, even before a vowel. That is, the rate at which the deletion affects a word depends upon how often the word occurs in the favorable environment, as if the word were gradually accumulating a reduced final consonant and then using it even where the phonetic conditions are not favorable.

Table 4.1 shows this relation between how often a word occurs in the environment for deletion. It happens that past tense verbs occur before vowels 40% of the time, while overall 21% of tokens occur before vowels. This distributional fact affects how past tense forms behave before vowels, giving them only a 7% deletion rate, but it also affects the rate of deletion before consonants, lowering it to 47% when the rate for all words is 59%. In contrast, the negative auxiliaries (*didn't, wasn't, isn't, shouldn't*, etc.) occur before consonants 80% of the time; they also have a much higher rate of deletion before consonants, at 84%, but also even before vowels, at 86%. So again it appears that the rate of deletion is affected by how often the word occurs in the right phonetic environment, then that affects the word when it occurs in other environments.

The next question to ask is why past tense verbs occur before vowels so often and why negative auxiliaries occur before consonants? To answer the second question first, the item that follows a negative auxiliary is most often a verb and verbs tend to begin with consonants. As for past tense verbs, they occur before prepositions and particles, such as *on, out, up, away*, and so on, and before vowel-initial pronouns such as *it* and *us*, as well as pronouns whose initial consonants tend to be deleted, *him, her*, and *them*.

Thus it appears that the particular distribution of words in spoken language affects how quickly they will be impacted by a sound change. If occurrence in the favoring environment is the major factor in how words undergo sound change, then in fact the phonetic conditions are really primary, even in these cases where it initially appeared as if the morphology were retarding the change.

4.7.2.   Changes at word boundaries

The effect of word boundaries on sound change has been discussed in the literature as an instance of grammatical conditioning of sound change, since word boundaries are not part of phonetic conditioning, but rather reflect the lexical structure of the language. An approach taken to explain how word boundaries function in sound change is to say that the sound change starts in pre-pausal position (before silence, which is a phonetic factor) and then generalizes to word-final position (Hock 1986). The example of German word-final devoicing is explained as follows: In Old High German, the word *tag* 'day' ends in a voiced stop. However, before a pause, it is devoiced (note the partial devoicing of voiced stops and fricatives in English words such as *and*, *bad*, *tab*, and *tag* before a pause). Hock proposes that this devoicing extends by analogy to word-final position, so that in New High German all obstruents are devoiced at the end of a word. His position is that the original phonetically conditioned sound change that took place pre-pausally has changed to include the grammatical information of word boundary.

Another approach to word-final phenomena is to recognize (as I proposed in the previous section) that word-final position is an alternating environment. With /t/, /d/ deletion we saw that the following context determined how the deletion would proceed, and that introduced lexical variation. Let us consider now another example, where the change occurs word-internally and also across word boundaries. Many Spanish dialects, especially in the Americas, have a debuccalized variant of /s/ that occurs word-internally before a consonant, as in *feli[h]mente* 'happily', *e[h]tilo* 'style', *denti[h]ta* 'dentist'. At the end of a word before a consonant, this reduction occurs as well: *animale[h] finos* 'fine animals'. If a vowel follows in the next word, some dialects have very little reduction, while others, where the change is more advanced, have variable reduction: *mientra[h] esa* 'while this', *no va[s] a encontrar* 'you are not going to find'. The question is why is there reduction across a word boundary before a vowel when this reduction does not happen word-internally?

As we noted in the previous section, the context between words is an alternating environment. In Spanish, as in many other languages, words begin with consonants much more often than with vowels. In running text, /s/ occurs before a C more than 50% of the time, the position before a vowel and before a pause being more evenly split (20–25% for vowels and 23–28% for pause) (Bybee 2000a). Thus, most words occur before a consonant twice as often as before a vowel, so the variant with the consonant is dominant and therefore extends to the context before a vowel, giving the reduced [h] before a vowel. As noted, word-internally before a vowel the [s] remains unreduced in most dialects. As a result, in the end we might have a change described as follows: /s/ becomes /h/ (or deletes) before a consonant and at the end of a word, as in these examples:

(57)   Word-final   Before a consonant   Before a vowel
        mientra[h] 'while'   *denti[h]ta* 'dentist'   *hermo[s]a* 'pretty'
        comemo[h] 'we eat'   *e[h]tilo* 'style'   *ca[s]a* 'house'

Then it would appear that the word boundary conditioned the reduction, but really it was the consonant at the beginning of the next word.

Such cases can also result in changes that appear irregular. For instance, in word-initial position Old Spanish /f/ became /h/ and now is not pronounced at all, but only in some words. Many scholars have tried to understand why some words still have /f/ while others do not. Consider these words in Modern Spanish, all with initial /f/ in Latin:

(58)   Initial f > h > Ø   Initial /f/ retained
              hijo 'son'   *fijo* 'fixed'
              hecho 'done'   *fecha* 'date'
              hallar 'to find'   *favor* 'favor'
              horno 'oven'   *foco* 'focus'
              humo 'smoke'   *fumar* 'to smoke'

Some scholars explain the words with /f/ as having undergone the reduction with subsequent reintroduction of the /f/ based on written language or other factors. Brown and Raymond 2012 suggest an explanation in terms of the phonetic contexts in which the words were used. The labio-dental /f/ is more likely to reduce (debuccalize) where an open vowel precedes it. They studied the contexts of use of words with initial /f/ in a text written during the period of variation, that is, while the sound change was in progress. For all words that began with /f/ in Latin, they checked to see how often the preceding word ended in a non-high vowel, that is, the favorable context for reduction. They found that the words that in Modern Spanish have the spelling *h* (not pronounced today) were significantly more likely to be preceded by a non-high vowel than the words that today still have /f/. So it appears that when the period of variation ended, the words that more frequently occurred in the environment for reduction ended up with the reduced sound, while the ones that occurred more often preceded by a sound that did not induce reduction ended up unchanged, with /f/. We conclude, then, that the change is not conditioned by the word boundary, but rather by the phonetic elements in the context.

4.7.3.   Alternating environments within words

Alternating environments can also occur word-internally. We have seen in earlier sections of this chapter that sound change can take place despite alternating environments and can create alternations that eventually become morphologized. But sometimes the effect of the alternating environment can be seen in the period where a change is still variable. Timberlake 1978 has found evidence for this in the Mazovian dialect of Polish, where a palatalization process was ongoing when the data was gathered.

In Timberlake's examples a sound change progresses more slowly in a morpheme which occurs in an alternating environment. Consider the following examples from the Mazovian dialect of Polish (Timberlake 1978: 313–314). Transcriptions are from Timberlake and his sources. The examples in (59) show that root-internal position velars are always more or less palatalized before /i/. (The symbol [ʲ] indicates full palatalization and ['] indicates partial palatalization; *c* stands for [ts].)

(59)   Mazovian Polish: uniform environment
            kʲij   'stick'
            skʲiba   'ridge'
            gʲipsu   'gypsum'
            k'ɪlômetr   'kilometer'
            g'ɲe   'bends'

In alternating environments, represented here by the position before a suffix, stops are palatalized before /i/ in only about half of the recorded examples as shown in (60):

(60)   Mazovian Polish: alternating environment
            prog'ɪ   'hearths' cf. progu (gen. sg.)
            drog'ɪ   'roads' cf. droga (nom. sg.)
            burak'ɪ   'beets'
            jarmak'ɪ   'fairs'
            morg'ɪ   'acres'
            rog'ɪ   'horns'
            gruskɪ   'pears'
            kackɪ   'ducks'
            zmarsckɪ   'wrinkles'
            drugɪ   'other'
            robakɪ   'worms'

When the velar is stem-final, it will sometimes occur in a palatalizing context and sometimes not. This is the reason, according to Timberlake, that the palatalization process is retarded even when the conditioning is present. It appears, then, that the different forms of the stem that occur in different environments have an effect on one another. From the situation described for this dialect, there are two possible outcomes: in the end an alternation is established for the forms in (60) or the palatalization fails for the forms in (60) and no alternation is established.

This case may be relevant to situations where it appears that an alternation fails to be established despite a regular sound change sweeping the language. An example comes from Romance, resulting from the palatalization of /k/ and /g/ before front vowels and glides in spoken Latin, which we discussed in Sections 2.2.5 and 4.6. This sound change produced some of the alternations in Spanish second and third conjugation verbs: for instance, the Latin verb *dīcere* 'to say, tell' has its stem-final /k/ before a front vowel in most of the paradigm, and occurs before a back vowel only in the 1st singular present indicative and the present subjunctive.

(61)   The Latin verb *dīcere* 'to say, tell'

Present indicative			Present subjunctive	
dīco	*dīcimus*		*dīcam*	*dīcamus*
dīcis	*dīcistis*		*dīcas*	*dīcātis*
dīcit	*dīcunt*		*dīcat*	*dīcant*

            Imperfect indicative: *dīceābat*
            Future: *dīcet*

When the /k/ palatalized, an alternation was established in this paradigm, which still remains in Spanish today, as shown in (62), where the orthographic *c* represents [s] in American dialects and [θ] in Peninsular Spanish.

(62)   Spanish *de[s]ir* 'to say, to tell'

Present indicative		Present subjunctive	
digo	*de[s]imos*	*diga*	*digamos*
di[s]es		*digas*	
di[s]e	*di[s]en*	*diga*	*digan*
Imperfect:	*de[s]ía,* etc.		

In first conjugation verbs, however, the phonetic conditions are just about reversed: the back vowels occur in the indicative and the front vowels in the subjunctive. While the conditions for an alternation exist for stems ending in velars, no such alternations arose. Thus the verbs *llegar* 'to arrive', *pagar* 'to pay', *negar* 'to deny', and *rogar* 'to beg' have subjunctive forms with the velar (indicated in the spelling by the presence of *u* after the *g*), *llegue, pague, niegue, ruegue*. In both cases there is an alternating environment, but in one case an alternation actually took hold while in the other case it did not.

Two approaches to explaining the lack of an alternation in first conjugation verbs may be taken. First, one could argue that the alternation was established, but then later was leveled (see Chapter 5) – that is, new forms with the velar were constructed; or second, that because of the alternating environment, the alternation was never established. At present, it is not known which approach is correct in this case or indeed in other such cases.

4.7.4.   Conclusion: sound change affected by grammar ▰▰▰▰▰▰

Given the many examples we have reviewed in the preceding sections, a strong case cannot be made for giving up the Neogrammarian hypothesis of the phonetic predictability of sound change. It appears instead that investigators need to recognize that the broader phonetic context in which words are used may be part of the conditioning environment. Given this broader context, words and morphemes occur with different probabilities in the phonetic environment for a change, which affects how likely they are to undergo the change. As sound change is phonetically gradual and characterized by much variation while it is ongoing, differences in the distribution of words may allow for some differences in outcome. But it is not the grammatical or lexical category of the word that matters; it is rather the contexts of use in discourse. Thus so far it appears that the Neogrammarians were right: changes occur within a phonetic context.

4.8.   Conclusion

While previous chapters addressed the phonetic reasons for sound change, this chapter has been concerned with the way sound change interacts with the grammar of a language. First, we considered how the alternations caused by sound change become a part of morphological paradigms. In Chapter 5 we will consider further analogical changes that affect such alternations. Second, we addressed the way that alternations caused by sound change can become part of morphosyntactic constructions. We also discussed some more specific changes such as rule inversion and the extension of the phonetic change in rule telescoping. We considered next the way exceptions to sound change can develop over time. Then we considered the other side of the coin: can grammatical factors affect sound change as it is ongoing? Here we saw a number of examples of changes that seemed to be affected by particular morphemes or by word boundaries. In each case, however, we were able to conclude that it was not the grammatical elements themselves that were affecting the sound change, but rather the phonetic contexts in which they occurred.

Questions for discussion

1.   Try to observe English speakers you listen to pronouncing words such as *houses*. Most older speakers use a medial [z] while some younger speakers use an [s]. Which pronunciation is older? Why would the two variants appear? Is there change in progress?

2.   Some speakers of American and British English have lost word-final and preconsonantal /r/ by a regular sound change. In some dialects that have lost /r/, speakers appear to add it back in at the end of a word before a vowel. They might say *the author can...* with no /r/ but *the author is...* with the /r/ present. This seems to be an insertion, because many of these same speakers add an /r/ after words like *idea*, as in *the idear is*. As there was never an /r/ at the end of *idea*, there seems to be an insertion. Try to explain in terms discussed in this chapter what is happening in these dialects.

3.   Does the special reduction discussed in Section 2.9 violate the Neogrammarian Hypothesis?

5   Analogical change

5.1.   Analogy

The term "analogy" as used in linguistics has a specific and a general meaning. In historical linguistics it usually applies to morphological change, more specifically, change within morphological paradigms; that is what this chapter is about. The broader use of the term applies in syntax and refers to a process by which innovative expressions are based on existing expressions rather than on rules, a point we return to in Chapter 8.

This chapter is concerned with changes in morphological form (rather than meaning, which we get to in the next two chapters). The definition of morphological analogy I will use is the following: the re-making of a word based on similarity to other existing words in the language. In the preceding chapter we saw that sound change introduces alternations and irregularities into morphological paradigms. Analogical changes are often a response to these alternations, either working to eliminate them or, less often, to extend them to new lexical items.

Analogical change is rarely lexically regular the way sound change often is. That is, while sound change tends to affect all the lexical items that have the appropriate phonetic conditions for the change, analogical change clearly works one item at a time and most commonly does not affect all lexical items or paradigms that have the requisite conditions. This property of analogical change makes it seem irregular and perhaps even unpredictable. However, when a broad view is taken of many documented historical analogical changes, and phenomena found in child language and experiments, some very general trends can be observed. This chapter reviews the types of changes traditionally grouped under analogy and discusses some general trends in the directionality of change.

5.2.   Proportional analogy

Have you ever paused to consider whether the nightmare you had the previous night was something you *dreamed* or something you *dreamt?* The existence of these two alternate forms is the result of analogy. Analogical change is often described as resulting from proportional or four-part analogy, a kind of reasoning often found in intelligence tests. Thus, in order to understand where the alternate form *dreamed* came from as it replaces older *dreamt*, the following four-part analogy might be proposed:

(63)   *seem* : *seemed* :: *dream* : *dreamed*

The problem with this account is that it very likely does not describe the cognitive mechanism by which changes such as this one are accomplished. For one thing, such changes are rarely based on only one other set of forms; when analogy occurs it is because there are multiple forms in the language with the pattern, as we see in most English verbs that add *–ed* for past tense without changing the vowel: *dimmed, tapped, changed, tweaked, passed*, and so on. Moreover, the speaker does not have to conjure up three forms to produce the fourth one, because the general pattern resulting from the many forms exhibiting it is available in memory as a generalization. In subsequent sections we will see that the mechanisms that produce analogical innovations are varied, but none of them requires a four-part proportional analogy.

5.3.   Analogical leveling

The change just illustrated of *dreamed* replacing *dreamt* is an example of analogical leveling. Leveling is said to take place when the new form eliminates an alternation that existed in the older form. Consider the following set of English present and past tense forms:

(64)   Base/Present   Past and Past Participle
         [iː]   [ɛ]
         keep   *kept*
         leave   *left*
         sleep   *slept*
         sweep   *swept*
         feel   *felt*
         kneel   *knelt*
         mean   *meant*
         dream   *dreamt*
         creep   *crept*
         leap   *leapt*
         weep   *wept*

In all of these forms (a verb class), the suffix *–t* is added (even in cases where the preceding consonant is voiced, as in *felt*, *knelt*, and *meant*), and the vowel of the present is [iː], but the vowel of the past and participle form is [ɛ]. So these verbs have a stem vowel alternation. (I am sure you will recognize that it was the result of the Great Vowel Shift discussed in Chapter 3; the vowel of the base was a long vowel and it had been shortened in Middle English when the cluster with *–t* followed.)

In Present Day English, the forms *dreamed, kneeled, creeped, leaped,* and *weeped* instead of *dreamt, knelt, crept, leapt,* and *wept* sometimes occur. Some dictionaries recognize these forms, and all five occur in corpora of American English. These forms exemplify analogical leveling. It is important not to think of this change as, for example, *leapt* [lɛpt] changing into *leaped*. Rather *leaped* is a new form created by taking the base form *leap* and applying the regular past tense pattern to it. One way we know this is that both forms still exist in variation today, even if at some point the older form might disappear. In some cases, when analogical change takes place, the older form stays around with a different meaning. For example, the comparative form of the adjective *old* used to be *elder*. Now *older* is the normal comparative form, but *elder* (and the superlative *eldest*) are still used in specific settings, usually when talking about siblings, as in *the elder sister*.

In the case of *dreamed, creeped, kneeled, leaped,* and *weeped* we can also talk about regularization. Since the suffix *–ed* and no stem alternation is considered regular in English, changes that move verbs from the more irregular classes to the regular ones can be considered regularization. When children during the acquisition process create regular forms such as *catched* or *sleeped*, researchers speak of overregularization. This process is more common among children than adults, but as forms such as *creeped, leaped,* and *weeped* show, adults participate as well. These verbs are not ones that would be used by very young children.

As you can note by looking at the verbs and their past tense forms in (64), only some verbs have a tendency to undergo leveling or regularization. As we noted at the beginning of the chapter, analogical change occurs one form at a time and rarely goes to completion, the way sound change does. Also, note that the mechanism described above, the creation of a new form (not the change of an old form) points to the change happening one verb at a time. Thus we could ask, what are the factors that determine which verbs undergo leveling?

One factor that has been identified is the token frequency of the irregular form. If a past tense form in English has an alternation and it is of very high frequency, then it is unlikely that it will regularize. The reason is that it will have a strong memory representation for speakers once they have learned the language, and that will make the past form easy to access (that is, easy to find in memory and retrieve for use). If the form is easy to access there will not be any chance for a new form to be composed or, if it is used, to be taken up by other speakers. In contrast, if a past form is low in frequency it might be more difficult to access, and if the speaker does not retrieve it immediately, the regular pattern could be activated and a new, regular form produced.

Now consider the list of past forms in (64) arranged in order of their token frequencies in the 450 million-word Corpus of Contemporary American English (COCA), as shown in (65).

(65) | Present | Past and past participle | Frequency per million in COCA |
|---------|-------------------------|------------------------------|
| *leave* | *left* | 310 |
| *feel* | *felt* | 253 |
| *keep* | *kept* | 139 |
| *mean* | *meant* | 91 |
| *sleep* | *slept* | 20 |
| *sweep* | *swept* | 19 |
| *dream* | *dreamt/dreamed* | 13.5 |
| *leap* | *leapt/leaped* | 9 |
| *kneel* | *knelt/kneeled* | 6 |
| *creep* | *crept/creeped* | 5.5 |
| *weep* | *wept/weeped* | 4 |

The frequency count of the past/past participle forms includes both the conservative and regularized forms, so they constitute a count of how often the verb appears in the past. As you see from (65), the six verbs that are highest in frequency in Present Day English do not have leveled or regularized variants, but the five that are of the lowest frequency all have such variants.

It appears, however, that frequency of use is not the only factor affecting leveling. The different verbs that have regularized variants behave differently. For instance, while *dreamed* and *leaped* are more frequent than the conservative variants, for the other verbs, the regularized variant is less frequent, much less frequent in the case of *wept/weeped*. Another indicator that token frequency is not the only predictor of leveling is that the difference in frequency between *slept* and *swept* on the one hand and *dreamt* on the other, is not that great, as shown in (65). What is clear, however, is that high-frequency verbs resist analogical leveling; good evidence for this is the fact that irregular verbs (and nouns and adjectives for that matter) are highly frequent in all languages. The other factors that may be at play are not known at the moment.

The example of *creeped* shows another way that a regular form can develop. In the COCA search for *creeped* there were 84 instances that occurred in the phrase *creeped (someone) out* or BE *creeped out* (which I did not count in [65]). In fact, in this phrase *crept* never occurred, only *creeped*. Here is an example.

(66)   *Truth was, receiving the dead roses <u>creeped me out</u>.*   (COCA 2008)

In this use, *creep* is not an intransitive verb meaning 'move slowly', but rather a transitive verb meaning something like 'to instill fear or disgust' in someone. The reason it is regular is that it is derived from a noun. Apparently *to creep someone out* is a remaking of the phrase *give someone the creeps*. The latter phrase has been around since the mid-nineteenth century, while the former one appears first in the late 1990s and becomes frequent after 2000. Examining data from the Corpus of Historical American English (COHA) reveals that *the creeps* referred to a crawling sensation of the skin when a person is afraid or disgusted.

When verbs are derived from nouns, they strongly tend to be regular. For example, *to ring* in the sense of 'to form a ring' in the following example is regular.

(67)   *Any Chinese city is <u>ringed</u> <u>with</u> appliance stores; where once they offered electric fans, they now carry vibrating massage chairs.* (COCA, National Geographic 2011, Bill McKibben)

It wouldn't do to say *Any Chinese city is rung with appliance stores* nor changing the sentence to active (from passive), *Appliance stores rang the city*; keeping the verb regular helps to maintain its relation to the noun. No doubt, the increase in frequency of the regular past tense pattern, which will be discussed more in the next section, is aided by the strong tendency of English to form new verbs from nouns. For present purposes, it is important to note that in these examples *creeped* and *ringed* are not instances of analogical leveling, but rather instances of new verbs formed from nouns.

We have seen, then, that analogical leveling is the loss of an alternation in which one form of the paradigm that has an alternation is used to create new forms that do not have the alternation. Analogical leveling affects low-frequency paradigms, and high-frequency paradigms tend to resist leveling. There will be more examples of leveling in sections that follow. One important question about leveling concerns which variant in the paradigm is the one that serves as the basis for creating new forms and thus is the one that survives. This question will be addressed in Section 5.5.

5.4.   Productivity

Another question that arises in the understanding of analogical leveling is what determines what the regular pattern will be. For instance, why is it that new forms such as *leaped* and *dreamed* appear rather than new forms such as *sept* from *seep* (replacing *seeped*) or *bept* from *beep* (replacing *beeped*) or *semt* from *seem* (replacing *seemed*)?

The reason is that some patterns are highly productive and some are less productive. Productivity is the likelihood that a pattern or construction will apply to a novel item. Right now in English, the past tense suffix *–ed* with no internal change of the verb stem is the productive pattern. Things were not always this way, which shows that productivity can come and go, as we will see below.

There is a strong relationship between the productivity of a pattern and the number of items it applies to, termed the *type frequency* of the construction. In Present Day English there are about 180 verbs with some kind of irregularity – no suffix (*cut*), vowel change (*break, broke*), consonant change (*teach, taught*) – but the vast majority of verbs form their past tense with the suffix *–ed* (the allomorphs [d], [t] and [ɪd]) and no other change. Because there are so many verbs with this pattern, it is the one most often applied to new verbs taken into the language by borrowing (*ski/skied* borrowed from Scandinavian, *waltz/waltzed* borrowed from German) or by derivation (*creep/creeped* from *the creeps*, *hammer/hammered* from the noun *hammer*). Of course, these and the many other additions to this pattern make it all the more productive.

In Old English the situation was quite different. The verbs that had vowel changes in the past (called the "strong" verbs) were more numerous than they are now. The "weak" pattern used the suffix *–ede* or *–ode*; such verbs were less numerous than they are now. Most of the vowel change patterns (called "ablaut") are very ancient, going back to vowel changes in Proto-Indo-European (see Chapter 10). The suffix developed later, probably in Proto-Germanic (since all the Germanic languages have such a suffix). Its source was very likely the past tense of the verb 'to do', which can be reconstructed as **dedō–* and **dedē–* with person/number endings attached. The use of a verb (or verbal noun) plus 'did' was probably meaningful at first, but later it became a way of forming the past tense of new verbs from nouns or from borrowed words (*ende* 'end, n.' > *endian*, *enede–* 'to end, ended'). The changes by which two words become a single word with an affix is *grammaticalization* and will be explained fully in Chapter 6. For now it is enough to say that both the loss of meaning and the reduction of phonological form are normal concomitants of grammaticalization.

Note that the OE strong verbs have lots of different vowel changes; in fact, they are usually divided into seven different classes. The following shows one representative verb of each class.

(68)　　　Old English Strong Verb Classes

Infinitive	3rd pres.	Past sg.	Past pl.	Past participle
rīdan 'to ride'	*rītt*	*rād*	*ridon*	*riden*
smēocan 'to smoke'	*smīecþ*	*smēac*	*smucon*	*smocen*
drincan 'to drink'	*drincþ*	*dranc*	*druncon*	*drunken*
brecan 'to break'	*bricþ*	*brœc*	*brœ̄con*	*broken*
etan 'to eat'	*itt*	*ǣt*	*ǣton*	*eten*
standan 'to stand'	*stent*	*stōd*	*stōdon*	*standen*
grōwan 'to grow'	*grēwþ*	*grēow*	*grēowon*	*grōwen*

Given the complexity of the system and the fact that vowel changes signaled the difference between present and past, it would have been difficult to incorporate new verbs into this system. Thus the weak verb suffix, *–ede*, *–ode* came in very handy, especially as more words were borrowed into English from French during the Norman Conquest, and the number of verbs using the suffix increased dramatically. This increase then gradually increased the productivity of the suffixing pattern. As this happened, some of the strong verbs regularized. From the list above, you see that *smoke* is now a regular verb; also *reap, shove, help, burn, mourn, heave, wax, flow, row, mow, seethe, delve* among others were strong verbs in OE but now are regular.

Leveling or regularization is one mechanism by which the strong verb classes shrink in size while the suffixed class grows. The other mechanism that increases the number of suffixed verbs is the complete loss of verbs from the language. Some strong verbs listed in *Sweet's Anglo-Saxon Primer* that are no longer used in PDE are: *hrīnan* 'to touch', *mīþan* 'to hide', *stīgan* 'to ascend', *brūcan* 'to enjoy', *beorgan* 'to protect', *weorpan* 'to throw', and *hātan* 'to call'. These verbs are lost as others come in to replace them (see Chapter 9 for more discussion), and their loss shifts the balance towards more verbs formed with the *–ed* suffix.

Derivational affixes also compete for productivity. The suffix for forming nouns from adjectives in English, *–ness* (*happiness, redness, creepiness*) is very productive today, and it apparently was also widely used in OE (Riddle 1985) alongside other suffixes such as the predecessors of *–ship* (OE *–scipe, –shepe*), *–hood* (OE *–hēd*), and *–dom*. According to Riddle, there was a lot of variation in OE with competing forms based on the same roots, as in these examples:

(69)   *raunesse, rauhede*   'rawness'
        gladness, gladscip   'gladness'
        wīsness, wīshede, wīsdom   'wisdom'
        blīnhēde, blindness   'blindness'
        dronkenesse, drunkenhede, drunkeshepe   'drunkenness'
        derkness, deorkhede   'darkness'

In PDE the suffixes *–ship*, *–hood*, and *–dom* are used in very few words (*fellowship, falsehood, freedom*) while *–ness* is relatively productive and used in many different words to produce an abstract noun from an adjective.

5.5.   Trends in analogical change: the basic–derived relation

In this section we treat some strong tendencies that appear in analogical change based on the structure of paradigms. These include ways of predicting which form will survive and serve as the basis for new forms in analogical change (Sections 5.5.1 and 5.5.2) and how the semantic categories expressed in the paradigm determine which forms are more likely to change.

5.5.1.   The basic form of the paradigm

The first question we consider is how to determine which form of a paradigm serves as the basis for new formations. Taking the example discussed earlier, we ask why in the leveling of *leaped, leapt* it is a new past form created on the basis of the present and not a new present form created on the basis of the past? That is, given that there are two stem forms – one with the tense vowel [iː] and one with the lax vowel [ɛ] – why is the alternation leveled by creating a new form of the past, *leaped*, rather than a new present, *lep, leps*, and even *lepping*?

One approach to this question is to point out that the more "basic" or simpler form of the paradigm serves as the basis on which new forms are created (Kuryłowicz 1947). This opens up the question of what constitutes the basic

Table 5.1: *Markedness relation for specific categories*

Unmarked member	More marked members
Nouns, pronouns and adjectives:	
singular	plural, dual, trial, paucal
direct cases (nom., acc.)	oblique cases
nominative	accusative
absolutive	ergative
masculine	feminine, neuter
simple adjective	comparative, superlative
normal size	diminutive, augmentative
cardinal numbers	ordinal numbers
lower numerals	higher numerals
3rd person, 1st person	2nd person
Verbs:	
active	passive, reflexive, middle, reciprocal
indicative	other moods
present	past, future
perfective	imperfective
affirmative	negative
declarative	interrogative

form of a paradigm, which may be different in different analyses. Another approach names the categories, noting that present tenses serve as the bases for pasts, indicatives for subjunctives, and 3rd singular for other person/number forms (Mańczak 1958). This approach is more concrete, but it fails to generalize over the various cases.

An approach that attempts a generalization over categories of different sorts invokes the concept of *markedness* based on semantic features as developed by Roman Jakobson (Jakobson 1939). Jakobson observes that the unmarked member of a category, such as gender (masculine) differs from the marked member (feminine), which states the presence of a property because it (the unmarked member) either indicates the absence of the property or says nothing at all about the property. That is why forms such as *waiter* or *actor* can be used to indicate both males and females, but *waitress* and *actress* are restricted to female referents. In some cases we can identify the literally "unmarked" form of a paradigm because it has no affix. Greenberg 1966 added the criterion of frequency to those proposed by Jakobson. He demonstrated that the unmarked member was usually the most frequent one. By taking these criteria into account, the markedness approach can generalize to other categories as shown in Table 5.1, which is based on Greenberg 1966.

Be aware, however, there are problems with applying the semantic definition (the presence or absence of a property) in many of the categories, and there are paradigms where no one member lacks an affix. So this approach also presents problems of generalizing in a definitive way to all categories. Nonetheless, the breakdown in Table 5.1 gives us a rough way of predicting how analogical leveling applies in inflectional paradigms.

Despite the relative success of this general breakdown, the approach based on semantic criteria is disproved by cases in which leveling for one lexical item's paradigm goes in the opposite direction of leveling for another paradigm. Mańczak 1958 notes one such example: for geographical names, leveling favors the locative case, the case used in the answer to "where?"

Tiersma 1982 has brought attention to an interesting pattern of leveling in the West Germanic language Frisian. In Frisian, nouns often have vowel alternations in the singular and plural, as shown in (70a), and this alternation is leveled as shown in (70b) with a new plural formed using the vowel of the singular.

(70)   Frisian nouns

      a. Conservative alternation   b. Innovative forms
         Singular/plural   Singular/plural
         hoer/hworren, 'whore'   *hoer/hoeren*
         koal/kwallen, 'coal'   *koal/koalen*
         miel/mjillen, 'meal, milking' *miel/mielen*
         poel/pwollen, 'pool'   *poel/poelen*

The leveling shown in (70b) is what would be expected given the markedness relations shown in Table 5.1. However, there are also some nouns undergoing leveling in which a new singular has been formed using the diphthong of the plural, as shown in (71).

(71)   Frisian nouns

      a. Conservative alternation   b. Innovative forms
         Singular/plural   Singular/plural
         earm/jermen, 'arm'   *jerm/jermen*
         goes/gwozzen, 'goose'   *gwos/gwozzen*
         hoarn/hwarnen, '(animal) horn' *hwarne/hwarnen*
         kies/kjizzen, 'tooth'   *kjizze/kjizzen*
         spoen/spwonnen, 'shaving, splinter' *spwon/spwonnen*
         toarn/twarnen, 'thorn'   *twarne/twarnen*
         trien/trjinnen, 'tear'   *trjin/trjinnen*

The examples in (70) and (71) demonstrate conclusively that an approach purely in terms of general categories as shown in Table 5.1 will not predict all cases of the direction of leveling. Tiersma points out that while the nouns in (70) show the usual pattern of distribution in which the singular is more frequently used than the plural, the nouns in (71) show the opposite distribution: the entities referred to by these nouns come in pairs or multiples so that the plural form is the more frequently used form. Tiersma argues that it is not semantic markedness that determines the direction of leveling, but rather the frequency of use. The more frequent form is not only less likely to change (as we noted in terms of which paradigms tend to level) but it is also most likely to serve as the basis of change. Since the "unmarked" form as shown in Table 5.1 is in most paradigms also the most frequent form, referring to frequency rather than semantic basicness can explain the changes found in (70), that is, those predicted by *general markedness*, and also the changes in (71), those predicted by *local markedness*, as Tiersma put it.

Thus what we learn from this excursion through various proposals is that there might be a very concrete and testable way to predict how leveling will turn out. Reference to frequency of use is much more testable than reference to markedness theory. Moreover, we can formulate a very general hypothesis that covers several types of cases beyond analogical leveling, as we shall see in the following sections. The principle is this:

(72)   High-frequency forms are resistant to change on the basis of the structure of other forms or patterns, and more likely to serve as the basis of such change in low-frequency forms.

We have already discussed the cognitive mechanism behind this hypothesis. Every token of a word or phrase strengthens its representation in memory, making it easier to access on subsequent occasions. The forms that are strongly represented in memory will be less likely to change, and they are likely to be the forms accessed and used when a less frequent form is difficult to access. This hypothesis applies to high-frequency paradigms with irregularities that resist change, and it applies to the relations among forms of a paradigm, with the more frequent ones being taken as the basis of change, if it occurs.

Returning to paradigms that resist regularization, consider the nouns in English that have the plural expressed by a vowel alternation: *foot/feet, tooth/ teeth, mouse/mice, goose/geese, child/children, man/men*, and *woman/women*. These plural nouns are either of high frequency (*men, women*) or the plural is of equal or greater frequency than the singular, as in the case of referents that tend to come in pairs or multiples, *feet, teeth, mice*, and *geese*.

The hypothesis in (72) has not been tested on enough cases to determine how reliably it predicts the direction of leveling. As usual, there are likely other factors that interact with frequency of use. However, it is the most promising as well as the most testable factor that has been proposed. In the next section we see how frequency of use may influence another type of morphological change – the creation of zero markers.

5.5.2.   Under-analysis and the creation of zeroes

In noun, verb, or adjective paradigms there is often one form that carries no affix or other marking, but nonetheless signals an inflectional meaning. For example, for English nouns, singular has no affix; thus *dog* has no affix, but it is interpreted as singular in usage such as *the dog gobbled up the pizza. The dog* is not just vague about whether it refers to one or to multiple dogs, it is quite definitely singular. In this section we consider how nothing – the lack of an affix – can have meaning.

The meaningful lack of an affix is an indicator of an obligatory category, a category that is required by the morphosyntax to have some exponent. Another example is the English simple present. If I say *I drink decaf* you know that I mean I habitually drink decaf coffee. The meaning of 'I am drinking decaf right now' is expressed by the progressive *be + ing* form, and the lack of that form signals habitual meaning. In contrast, in the simple past, the lack of the progressive form does not require a habitual aspectual meaning. The sentence *he drank decaf* could be either habitual in meaning or it could mean just one instance, such as *last night he drank decaf* compared to *he always drank decaf.* So the progressive/habitual distinction is not obligatory in the past tense, only in the present.

Following from what we noted above about the relative frequency of forms, the zero-marked form of a paradigm tends to be the most frequent form (Greenberg 1966). There are two diachronic trends that account for this correspondence. One concerns what types of items tend to undergo grammaticalization, the process that creates affixes. This will be discussed in the next two chapters. The other way that zeroes arise in the most frequent forms is by the under-analysis of forms that earlier had affixes, a process we will now examine.

In many languages the 3rd person singular form in verbal paradigms is zero-marked, but in other cases it does have a marker. Our interest here is in cases where an overt affix appears, but the form is reanalyzed as having a zero-marker. Watkins 1962 presents several examples from the development of the Celtic languages, which show a restructuring of whole paradigms based on an analysis of the 3rd singular form as having a zero-marker for person and number. The following examples illustrate such a restructuring in preterit verbal forms of the Occitan dialects of southern French. The Old Provençal forms in (73) can be taken as a starting point. Here it appears that the stressed vowel could be considered the marker of preterit with person/number suffixes *–i, –st, –t, –m, –tz, –ren* added to the sequence *canté–.* (Present forms differ because they have stress on the stem vowel: *cántat* 3rd sg. pres.)

(73)   Old Provençal preterit forms (Anglade 1921: 262, 294) *canta* 'to sing'
         1st sg. *cantéi*   1st pl. *cantém*
         2nd sg. *cantést*   2nd pl. *cantétz*
         3rd sg. *cantét*   3rd pl. *cantéren*

In the Charente dialect shown in (74) a *t* appears in the 2nd singular and all the plural forms. The 1st singular is changed only in that the *–éi* diphthong has simplified to *–í.* The intriguing question is where the *t* in the 2nd singular and plural forms came from. In view of the high frequency of the 3rd singular form, Bybee and Brewer 1980 propose that the 2nd singular and all the plurals were remade using the 3rd singular as the base and adding person/number suffixes: for instance *cantét + em* gives the 1st plural form.

This change comes about because the high-frequency 3rd singular form is taken by speakers to be the basic form of the preterit paradigm. Thus the *–t* on that form is taken to be a marker of preterit, not a marker of 3rd singular. Once the person/number markers are added, then indeed, the –*t*– becomes the sign of the preterit. The fact that the 1st singular does not change also follows from hypothesis (72): as 1st singular forms are also of high frequency, this form resists reformation and remains.

(74)   Charente dialect
        1st sg. *cantí*   1st pl. *cantétem*
        2nd sg. *cantétei*   2nd pl. *cantétei*
        3rd sg. *cantét*   3rd pl. *cantéten*

A slightly different outcome is found in another dialect in southern France, Clermont-Ferrand. In this case the 1st singular is remade along with the other forms, but the 3rd singular has lost its –*t*, by regular sound change.

(75)   Clermont-Ferrand dialect
        1st. sg. *cantéte*   1st pl. *cantétem*
        2nd sg. *cantétes*   2nd pl. *cantétetz*
        3rd sg. *canté*   3rd pl. *cantéton*

These examples and many similar ones show that the high frequency of a morphologically complex form can lead to it being under-analyzed or taken to be a simpler unit than it was earlier. That is, the 3rd singular preterit forms had three morphemes: the stem, the stressed vowel for the preterit, and the final –*t* for the 3rd singular. In the reanalysis, the word has only two parts, the stem and the –*ét*, which is now considered to signal preterit. We will see in the following examples, and also in other contexts in this book, cases in which a high-frequency form becomes *autonomous* in the sense that its component parts are no longer associated with these parts used in other words or phrases (see also Section 9.5).

The creation of double-marked forms also illustrates the effect of autonomy. Tiersma 1982 brought up double-marked plurals to underscore his point about nouns that more often occur in the plural being taken as autonomous and thus under-analyzed. In Middle Dutch, the word for 'shoe' was *schoe*, but the modern singular is *schoen*. This was the earlier plural form and now there is a new plural, *schoenen*. The plural form was taken as basic and used for singular because shoes ordinarily come in pairs. Other examples of double-marked plurals in Dutch are shown in (76), although in these cases the singular remains unchanged.

(76)   Dutch double plurals

Singular	Older plural	Modern plural	Gloss
blad	*blader*	*bladeren*	'leaf'
ei	*eier*	*eieren*	'egg'
hoen	*hoender*	*hoenderen*	'hen'
kalf	*kalver*	*kalveren*	'calf'
kind	*kinder*	*kinderen*	'child'
lam	*lammer*	*lammeren*	'lamb'
rad	*rader*	*raderen*	'wheel'

These nouns all refer to items that tend to be referred to in the plural. Perhaps aided by the fact that the plural marker *–er* was only one of several plural markers, and less productive than the *–en* plural, the older plural noun was taken to be a single unit rather than a stem plus an affix. As a result, speakers added a plural affix in accord with the meaning of the word, resulting in what appears from an etymological point of view to be two plural markers. Old English created some double plurals, too, but the only one remaining in the language is the plural of *child, children* – which contains both the *–er* plural (now extinct in English) and *–en* plural, now rare in English.

In this section we have seen that high-frequency complex forms are sometimes taken to be unitary (not consisting of component parts) and used as the basis for creating new forms within inflectional paradigms. We have also noted that some high-frequency forms resist change as predicted by the hypothesis given in (72).

5.6.   Change within more related categories

The examples just discussed show change within inflectional paradigms from a more basic form to other forms. Now we need to say a bit more about how the forms of paradigms are organized such that they can affect one another. Many inflectional languages have categories of tense, aspect, and modality as well as person and number. These categories differ from one another in the extent to which they affect the meaning of the verb, with aspectual differences having the greatest effect followed by tense, mood, and person/number (Bybee 1985). It follows, then, that the forms most closely related to one another semantically occur within the same aspect, tense, or mood, while verb forms in different aspects will be the most distantly related of the inflectional forms of a paradigm. In terms of leveling of alternations, it is most likely that alternations among forms that are the most closely related will be the first to be leveled while alternations among forms that are less closely related will be more stable.

This point can be illustrated with the forms of the verb 'to do' in Old and Middle English as shown in (77) (Moore and Marckwardt 1951).

			Old English	Middle English
(77)	Pres. ind. sg.	1	*dō*	*do*
		2	*dēst*	*dost*
		3	*dēþ*	*doth*
	Plural		*dōþ*	*do*
	Pret. ind. sg.	1	*dyde*	*dide, dude* [dyde]
		2	*dydest*	*didest, dudest*
		3	*dyde*	*dide, dude*
	Plural		*dydon*	*dide(n), dude(n)*

Note that in OE there is a vowel alternation in the present indicative, which has /oː/ in the 1st singular and the plural, and /eː/ in the 2nd and 3rd singular. In addition, the vowel of the preterit is different from either of the vowels of the present; it is a high front rounded vowel. The change that took place during the ME period eliminated the vowel alternation in the present but did not affect that vowel of the preterit. In the present, the vowel of the 1st singular (a highly frequent form) and plural replaced the vowels of the 2nd and 3rd singular. The variation you see in the preterit in the ME period was due to the fact that the front rounded vowel was being gradually lost. As in other verb paradigms of the OE and ME periods, any alternations among the vowels of the present were gradually leveled, but often the difference of vowels between the present and preterit remained.

This tendency by which forms that are more closely related to one another tend to have the same stem forms can be seen in synchronic paradigms where alternations are more common across aspect, tense, and mood forms than across person/number forms within the same aspect, tense, or mood. For example, the most extreme stem change in Spanish verbs is between the present/imperfect stem vs. the preterit stem in certain verbs, as shown in (78). Most of these alternations date back to Latin or beyond. The person/number forms within the present and the preterit use the same stem form. The stability of these alternations provides evidence that the structure of paradigms is one determinant of the likelihood of analogical changes taking place, along with the frequency distributions of forms within the paradigm.

(78)   Spanish

3rd sg. present	3rd sg. preterit	Gloss
pone	*puso*	'put'
tiene	*tuvo*	'have'
hace	*hice*	'make, do'
está	*estuvo*	'be (located)'
quiere	*quiso*	'want'
dice	*dijo*	'say'
sabe	*supo*	'know'

5.7.   Extension

Analogical extension is the opposite of leveling in the sense that through extension an alternation begins to appear in a paradigm that previously had no alternation. Leveling is much more common than extension because there is a strong tendency towards having one form for one meaning. However, extension does occur under certain circumstances. In this section we will consider two quite different types of extension, one in which a stem alternation that expresses a meaningful distinction is spread to other lexical items and one in which an alternation is introduced by the extension of an allomorph of an affix.

Table 5.2: *A semi-productive verb class of English*

	/ɪ/	/æ/	/ʌ/	/ɪ/	/ʌ/
–m	swim	swam	swum		
–n	begin	began	begun	spin	spun
	run	ran	run	win	won
–ŋ	ring	rang	rung*	cling	clung
	sing	sang	sung	fling	flung*
	spring	sprang	sprung	sling	slung*
				sting	stung*
				string	strung*
				swing	swung
				wring	wrung
				hang	hung*
				bring	brung**
–nk	drink	drank	drunk	slink	slunk
	shrink	shrank	shrunk		
	stink	stank	stunk		
–k				strike	struck*
				stick	stuck*
				sneak	snuck**
				shake	shuck**
–g				dig	dug*
				drag	drug**

*Not a strong verb in Old English, but made strong by analogy, according to (Jespersen 1942).
**Dialectal, not a strong verb in Old English

In both cases, the type frequency of the extended pattern is a strong determining factor in the change.

The first case involves a vowel alternation in a class of verbs that were strong in OE. As mentioned above, the development of past tense forms from OE to PDE predominantly involves the regularization or loss of such verbs, though token frequency is one factor in their preservation. In defiance of this general trend, one class of verbs has expanded by adding new members, mostly verbs that were previously regular. In Table 5.2 we see examples of these verbs. The past forms marked with an asterisk were not original members of this class but have come to have the vowel alternation by analogical extension. The discussion of this class is based on Bybee and Moder 1983.

A few interesting points about the verb class should be mentioned. First note that the verbs in the left column have three forms, one for present/infinitive, one for past and one for the past participle. The verbs in the right column have only two forms, having replaced the past form with the participle form. This is a general trend in English verbs, though in some cases it is the past form that replaces the participle, as when *shown* is replaced by *showed*, or *proven* by *proved*. All the verbs newly added to the class have only the two forms. No one has yet explained why the participle form replaces the past in this class.

As seen in the left column, historically this class had verb stems that ended in any one of the three nasal consonants. In OE the final –*g* after a nasal was very likely pronounced. The class also included verbs ending in –*nd* such as *bind, grind, find,* and *wind.* These verbs underwent a lengthening of the vowel because of their final consonant clusters and after the Great Vowel Shift ended up with past forms *bound, ground, found,* and *wound.* This vowel lengthening removed the verbs ending in alveolars from the class and left the ones with velars as the most common type, especially since there were also class members ending with –*nk* as in *drink.* After this change, most of the verbs in this class had a similar phonological shape. Given the new verbs that have joined the class, it is clear that this phonological definition of the class was very important in attracting new members, as all the new members have a final velar consonant or cluster.

Another important observation about the new members of the class is that they do not all have nasal consonants in their codas. The original class was defined by the nasal consonant at any point of articulation in the coda, but now the class is defined by a velar consonant in the coda, as shown by *struck* and *dug* and other similar verbs. So the phonological shape of the verb is very important, but it can also change over time as the membership in the class changes.

Notice also that, in the OE class, all the present forms had the vowel /ɪ/, but among the innovative forms the vowel of the present is not so important. *Strike, hang, sneak,* and *drag* have the "wrong" vowel. This means that it is the final shape of the past form that determines class membership, not the relation between the present and the past. Thus no four-part proportional analogy could be constructed to explain these innovations. Rather the innovative past forms are constructed based on a generalization over the existing past forms.

Since no other OE strong verb alternations extend to new verbs, we must ask what makes this class special. First, we have already seen that there is a firm phonological characterization of the shape of the verb stem (which, by the way, includes a strong tendency to have an initial consonant cluster with *s*–). A second factor may be the type frequency of this class. Of all the OE strong verb classes that survive today, this one has the most members. The type frequency of the pattern as well as its strong phonological definition makes it applicable to other verbs that fit the phonological definition. Note that there is no tendency to extend the vowel /ʌ/ to verbs such as *fit* or *sip.*

The second example of the extension of an alternation involves alternations among suffixes marking noun plural in Brazilian Portuguese (BP). In Portuguese, nouns are usually made plural by adding an /s/, as in *janela, janelas* 'window, windows'. However, for singular nouns ending in –*ão* there are three ways to form the plural: one adds –*s* as expected, but in the other two the nasalized diphthong undergoes a change:

(79) Brazilian Portuguese

Singular	Plural	Gloss
irmão	*irmãos*	'brother'
leão	*leões*	'lions'
pão	*pães*	'bread', 'loaves of bread'

Even though it would seem that the regular pattern of adding –*s* to the singular would be the favored pattern here, for these nouns ending in –*ão* the plural with –*ões* is by far the most common, as 97.8% of the nouns with this singular form (over 7000 different nouns) use –*ões* as the plural (Huback 2011). For that reason there is a tendency to use the –*ões* plural in words that by normal sound change should have –*ãos*, such as *cidadão* 'citizen' which historically has the plural *cidadãos* but now is sometimes *cidadões*.

There are two ways to look at this change. One could say that the alternation between the singular and plural noun stem has been extended to nouns that did not have it before, in which case it would be similar to the example discussed just above. The other way to analyze this change is to say that the nasal diphthong plus –*s* marks plural, and there are allomorphs of the plural affix, which include –*ãos*, –*ões*, and –*ães*. This seems like a more complex analysis since most nouns pluralize by just adding –*s*, but if we do not consider the three nasal diphthong allomorphs to be in competition, we cannot explain why the change is not simply the elimination of the alternation in favor of just adding –*s*.

In both cases of analogical extension discussed here, the pattern that extended to new paradigms is the one with the highest type frequency, that is, the highest number of distinct lexical items subject to the pattern. In the case of the BP plurals, Huback 2011 finds that nouns with high token frequency tend not to undergo the change. This is the same pattern that is commonly found when analogical leveling is occurring.

5.8.   The development of suppletion

Have you ever wondered why the past tense of *go* is *went*, rather than a form more similar to *go*? In this section we deal with another way that irregularities can be introduced into a paradigm: by suppletion. The term *suppletion* can be used to refer to any kind of synchronic irregularity in the stem forms in a paradigm, but its original meaning was stricter: it refers to paradigms whose members originally came from entirely different lexical stems. *Go* fits the historical definition because *go* was one verb with its own past tense and *went* was the past tense of *wend*, which means 'to go turningly'. Now, however, the only possible past form for *go* is *went*, and *wend* has its own past form, *wended*.

So *go* and *went* are in a perfectly normal present/past relation even though their forms are wildly different. It is a suppletive paradigm.

There is much discussion of how irregular and suppletive forms should be treated in synchronic grammars, but our interest here is in how suppletive paradigms arise diachronically. First let us consider what types of examples of suppletive paradigms are found in languages around the world. Some generalizations are possible. First, suppletive paradigms are most common in inflectional languages and occur less frequently in agglutinative languages. Second, most languages that have suppletion have only a few cases. Third, suppletive paradigms are usually among the most frequently used paradigms. Finally, there are several generalizations that can be made about what categories tend to be expressed by suppletive forms, as we see in the following.

Suppletion is particularly common in verbal paradigms and favors tense and aspect distinctions (Veselinova 2003). In other words, there are more cases of suppletion like that found in *go/went* where the different stems correspond to different tenses than other types. A suppletive distinction between perfective and imperfective is also common. For instance, in Spanish the preterit (perfective) of the verb 'go' is *fue* (3rd sg.) while the imperfect (imperfective) is *iba* (3rd sg.). The Central American language Chalcatongo also has suppletion corresponding to aspect.

(80)   Chalcatongo (Oto-Manguean, Mixtecan) 'to come' (Veselinova 2003: 97)

Habitual	Progressive	Perfective
nbíí	*bèi*	*na-kii*

The Irish verb 'to go' also shows suppletion for tense and aspect. The imperfective aspect stem is derived from the present by sound change, but the past and future forms come from different lexical sources.

(81)   Irish (Celtic) *teim* 'to go'

	Present	Imperfective	Past	Future
1st sg.	*téim*	*théinn*	*chuas*	*raghad*
2nd sg.	*téann*	*théithéa*	*chuais*	*raghair*
3rd sg.	*téann*	*théadh*	*chuaigh*	*raghaidh*

In nouns, the most common distinction marked by suppletion is the singular/plural distinction, as in English *person/people*. One study finds that the most frequent noun to have singular/plural suppletion means 'child', with nouns meaning 'woman', 'man', and 'person' also often suppletive (Vafaeian 2010). Adjectives are also subject to suppletion, as we see in English *good, better, best* and *bad, worse, worst* or Latin *bonus, melior, optimus* 'good, better, best' or *malus, peior, pessimus* 'bad, worse, worst'.

It also happens occasionally that one or more person/number forms in a tense/aspect category of a verb may have forms from a different lexical stem. In German the present of the verb *sein* 'to be' consists of 1st singular and 2nd singular *bin* and *bist* from a verb cognate with *be* in English (PIE **bhew-*) and a

3rd singular *ist* from another stem (PIE **es-*). French *aller* 'to go' in the present has the following forms, where the singular and 3rd plural forms derive from Latin *vadere* 'to go', while the other forms come from Latin *ambulare* 'to walk'.

(82)   French *aller* 'to go' present tense

	Singular	Plural
1st	*vais*	*allons*
2nd	*vas*	*allez*
3rd	*va*	*vont*

In a way, the joining of forms from different paradigms into one paradigm is a strange development. It requires that a form leave its home paradigm and join another one, replacing a form that was already there. It also requires some meaning change, since the contributing lexical items probably were similar semantically but not identical. Some of the properties of suppletive forms help us understand how this process occurs. First, the fact that suppletive paradigms are all highly frequent and involve verbs with very general meaning such as 'be', 'go', 'come', 'say', 'do', 'see', 'give', 'sit', 'have', 'eat', and 'die' (Veselinova 2003) means that in any language there is likely to be more than one verb in each of these semantic domains. Also, highly frequent verbs are likely to have multiple meanings and uses, which leads to a situation where two or more verbs might be competing for a particular use, and thus might come to be used in one tense or aspect more than another (Rudes 1980). Related to the last point is the tendency for suppletion to occur along category lines that express larger changes in meaning, such as tense and aspect rather than person and number, except for the most frequent verbs.

Another interesting point is that some of the documented cases show that currently existing suppletive forms replaced other forms that were suppletive. For example, in OE, *gān* 'to go' had a suppletive past tense *ēode*. That is the form *went* replaced in ME. The evidence suggests that *ēode* was undergoing reduction, as it is documented in a number of forms, such as *ȝede, yode, yude*. Perhaps because the form was undergoing some reduction, speakers may have preferred to use a fuller form such as *went*. In that regard, it should be noted that Latin *ēo* 'I go' with the present and perfect forms shown in (83), really had no stem in the present and only the vowel *ī* for a stem in the perfect. The replacement by other verbs such as *ambulare* and *vadere* thus put some phonological material back into the paradigm.

(83)   Latin *ēo* 'I go'

	Present		Perfect	
	singular	plural	singular	plural
1st	*ēo*	*īmus*	*iī*	*iimus*
2nd	*īs*	*ītis*	*iistī*	*iistis*
3rd	*is*	*eunt*	*iit*	*iērunt*

Along with the other points we have mentioned about high-frequency verbs – that they have general meaning and different meaning in different contexts – the other reason that high-frequency verbs develop suppletion could be that they tend to be reduced, and the addition of forms from other paradigms gives them a more explicit phonological form.

5.9.   Morphological reanalysis

Other types of change in word structure fit the definition of analogical change as the remaking of a form based on other forms or patterns existing in the language. One type is reanalysis or metanalysis, in which some of the phonological material in a sequence is assigned to a different morpheme or word than it originally belonged to. For example, because of the alternation in the English indefinite article between *a* and *an*, some nouns have lost their initial *n–* while others have added an *n–*. The French word *naperon* 'apron' was borrowed into ME as *napron*, but the sequence *a napron* was reanalyzed as *an apron*, with the *n–* being interpreted as belonging to the indefinite article. The related word *napkin* was not subject to this reanalysis. In the other direction, the compound word *ekename* literally 'added name' acquired an initial *n–* from the indefinite article, yielding *nickname*.

A similar kind of reanalysis also occurs between morphemes within a word. French adds a suffix *–ier* to form an agentive noun as in *charpente* 'frame', *charpentier* 'carpenter', *cheval* 'horse', *chevalier* 'knight'. Given the number of nouns that lost their final consonant by sound change, for instance, *argent* 'silver', where the final /t/ remains in the agentive formation, *argentier* 'silversmith', it has become common to add *–tier* to nouns that have no final consonant, such as *clou* 'nail' giving *cloutier* 'nail maker', even if the noun originally had a consonant other than /t/, as in *tabac* 'tobacco, snuff', *tabatier* 'snuff box'. Note that this reanalysis is similar to the case of Maori passives discussed in Section 4.2.

A more extreme mis-segmentation occurs occasionally in the creation of new derivational morphemes. The word *alcoholic* is very transparently divided into two morphemes as *alcohol + ic*. Yet a new suffix has been created by taking much more of the word and adding it to other words or pseudo-stems: *chocoholic*, *foodaholic*, *workaholic*. By taking more than just the *–ic* from *alcoholic* a new morpheme emerges that has some of the meaning of *alcoholic*, in particular, the meaning of an addiction to the substance or activity named by the stem noun.

Some motivation for reanalysis comes from *folk etymology*, a kind of analysis that tries to establish the meaning of the whole word from the meaning of the parts. Borrowed words are often subject to the kind of reanalysis called folk etymology. A famous example is the word *hamburger* which originally referred to the German city Hamburg plus the agentive suffix *–er*. In English the word came to be used to refer to a ground beef sandwich on a bun. Because of its overall meaning, speakers interpreted the *ham* syllable as standing for a meat (though of course it is the wrong meat), leaving the *burger* part to stand for 'sandwich on a bun'. Thus a new morpheme was created that was extended to many other compounds: *fishburger, tofuburger, veggie burger*, or just *burger*.

Some examples from other languages are reported in Campbell 1999. The Spanish word *vagabundo* 'vagabond, tramp' has been more transparently reformed as *vagamundo* incorporating the word *mundo* 'world', as a vagabond wanders (Spanish *vagar*) the world. *Jerky* as in *beef jerky* has been borrowed from Spanish *charqui*, which in turn was borrowed from Quechua *č'arqi* 'dried meat'. English speakers interpreted this as related to *jerk* and use this verb to designate the processed meat, giving the phrase *jerked meat*.

A final type of change through morphological reanalysis is *back formation*, by which a new word is formed through stripping affixes or what appear to be affixes from a word. A contemporary example is the use of a verb *to orientate* from *orientation*. English already had a verb *to orient* but this new verb has arisen by back formation, taking the *–ion* off *orientation*. Both the words *cherry* and *pea* earlier ended in *–s* (*cherry* came from French *cherise* and *pea* from OE *pise*). Since these are items that tend to occur in the plural, it would be normal to interpret the simple form as plural and pull the *–s* off to make a singular.

5.10.   Parallels between analogical change and child language

It is likely that the reader noticed that some of the examples given of analogical change are somewhat familiar in the sense that they are like errors that children make when acquiring their language, or errors that second language learners make. Sometimes native speaker adults make analogical errors as well. Such errors generally follow the tendencies outlined here. A common error found in both children and adults is regularization or leveling, as when children say *sweeped* rather than *swept*. Such errors can be induced in adults by putting them under pressure in an experimental situation (Bybee and Slobin 1982). Children tend to regularize with the pattern that has the highest type frequency, not just in English, but in other languages such as French and Hungarian (MacWhinney 1978). Also extensions occur in both children and adults with errors such as *struck* for *streaked*; when presented with novel verbs, children and adults produce forms such as *sping/spung*. Note that the most common examples involve the extension of the vowel pattern found in the semi-productive verb class described earlier.

Children acquiring inflectional languages tend to use the 1st and 3rd singular forms earlier than other forms. Their errors show that they use these forms as the base for creating other forms, especially within the same tense and aspect. For example, in Polish a child confronted with the three conjugation classes of Polish verbs as shown in (84), consistently produced 1st singular forms that were made up of the 3rd singular stem plus the suffix *–m* (from Conjugation 3). Note that this strategy led to the leveling of the stem alternation in favor of the alternant in the 3rd singular (Smoczynska 1985): $sz = [\int]$, $cz = [t\int]$, $rz = [\mathfrak{z}]$, $\varrho = [\tilde{\varepsilon}]$.

(84)   Polish present forms in the singular

	Conjugation 1		Conjugation 2		Conjugation 3
	'write'	'take'	'do'	'see'	'read
1st	*pisz-ę*	*bior-ę*	*rob-i-ę*	*widz-ę*	*czyt-a-m*
2nd	*pisz-e-sz*	*bier-e-sz*	*rob-i-sz*	*widz-i-sz*	*czyt-a-sz*
3rd	*pisz-e*	*bierz-e*	*rob-i*	*widz-i*	*czyt-a*

Child's 1st singular forms

1st	*piszem*	*bierzem*	*robim*	*widzim*	*czytam*

Children also display local markedness – using a high-frequency form to make other forms even when it is not the most 'basic'. For example, children learning Hebrew generally form the plural from the singular, for instance forming from *simla* 'dress' a plural *simlot* (cf. adult plural *smalot*), but in cases where the plural is more frequent than the singular, they form a singular from the plural, as shown in (85) (Berman 1985); $c =$ [ts].

(85)   Hebrew

Adult forms		Child's singular	Gloss
singular	plural		
cédef	*cdafim*	*cdaf*	'seashell'
dim'a	*dma'ot*	*dma'a*	'teardrop'
écem	*acamot*	*acama*	'bone'

Other innovations by children also parallel some other changes we have discussed here. Children produce double-marked forms such as *feets* and *broked*. Children also give evidence that they are working to analyze the parts of words and compounds. Parents can cite many examples of their children's folk etymology, such as the period in which my son analyzed *Tuesday* as *Two-s-day* and then changed *Monday* to *One-day*.

The fact that in the acquisition of morphology children often produce forms that comply with the types of morphological change that occur in diachrony does not necessarily mean that the changes come about through language acquisition (see the discussion in Section 11.1.4). Children usually correct their innovations when they do not match their peers' or adult speech. What the parallels show is that the same kinds of analysis and pattern formation occur in both children and adults, and these patterns can become the source of change in the language.

5.11.   Conclusion

In summarizing this discussion of analogy, it is worthwhile noting the many differences between sound change and analogy that result from the very different mechanisms of change that are applied in each case. Sound change can be characterized as changes in the articulatory habits guiding the formation and timing of the gestures that form words and phrases. While at least some sound change affects high-frequency words earlier than low-frequency words, there is a very strong tendency for the outcome of sound change to affect all the words of a language in a uniform manner. Analogy applies at what might be considered a higher cognitive level, since it involves generalizations over the structure of words that are morphologically complex. It tends to affect one paradigm at a time, and it often leaves some paradigms unaffected, as when high-frequency paradigms resist change because of their greater strength in memory. While sound change is governed by phonetic factors, analogy is governed by semantic factors (the meaning of the morphological categories) as well as by phonological similarity. One way of summing up these differences is a statement now called "Sturtevant's Paradox": sound change is regular but produces (morphological) irregularity; analogy is irregular but produces regularity (within paradigms) (Sturtevant 1947).

In the past it has seemed that analogical change is also "irregular" in the sense that one cannot predict the direction of change, that is, which variant will prevail when an alternation is leveled, or whether leveling or extension will occur. In this chapter several general tendencies of analogical change have been discussed, and all of these tendencies have strong support. However, sometimes they are in competition with one another, which makes it difficult to predict what changes will occur for any particular paradigm. Consider this example of analogical changes that move in two directions: Spanish has some 3rd conjugation verbs that have a stem alternation of /i/ with /e/, e.g. *pedir* 'to ask' has 1st singular present *pido*, but 1st plural *pedimos*. It is common in Spanish dialects to find this alternation has been leveled to *pidir*, *pido*, *pidimos*. On the other hand, there are dialects in which this alternation has been extended to verbs that earlier had no alternation, such as *escribir* 'to write' with 1st singular Present *escribo*, 1st plural *escribimos*. In some dialects these forms are *escrebir*, *escribo*, *escrebimos*. Two different pressures are operating here: one is the tendency towards leveling (creating one form for one meaning) and the other is the semi-productivity of a class with reasonable type frequency – there are more than twenty verbs with the alternation. These competing tendencies make it difficult to predict analogical change. However, there is one logically possible change that does not occur: there are no reports of leveling of the alternation in favor of the forms with /e/. That is because /e/ only occurs in the lower frequency and less basic forms of the paradigm. So even if we cannot arrive at a unique prediction, we can at least rule out some possibilities by what we know of the general tendencies in analogical change.

Suggested reading

Bybee, J., 1985. *Morphology: a study of the relation between meaning and form*, Amsterdam: John Benjamins. Especially chapters 1–5.

Greenberg, J., 1966. *Language universals: with special reference to feature hierarchies*, The Hague: Mouton.

Hock, H.H., 2003. Analogical change. In B.D. Joseph and R.D. Janda (eds.) *The handbook of historical linguistics*, Oxford: Blackwell, 441–460.

Rudes, B.A., 1980. On the nature of verbal suppletion. *Linguistics*, 18(7/8), pp. 665–676.

Questions for discussion

1. What are some words that have the suffixes *–hood*, *–dom*, and *–ship*? Check the OED to see if they had these suffixes in OE. Can you find words such as *creepiness* in a dictionary?
2. Use an online corpus to check the frequency of the singular/plural pairs, *foot/feet*, *tooth/teeth*, *mouse/mice*, *goose/geese*, *man/men*, and *woman/women*. What is the relation between the frequency of these nouns and their irregularity?
3. Use a dictionary to determine the earlier relation between *louse* and *lice* (if you don't already know what it is). Explain how and why this relationship has changed over time.
4. In Spanish and French the verb 'to go' is even more complex than is indicated in the text. Look up the full paradigms for these verbs (Spanish *ir*, French *aller*) and determine how many different verbs came together to make these paradigms.
5. Are pairs such as *cow*, *cattle* suppletive?

6 Grammaticalization: processes and mechanisms

6.1. Introduction

In this chapter and the next we examine the process of grammaticalization (sometimes also called "grammaticization"), the process by which new grammatical morphemes come into being. As mentioned before, grammatical morphemes (= grams) can be contrasted with lexical morphemes (such as nouns and verbs) in that lexical morphemes are considered "open class" items, meaning a language can easily add new members to the class, while grams are considered "closed class" morphemes because once a class is established it does not easily add new members. As our discussion unfolds it will become clear why this is.

Examples of grammatical morphemes are affixes, auxiliaries, articles, pronouns, prepositions, and postpositions. All grammatical morphemes are very restricted in where they can occur – affixes are attached to stems, auxiliaries occur with main verbs, articles with nouns, pronouns in place of noun phrases, prepositions and postpositions with noun phrases. That is, grams occur in particular constructions. Part of the story of how they develop concerns how the constructions they are in develop.

In this chapter and the next we will discuss how these grammatical forms develop over time. You might be surprised to learn that they almost all come from lexical items, such as nouns and verbs, or combinations of lexical and grammatical items. Indeed, this idea has only gained currency in the last few decades, as more and more studies demonstrate that, across languages, grammatical morphemes develop in much the same way. The chapter begins with a summary of the way the future auxiliary *will* developed in English and continues with observations about how futures in Romance languages developed. After that, we discuss general processes and mechanisms that apply in grammaticalization. In Chapter 7 there is a discussion of the many paths of change that lead to the establishment of grammatical morphemes of different types in the languages of the world.

PART I: HOW FUTURE TENSE MARKERS DEVELOP

6.2. Case study: *will* in English

In studying how *will* became a future auxiliary in English, we will note changes that occurred in its phonetic form, its morphosyntactic properties, and its meaning or function. All of these changes occur together in the long, gradual process of grammaticalization. Given that there are changes that affect different types of behavior, one can say that grammaticalization is not just one process, but many processes that occur together.

We pick up the story of *will* when extensive texts in Old English began to appear, in the ninth century AD, though we can tell something about changes that had already occurred by that time. *Willan* (*will* + *an* 'want' + infinitive suffix) was a verb that was frequently used and had a variety of uses already. It could be used as a main verb with a direct object, as in example (86) where the object is a noun phrase and (87), where the object is a clause with *that* (*ðæt*). In these examples, which show that *willan* was once a main verb, the meaning is very much like the PDE main verb *want* (Examples 86–89 taken from the OED).

(86)   *Ne drincð nan man eald win, & wylle sona þæt niwe.* (1000 WS Gospels: Luke)
          'No man drinks old wine and immediately wants some new (wine).'

(87)   *Hē cwæð: Hwæt wilt ðū ðæt īc ðē do?* (Blickling Homilies 19.33)
          'He says: What do you want me to do for you?'

Willan was also used commonly with an infinitive complement, as in examples (88) and (89), where its meaning was 'want to'. This use sometimes expressed the intention of the subject to do something.

(88)   *Hwyder wilt þu gangan? Min Drihten, ic wille gangan to Rome.*
          (The Blickling Homilies 191)
          'Where to you want to go? My Lord, I want to go to Rome.'

(89)   *Ic wille mid flōde folc ācwellan.* (1296 Genesis)
          'I intend to kill the people with a flood.'

In addition to these uses, it could indicate willingness and even sometimes be interpreted as expressing future.

In ME, the frequency of use of *will* with an infinitive complement increases and use with an accusative object decreases significantly. With a verbal complement (an infinitive, but without *to*) the meaning is usually willingness or intention, and the phrase is used by a first person to express resolution or to make a promise. The examples below are from *Sir Gawain and the Green Knight* (mid-fourteenth century). While in OE singular and plural were distinguished and 2nd singular was *wilt*, in ME the plural marking has been lost, and the final vowel is variably deleted. The 2nd singular form, *wilt* continues to be used. *Wil* and *wyl* are variant spellings, but probably do not indicate different pronunciations (Bybee and Pagliuca 1987).

(90)   Intention
          Now wyl I of hor seruise say yow no more (line 130, narrator speaking)
          'Now I will not say more of their (table) service.'

(91)   Willingness
            And ʒe wyl a whyle be style
            I schal telle yow how þay wroʒt. (lines 1996–1997, narrator speaking)
            'And (if) you will be still (silent) a while, I shall tell you how they acted.'

The true hallmark of a future tense is the expression of a prediction about the future made by the speaker. This use was not common in ME and occurs only once in the *Gawain* narrative from which our examples come. Here is the one prediction example:

(92)   Prediction
            For mon may hyde his harme, bot vnhap ne may hit,
            For þer hit onez is tachched twynne wil hit never. (lines 2511–2512)
            'For a man my hide his misfortune, but he cannot undo it.
            For once it is attached there, it will never come apart.'

At the next stage of development, Early Modern English, some changes in form occur. The contracted spellings have begun to be used, giving *I'll, we'll, you'll,* and *thou'lt,* and less often *he'll* and *she'll.* The contractions (including *'twill* for *it will*) indicate a phonological reduction which goes along with the increase in frequency. As for function, most examples still express intention, promise, or willingness, though there are more instances of prediction. The following examples are all from Shakespeare's *The Merchant of Venice* which was written around 1600.

(93)   Intention
            Well, old man, I will tell you news of your son: (2.2)

(94)   Intention
            I'll end my exhortation after dinner. (1.1)

(95)   Willingness
            Yet, to supply the ripe wants of my friend, I'll break a custom. (1.3)

(96)   Prediction
            I fear he will prove the weeping philosopher when he grows old, being
            so full of unmannerly sadness in his youth. (1.1)

(97)   Prediction
            I am half afeard
            Thou wilt say anon he is some kin to thee,
            Thou spend'st such high-day wit in praising him. (2.9)

One prominent difference between Early Modern English and PDE is that the prediction uses have become more common, though the uses for intention and willingness continue to occur. An informal count that I did myself of about 100 instances of *will* in two Shakespearean plays (*The Comedy of Errors* and *The Merchant of Venice*) shows pure prediction uses such as (96) and (97) account for fewer than 20% of the uses, compared to a count of PDE (British) by Coates 1983, which found prediction in 50% of all uses of *will*. So we note that when meaning changes in grammaticalization, new meanings develop (e.g. prediction), and subsequent changes show the new meanings becoming more frequent. All along the grammaticalization path, polysemy exists and meaning changes consist of changes in the frequency of certain of the meanings. Note that in PDE, *will* is still used for intention, willingness as well as prediction. Here are some examples from Coates' British English corpus:

(98)   Intention
         I'll put them in the post today.

(99)   Willingness
         *Give them the name of someone who <u>will</u> sign for it and take it in if you are
         not at home.*

(100)   Prediction
         I think the bulk of this year's students <u>will</u> go into industry.

In terms of morphosyntactic properties, *will* is a member of the class of modal auxiliaries in English, a class that has properties distinct from main verbs. This class did not exist yet in OE, but the class developed as *will* and the other modal auxiliaries (*shall*, *may*, *can*, *must*, *should*, *might*, *could*, and *would*) grammaticalized. The properties these auxiliaries have is that they invert with the subject in questions, the negative *not* follows them, they take an infinitive without *to* and they do not have the 3rd singular suffix *–s*. The first three of these properties are ancient properties that all verbs had in OE or ME. While other main verbs lost these properties, the modal auxiliaries were highly fixed in their constructions as a result of their high frequency and grammaticalization and thus retained these properties (cf. the hypothesis of the last chapter, that high-frequency forms resist change). The lack of a 3rd singular suffix is an ancient property of a small class of highly frequent verbs whose present tense forms were formerly past tense. The other property that modal auxiliaries have – that they do not have infinitive or participle forms – is a more recent development and is linked to the meaning changes they have undergone. Because of the loss of their earlier lexical meaning, they are no longer used as main verbs and cannot enter into the main verb position in constructions.

6.3.   Romance inflectional futures

The development of the future tense in Western Romance is a famous case of grammaticalization, because in this case we see the complete track of change from a lexical item (*habēre* 'to have, hold') in construction with a main verb infinitive all the way to suffixed inflections for the future. The development starts with a Latin construction in which an infinitive occurs with the inflected forms of the verb *habēre*. The earliest meaning of the construction indicates a predestination for a certain situation to hold (Benveniste 1968). Interestingly, English *shall* in early uses also often hinted at predestination but went on to indicate a sense that an arrangement has been made and will therefore be followed. A similar change occurred with the Latin periphrasis as it gained currency in the sixth and seventh centuries and came to be used for shades of obligation, intention, and eventually prediction.

In terms of the form of the construction, the infinitive tended to precede the inflected forms of *habēre* and the /h/ in these forms tended to be lost, *essere habetis* 'you (sg.) will be' or *venire abes* 'you will come' and *videre habe* 'he will see' (sixth century, Benveniste 1968). Further reduction of the forms of *habēre* occurred, including the loss of the medial /b/, giving future forms for French such as *chanterai*, Spanish *cantaré*, Italian *canterò*, Portuguese *cantarei* 'I will sing'. To illustrate more fully with Spanish, the future is formed by adding the reduced form of *haber* to the infinitive (a form ending in *–r*).

(101)   Spanish inflectional future of *cantar* 'to sing'
          1st sg.   *cantar + é*   1st pl.   *cantar + emos*
          2nd sg.   *cantar + ás*   2nd pl.   *cantar + éis*
          3rd sg.   *cantar + á*   3rd pl.   *cantar + án*

The process by which the forms of the auxiliary became attached to the infinitive was long and gradual. At the beginning of the process other items could occur between the infinitive and the auxiliary. Then in Old Spanish when the clitic object pronouns developed, they tended to occur before the finite verb and after a non-finite form. That would put them in between the infinitive and the auxiliary. This was commonly their position in Old Spanish. In fact, it seems after a time that clitic pronouns were the only items that could separate the infinitive and auxiliary. Here are some examples from the fifteenth century that show the object pronoun *lo* (3rd singular masculine) separating the two parts of the construction. Note that in (102) the first verb (*diesmará*) is in the future tense and has the affix, while the second verb (*dar* is followed by the object pronoun and then the auxiliary):

(102)   *diesmará vuestro pan y vuestro vino. y dar lo ha a sus vasallos*
          (Mejia, fifteenth century)
          'he will take a tenth of your bread and wine and he will give it to his vassals'

(103)   *todo sarmiento que en mi no lleuare fructo cortar lo ha*
          'all the vine shoots that do not bear fruit (for me) he will cut'
          (Meditaciones de Pseudo-Augustine)

Eventually this syntactic pattern disappeared and the object pronoun came to appear before the whole verbal sequence, as in *lo dará* 'will give it, 3rd sg' or *lo cortará* 'will cut it, 3rd sg.'. At this point the sequence is consistently written as one word and the auxiliary has become a suffix.

The case of the Romance futures illustrates three points. First, future tense grams can develop from constructions that indicate obligation as well as from constructions that indicate volition. Second, if conditions are right, grammaticalizing elements can become affixed to the lexical item in the construction. Third, even the affixation process is gradual and characterized by variation while it is ongoing.

6.4.   Future markers from movement verbs

So far we have seen future grams develop from volition and obligation verbs in English and in Romance languages. But this is not the end of the story for English or Spanish, French or Portuguese. Just when you think that the language has established a very functional way to signal future tense, along comes another construction grammaticalizing and pushing the older future out of the way. In English and the Romance languages named, a construction using the verb 'go' arises and begins to move into the function of signaling future meaning. The English construction consists of the verb *go* in the Progressive construction with *to*-infinitive.

(104)   SUBJECT + *BE* + *going* + *to* + VERB

Note that the whole construction enters into the grammaticalization process and that all the components of meaning are necessary to create the new meaning. The verb *go* in the progressive with an infinitive provides the sense that the subject is moving towards a goal signaled by a verb. This amounts to a purpose meaning, such as *I am going to Santa Fe to see my sister*. This is a common enough kind of expression to have in English, and indeed it can occur with other verbs as well, such as *I'm walking to the drugstore to get some aspirin*. But *go* is the most frequent verb to occur in this construction and it expands to express functions such as intention, as in *I'm going to mail these letters today*, and even prediction, *it's going to rain tomorrow*.

This grammaticalizing construction also undergoes considerable phonetic reduction in American English, and the *going to* part is now sometimes spelled as *gonna*, indicating a reduction of the vowel in the stressed syllable and the reduction of [ŋtʰu] to a nasal flap with a schwa vowel. In phrases with *I* it reduces even further, to something like [aimə̃ɾə]. Over the last two centuries this construction has undergone extreme increases in frequency of use and is now used in many places where *will* would have been used earlier.

As mentioned above, a similar path of change is occurring in French, Spanish, and Portuguese, with the result that the inflectional future we discussed in the last section is now being replaced with a future construction made up of the verb 'go' plus the preposition *a* 'to, towards' in Spanish and just the infinitive in Portuguese and French. In Spanish this new *go*-future occurs in 67% of future expressions, in French in 78%, and in Portuguese in 99% (Poplack 2011). So in all cases, the grammaticalizing construction is already used in the majority of cases where future is expressed; indeed, in Portuguese the replacement process is almost complete.

6.5.   Some generalizations concerning futures
and grammaticalization

In the preceding three sections three different sources for future grams have been presented: volitional verbs, obligation constructions, and movement-towards constructions. This might lead us to believe that each language we examine might have a different source for future grams. However, this is not the case. The three sources we have just considered are the main ones occurring in many languages of the world. Here is a (non-exhaustive) list of languages with each type of future gram (data primarily from Bybee et al. 1994):

(105) a.   **Volition futures**: English, Inuit, Danish, Modern Greek, Romanian, Serbo-Croatian, Sogdian (East Iranian), Tok Pisin
   b.   **Obligation futures**: Basque, English, Danish, Western Romance languages
   c.   **Movement futures**: Abipon, Atchin, Bari, Cantonese, Cocama, Danish, English, Guaymí, Krongo, Mano, Margi, Maung, Mwera, Nung, Tem, Tojolabal, Tucano and Zuni; also French, Portuguese, and Spanish.

As this list shows, one very astonishing thing about grammaticalization is that, in completely unrelated languages, grammaticalization uses the same lexical material and proceeds in very much the same way. In the next chapter we will discuss common grammaticalization sources for many kinds of grammatical morphemes, but for now we continue to examine the properties of grammaticalizing constructions.

Even though these sources for futures are quite different from one another, the way they gradually evolve into the expression of future meaning is quite similar. It seems that they usually go through the important stage of first expressing "intention of the subject" and only after that, "prediction", giving the following grammaticalization path:

(106)   volition
          obligation   >   intention   >   future (prediction)
          movement towards

Despite some language-specific variation in how this path develops, the general trend, and certainly the directionality of semantic change, appears to be the same across languages.

In addition, the formal properties of grammaticalizing items and their constructions undergo similar changes. There is also directionality in these changes. Givón 1979 proposes a path of change that is applicable across grammatical constructions and also across languages. This path starts with "discourse", by which he means loosely connected sequences of words; it continues to "syntax", by which he means constructions with more fixed structure and meaning, and then to "morphology", that is, affixed morphemes, as we saw in the case of the Romance inflectional future.

(107)   discourse > syntax > morphology

With this path of change in mind, Givón 1971 proposes his now-famous slogan: 'today's morphology is yesterday's syntax'. Think of the example of Romance futures: when the infinitive occurred with an auxiliary (*cantar ha*) we speak of syntax; when the auxiliary becomes a suffix (*cantará*) we speak of morphology.

The fact that such general principles seem to hold across many instances in many languages means that the mechanisms of change that affect grammaticalizing constructions are the same across languages. In the remainder of this chapter we explore the mechanisms of change that together create the process of grammaticalization.

PART II: MECHANISMS OF CHANGE

As we have seen, grammaticalization involves changes of different aspects of the affected construction: its phonetic form, its grammatical behavior, and its meaning. In the following sections various aspects of grammaticalization are discussed separately with an eye to identifying the mechanisms of language use that underlie each aspect of the change. Sections 6.6–6.10 contain discussions of changes in phonetic and morphosyntactic form and Sections 6.11–6.13 focus on changes in meaning.

6.6.   Chunking and phonetic reduction

One factor that promotes reduction in grammaticalization is chunk formation. A chunk is a sequence of elements that is processed together. Words and morphemes that are used repeatedly together form chunks, and the words and morphemes in grammaticalizing constructions make especially good examples. As the chunk is used more and more, it tends to undergo more and more internal phonetic reduction and fusion. The invariant parts of these chunks undergo more change. Consider the movement-future construction of English:

(108)   SUBJECT + BE + *going to* + VERB

The invariant parts of this construction, *going to*, are the parts that change the most. This sequence undergoes vowel reduction to schwa, which is common in English, resulting in a schwa in the first (stressed) syllable and the last (*to*): [gə̃ɾ̃ə]. The [ŋ] assimilates to the [t], but the latter, prone to flapping in this context, fuses with the preceding nasal to form a nasalized flap. The vowel preceding the nasal is nasalized. The other parts of the construction are schematic, meaning that multiple different items can occur in these positions: the subject can be any pronoun or noun phrase, the verb BE has multiple forms depending upon the subject and any verb can occur in the VERB position. The forms of BE contract with the subject (especially if it is a pronoun) as they do when BE has other functions, but no other parts of the construction reduce. Thus we can conclude that the parts of the construction that are most likely to reduce and fuse are the ones that are most commonly used together.

Because the different future grams we discussed above come from different constructions and occur in different languages, they have different patterns of reduction. The English future *will*, like the BE in the movement future and auxiliaries in general in English, fuses with the preceding pronoun, giving *I'll*, *you'll*, *he'll*, *she'll*, and *they'll*, as well as *that'll* and *what'll*. The contracted form also occurs variably with full noun phrases. In contrast, the Romance future inflection, which occurs after the infinitive form of the main verb, fuses with the lexical verb, despite the fact that a very large number of distinct verbs (really, all verbs!) occur in this position. In general it appears that when a developing gram occurs **after** the lexical item it belongs with, it is much more likely to form an affix (a suffix, that is) than if it occurs **before** the lexical item. This is one of the factors that explains why there are so many more suffixes in the languages of the world than there are prefixes.

When we discussed sound change in Chapter 2, we observed that sound changes of a reductive nature tend to occur earlier in high-frequency words than in low-frequency words. The reductive changes we see in grammaticalization are just extreme instances of this pattern. Also, the specific phonetic changes that occur, as we have just seen, are usually just more extreme instances of reduction seen elsewhere in the language.

Some researchers, such as Bisang (2004), note that in some languages, especially those non-affixing languages (isolating or analytic languages) of Southeast Asia, phonetic reduction does not occur in grammaticalization. It should be noted, though, that some phonetic reduction is subtle and could only be identified by looking carefully at the phonetic shapes of lexical and grammatical morphemes, such as their duration, tone, and the phonetic properties of consonants and vowels. Since in Vietnamese, as we saw in Chapter 3, high-frequency words are shorter and have more tone reduction, it is likely that there is some phonetic reduction, even if it is minimal. Bybee et al. 1994 find that the extent of phonological fusion and reduction of developing grams parallel the extent of semantic change, and that some languages have more of both and some less of both. The languages Bisang discusses are examples of languages that undergo less grammaticalization of both form and meaning.

6.7.   Specialization or loss of paradigmatic contrast

Grammaticalizing constructions undergo changes affecting the items that can occur in the different positions of the construction. Some positions narrow the range of items that can occur, sometimes to only one (specialization), while other positions expand the range of items (category expansion). I treat the first phenomenon in this section and the second in the next section.

Hopper 1991 discusses specialization using the example of the negative construction in French. French inherited the Latin negator, which in Old French was *ne*. It appeared before the verb. In addition, a construction arose in Old French by which the preverbal *ne* was supplemented by a noun denoting a 'least quantity'. This construction survives into Modern French as the main form of negation, as in (109), where *pas* 'step' occurs after the verb *boit*.

(109)   *Il ne boit pas de vin*   'He doesn't drink wine'

In Old French *pas* was not the only noun to occur in the negative construction. Other nouns were:

(110)   *point* 'dot, point'   *mie*   'crumb'
             gote 'drop'   *amende*   'almond'
             areste 'fish-bone'   *beloce*   'sloe'
                                      eschalope 'pea pod'

In the sixteenth century, this group of nouns had reduced to only the following, among which *pas* and *point* were the most commonly used:

(111)   *pas* 'step, pace'   *point* 'dot, point'
             mie 'crumb'   *goutte* 'drop'

Today, only *pas* and *point* are used, and the former is the neutral negator. This is a case of specialization in the sense that of the group of words that once appeared in the construction, only two remain. The older means of negation with only *ne* is no longer available. It is characteristic of grammaticalization that *pas* has lost its meaning of 'step', as shown in example (109). Because it occurs in the negative construction, it has taken on negative meaning. Now it is common for the *ne* to be deleted or omitted from the construction, with only *pas* indicating negation. *Pas* also occurs in other constructions to indicate negative, such as the phrase *pas beaucoup* 'not much'.

Another example of specialization is found in the development of the perfect construction in English. Today the perfect construction uses a form of *have* plus the past participle to signal a meaning of past with current relevance, or a past continuing into the present, as in the following:

(112)   *For centuries children have learned to walk with push toys and have played*
             with rattles.   (COHA 1980)

This construction began to grammaticalize in Old English from a possessive construction with *habban* 'to have' with transitive verbs in an adjectival form, giving a resultative meaning, as in (113) from Traugott 1972.

(113)   *Ic   hæfde   hine   gebundenne.*
             I   have   him   bound + ACC

According to Traugott, this construction gave rise to a similar one using the past participle, as in (114). This construction becomes our perfect construction.

(114)   *ic hæbbe nu gesæd hiora ingewinn*
             I have now told their inner struggles

With verbs indicating a change of state and some other intransitives, the construction contained the verb 'to be' rather than 'to have'. Both adjectival and participial forms occur; (115) contains the participle.

(115)   *Hie wæron cumen Leoniðan to fultume*
          They were come to help Leonitha.

So there were two different auxiliaries used in the perfect, 'be' and 'have'. This situation occurs in other languages, such as French and German, where the 'be' auxiliary is used with certain intransitive verbs and the 'have' auxiliary with all other verbs. In English, however, the 'have' auxiliary has taken over even with intransitive verbs. As late as Early Modern English, there were still some expressions with the 'be' verb, as in *he is risen* or *he is come* as found in certain early Bible translations. Also, one lone high-frequency verb maintains a 'be' form: *he is gone* contrasts with *he has gone*. The former has a resultative meaning in that it means 'he is gone and he is still not here' while the 'have' form has the standard perfect meaning. The loss of the 'be' auxiliary in the English perfect is another example of specialization.

Specialization occurs because one variant increases in frequency more than others, beginning a self-feeding process. The more frequent variant is more accessible and thus used more often, increasing its accessibility. Its meaning generalizes or bleaches more (see Section 6.9) and it becomes entrenched in the construction. The less-frequent variants decrease in frequency and may eventually be lost. The item that remains in the grammaticalized construction is the one that earlier had a higher type frequency, which made it the more productive variant. As with cases of analogical leveling (see Section 5.3), high-frequency lexical items with the less-productive variant nevertheless can resist being taken over, at least for a while.

6.8.   Category expansion

Grammaticalizing constructions also have slots or categories that start out as semantically restricted, but expand or become more schematic (covering more meanings) during the process. Our first example is the English modal auxiliary *can*, which was earlier a verb meaning 'to know (how)' and was used only with a small number of infinitives; today it can be used with any verb. We will compare the situation in OE with that of PDE, based on Bybee 2003.

In OE texts, the verb *cunnan*, from which *can* derives, was used with a noun phrase object, as in to know a person, language, book, or skill. It was also used in the sense of understanding, as in this example.

(116)   *Ge dweliaþ and ne cunnon halige gewritu.* (Ags. Gospel of Matthew xxii)
          'You are led into error and do not know the holy writing.'

It was not very frequently used with an infinitive complement, but when it was, the infinitive complement could denote a skill, as in (117).

(117)   *mid hondum con   hearpan grētan* (c. 1000 Versus Gnom. 172)
          with hands   know harp   to touch
          'with his hands he knew how to play the harp'

Note that you could also say 'he can the harp', so this example is not far from one in which there is a noun phrase object.

Somewhat surprisingly, *cunnan* was also used with verbs that indicate understanding, as if its sense of 'know' was not strong enough and another verb had to be added to expand on what it meant, as in this example:

(118)   *Nu   cunne ge   tocnawan   heofenes hiw.* (Ags. Gospel Matthew xvi)
'Now can   you distinguish heaven's hue?'

In this vein also are examples with verbs of communication where *cunnan* means 'have the knowledge to say truthfully', as in this example:

(119)   *Weras þa   me soðlice secgan cunnon.* (c. 1000 Elena 317)
Men   then me truly   say   can.
'Then men can truly say to me.'

In all of these cases, which are representative of the use of *cunnan* with an infinitive in OE, the meaning of knowing or knowing how to is very strong. One of the ways *can* changed in ME was by expanding these verb classes from intellectual states of mind to more emotional states (such as 'love'), from communication to verbs including teaching and comforting, and from special skills to more general overt action. In all these cases, a human subject is still necessary. This expansion indicates that *can* moved from the meaning of mental ability to a more general meaning of 'ability'. Later, in the Early Modern period, examples with the meaning of 'root possibility', which means 'it is possible to' began to appear, as in (120).

(120)   *Til we be roten, kan we nat be rype.* (A. Rv. 3875)
'Until we are rotten, it is not possible for us to be ripe.'

Once the possibility meaning occurs, then the subject position opens up to non-human, inanimate subjects, as in (121).

(121)   *There is a great number that fayne would   aborde, our ship can holde
no more.* (Barclay, *Ship of Fooles* 1570)
'There is a great number that want to come aboard, our ship can hold
no more.'

Thus both the class of verbs possible in the infinitive has expanded to include all verbs of English, and the subject position has also expanded from just humans to all entities. This expansion is indicative of meaning change, in particular, generalization or bleaching, which we discuss in Section 6.11.

A second, somewhat different example comes from the languages of West Africa, where a verb meaning 'to say' has become a complementizer. Lord 1976 demonstrates that the complementizer *bé* in Ewe (Niger-Congo, Kwa) came from the verb 'to say' (see also Lord 1993). When *be* is used as a verb, no complementizer is necessary as shown here:

(122)   *me-be   me-wɔ-e*
1s-say   1s-do-it
'I said that I did it'

However, with other verbs with similar meaning, the complementizer *bé* 'that' appears:

(123)   me-gblɔ   bé   me-wɔ-e
         1s-say   that   1s-do-it
         'I said that I did it'

Ewe is a language with serial verb constructions, meaning that it is common to have two or more verbs in sequence that share the same subject. Apparently *bé* grammaticalized from a construction in which two saying verbs occurred in sequence. The second one has lost its ability to take inflection (note, no subject marker on *bé*) and has lost its meaning. Now *bé* also occurs with verbs other than those of saying, such as those in (124), to introduce a sentential complement, as in example (125).

(124)   Ewe verbs taking the complementizer *bé*
         gblɔ 'say'   *ŋlɔ*   'forget'   *ŋlɔ* 'write'
         kpɔ 'see'   *se*   'hear, perceive'
         bu 'think'   *dí*   'want'   *xɔse* 'believe'
         nyá 'know'   *kpɔ́ mɔ́* 'hope'   *ná* 'make sure'
         vɔ 'fear, be afraid'

(125)   *atá   kpɔ   bé   kofí   wɔ   dɔ́a*
         'Ata   saw   that   Kofi   did   the work'

As the source verb meant 'say', we assume that at first *bé* was used with verbs of saying. However, the class of verbs that takes this complementizer has expanded greatly to verbs and phrases that introduce sentential complements. As in the case of *can*, the expansion of the accompanying lexical items goes along with the loss of the earlier meaning of the grammaticalizing element.

6.9.   Decategorialization

As we have seen, when a noun or verb becomes fixed in a grammaticalizing construction, it loses aspects of its meaning and can become disconnected from instances of the same noun or verb used in other contexts. As it is more fixed in the grammaticalizing construction, it loses the morphosyntactic properties that designate it as a noun or verb. The loss of morphosyntactic features indicative of its lexical class is called "decategorialization" (Hopper 1991). We can illustrate this process by looking at the modal *can* and the connective *while*.

Consider the modal auxiliary *can*. In OE *cunnan* behaved more like a main verb, but in PDE it is strictly an auxiliary. What properties of main verbs did it lose?

1. The ability to take an object: in example (117) we see *cunnan* occurring with a noun phrase object. This use continued into ME but does not occur in PDE: **I can the piano.*

2. The loss of the infinitive form: In OE the infinitive form *cunnan* was sometimes used, and in ME there are instances such as (126) where *conne* must be considered an infinitive because it is used with the auxiliary *shall*.

(126)   *Criseyde shal not conne knowen me.* (Chaucer, *Troilus and Cressida*, l. 1404)
         'Cressida will not be able to recognize me.'

In PDE instances of two modal auxiliaries occurring together are quite uncommon, occurring only in certain dialects in certain combinations. As can be seen from the translation of (126), the problem is not so much a semantic incompatibility, as the future with *be able to* is quite acceptable and semantically sound. However, if *can* has lost much of its ability meaning, so that it now signals root possibility, which itself can refer to the future, the combination of future with *can* becomes exceedingly rare and unfamiliar, thus passing out of existence.

3. The loss of verbal inflection: OE *cunnan* was a verb that did not have a 3rd singular inflection in the present tense. It was a member of the class called "preterit-present verbs" because the present was inflected as if it were a past or preterit form. Most of the other modern modal auxiliaries were members of this class as well. So even by the OE period, these verbs had some unusual characteristics. As they continue to change and grammaticalize, they lose even more inflectional possibilities because they drift apart from their past forms semantically. The past form of *can* etymologically is *could* and, indeed, *could* is sometimes used as the past of *can* in context, as in *When I was seven I could do a back bend*. But it is also used with a hypothetical meaning, as in *You could come with us*, where it does not indicate past tense at all, but rather situates the time reference in the future. So *can* and *could* have moved away from one another and are no longer in a strictly present–past relation.

As an example of decategorialization of a noun, consider the conjunction *while*. *While* (*hwil* in OE) meant 'a length of time', and we can still use the noun this way in some fixed expressions, such as *all the while, a long while*. However, when it is used to introduce a clause, as in (127) and (128), it is not functioning as a noun and therefore cannot take any noun characteristics. That is, in neither (127) nor (128) can you add an article (*a* or *the*), a demonstrative, or an adjective. Also in these examples, *while* is not in any of the usual noun positions – it is not the subject or object of the verb, nor the object of a preposition.

(127)   *He crosses the street in search of help while she tries one final approach.*   (COCA, Spoken, 2012)

(128)   *And while they weren't making a fortune, it was enough for the down payment*   (COCA, Spoken, 2012)

The extent of the grammaticalization of *while* is indicated by the two examples. Example (127) shows the meaning of time – the first clause describes a situation that occurs at the same time as the second clause. Example (128) also has temporal value, but in addition it has the meaning of concessive – that despite the counter-indications of the first clause (they weren't making a lot of money), the situation in the second clause still occurred.

It happens in the case of *can* that the verb it derived from is no longer used as a main verb. In the case of *while*, the noun it came from is still used in a limited fashion in fixed phrases (thus *a long while* and *a short while* are possible, but not *a boring while). In other cases, however, the lexical item that gave rise to a grammatical morpheme may still exist in full form. The Ewe complementizer has lost its verbal properties (it cannot take prefixes or suffixes), but the verb it derived from has not changed. English *have* in the perfect construction discussed in Section 6.5 is clearly grammaticalized in that construction, yet the lexical verb "possessive" *have* still exists and is used as a main verb. In fact, the grammaticalized perfect *have* behaves like an auxiliary in that it contracts with the negative *not* to form *hasn't*, *haven't*, and *hadn't*, but the main verb does not in American English:

(129)   *I was shocked to hear that school lunches <u>haven't</u> changed in fifteen years.*   (COCA, Spoken 2012)

(130)   *Obviously most people <u>don't have</u> (*haven't) four or five cars*   (COCA, Spoken 2012)

Also, the auxiliary contracts with the subject (131) but the main verb does not (132).

(131)   *I mean, <u>I've</u> said that from the very beginning.*   (COCA, Spoken 2012)

(132)   *You know what? <u>I have</u> (*I've) an amazing, yummy, big old car.*   (COCA, Spoken 2012)

So both situations can exist: the lexical item that entered into the grammaticalizing construction can cease to be used in other contexts, or it can remain in the language with its lexical function and meaning. In either case, however, the erstwhile lexical item in the grammaticalizing construction loses its earlier morphosyntactic properties because of the meanings and functions that the construction as a whole takes on.

Some researchers view decategorialization as an instance of reanalysis because an item that was previously a member of one linguistic category has joined another category. One could say the language users have reanalyzed it. In fact, some researchers define grammaticalization as the reanalysis of a lexical item as a grammatical item. The original definition of grammaticalization by Antoine Meillet "l'attribution du caractère grammatical à un mot jadis autonome" (Meillet 1912) or "the attribution of a grammatical character to a formerly autonomous word" seems to emphasize reanalysis. However, as used in this context, "reanalysis" is just a cover term for the outcome of the multiple changes that occur in grammaticalization. (See Section 11.1.3 for another view of how reanalysis and grammaticalization are related.)

6.10.   Fixing of position

Another morphosyntactic change that accompanies grammaticalization is the fixing of position. Often the lexical source for a developing gram was a word that could occur in different positions in the clause. The following example shows another, much less common, lexical source for a future gram, though one that would seem to be quite logical – a temporal adverb. In Tok Pisin (a creole language of Papua New Guinea), the English phrase *by and by* is grammaticalizing into a marker of both intention and future. It was earlier a full form, *baimbai*, but now it most commonly occurs in the reduced form *bai*. In the oldest records it occurs at the beginning of a clause, as in (133) and (134); subsequently a preverbal variant appeared. Romaine 1995 studies the clause-initial and preverbal occurrences of *bai* in a large corpus of children and adults of different dialects, including both first- and second-language speakers of Tok Pisin and finds that the trend is towards more and more preverbal instances.

(133)   Oldest form: *baimbai mi go*   'By and by I go'

(134)   Current variable form: *bai mi go*   'I'll go'

(135)   Innovative form: *mi bai go*   'I'll go'

In general, during grammaticalization there tends to be the stabilization of a single variant. In this case, the variant takes up the position closer to the verb, as its semantics are relevant to the verb. Here is an example from Romaine's corpus:

(136)   *Supos sios i kamap bikpela, em bai gim graun long ol bai sanapim aus lotus*
         'If the church (membership) gets big, it will give land for them to build a church'

A similar development in the African language Bari (Nilo-Saharan), puts the future gram *dé* before the verb when it indicates tense, but at the beginning of the clause when it functions as an adverb, 'then' (Heine and Reh 1984; Spagnolo 1933).

6.11.   Meaning change: bleaching or generalization

One early observation about the meaning change that lexical items in grammaticalizing constructions undergo is that the lexical meaning is *bleached* of specificities of meaning, or generalized as specific components of meaning are lost. A good example is the meaning change in the development of OE *cunnan* 'to know (how)' into PDE *can*. As we saw in Section 6.8, *cunnan* meant 'know' and thus was used in contexts that indicated a subject possessed mental ability or knowledge. During the ME period, as *can* was spreading to use with more and more verbs, it lost the "mental" component of its meaning and came to indicate the internal ability of an agent encompassing both mental and physical ability. This semantic step is considered bleaching or generalization. There is an intimate

Table 6.1: *Stages of development for* can

a.	*mental ability*:	mental enabling conditions exist in the agent
b.	*ability*:	—— enabling conditions exist in the agent
c.	*root possibility*:	—— enabling conditions exist ——

relation between the expanding contexts of use and the generalization of meaning such that expanding contexts lead to generalization which then leads to further expansion of contexts. Table 6.1 (a) and (b) show these two stages.

The third stage illustrated in Table 6.1 is the change to root possibility. At this point, no agent is necessary; rather *can* indicates general enabling conditions, as in (137), where the subject is impersonal *you*, and *can* means 'it is possible to'. Here possibility does not depend just upon the abilities of the subject, but, rather more generally, the properties of the transcript as well.

(137)   *if you – you know, go through the transcript, you can find little bits here and there*   (COCA, Spoken 2012).

Thus in this third stage the context is opened up to all kinds of subjects and verbs.

Increase in frequency of use that typically accompanies grammaticalization also contributes to bleaching or generalization. When a word or phrase is used repeatedly, we grow habituated to it and it loses some of its impact (Haiman 1994). A good example in lexical change is found with swear words. In social contexts where they are rarely used, their use carries a lot of force, but in contexts where they occur repeatedly, they lose their impact. In addition, as we have noted in previous chapters, words, phrases, and constructions that are frequently used are easier to access from memory than infrequent ones. The easier access means that frequent constructions that are grammaticalizing will in turn increase in frequency of use. This leads to more habituation and thus to more bleaching. The bleached meaning and easier access that comes along with frequency of use leads to further increases in frequency as does the expansion to new contexts. These factors working together propel grammaticalization along, creating the directionality effect which we will discuss in Section 6.14.

6.12.   Semantic change by adding meaning from the context

Not all meaning change for a grammaticalizing construction consists of loss of lexical meaning; in some cases meaning is added because of the interpretation that construction takes on in context. The most common means of adding meaning is by inferences made by the listener in the particular context in which the construction is used. Changes due to inferences can occur multiple times along a grammaticalization path. For instance, the English futures *will* and *be going to* that we discussed in Sections 6.2 and 6.4 respectively went through a stage of expressing intention. This function came about via inference.

Speakers and listeners are continually making inferences as they communicate. Speakers cannot put everything they mean to convey or describe into language; rather, they rely on the listener's knowledge of the world and knowledge of the context to make themselves understood. Listeners work to extract the main message from what they hear. Not only do they decode words and constructions, but they also continually ask themselves "Why is s/he telling me this?" That is, the listener tries to discern the speaker's motives and goals in the communication: this is inference.

The following is a conversation from a play by William Shakespeare in which we see clearly that the literal meaning of the lines is not what is really conveyed by the speakers.

(138)   Duke: *Sir Valentine, whither away so fast?*
         Valentine: *Please it your grace, there is a messenger*
                  That stays in to bear my letters to my friends,
                  And I am going to deliver them.
         Duke: *Be they of much import?*
                  (1595, Shakespeare, *Two Gentlemen of Verona*, 3.1.51)

The Duke's question means 'Where are you going so fast?' (*whither* means 'to-where' and it was possible in Early Modern English to leave out the verb *go*). Notice that Valentine's answer does not really give the location he is going to, but rather his goal or intention: to deliver some letters to a messenger. Notice further that that response is fine with the Duke: he apparently did not really want to know the exact location of the errand, but rather its goal or intention. We can tell this by his next question, which is about the letters. So while the two characters are talking about "going to", which in a literal sense would require information about location, in fact, they are both talking about intention and not movement in space. In other words, Valentine inferred that the Duke was asking about intention and not movement in space and he was correct in this inference.

If inferences about intention commonly accompany a construction such as *going to* VERB, these inferences can become conventionalized as part of the meaning of the construction. The result is a new meaning expressed by the construction. Note that in many cases both the movement in space meaning and the intention meaning occur together, as in (138). But at some point the intention meaning comes to be used where movement in space is not necessarily expressed, as in (139):

(139)   *You see I am going to make you a wampum belt of the shells you brought,*
         and I want you to tell me how to put them together.   (COHA 1824)

The intention use of *be going to* is particularly common with the first person. When it is used with the third person it can express intention as well, but in that case there is an inference of prediction (pure future), as in (140). That inference also becomes part of the meaning of the construction. The next step is its use for prediction when intention is not expressed, as in (141). Note that in this example an inanimate object is the subject of *be going to*.

(140)   *Most charming young lady, I must plead your cause; they are <u>going to</u>*
         disinherit you.   (COHA 1814)

(141)   *It's <u>going to</u> be a fair job to cut it out, but when it comes, it is not only*
         beautiful, but worth a price (speaking of a cocoon)   (COHA 1909)

These examples are just illustrative; they are not the examples in which the
change occurred necessarily. Note also that with all the types of meaning change
we discuss here the introduction of a new meaning does not necessitate the loss
of the old meanings. That happens gradually over time. Thus grammaticalizing
constructions and grammatical morphemes in general are usually polysemous;
that is, they have multiple meanings and uses at any given time. The *be going to*
construction in PDE can express movement in space for a purpose, intention of
the subject, or prediction by the speaker, or any of these at the same time!

6.13.   Metaphor

         Another source for new meanings for grammaticalizing construc-
tions is metaphorical extension. A metaphor maps a structural relationship from
one (usually more concrete) domain to another (usually more abstract) domain.
Spatial metaphors based on the human (or, less frequently, animal) body are
particularly frequent in the development of prepositions and postpositions.
Heine et al. 1991b find African languages to be especially rich in this sort of
metaphorical development. For instance, they cite the Swahili noun *mbele*
which means 'breast' but also 'frontside, front part' when it applies to non-
human objects. The spatial relationship between the breast and the whole human
body is mapped onto other objects by metaphor. *Mbele* is also used as a locative
preposition meaning 'in front of' and even as a temporal adverb meaning
'before'.

    Heine et al. 1991b survey 125 African languages and find that the most
common body parts used for relational constructions are 'head' for 'on', 'back'
for 'back', 'face' for 'front', 'belly, stomach' for 'in', and 'buttocks, anus' for
'under' or 'back'. The metaphor allows the body-part term to become more
general and abstract, as it can apply to objects of all types. Human bodies and
certain other objects, such as clocks, televisions, or houses, have intrinsic fronts
and backs, and terms such as 'face' can be applied to them metaphorically, as in
this example from Svorou 1994:

(142)   Bari (Nilo-Saharan, Spagnolo 1933)
         i   kɔmɔŋ   na   kadi
         in   face   POSS   house
         'in front of the house'

In contrast, other objects such as trees and mountains do not have intrinsic fronts
or backs. These relational terms are extended to "frontless" objects by taking

into account the perspective of the viewer. An object that is between the viewer and a tree is taken to be in front of the tree and an object that is farther away than the tree is taken to be at the back of the tree. (See Section 7.7 for more examples of sources for locative terms.)

A well-known lexical metaphor bases temporal words on spatial ones, including spatial movement, as in *the time is coming* or *time is going by too fast*. Thus one might argue that the change in a preposition such as Swahili *mbele* or English *before* or *behind* from a spatial sense to a temporal one could be a metaphorical extension. The problem with this argument is that the spatial sense could also give rise to inferences about the temporal domain (Svorou 1994). If someone arrives *in front of* someone else, s/he also arrives *before* that person. In other words, movement through space and movement through time are inextricably linked. For that reason, the English movement towards a goal construction *be going to* does not become a future through metaphorical extension, because the temporal sense was already there. Rather, as we saw in Section 6.12, the *be going to* construction goes through a stage in which it signals intention, an inference from movement towards a goal, and then eventually another inference of prediction becomes associated with the construction, yielding future meaning. Thus it is important to study intermediate stages in the development of meaning to find out what mechanisms apply. Just looking at an earlier and later stage could lead one astray in trying to determine how the change occurred.

6.14.   Other general properties of grammaticalization

In the next chapter we will see the full impact of grammaticalization by examining how demonstratives, determiners, passives, case markers, discourse markers, and others constructions grammaticalize in addition to the examples of tense, modality, complementizers, negatives, and conjunctions we have looked at in this chapter. What these examples show is that in all languages at all times grammaticalization is a major factor in creating grammatical morphemes and grammatical constructions. In this section we consider a few general properties of grammaticalization.

The grammaticalization process is **gradual** and characterized by **variation** in both form and meaning. Grammaticalizing constructions can and usually do express two or more meanings. The forms in the construction may have variants in their phonetic shape as well as in other morphosyntactic properties.

Grammaticalization is a **continuing process**. Once a construction is formed and a grammatical morpheme is created, one can say that grammaticalization has occurred, but usually change does not stop there, and the construction continues to become more and more grammatical until it is eventually lost or replaced by another construction with a similar function.

Grammaticalization processes **move in one direction**, a property called "unidirectionality". Of course, this is true by definition, since if a construction were becoming less grammatical we would not call the process "grammaticalization". However, it is true that thousands of cases of constructions becoming more grammatical over time have been documented, and many fewer cases of grammaticalization being stalled and vanishingly few cases in which grammaticalization appears to be reversed have been reported. For this reason, grammaticalization is often thought of as a pervasive process affecting many constructions of a language, moving them in the same direction – towards being more grammatical.

This chapter began with a discussion of the grammaticalization of future grams in English and Romance. What we saw there was that the *go*-future in English, Spanish, Portuguese, and French is replacing an earlier future (*will* in English and infinitive + *haber* in Romance languages). Thus we sometimes speak of cycles of grammaticalization: one construction developing only to be replaced by yet another. These cycles may occur fairly quickly or quite slowly. Once a gram has progressed to a point where its meaning is quite generalized, a new gram in a new construction arises with the more specific meaning, and as it gains in usage, it progresses down the same path as the previous gram. Thus when *will* no longer expresses intention strongly enough, *be going to* takes up this use, which then leads it to the inferences that dilute its intention meaning, leaving a need for a new way to express intention and so on. It is important to note that the language is not "trying" to get a new future gram. Speakers are trying to find ways to express the more specific meanings, but as soon as these become highly frequent, their meaning also changes. Thus we have cycles of change and replacement. Eventual loss occurs when the meaning becomes so generalized as to make little contribution and comes to be replaced. In some cases this is accompanied by so much reduction in form that the gram itself appears to have been deleted.

Suggested reading

Bybee, J., 2003. Cognitive processes in grammaticalization. In M. Tomasello (ed.)
    The new psychology of language, Mahwah, NJ: Lawrence Erlbaum,
    pp. 145–167.
Haiman, J., 1994. Ritualization and the development of language. In W. Pagliuca (ed.)
    Perspectives on grammaticalization, Amsterdam: John Benjamins,
    pp. 3–28.
Hopper, P.J., 1991. On some principles of grammaticization. In E.C. Traugott and
    B. Heine (eds.) *Approaches to grammaticalization*, Amsterdam: John
    Benjamins, pp. 17–35.
Hopper, P.J. and Traugott, E.C., 2003. *Grammaticalization*, Cambridge: Cambridge
    University Press.

Questions for discussion

1. Consider the many ways that repetition or frequency increase affect the mechanisms of change. Is frequency both a cause and a result of grammaticalization?
2. Consider habituation, inference, chunking, and reduction: are these processes that apply only in language, or can you find examples of how they might apply in other cognitive domains?
3. The Latin word *unde* meant 'from where, whence'. The Spanish word for 'where' is *donde* and for 'from where, whence' is *de donde*. *De* is a preposition meaning 'of, from'. Postulate the diachronic development of *de donde*.
4. Many American speakers use *you guys* to just mean *you*-plural regardless of the gender of the addressee. Is grammaticalization going on with *you guys*? What properties would you look for to answer this question?
5. What are the many uses of the adverb or preposition *ahead*? How do each of these relate to the body part noun *head*?

7 Common paths of grammaticalization

7.1. Introduction

Grammaticalization is interesting enough as a language-specific phenomenon but it becomes all the more important and interesting with the discovery that very similar paths of semantic change can be documented in unrelated languages. Indeed, large-scale crosslinguistic studies of grammaticalization reveal that for each gram type there are only a few possible lexical sources (Bybee et al. 1994; Heine et al. 1991b; Heine and Kuteva 2002). In Chapter 6 we saw that future grams can develop from verbs or constructions with meanings of volition or obligation, from constructions signaling movement towards a goal, and in a few cases from temporal adverbs, such as Tok Pisin *baimbai*. These four sources account for the vast majority of future grams whose sources are known.

The consequence of these facts is that in all languages at all times the same mechanisms of change are operating on very similar lexical and grammatical material and thus producing similar results. This is not to say that grammaticalization is exactly the same across languages. Poplack 2011 compares the grammaticalization over two centuries of the movement futures in French, Portuguese, and Spanish and demonstrates that not only are the rates of change different, but the contextual factors that influence the use of the movement future are different across these languages. What this means in terms of the universality of grammaticalization paths is that the conceptual sources are similar (they are probably never exactly the same), and the mechanisms of change such as bleaching and inference are very similar across languages, but in each language there will be some specific conditions that push the long-term development more in some contexts than in others. These language-specific factors may be the existence of other, competing forms, the attachment of social meaning to one variant or another, or particular patterns of usage that skew distributions. Despite these language-specific factors, broad patterns of change that are similar across unrelated languages can still be identified.

In this chapter we examine what is currently known about these broad patterns of change, termed "grammaticalization paths". In each case we see examples from unrelated languages and consider briefly what mechanisms of change appear to be operative. We begin with the grammaticalization of the inflectional categories of verbs, the temporal categories of tense and aspect in Section 7.2, followed by mood and modality in Section 7.3, personal pronouns in Section 7.4, and finally person–number agreement in Section 7.5. Sections 7.6–7.8 treat the nominal categories of articles, adpositions, and case markers and Sections 7.8–7.11 deal with the grammaticalization of larger constructions. We end the chapter with a discussion of what happens at the very end of the process.

7.2.   Tense and aspect

The terms "tense" and "aspect" refer to the grammatical expression of the conceptual category of time. It is important to distinguish concepts from their linguistic expression because there are different types of linguistic expression. The temporal domain includes notions that are coded as lexical items, such as *now, today, yesterday, then, on Wednesday,* etc. as well as notions that are coded in periphrastic constructions such as *be going to* or inflections such as past tense *–ed.* Thus we have the conceptual area of time and language-specific expressions of time, both lexical and grammatical. In addition, crosslinguistic research has shown that certain types of grams occur consistently across languages, and these are called "gram-types" (Bybee 1985; Dahl 1985; Bybee and Dahl 1989). In the discussion below, I will follow Comrie 1976 and designate language-specific names, such as "Preterit", by using an initial upper-case letter and the universal category name with a lower case initial letter, "perfective". Thus one can say, the Spanish Preterit is a perfective and the OE Preterit is a past tense. This convention helps us distinguish between language-specific grams, whose names were devised before the crosslinguistic similarity and differences among grams was recognized, from those gram-types that have definitions independently of specific languages.

The meaning of tense grams is deictic; this means that the actual temporal reference changes according to the moment of speech or some other reference point. That is, if I use the present tense today I do not mean exactly the same time as if I used it yesterday. Temporal words such as *now* and *today, next week* are also deictic in that the time they refer to depends upon the time at which they are uttered. The most common tenses are past, present, and future, though some languages also express meanings such as recent or remote past or future. The future is often not strictly a tense, since future grams also commonly express other meanings, such as intention, as we saw in the last chapter. Present tense is somewhat problematic as well, since it is used mostly with states and conditions that last over a period of time which includes the present. Only the past is strictly tense-like when it refers only to situations occurring prior to the moment of speech, as it does in English.

Aspect refers to the different ways that the internal temporal structure of a situation can be viewed (Comrie 1976). For example, the progressive in English (*BE* + VERB + *ing*) looks at a situation that is ongoing at the moment of speech, *he is swimming*, or at a moment in the past, *he was swimming*. This is different than viewing the situation as a completed whole, as in *he swam across the pool.* Habitual aspect, such as expressed by the simple present in English when used with a dynamic verb or in the past with *used to*, views a situation as repeated over time and characteristic of a period of time, as in *he swims every day* or *he used to swim every day*. Some languages have a major aspectual distinction of perfective vs. imperfective, where perfective views a situation as a completed whole (usually in the past) and the imperfective views the situation as ongoing in some sense – either as in progress or repeated or habitual. This is the distinction found in the Spanish Preterit vs. Imperfective or Present. The Preterit is a perfective, viewing the situation as whole and completed, the Imperfective is a past imperfective, viewing a past situation as ongoing (progressive or habitual) and the Present is inherently imperfective (as something truly simultaneous with the moment of speech is either a state or a progressive or habitual situation). In discourse, perfectives are used to give the main line of the narration and imperfectives describe background situations.

While linguists would like to draw a firm line between tense and aspect, in most languages and in diachrony the two are deeply interrelated, and often one gram expresses both a tense and an aspect notion, as the Spanish Imperfective does by describing imperfective situations in the past. In terms of grammaticalization paths, past and perfective are related as are present and imperfective. Thus our discussion of grammaticalization paths will treat tense and aspect together.

7.2.1.   The past/perfective path

In this section we will examine some of the ways that a set of related grams develop: resultative, anterior (perfect), perfective, and past. There are several source constructions for these senses; we begin with one common in Indo-European languages.

As we saw in Section 6.7, a resultative construction can change to express anterior (also often called "perfect", though this term can be easily confused with "perfective"). This construction consists of a stative verb, such as *be* or *have* with a past or passive participle as shown in the Old English examples in (143) and (144).

(143)   *ic   hæbbe   nu   gesæd   hiora   ingewinn*
        'I   have   now   told   their   inner struggles'

(144)   *Hie   wæron   cumen   Leoniðan   to   fultume*
        They   were   come   Leonitha   to   help
        'They had come to help Leonitha'

The resultative meaning is that a situation (or action) occurred that resulted in a current state of affairs. For instance, in example (144), that would mean that they have come and they are still here.

The resultative meaning has a tendency to generalize to the meaning of a past action with current relevance, so from a resulting state (in the present) to a more general meaning of relevance to the current situation. That is the meaning of anterior or perfect. One way to understand the anterior or perfect is to note that it is not used for narrating sequences of events. Narrating is the function of past or perfective. Compare example (145) with the English anterior, where the proposals being pushed are still relevant, that is, they could still be adopted, to example (146) which just states facts about past events.

(145)   *Some officials have pushed for cleaner, city-owned*
          generators that would still run on fossil fuel. Others have called
          for retrofitting the current power plant and keeping it open while
          alternative power options are explored. (COCA 2009)

(146)   *The local city councilman pushed successfully for a*
          moratorium on opening large stores in downtown, although Wal-
          Mart got around that by pulling its permits before the ordinance
          took effect. (COCA 2012)

Anterior constructions derived from a resultative meaning are composed of a stative verb plus a participle as in English; such constructions are found in Spanish and other Indo-European languages such as Danish, Modern Greek, and Baluchi, as well as languages of other families, such as Basque, Tigre, Mano, and Buriat (Bybee et al. 1994).

In many languages, the source for the anterior or perfect is an active verb such as VERB + 'finish' or a motion verb construction such as 'come from' + VERB. Such constructions do not always have a resultative meaning or source, but rather can move directly from the sense of finishing one situation before beginning another to a sense of a past situation with current relevance. Here is an example from the Central African creole language Sango (Samarin 1967).

(147)   *eh bien,   lo tɛ ungunzá ní   kóé awe, mɔ goe mɔ mú na lo   ngú*
          well then 3.s eat greens the.one all finish 2.s go 2.s take with 3.s water
          'then, when he has eaten up the manioc greens, you go give him water ...'

Some languages that have anteriors from a verb or auxiliary meaning 'finish' are Bongu, Temne, Tok Pisin, Lao, Kammu, Mandarin, and Palaung.

Thus we have three common sources for anteriors: resultatives (formed with a stative verb and a participle), 'movement from', and 'finish'. These constructions converge on the meaning of 'anterior' as shown in the partial path of change in (148).

(148)   resultative
          movement from   >   anterior
          finish

Subsequent changes in anterior grams lead to the development of the more generalized meanings of perfective or past. That is, an anterior loses the 'current relevance' part of its meaning and simply signals a whole or completed situation in the past. For instance, the French *passé composé*, which is formed with *avoir* 'to have' or *être* 'to be' plus a participle form, started as an anterior and has now become a perfective, used for simple completed situations in the past. It has replaced the perfective inherited from Latin (the *passé simple*) in speech and some forms of writing. Some evidence exists for how the change from anterior to perfective might happen. In a description of seventeenth-century French, the Port-Royal grammar (Lancelot and Arnould 1660), the *passé composé* is described as being used for actions and events that occurred on the same day. So from 'past action with current relevance' the meaning changed to 'past action on the same day' and from there it extended to past actions in general. Interestingly, a study of the current use of the Spanish Perfect in the dialect of Alicante in Spain also shows that it has come to be used for past actions on the same day (Schwenter and Torres Cacoullos 2008). Perhaps the Perfect in Spanish is following the same path as the cognate construction in French and will end up as a perfective.

Anteriors that come from verbs meaning 'finish' can also develop into perfectives. This has occurred in Lhasa, Burmese, Kongo, and Mandarin Chinese (Heine and Kuteva 2002). The path in (148) can now be expanded as in (149):

(149)   resultative
         movement from   >   anterior > perfective
         finish

Another related development is from anterior to simple past. A simple past and a perfective are very similar in that they are both used to narrate past events. However, a simple past differs from a perfective in several ways (Bybee et al. 1994; Section 3.14), primarily in that a simple past does not contrast with a past imperfective, but can be used to express imperfective as well. An example is the English usage such as *he washed his car every week*, which describes a habitual (imperfective) situation. Also the simple past can be used with stative verbs to give past tense meaning, while perfective inflection on statives changes the meaning of the verb. Thus in Spanish the Preterit (perfective) form of the verb *saber* 'to know' is *supo* (3rd sg.) and it means 'found out'. To express 'he knew' one has to use the imperfective form *sabía*.

There is evidence that anteriors have become simple pasts in a few languages. In German the 'have'/'be' + PARTICIPLE construction that was formerly an anterior, is now used for simple past. Heine and Reh 1984 report that in the Dahome dialect of Ewe (West Africa) the verb 'finish' has developed from an anterior to a past tense marker. In Atchin (Austronesian) the auxiliary *ma* 'come' merges with the pronominal forms to make a past tense auxiliary. In the neighboring dialects of Vao and Wala, this same auxiliary is still used as an anterior (Capell and Layard 1980). Thus all three sources of anteriors are documented as becoming simple pasts, as shown in (150). Note that for both perfectives and pasts we have fewer clear cases of documented source constructions. The reason is that as grammaticalization advances, and as time goes by, the connection to the earlier source construction becomes less obvious and that construction might be lost.

(150)   resultative
         movement from   >   anterior > perfective/simple past
         finish

The factor that seems to determine whether an anterior will become a perfective or a simple past is the prior existence of an imperfective in the language. French already had an imperfective (the *imparfait*) so the new *passé composé* is restricted to perfective uses; Dutch and German have no imperfective, so the compound past is free to spread into imperfective contexts. This is an issue that should be studied more, taking into account a broader range of languages.

7.2.2.   The present/imperfective path ▬▬▬▬▬▬▬▬▬▬▬▬▬▬▬

On the other side of the aspect domain are grams that express ongoing or habitual actions and states. One of the most frequently grammaticalized categories in this domain is the progressive. The progressive is important because it feeds into the chain of developments that eventually led to present tense and imperfective aspect.

The most common source constructions for progressives contain locative verbs and/or adpositions indicating that the subject is located in a space (standing or sitting, perhaps) where the verbal action is taking place. For instance, the Spanish progressive uses the verb *estar* 'to be located' from the Latin verb *stāre* 'to stand' with the gerund form of the main verb. In early examples such as (151) (from the thirteenth century) the locative meaning is still quite apparent (Torres Cacoullos 2000):

(151)   *Et alli estaua el puerco en aquella llaguna bolcando se*
         (GE.II)
         'And there was the pig in that pond turning itself'

In modern texts, however, the locative context is not present, and instead we get a purely aspectual sense of an ongoing process.

(152)   *todo hombre tiene un precio; y estoy hablando desde una*
         – perspectiva económica, hay gente que no tiene precio
         (COREC, AHUM019A)
         'every man has his price; and I am speaking from an economic
         perspective, there are people that don't have a price'

Another type of locative construction, found across the Kru languages of Africa, uses a locative verb and a nominalized form of the main verb. In some cases the nominalizer itself is identifiable as expressing location, as in this example from Godié (Marchese 1986):

(153)   ɔ   kù   sʉkĀ dɪ dʌ
         she be-at rice cut place
         'She is cutting rice'

Some other languages that use locative constructions to form the progressive are Basque, Island Carib, Cocama, Jivaro, Alyawarra, Tahitian, Tohono O'odham, Abkhaz, Baluchi, Mwera, Ngambay, Shuswap, Haka, Lahu, Cantonese, Dakota, and Tok Pisin (Bybee et al. 1994).

Another related source for progressives can be found in constructions using movement verbs such as 'walk', 'go', or 'come'. The Turkish progressive suffix *–yor* comes from a verb meaning 'walk, go'. In Spanish, a progressive construction that is less frequently used than the one with *estar* uses the verb *andar* 'to walk' as an auxiliary; *ir* 'to go' is also used with some main verbs. Consider this twentieth-century example where progressive is the meaning, not movement in space 'walking':

(154)   *ya no me interesa tanto el teatro, y por eso <u>ando aquí</u>*
          <u>cambiando</u> de pintura a música; de música a coreografía,
          y de coreografía a cine
          'now the theater doesn't interest me much and therefore <u>I am</u>
          <u>here changing</u> from painting to music, from music to
          choreography and from choreography to cinema'

Progressives such as the ones just illustrated have a strong tendency to have periphrastic expression, which is one indication that they are newly grammaticalized. They are also most commonly used with an agentive meaning (the subject is actively doing something) and with dynamic verbs rather than stative verbs. As progressives continue to develop, they extend to use in habitual contexts and eventually to use with stative verbs. The extension to habitual contexts has occurred in some dialects of Yoruba, in Scots Gaelic (Comrie 1976), Punjabi, and Hindi-Urdu (Dahl 1985). In addition, the Turkish progressive *-yor* (< 'walk' just mentioned) is used as a habitual marker in the spoken language (Underhill 1976). When a gram serves the functions of both progressive and habitual, it has become an imperfective if it can be used with both present and past tense (and future, if applicable) or it becomes a present tense, if it happens to be restricted to the present from the beginning. As presents and imperfectives are more grammaticalized, they strongly tend to be expressed as affixes on the verb.

7.2.3.   The future path

The various paths that create future grams were discussed extensively in the preceding chapter along with the mechanisms of change that move grams along the path of change. The future path that was presented in Chapter 6 is repeated here as (155).

(155)   volition
          obligation   >   intention   >   future (prediction)
          movement towards

These sources are documented in the following languages:

a.   Volition futures: English, Inuit, Danish, Modern Greek, Romanian, Serbo-Croatian, Sogdian (East Iranian), Tok Pisin

b.   Obligation futures: Basque, English, Danish, Western Romance languages

c.   Movement futures: Abipon, Atchin, Bari, Cantonese, Cocama, Danish, English, Guaymí, Krongo, Mano, Margi, Maung, Mwera,

Nung, Tem, Tojolabal, Tucano and Zuni; also French, Portuguese, and Spanish.

Dahl's 1985 study found that future grams are fairly evenly split between periphrastic and affixal expressions. Later studies demonstrate that future grams that are less grammaticalized in meaning (for instance, also expressing "intention") tend to be periphrastic and in general less fused with the verb, while futures that are more grammaticalized (for instance, expressing epistemic modality [see below]) tend to be affixed to the verb and show more fusion (Bybee et al. 1991).

7.2.4.   Derivational aspect

Another way that aspectual markers can develop is through derivational processes. Derivational affixes grammaticalize in a slightly different way than inflectional affixes do. Certain affixes or particles develop from adverbs indicating locative direction. English examples are the particles that go with certain verbs, such as *up*, *down*, *over*, and *through*. When added to verbs that are atelic (verbs that describe situations without necessary end points), they change the expression to indicate that an endpoint has been attained. For example, *eat up* indicates the attainment of a limit, i.e. the complete consumption of the object. Consider also phrasal verbs such as *write up*, *write down*, *burn up*, *burn down*, *think over*, and *think through*. All of these phrases express an endpoint that the verb alone does not express. While these English phrases are better described as "completives", when such formations become very general in a language, they begin to resemble perfectives. In contrast to the perfectives described above, these can be designated as perfectives that develop from "bounders", grams that indicate that the action of the verb is carried to completion (Bybee and Dahl 1989).

In languages that have perfectives from bounders, there are usually several different bounders used, and these occur in specific combinations with verbs; thus in English we have *write down* and *burn down* but not **eat down* or **think down*. In some languages such processes have generalized and grammaticalized to the extent that almost all verbs have a form with and without a bounder. In this case the verbs without bounders may be viewed as imperfective and the verbs with bounders as perfective. An important way that such perfectives resemble the ones we discussed earlier is that they are used for narrating sequences of events. This type of perfective/imperfective distinction occurs in Russian and to varying degrees in other Slavic languages; it also occurs in Georgian (Kartvelian), Margi (Chadic), and Mokilese (Oceanic) (Dahl 1985). In all known cases, several bounders exist, and some verbs occur with more than one bounder; these systems thus exhibit much lexical idiosyncrasy. Here are some examples from the Chadic language Margi (North Africa; Hoffman 1963):

(156)   Derivatives of –bá 'out'

də̀m	'to pick, to gather'	də̀mbá	'to pick out, gather out of'
ndàl	'to throw'	ndàlbá	'to throw out'
ŋà	'to call'	ŋabá	'to call out'
'ùtlà	'to cough'	'ùtlàbá	'to cough up'

Derivatives of –ía 'downward'

ndàl	'to throw'	ndàlía	'to throw down'
dùgù	'to find, come upon'	dùgùwía	'to come upon, to attack'
vɔ̀lía	'to jump, fly'	vɔ̀lía	'to jump down'

Derivatives of –na 'away'

ndàl	'to throw'	ndàlnà	'to throw away'
ŋgùshí	'to laugh'	ŋgùshiná	'to laugh at, make fun of'
6ə̀l	'to break'	6ə̀lnà	'to break off'

Hoffman notes that the derivative suffix –bá is probably related to the verb bá 'to go out' and to the adverb àbá 'outside'. The suffix –ía may be related to the verb suffix –ghì in the related language Bura, which in turn is probably related to the adverb ághì meaning 'down'. Hoffman gives no indication of the source of the third suffix in (156).

Though these suffixed forms can be called perfectives just as the inflectional Spanish Preterit or periphrastic French passé composé can be called perfectives, they have different properties because of their diachronic sources. As we have already noted, none of the bounders is lexically general as the inflectional or periphrastic perfectives are. They differ slightly in meaning, as they include the sense that a limit has been attained, while the more usual perfectives simply view the situation as a whole (Dahl 1985). This is an excellent example of how the diachronic source of a construction or form highly determines its later uses and meanings.

7.3.   Grams indicating modality and mood

The semantic territory covered by modality is rather difficult to define, and some linguists include more in this territory than others. To get a feel for what is often included, consider the meanings of the PDE modal auxiliaries can, could, may, might, should and must. (Even though they have some modal uses, I have left out shall and will because will is a future now, and shall is infrequently used except as a future.) In the last chapter we saw some examples of the development of OE cunnan into can. There we noted that cunnan indicated mental ability or knowledge but then generalized into all kinds of abilities. It thus predicated certain conditions on the agent with respect to the main verb; it could be called an "agent-oriented" modality. Here is an example of the ability use of can from PDE.

(157)   *You are the one who can play the piano and knows how to tie a bow tie.* (COCA 2012)

(158)   *I can read the human body the way you read the*
             machinery on the ship. (COCA 2012)

Nowadays, *can* is most commonly used in a much more generalized sense that is called "root possibility". This type of possibility predicates enabling conditions on the agent, but also more general enabling conditions that are external to the agent, including both physical and social conditions. In the following example, it is not just the driver's skill that is at stake, but also the physical conditions, such as how much space there is for the vehicle off the road:

(159)   *I think I'll pull over as far as I can and let that whole herd*
             of cars behind me pass. (COCA 2012)

Root possibility is also the sense of *can* when it occurs in passive clauses, such as the following:

(160)   *I question whether it can even be called cruelty when any*
             other action would have meant our certain death. (COCA fiction)

Another modal meaning is obligation (sometimes called "necessity"), which comes in both strong and weak varieties. *Should* indicates a weaker obligation than *must*. Consider these examples:

(161)   *A little voice in my head warned me I should keep our*
             interaction all business. (COCA 2012)

(162)   *And so pilots must be qualified to handle whatever may*
             come. (COCA 2012)

These are also "agent-oriented" because they predicate conditions on an agent with respect to the main predicate. These obligations can be moral, legal or social. Often *should* is also used just to make a suggestion, as in (163):

(163)   *Maybe she and her sister should try and find a signature*
             brand of coffee to sell in the shop. (COCA 2012)

The lexical sources of obligation grams include main verbs meaning 'owe', such as *shall*, which in OE meant 'to owe' (money or allegiance). *Should* was the past tense of *shall*. Other languages with an obligation gram from 'owe' are Cantonese and Danish. Other periphrastic sources are verbs such as 'have' and 'be' plus an infinitive, as in English *have to* and *be to*, both of which signal obligation or arrangement. Such constructions also occur in Abkhaz, Baluchi, Temne, and Chepang. Impersonal phrases such as 'be good' or 'be fitting' can also become obligation markers, as shown in Lahu, Palaung, and Mwera (Bybee et al. 1994).

Obligation modals often undergo a semantic change in grammaticalization that leads to their expressing epistemic meaning, which indicates the degree of commitment the speaker has to the truth of the asserted proposition. When *should* and *must* are used as epistemics, they maintain their relative degree of strength. *Should* indicates probability, based on some evidence, as in (164), and *must* indicates strong probability, based on inference from evidence, as in (165):

(164)   *I have given her an injection. She should sleep through the night.* (COCA 2012)

(165)   *I know, he must think I am a billionaire.* (COCA 2012)

In fact, we can generalize and say that agent-oriented (or root) modals can become epistemic, because root possibility can also evolve into expressing epistemic possibility. This has not yet happened with *can*, but in the past it occurred with English *may*. Originally *may* expressed physical ability or might, and it generalized to ability and root possibility. We still use *may* for root possibility in writing. In the following example the authors are making a proposal, not stating an uncertainty. Note that *can* can be substituted for *may* without changing the meaning.

(166)   *We propose that the correlations shown in the literature between lexicon and syntax may reflect two different types of interactions.* (COCA 2012)

However, in spoken language, *may* is often used for epistemic possibility, meaning 'it is possible that'. In the following example, we see that the speaker is expressing uncertainty.

(167)   *Yes, the brooch is important, but getting it back may not solve everything* (COCA 2012)

(168)   *they may have moral concerns and they probably do* (COCA 2012)

Thus we see that root possibility can give rise to the meaning of epistemic possibility.

To summarize this part of the discussion of modality, here are the paths of change for ability and obligation meanings:

(169)   ability > root possibility > epistemic possibility
          weak obligation > probability
          strong obligation/necessity > inferred certainty or strong probability

The modalities of ability and obligation tend to have periphrastic expression as they are not highly grammaticalized; the epistemic modalities sometimes have inflectional (affixal) expression. Other categories related to modality that have inflectional expression are usually called "moods" and include subjunctives (special forms for subordinate clauses) and imperatives. As indicated by their expression type, these categories are often highly grammaticalized. Since they come from various sources and often have long histories, they will not be further treated in this chapter. More detailed discussion can be found in Chapter 6 of Bybee et al. 1994.

7.4.   Personal pronouns

Personal pronouns (such as English *I*, *me*, *you*, *he*, *she*, *it*, *they*) form a grammatical category that behaves in some ways similar to a noun phrase in that members of this class serve as the subject, direct or indirect object of the verb, or the object of a pronoun. In contrast with lexical nouns, they do not take modifiers such as articles, demonstratives, or adjectives. They constitute a closed class (though new members may arise through grammaticalization, as we will see here). In this section we will briefly survey the sources of personal pronouns in the languages of the world, starting with third person pronouns. Much of this discussion is based on Heine and Song 2011.

7.4.1.   Third person pronouns

Third person pronouns derive from demonstrative pronouns, nominal concepts or intensifiers, according to the research of Heine and Song 2011. Demonstrative pronouns are words such as *this* and *that* which distinguish referents according to spatial location. Some languages do not have a separate category for third person pronouns but instead use the same forms as are used for demonstratives (Latin, Cora [Uto-Aztecan], Yindjibarndi [Pama-Nyungan], Turkish [Altaic], and Ancient Egyptian [Afro-Asiatic]). The forms of the Latin distal demonstrative pronoun *ille* 'that one, m. sg. nom.' became third person pronouns in Romance languages, e.g. French *il*, Spanish *él*, Portuguese *ele*; Latin *illa* 'that one, f. sg. nom.' became French *elle*, Spanish *ella*, Portuguese *ela*. The object pronouns in these languages derived primarily from the accusative case, but with more phonological reduction, French *le*, *la*, Spanish *lo*, *la*, and Portuguese *o*, *a*.

The nominal concepts giving rise to third person pronouns usually denote 'male person, man'. For example, in the ǀAni language of Botswana (Central Khoisan), the noun *khó(e)-mà* 'person, m. sg.' has become the third masculine singular pronoun *khó(e)ma* and has further reduced phonologically to *khóm* (Heine and Song 2011). Other examples from African languages in which the word for 'man' has become a pronoun are Lendu (Central Sudanic), Zande (Ubangi), Alur, and Adhola (Nilotic Southern Lwoo). Other nominal sources are nouns denoting ranks or social positions, especially in languages with honorific systems.

Intensifiers, such as 'head' and 'self', can also be added to pronouns to create new ones. The English reflexive with *self* is used as an intensifier, as in *President Obama himself tipped off the entire world to the rescue*. This type of use can be the source of a new pronoun, as in Turkish where the noun *kendi* 'self' can be used as a third singular pronoun.

7.4.2.   Second person pronouns

Second person pronouns may derive from spatial deictic terms, lexical nouns, or intensifiers as third person pronouns do, but in addition there are two other important sources for second person pronouns: plural pronouns and third person forms. The substitution of plural or singular forms in the second person is common. In the last few centuries this process has occurred in a number of European languages. It can be seen in progress today in French where there is a familiar second singular pronoun, *tu*, and a more formal one, *vous*. The latter form was earlier the second person plural (from Latin *vōs*), but it has come to be used with a singular referent to indicate politeness or formality, leaving the original singular to indicate familiarity. A similar change occurred in English, when *you*, which was originally only plural, came to replace *thou* in polite or formal situations. This replacement has been carried to its logical conclusion and *you* has become the only way to express second person singular, while still being used for the plural. (A result of this change is that now various ways of expressing the plural are arising: *you all, you guys, youse*, etc.)

Another strategy for addressing a second person politely is to use a nominal phrase that is actually a third person form. Spanish *vuestra merced* and Portuguese *vossa mercê*, which both mean 'your grace', were grammaticalized to second person polite pronouns (*usted* and *você*, respectively), and in Dutch *Uwe Edelheid* 'your nobility' became the second person polite form *u*. According to Heine and Song 2011, the Portuguese form *vossa mercê* was used first around 1460 to address the king, then it was extended to use in addressing dukes and further extended to the rest of the population, replacing the form *vós* that was inherited from Latin. In general, it appears that second person forms are highly affected by the polite trend to honor the addressee and elevate his or her status. The complementary trend of the speaker to express humility affects forms that grammaticalize into first person pronouns.

7.4.3.   First person pronouns

Both first and second person pronouns are fairly conservative, meaning the inherited form can remain in a language and its daughters for a very long time. This is illustrated in Tables 7.1 and 7.2, where the nominative and accusative forms of first and second singular are given for languages representing the major branches of Indo-European.

What you can see in Table 7.1 is that across these languages, representing more than a 2000 year time-depth in some cases, the first person forms are cognates, meaning they are all descended from a common ancestor form. The best evidence for this is found in the consonants. The nominative form has a medial or final velar consonant in most forms, with a palatalized consonant in Old Church Slavonic and Lithuanian and a weakened velar in Sanskrit. The accusative form maintains an /m/ as the initial consonant in all the languages. When you add the 2000 years since, for example, Latin was spoken and note that Romance languages generally still have /m/ in first person accusative and /t/ in second person, you can see how long these forms stay around.

Table 7.1: *Nominative and accusative forms of first person singular in the major branches of Indo-European* (Beekes 1995)

'I'	Sanskrit	Old Church Slavonic	Lithuanian	Hittite	Greek	Latin	Gothic
nominative	*ahám*	*azʋ*	*àš*	*uga*	*egō*	*egō*	*ik*
accusative	*mā́m*	*mene*	*manè*	*ammuk*	*emé*	*mē*	*mik*

Table 7.2: *Nominative and accusative forms of second person singular in the major branches of Indo-European* (Beekes 1995)

'thou'	Sanskrit	Old Church Slavonic	Lithuanian	Hittite	Greek	Latin	Gothic
nominative	*tvám*	*ty*	*tù*	*zik*	*sú*	*tū*	*þu*
accusative	*tvā́m*	*tebe*	*tavè*	*tuk*	*sé*	*tē*	*þuk*

Because these forms tend to stick around in a language a long time, we do not know what their original lexical sources were, and this is true of first and second person pronouns in many languages of the world. In a few cases, we have lexical sources for first person. For example, in Indonesian the first person pronoun is *saya*, and it is documented that *sahā ya* 'servant' was also used for 'I (humble/polite)'. In this language, one uses different forms for different social relations, but now *saya* is a neutral, non-familiar 'I' (Lehmann 1982).

First person plural pronouns can be bolstered by adding intensifiers, as when Spanish *nos* 'we' adds *otros* 'others' to become *nosotros* 'we'. First plural pronouns also arise from indefinite pronouns. In French the indefinite pronoun *on* is often used to indicate 'we' as in *on y va* 'let's go'. In Portuguese the noun phrase *a gente* 'the people' came to be used as an indefinite pronoun and has further extended to use for first plural competing with the inherited form *nós* (Travis and Silveira 2009).

7.5.   Person–number agreement

Personal pronouns have various uses and often have both full forms (tonic forms) for more emphatic uses and reduced forms (atonic forms). Thus, once they are formed, pronouns tend to continue undergoing grammaticalization. One outcome can be affixation of the atonic forms to the verb. In many languages one can observe phonological similarity between the person–number agreement affixes on verbs and the personal pronouns. Consider the pronouns of Buriat (Altaic) in (170) and compare them to the suffixes for agreement in (171) (Poppe 1960).

(170)   Buriat: Personal pronouns, nominative case
          1st sg. *bi*   1st pl. *bide* or *bidener* (with plural suffix *–nar*)
          2nd sg. *si* 2nd pl. *ta*

There are no special third person pronouns, instead the demonstratives, 'this' and 'that' are used.

(171)   Subject agreement suffixes on verb: *jaba–* 'go' + *–na–* present tense
          1st sg. *jabana-b*   1st pl. *jabana-bdi*
          2nd sg. *jabana-s*   2nd pl. *jabana-t*
          3rd sg. *jabana*   3rd pl. *jabana-d* (cf. *ede* 'these')

7.6.   The development of definite and indefinite articles

Definite articles most commonly develop from demonstratives ('this' or 'that') and usually the distal demonstrative 'that'. This development can be observed in the Romance languages, where the definite article develops from the same demonstrative as the third person pronouns discussed above. Latin *ille, illa* 'that, m., f.' developed into the Spanish articles *el, la*, French *le, la*, Portuguese *o, a*, and their corresponding plural forms. The demonstrative originally had deictic or spatial meaning, distinguishing near (Latin *hic* [the speaker] and *iste* [near the addressee]) from far. When the demonstrative *ille* is used within a text to denote a referent that has previously been identified, the meaning is generalized from reference in space to reference within a discourse. From that the definite meaning, which indicates that the referent of the noun is known to the addressee, can arise. Similar developments have taken place in English (where *the* derived from *that*), in Bizkaian Basque, Vai (Niger-Congo), and Hungarian (Finno-Ugric) (Heine and Kuteva 2002).

Indefinite articles derive primarily from the numeral 'one', as seen in many European languages, such as English, German, Spanish, French, Greek, Albanian (Indo-European), Hungarian (Finno-Ugric), and also Turkish (Altaic), Lezgian (North Caucasian), Tamil (Dravidian), and Easter Island (Oceanic) (Heine and Kuteva 2002). In this process, the singular sense is usually maintained, but the contexts of use change from cases where the designation of one and only one referent is highlighted to one in which the speaker is introducing a new referent into the discourse. In some languages, evidence that the notion of 'one' has been generalized comes from the fact that the article may be pluralized, as in Spanish *unos, unas*. In English, there is considerable phonological reduction of the indefinite article *a/an* that distinguishes it from the numeral and indefinite pronoun *one*.

7.7.   The sources of adpositions

The term "adposition" is used to cover both prepositions (which occur before their noun object) and postpositions (which occur after their object). As we will see in the next chapter, postpositions generally occur in languages in which the nominal object precedes the verb (OV languages, such as Japanese), while prepositions occur in languages in which the object follows the verb (VO languages, such as English). Adpositions can derive either from noun or verb constructions.

The grams that derive from noun constructions start out with meanings that specify spatial positioning. They are usually in a construction with an established adposition and a noun in the genitive comparable to English complex prepositions such as *in front of* N. Crosslinguistic studies (Heine et al. 1991b; Svorou 1994) find that the nouns that grammaticalize in such constructions are most frequently nouns for human body parts such as head, eye, mouth, face, back, and others, but they can also be environmental landmarks such as sky, track, field, or doorway, or relational object-part names, such as side, top, middle, or interior (and some of these may derive from body-part terms). Here are some typical examples:

(172)   Abkhaz (North Caucasian)
        a-vok'zà   *a-ç'ə*
        the-station   3SGPRO-mouth
        'at the station'

        Car Nicoborese (Austro-asiatic)
        i   *kúːy* *řɔ́ːŋə*
        on head hill
        'on top of the hill'

        Bari (Nilo-Saharan)
        i *kɔmɔŋ ŋa kadi*
        in face   of house
        'in front of the house'

When body-part nouns are used they usually refer to the position of the noun on the human body: head > top, face > front, back > back, buttocks > bottom. However, there are some languages in which head > front, buttocks > back, back > top, and belly > bottom. In this case, the spatial relations of the part to the whole are based on the body of a four-legged animal (Heine et al. 1991b; Svorou 1994). Heine suggests that such *pastoralist* models are most common in cultures where animal husbandry is an important source for food.

Svorou (1994: 90) proposes that the stages of semantic change that body-part terms undergo in their evolution to spatial adpositions is as in (173):

(173)   body part term > relational   > location   > location
                           part of object   near object   in region of
                                        part   object part

This trajectory is illustrated with the English phrase *in front of*. The noun *front* was borrowed from Latin *frontis* meaning 'forehead' in the thirteenth century and a century after that was found in the phrase *the front of* to denote the foremost part of an object, such as a house, where the side with the door was considered the front. As I mentioned in Section 6.13, this semantic extension can be considered metaphorical, since the relational structure extends from one specific domain (the human body) to other domains. Later it was extended to denote any side, depending upon the speaker's perspective. In the seventeenth century it is found in the expression *in the front of* to indicate a location in contact with the front part of an object. In the eighteenth century *in front of* was finally used to indicate an area near the front of an object, taking on its current meaning. These last two steps may be considered instances of metonymical change (by which the part comes to stand for the whole), as the region indicated expands from an object being a part of an entity to being in contact with it and, finally, to being in a region adjacent to it.

Another source of adpositions are verbs, especially in serial verb constructions. Recall that languages with serial verbs allow sentences in which two verbs that share the same subject can be sequenced without added markers. Givón (1975) discusses this source for Yoruba (Niger-Congo) where the verb *fi* 'take' becomes an instrumental marker as in (174) and then generalizes, as in (175):

(174)   *ma fi   àdá   gé igi*
             I   took machete cut tree
             'I cut the tree with the machete'

(175)   *mo fi   ọgbọn gé igi*
             I   took clever cut tree
             'I cut the tree cleverly'

Also in Yoruba the verb *fún* 'give' is used to signal a beneficiary, as in these examples:

(176)   *mo   mú   ìwé   wá   fún   ọ*
             I   took   book   came   gave   you
             'I brought the book for you'

(177)   *mo   sọ   fún   ọ*
             I   said   gave   you
             'I said to you'

Prepositions derived from verbs can also be found in other languages, for instance the Malayo-Polynesian language To'aba'ita discussed in Lichtenberk 1991. In fact, English also has some prepositions derived from a present participle + noun object construction. The preposition *during* as in *during the night* is the present participle form of the obsolete verb *duren* 'to last, to endure'. Another present participle that may be becoming a preposition is *considering* as in *considering the cost* or *following*, as in *following dinner*.

7.8.   The development of case

As we saw in examples (174)–(177) markers of grammatical relations, such as case markers, also arise from the grammaticalization of adpositions. Givón 1975 points out that an accusative case marker in Yoruba probably came from a verb meaning 'get' or 'take' even though no such meaning is discernible today.

(178)   *bólá   gbà   adé   gbó*
         Bola   ACC   Ade   believe
         'Bola believed Ade'

Another source for accusative case is a long chain of grammaticalization starting with a preposition meaning 'towards' or 'to' (allative case). In Latin the preposition *ad* first meant 'towards' (as in *going towards Rome*) and then 'to' (as in *going to Rome*). Later, in Spanish it came to be used to indicate dative case (the case of the indirect object) as in *dió el libro a Juan* 'gave 3rd sg. the book to John'. In the next step, the preposition *a* is used with direct objects if they are human and definite, as in *ví a Juan* 'I saw John'. At this point, *a* marks accusative under certain circumstances, but it is spreading to a more general use (Company Company 2002). Other languages in which an allative becomes a dative are Tamil (Dravidian) and Lezgian (North Caucasian). Another case where a dative comes to mark the patient (direct object) is Dolakha-Newari (Tibeto-Burman). Also, the English object pronoun *him* was formerly a dative pronoun (Heine and Kuteva 2002). Other sources of case markers will be discussed in the next chapter in relation to the development of passive and ergative constructions.

7.9.   Discourse markers and subjectification

Discourse markers are usually outside the clause or main predication and indicate the speaker's attitude towards the material in the clause. Discourse markers derive diachronically from verbs or even from whole clauses, but as with other sequences undergoing grammaticalization, they lose their syntactic and morphological flexibility, become fixed, undergo phonetic reduction, and take on pragmatic functions. Some English examples are phrases such as *you know* and *I think*. The example we will examine here is from Spanish: the phrase *dice que* 'say 3rd sg. that' becomes *dizque*, a marker of doubt expressed by the speaker about the proposition. The following examples from Company Company 2006 show first the ordinary verbal use of *dice que* in (179), then a case in which what is said may not be true (180) followed by examples where *diz que* comes to express some speaker doubt (181) and finally a case (182) where *dizque* is used twice; the second time as a pure discourse marker expressing doubt about the preceding statement.

(179)   *Ya Plinio, en su Historia Natural, dice que las palmas*
          datileras dan en las costa de España un fruto.
          'Pliny, in his Natural History, has already said that on
          the coast of Spain date palms give a fruit.'

(180)   *Se dice que la prosperidad material trae la cultura y la*
          dignificación del pueblo, mas lo que realmente sucede...
          'It is said that material well-being brings with it culture
          and dignity of the people, but what really happens...'

(181)   *Se trajo todo al instante y con estos y otros auxilios, diz*
          que se alivió el enfermo.
          'Everything was brought at once and with these
          and other remedies it is said that the sick one got better.'

(182)   *Sí, sí, dizque estamos progresando, dizque.*
          'Yes, yes, they say things are getting better,
          supposedly.'

When *dizque* is used as a discourse marker, it is fixed in the third person present form and cannot be conjugated. Now it is syntactically autonomous, too, in that it does not take an object for the complementizer *que*. It has also undergone phonetic reduction, losing the final /e/ of the verb. In this function it is written as one word.

Discourse markers change their meaning and function by becoming more subjective (Traugott and Dasher 2002; Company Company 2006). As *dizque* changed from a lexical verb + complementizer, it took on the function of expressing an evidential function, of attributing a statement to other parties, and it also came to express some doubt on the part of the speaker. This change occurs as the phrase is used frequently in cases where indeed the speaker has some doubts and the listener then attributes the speaker's use of the phrase to indicate doubt. So the greater subjectivity of the discourse marker function is due to an inference by the listener that if the speaker uses this form, s/he is expressing some doubt about the truth of the statement. Thus, while the subjectivity is attributed to the speaker, it is actually the listener that adds in this meaning because listeners are always trying to understand the subjective opinion of the speaker.

Another discourse marker that has been studied extensively by Traugott and Dasher 2002 is English *indeed*. OE *dede* was a noun related to the verb *to do* meaning 'action'. The PDE meaning of *deed* is not too different from this older meaning. As a noun it could take modifiers just like any other noun and could serve as the subject or object of a verb. It also occurred in prepositional phrases, and *in dede* was such a phrase, which meant 'in action', often used in contrast to *in speche* 'in speech'. From this sense it evolved into a meaning of 'in truth' in the fourteenth century (since observed actions verify the truth more than words). Our current usage of *indeed* as an emphatic derives directly from this use, as in this example:

(183)   *I mean, that would be very exciting, indeed.* (COCA 2012)

Traugott and Dasher find that epistemic markers high on the scale of certitude are often used in contexts in which one statement contrasts with another, as if the statement modified by *indeed* were not expected. In the following sequence, it appears that there was an assumption that poltergeists were the only kind of ghost.

(184)   *Polter-geist means noisy geist, in ghost language. It's*
          just mischievous. Indeed, there are many other kinds of geists
          out there in the spirit world. (COCA 2012)

This use states a relation between two statements, and from this usage, according to Traugott and Dasher, we get a discourse marker usage in which *indeed* occurs at the beginning of a clause that adds more information and more punch to the preceding clause as in this contemporary example.

(185)   *First of all, it creates not one new job. Indeed, it will hit*
          some small businesses. (COCA 2012)

So again we see that a phrase with original lexical items with fairly concrete meaning can undergo subjectification and grammaticalization to become markers of the speaker's evaluation of the truth of the proposition or the speaker's positioning of the proposition in discourse in relation to other statements.

Some argue that the development of discourse markers is similar to, but not identical with, grammaticalization (Company Company 2002). One apparent difference is that the discourse marker is outside the clause, rather than inside it as tense and aspect markers are. And one might argue that it is not part of a construction. On this point, though, one could consider the construction to be the discourse marker plus the clause it modifies, so it is just a very inclusive construction. Also, discourse markers are characterized by subjectification, which is not always present in the grammaticalization of other constructions.

7.10.   The end of the process of grammaticalization

It is reasonable to ask what happens to grams at the end of the long process of grammaticalization. In general we can say that as grams become more and more bleached, the tendency is to replace them with more recently grammaticalized items that have somewhat fuller meaning. This replacement process can move very slowly, so that it often happens that older and newer grams fulfilling similar functions co-exist in a language. For instance, OE had case suffixes for nominative, accusative, dative, and genitive, but it also had developed prepositions that signaled many locative relations in conjunction with the case suffixes. Thus *to* is used with the dative case for NPs that are goals, as in (186) (Traugott 1972).

(186) | *his* | *suna* | *twegen* | *mon* | *brohte* | *to* | *þæm* | *cyninge* |
          |--------|--------|----------|-------|----------|------|-------|-----------|
          | his | sons | two | one | brought | to | that-DAT | king-DAT |
          'someone brought his two sons to that king'

Prepositions and case suffixes co-existed in a similar way in Latin. In English and in Latin the case suffixes were gradually lost with word order signaling subject and object relations and prepositions taking over other functions. Some researchers attribute this loss to phonetic reduction that eventually obliterated the suffixes; for instance, in English final vowel contrasts were lost when unstressed vowels were reduced to schwa and final consonants were deleted (Vennemann 1975). However, we should not lose sight of the fact that these highly grammaticalized suffixes had also lost most of their meaning as well. So in this case in the end of the process, both form and meaning are so reduced that they are both lost.

Sometimes when a gram is replaced by a more recently developed gram, the older one stays in the language, usually in a more marginal function. In American English, *will* and *be going to* are frequently used to express future (as discussed in Chapter 6) and the older future, *shall*, is much less frequently used, and it is rarely now used with future meaning. Its current uses reflect some of its earlier distribution because *shall* has always had a split in function depending upon the person of the subject: the first person is the only one with future meaning; when used in the second or third person, its older obligation meaning has been retained. So today we find *shall* used in the statement of laws *Congress shall make no law...* and also in Biblical language. We also find it used with first person, especially in the plural in questions, such as *shall we open it up?* and in certain formulae, such as *shall we say?*

Another possible development at the end of a long path of grammaticalization is that the very bleached out or generalized meaning of a gram takes on new meanings from the contexts in which it is used. As reported in Bybee et al. 1994: 230–234, there are cases where an old present tense has been replaced by a grammaticalizing present progressive. For example, in Armenian and Cairene Arabic, an expanding progressive has taken over most of the present indicative uses in main clauses and assertions, leaving the older present in contexts such as purpose clauses, adverbial clauses after certain temporal conjunctions, and certain complement clauses. As a result, what used to be a simple present or imperfective indicative is now used in contexts that are often associated with the subjunctive across languages. Indeed, Fairbanks and Stevick 1958 describe the Modern Armenian indicative form in question as having the function 'present optative'. Apparently, this present inflection took on the meaning of the constructions it occurred in and carried this non-assertive meaning with it to its use in main clauses.

A final repository for old grams is the lexicon, where bits and pieces of old grams augment lexical items. For instance, the final *-om* on *seldom* was a dative plural case marker from OE on the noun *selda-* 'rare' (Hopper 1994). A more systematic case concerns the end state of the development of definite articles. Greenberg 1978b argues that noun markers are the fossilized version of definite articles, spread to almost all uses of the noun. He gives the example Hausa (Chadic) in which all nouns end in a vowel and in most cases the vowel is long. He suspects that the long vowel is the relic of a definite article suffix that generalized to almost all cases. The nouns that do not have a long vowel are proper nouns (which are already specific and usually do not take articles) and nouns in adverbial expressions, both locative and temporal, such as ʔà ʔídó 'in the eye' compared to ʔídòò 'eye', and words like jíyà 'yesterday' which end in short vowels (Greenberg 1978b: 71–72).

7.11.   Conclusion

The examples in this chapter are meant to demonstrate how pervasive the grammaticalization process is, leading to the development of grams for all aspects of grammar. In every case, the mechanisms cited in Chapter 6 apply to different lexical material and different constructions with a similar effect: the creation of grammatical morphemes that do the work of grammar, whether within the verb phrase, the noun phrase, or the discourse as a whole. The examples also demonstrate that very similar paths of change (for both form and meaning) exist for many unrelated languages, showing that the process is not restricted to languages of a certain type, but rather that the potential for grammaticalization resides in the social and cognitive context in which language is used, which is similar across cultures.

Suggested reading

Bybee, J.L., Perkins, R.D., and Pagliuca, W., 1994. *The evolution of grammar: tense, aspect and modality in the languages of the world*, Chicago: University of Chicago Press.

Heine, B. and Kuteva, T., 2002. *World lexicon of grammaticalization*, Cambridge: Cambridge University Press.

Hopper, P.J., 1994. Phonogenesis. In W. Pagliuca (ed.) *Perspectives on grammaticalization*, Amsterdam: John Benjamins, pp. 29–45.

Questions for discussion

1.   What are the diachronic factors that determine differences and similarities of grammatical categories across languages? How do the French and Spanish 'have done' constructions differ from one another? How does the Slavic perfective differ from these?

2.   If you have learned a language with person–number agreement on verbs, see if you can find any similarities between these affixes and the personal pronouns in the language. For example, you might consider Latin.

3.   Check *shall* in COCA and compare its frequency to *will*. Also check the contexts in which *shall* is now used, to see if it concurs with the description in the text.

4.   A lot of information about grammaticalization can be found in the *Oxford English Dictionary* (probably available online from your university library). Check the entry for *however* to see how the current meaning and use of this word evolved over time.

8   Syntactic change: the development and change of constructions

8.1.   Introduction

Syntactic change will be treated here as consisting of changes in syntactic constructions, including the creation of new constructions and changes in constructions once they come into existence. The term *construction* will be used here both in its very traditional use, where one speaks of "the passive construction" or a "relative clause construction" and also in the way it is currently used in syntactic analysis by linguists such as Goldberg, for whom a construction is a form–meaning relation (Goldberg 1995, 2006). For Goldberg, words and morphemes as well as phrases and syntactic patterns are form–meaning mappings, but in this chapter, we will consider syntactic patterns that are conventionalized. Such patterns have slots or positions within them that can be filled by a range of different words or morphemes and are thus *schematic*. So, for example, a prepositional phrase is a construction consisting of a preposition and an NP object. Both positions are schematic in the sense that many different items can occur in each *slot*. The preposition slot, say in English, is schematic since any preposition can occur in it. The NP slot is even more schematic because the range of possible NPs in English is enormous. Viewing a construction as a form–meaning mapping means that we take constructions to convey an overall meaning that goes beyond just the meaning taken from the words and morphemes that comprise them.

The phenomena treated under syntactic change are intertwined with grammaticalization in two ways. First, many constructions have specific grammatical morphemes in them and they have developed by the process of grammaticalization. Thus, all the prepositions found in English (*in, to, of, behind, below, after*, and so on) have undergone grammaticalization giving rise to new preposition constructions. When a unit or set of units changes category, we can speak of syntactic change. For instance, if a verb in construction with another verb becomes an auxiliary, not only has grammaticalization taken place, but syntactic change has also occurred. Second, the creation of new constructions is driven by some of the same processes that drive grammaticalization: chunking, category expansion, generalization, and inferencing. Thus many of the themes of this chapter are familiar from the last two chapters.

In addition, here we treat word-order typology and the phenomenon of word-order change, reviewing some of the accounts for the way a language can change from one word-order type to another. While change in word-order type is not common, it has

161

apparently occurred in the Indo-European language family and thus has received a lot of attention from historical linguists, especially in the twentieth century.

8.2.   From paratactic to syntactic

In his 1979 book *On Understanding Grammar*, T. Givón made a case for the development of grammar out of discourse by showing that loosely joined strings of words (paratactic combinations) over time become more tightly joined together to form syntactic units. In this connection, Givón proposed his famous cline, saying that change occurs in "cyclic waves" repeating the following pattern (1979: 209):

(187)   Discourse → Syntax → Morphology → Morphophonemics → Zero

In our discussion of grammaticalization we have dealt with the shift from syntax to morphology, as when periphrastic expressions become affixes. In Chapter 4 we saw examples of the development of morpho-phonemics, and at the end of Chapter 7 we saw briefly how inflections can disappear. Here we will see examples of the first step, in which words that are loosely strung together in discourse, with repetition, come to be more tightly joined into conventionalized constructions, with meanings that are different from just the sum of the meanings of the words.

8.2.1.   Topics become subjects

One example that Givón gives that exemplifies the change from discourse to syntax concerns a topicalization construction in the Bantu language Kimbundu, in which the object NP can occur at the beginning of the sentence. In the following, examples (188) and (189) show the usual word order and agreement, and (190) shows the topicalized object NP (Givón 1976).

(188)   *aana*   *a-mono*   *Nzua*
children   3PL-SUBJ-saw   John
'The children saw John'

(189)   *mwana*   *u-mono*   *Nzua*
child   3SG-SUBJ-saw   John
'The child saw John'

(190)   *Nzua,*   *aana*   *a-mu-mono*
John   children   3PL-SUBJ-3SG-OBJ-saw
'John, the children saw him'

Example (190) can be regarded as a discourse pattern in the sense that the appearance of the object at the beginning of the sentence produces a loosely joined or paratactic structure whose function is to draw attention to the object, *Nzua*, as the topic of the discourse.

Throughout this chapter I will make reference to studies that rely on a discourse notion of "topic". Despite many attempts, there is no general agreement on the meaning of this term, nor have there been enough studies of how constructions function in discourse context. For our purposes we will assume the topic is what the sentence is about, which is determined by the discourse context in that the topic has in most cases already been identified in the discourse. The topic is considered distinct from the comment, which is the new information presented in the sentence. Be aware that these terms may be used in different ways in different studies. Note also that the topic is not always the subject of the clause: the subject usually has a syntactic rather than pragmatic definition: it might trigger verb agreement, it may have a distinctive case marking, and it may occupy a certain position in the clause. In the cases we study here and in subsequent sections, we see a trend for the topic to become the subject.

In Kimbundu, other examples show that this originally loose structure has become "syntacticized" or made into a more cohesive construction that has the function of a passive in Kimbundu. In this construction the original 3rd plural subject prefix *a*– has become fixed as an invariant marker – probably developing from an impersonal 'they' to a marker of passive. This is shown in (191) and (192) by the fact that the *a*– occurs even when the agent of the verb is not 3rd plural.

(191) *Nzua   a-mu-mono   kwa   meme*
       John   a-3SG-saw   by   me
       'John was seen by me'

(192) *Nzua   a-mu-mono   kwa   mwana*
       John   a-3SG-saw   by   child
       'John was seen by the child'

(193) *meme   a-ngi-mono   kwa   Nzua*
       I   a-1SG-saw   by   John
       'I was seen by John'

As seen in (193), the former topicalized object 'I' is now functioning as the subject and controls subject agreement, making the construction a passive construction. In addition, the agent of the verb, if added, is marked by the preposition *kwa* 'by'. So from a loosely joined discourse sequence, over time, with repetition, a new more tightly joined construction has developed. In the course of this development, a new gram has emerged: the 3rd plural prefix has become a marker of the passive construction. This type of change is often referred to as "reanalysis" because of the extreme shift from a 3rd plural prefix to a passive prefix. Of course, it is the context of the whole construction and the uses to which it is put that determine how this prefix was reinterpreted.

8.2.2.   Two clauses into one

In Sections 6.8, 7.7, and 7.8 we saw how serial verb constructions (two verbs sequenced with the same subject) can give rise to complementizers, adpositions, and case markers. Many researchers have further noted that serial verb constructions derive historically from conjoined clauses that share the same subject as well as the same tense, aspect, mood, and polarity (affirmative/ negative). Lord 1993 describes the evidence for this development in the Kwa languages as well as other languages of West Africa. First, she points out that a marker (*de*) in the Twi language (Kwa, Niger-Congo) with a wide range of grammatical functions including the marking of direct object, was used as a verb in conjoined sentences such as these reported in 1881 and 1875:

(194)   ɔ-n-dé   apèmpensí nà´   ɛ-pè   n'-ádé
         3SG-NEG-use extortion   CONJ 3SG-seek 3SGPOSS-thing
         'It is not his manner or way to enrich himself by extortion'

(195)   anoma de ako-ne-aba   na enwene   berebuw
         bird   *de* going-and-coming   CONJ 3SG-weave nest
         'By going and coming a bird weaves its nest'

These examples show that *de* was a verb at one time as it could occur in clauses conjoined to other clauses with full verbs by the conjunction *na*, which like English *and* can conjoin parallel clauses. Second, Lord points out that these examples also represent a possible source structure for the serial construction because the conjoined clauses are not parallel pragmatically, but rather express other functions, e.g. means-end and action-result, which are typical functions for serial verb constructions. Lord presents the following diachronic progression of sentence types, as in (196), which shows that the conjunction is lost first, then the subject pronoun is omitted, leaving in (c) only the two verbs in sequence.

(196) a.   NP   VP   CONJ   NP   VP
      b.   NP   VP   ∅   NP   VP
      c.   NP   VP   ∅   ∅   VP

An example of (c) from Twi with *de* functioning as a verb is:

(197)   ɔ   de   sika   ba-ae
         he   *de* money   come-PAST
         'He came with money'

So the changes described in (196) have the effect of reducing two full clauses to a much more tightly joined structure. In the case of (a) there are two conjoined clauses, in (b) there are two clauses juxtaposed, but in (c) there is a different construction, which could be argued to be only one clause. As we have noted in other chapters, it is common for one of the verbs in (c) to further grammaticalize and lose its status as a verb, and that is what has happened to *de* in Twi. This example, then, spans the diachronic sequence from two conjoined clauses to a single clause.

There are also different sorts of examples that show the development of two clauses into one. Heine et al. 1991a report that in Teso (a Nilo-Saharan language of western Kenya and eastern Uganda) the negative construction (198) derived from a construction with a main clause and subordinate clause, as in (199).

(198)   *mam petero   e-koto   ekiŋok*
          not Peter   3SG-want   dog
          'Peter does not want a dog'

(199)   *e-mam   petero   e-koto   ekiŋok*
          3SG is not   Peter (who)   3SG-want   dog
          'It is not Peter who wants a dog'

The sentence in (199) consists of the main verb *–mam*, which originally meant 'not to be', with Peter as its object and a relative clause modifying Peter. In the current construction, as in (198), the verb *–mam* has lost its subject marking and has become a negative particle. The result is that the negative sentence consists of one clause rather than two. As this happens, what was formerly the subordinate clause has become the main clause.

8.2.3.   Reorganization within the clause: how ergatives develop ▰▰▰

As our first example in this chapter we discussed a construction in Kimbundu that started as a topicalization construction and has now become a passive, due to the reanalysis of the topic as the subject of the sentence. In this section we discuss a development that produces a new organization of arguments in the clause: the ergative construction. There are two principal types of case marking or alignment: accusative and ergative. Accusative marking is familiar from most European languages; the subject of both transitive and intransitive verbs behaves the same and is distinguished from the object of transitive verbs. In case marking, the subject case is the nominative and the direct object case is the accusative. For instance, English *he* and *him* are distinguished by case. *He* is used for the subject of both transitive (*he saw the deer*) and intransitive clauses (*he walked away*) and *him* is used only for the object (*the deer saw him*). In addition, in languages such as English the subject of both transitives and intransitives behave the same, for instance, in triggering verb agreement in the present tense. In contrast, ergative alignment means that the subject of the intransitive and the object of the transitive behave the same, for example in their case marking or lack of it. Together they constitute the absolutive and contrast with the subject of the transitive verb, which is the ergative and often has distinctive marking by case affix or a particle.

Ergative constructions occur in many of the world's languages. Often a language has an ergative construction as well as a nominative/accusative construction. These 'split ergative' systems give us some clues into how ergatives develop diachronically. For example, in Hindi (Indo-Iranian), clauses in the imperfective aspect have a nominative/accusative pattern, as in (200), where it can be seen that the transitive subject has no marker, but the object has the marker *–ko* if it is definite and animate. In addition, the verb agrees with the agent in gender and number, as in (200c) and (200d) (Allen 1951, Anderson 1977).

(200) a. *laṛkā   kutte-ko   dekhtā   hai*
      boy   dog-DEF-ACC   see-MASC-SG   AUX-SG
      'The boy sees the dog'

   b. *laṛkā   kutte   dekhtā   hai*
      boy   dog-PL   see-MASC-SG   AUX-SG
      'The boy sees some dogs'

   c. *laṛkī   kuttā   dekhtī   hai*
      girl   dog   see-FEM-SG   AUX-SG
      'The girl sees a dog'

   d. *laṛke   kuttā   dehkte   hāi*
      boy   dog   see-PL   AUX-PL
      'The boys see a dog'

In contrast, clauses in the perfective aspect have an ergative pattern, as shown in (201), where it can be seen that the transitive subject is marked with the particle *–ne* and the verb agrees with the object.

(201) a. *laṛke-ne   kuttā   dekhā   hai*
      boy-ERG   dog   see-PTCP   AUX-SG
      'The boy has seen a dog'

   b. *laṛkõ-ne   kuttā   dekhā   hai*
      boy-PL-ERG   dog   see-PTCP   AUX-SG
      'The boys have see a dog'

   c. *laṛkī-ne   kuttā   dekhā   hai*
      girl-ERG   dog   see-PTCP   AUX-SG
      'The girl has seen a dog'

   d. *laṛke-ne   billī   dekhī   hai*
      boy-ERG   cat (fem)   see-PTCP-FEM   AUX-SG
      'The boy has seen a cat'

   e. *laṛke-ne   kutte   dekhe   hāi*
      boy-ERG   dog-PL   see-PTCP-PL   AUX-PL
      'The boy has seen some dogs'

Intransitive clauses are treated the same way in both aspects, that is, the subject is not marked and the verb agrees with it.

The history of Hindi shows how this situation arose. The perfective arose from the grammaticalization of a periphrastic construction that used the verbal adjective or participle form plus a copula that had a passive sense. This passive sense described a present state that was the result of a past action or a resultative meaning. As we saw in the last chapter, resultative meaning tends to develop into anterior and further into perfective. Because the perfective developed from a passive, the notional object appears in the nominative, and the agent of the action has a special marker *–ne*. Thus, along with the grammaticalization of the perfective came a change from a passive to an ergative, but only in the perfective. The result is an ergative/accusative system that is split on the basis of aspect (Anderson 1977; Garrett 1990; Harris and Campbell 1995).

Another interesting case occurs in the Polynesian languages, where the East-ern Polynesian languages, such as Maori and Hawaiian use accusative alignment, while some of the other languages of the family, particularly the Tongic and Samoic-Outlier languages such as Samoan, have ergative alignment. From the existing languages, researchers hope to reconstruct the earlier patterns. While there is still debate on whether the earlier language was accusative or ergative (see Ball 2007 and Otsuka 2011), the proposal by Chung 1977 will be presented here. She argues that the evidence points to a change within the latter languages in which a passive construction develops into an ergative construction, as in the Hindi case, but without consequences for the aspectual system. The Eastern Polynesian languages, which are accusative, have the pattern shown in (202). Note that all of these languages are VSO and have tense and aspect marked in a particle preceding the verb and case marking in a preposition. DO stands for direct object.

(202)   Accusative languages
         Tense   Verb   Subj   (intransitive)
         Tense   Verb   Subj   *i* DO   (transitive)

An example of a transitive sentence from Maori is in (203).

(203)   *Ka*   *inu*   *te*   *tangata*   *i*   *te*   *wai*
         TNS   drink   the   man   ACC   the   water
         'The man drank the water'

Here one can observe that the DO is marked by a preposed *i*.

In the ergative languages of the group, the main pattern is shown in (204). This pattern applies to transitive verbs whose object is affected by the action of the verb.

(204)   Ergative languages:
         Tense   Verb   Subj   (intransitive)
         Tense   Verb   *e* Subj   DO   (transitive)

An example of a sentence with a transitive verb from Samoan is in (205). We see that the expression of transitive sentences is quite different than in Maori, and the ergative NP is marked by a preposed *e*.

(205)   *'Ua*   *tipi-(ina)*   *e*   *le*   *lo'omatua*   *le*   *'ulu*
         TNS   cut-PASS   ERG   the   old-woman   the   breadfruit
         'The old woman cut the breadfruit'

To understand the development of the ergative construction in Samoan, consider the passive construction in Maori and the other accusative languages, as shown in (206).

(206)   Passive:
         Tense   Verb-C*ia*   *e* Agent   Subject

Here is a Maori example:

(207)   *Ka   inu-mia   te   wai   e   te tangata*
         TNS   drink-PASS   the   water   AGT   the man
         'The water was drunk by the man'

The passive in the accusative languages is quite similar to the ergative in the ergative languages. Chung argues that the passive is the diachronic source for the ergative construction. The only difference between the two constructions is that the passive suffix on the verb is variably deleted in the ergative construction and the ergative NP precedes the absolutive in the ergative construction while the agent follows the object in the passive construction.

The ergative languages also have an alternate pattern used with a restricted class of verbs which do not have an affected object (verbs of emotion, perception, and communication) called the middle, as shown with the Samoan example in (208).

(208)   *'Ua 'alo   le fafine   i   le teine*
         TNS ignore the woman ACC the girl
         'The woman ignored the girl'

Comparing (208) to (203) it is clear that the middle construction in the ergative languages corresponds to the accusative construction in the accusative languages. Thus Chung's argument is that passive constructions such as are found in Maori have evolved into the ergative construction in languages such as Samoan, where it is used with transitive verbs that have an affected direct object. Other transitive verbs still use the older accusative construction (now called the middle).

In most languages passive constructions are used much less frequently than active constructions. Passives are used if the speaker chooses to frame the clause from the perspective of the semantic object of the verb. However, Chung notes that in Maori the passive construction is very frequent. If this passive construction becomes frequent enough to be the normal way of expressing transitive situations, then the language begins to shift toward having basic ergative alignment. This has apparently occurred in Samoan, along with a trend towards using the verb stem without the passive suffix. In addition, the ergative construction in Samoan is extending to verbs that more traditionally were found in the middle construction. Chung reports that today many younger speakers use a wide range of verbs either in the middle (as in 209), as is expected, or the ergative (as in 210), which would be an innovation. Samoan, then, also has a split ergative system based on the lexical verb.

(209)   *na   tofo   'oia   i   le   kuka*
         PAST   taste   he   DO   the   cooking
         'He tasted the cooking'

(210)   *na   tofo   e   ia   le   kuka*
         PAST   taste   ERG   he   the   cooking
         'He tasted the cooking'

In this case it is argued that the ergative construction developed out of a passive construction. (There are also other sources for ergatives; see Harris and Campbell 1995 chapter 9.) The accusative and passive constructions co-exist in the language, but as the passive comes to be used more frequently it can become the more basic construction. It can also extend to use with more and more transitive verbs, gradually replacing the older accusative construction.

8.3.   Development and change in constructions

In the previous two sections we have seen several examples of the way more loosely joined word combinations develop into more tightly organized constructions. This process has recently been called *constructionalization* (Noël 2007). Once constructions are formed, they go through changes, which can include expanding their range of use, expanding the set of lexical items that occur in them, as well as decreasing their range of use when other constructions compete with them. It is also possible for constructions to completely disappear from a language, as other constructions take over their functions. These stages in the life cycle of constructions will be discussed in the following subsections.

8.3.1.   How constructions begin and expand

Some of the constructions discussed so far (topicalization into passives, passives into ergatives) originate in discourse-based strategies for topicalizing or positioning the speaker's perspective on one or another noun in the clause. However, there are lots of types of constructions and many of these involve particular lexical items or combinations of lexical items. The study of the origins of these types of constructions is still in its infancy, but historical information on a few of them has been presented in the literature. In this section, we will see an example of a productive Spanish construction that developed from a simple combination of a verb and an adjective.

In Modern Spanish there are several verbs that can be used in a construction with an adjective to mean 'become, enter into a state'. Wilson 2009 traced the development of one of these constructions, *quedarse* + ADJECTIVE, from its beginning in the twelfth century to the current era. The verb involved is the reflexive form of *quedar* meaning 'to remain'. It first appears in a construction meaning 'to become' in the twelfth century. Note that in this early example (211), either the notion of remaining or becoming could have been expressed.

(211)   *E el conde quando vio que de otra manera no podia ser sino como queria*
          el comun delos romeros no quiso ay quedar solo & fazia lo mejor &
          cogio sus tiendas & fue se empos delos otros.
          'And when the count saw that there could be no other way than the
          common wishes of the pilgrims to Rome wanted it, (he) didn't want
          to be left alone and did his best and gathered his tents and went after the
          others.'   (Gran conquista de Ultramar, anon., thirteenth century)

In twelfth- and thirteenth-century texts there are only a few examples of this construction, but by the seventeenth century it had become very productive and was used with a range of adjectives. Wilson studied how this expansion occurred over the centuries. He found that the construction occurs with certain adjectives as conventionalized collocations; for instance, *quedarse solo* 'end up alone' is the most frequent combination in twelfth-century texts examined. The construction occurs only twelve times, but three of these are *quedarse solo*, and all other combinations occur only once. This same combination continues to occur throughout the centuries. For these reasons it could be considered conventionalized. The construction also occurs with some other adjectives, which may or may not be conventionalized. To say that a word sequence is conventionalized, or a collocation or prefabricated sequence, means that this word combination is the idiomatic or native-like way to express an idea (Pawley and Hodgetts Syder 1983; Erman and Warren 2000). Thus I translate *quedarse solo* with 'end up alone' in English because that is the conventionalized expression in English, rather than the semantically coherent but rather odd 'become alone'.

The importance of the conventionalized VERB + ADJECTIVE combinations is that they serve as a semantic model for other adjectives that are drawn into the construction. As an illustration, in the fourteenth and fifteenth centuries, examples such as (212) appear. Wilson argues that, in this example, being left widowed or becoming a widower occurs with *quedar* because it is semantically similar to the earlier, conventionalized and entrenched expression for being left alone (remember, there are other verbs of becoming that it could have occurred with).

(212)   *Enla tierra de ansaj avia vn potente rrey al qual no avia quedado sy no*
vna hija la qual avia avido de su muger que enel ora del parto murio
& quedo biudo mas el rrey hjzo criar la hija muy honorable mente.
'In the land of Ansaj there was a powerful king to whom no one was left
but a daughter who he had had from his woman who in the moment of
birth died & (he) became widowed, but the king had the daughter raised
honorably.'   (Historia de la Linda Melosina, anon., fifteenth century)

Also during this period, the adjective *huérfano* 'orphaned' is used with *quedar* as well as a series of prepositional phrases with *sin* 'without', e.g. *sin heredero* 'without heirs', *sin armas* 'without weapons', *sin pluma* 'without a pen', and even some more abstract notions, such as *sin dubda* 'without doubt' and *sin pena* 'without grief'. It appears, then, that in this period, the category of adjective or prepositional phrase that can be used with *quedar(se)* expands because of semantic similarity with the early expression with *solo*, which gives rise to expressions describing the loss of a family member, then other physical deprivations, such as lacking weapons to more abstract expressions. Thus a more general construction is formed from a beginning with a single entrenched example. It is also interesting that this conventionalized expression *quedarse solo* is still quite frequent in the twentieth and twenty-first centuries.

Other conventionalized collocations develop with *quedarse* + ADJECTIVE. In the fifteenth century, the expression *quedarse confuso* 'become confused' is found, and by the seventeenth century there are quite a number of adjectives in this semantic domain that are used with *quedarse*: *suspenso* 'astonished', *embelesado* 'captivated', and *absorto* 'engrossed', for instance. The category centered on the expression of surprise expands even more in the nineteenth century and still exists today. The conventionalized way of saying 'to be surprised' in Modern Spanish is *quedarse sorprendido*.

This construction in Modern Spanish is quite productive, meaning that it can apply to new items. It also has a very high type frequency, which means that it occurs with a large number of adjective types (different adjectives). Most of these adjectives, however, belong to one of several semantic clusters, so that the productivity of the construction is highly constrained semantically. Interestingly, it appears that this construction was more productive in the seventeenth and eighteenth centuries than it is now. What is currently restricting its use is the development of other verbs of becoming, which have taken over some of the functions of the *quedarse* construction: one such construction is *ponerse* + ADJECTIVE.

Another construction whose origin and development have been studied across time is the *way*-construction in English, as shown here (Israel 1996):

(213)   *The wounded soldiers limped their way across the field.*

Israel notes that this construction with *way* was a specific instance of a more general construction in Middle English which he describes as the *go-your-path*-construction, because nouns other than *way* could be used in it, as in these two examples:

(214)   *To madian lond, wente he his ride* (c. 1250)
          'He rode off to Madian land'

(215)   *Tho wente he his strete, tho flewe I doun.* (1481)
          'He went straight while I hurried down.'

The most common noun to be used in this construction was *way* and the most common verb was *wend* 'to go turningly'. In fact, *wend one's way* is still a frequent idiomatic expression in English. Here are other ME examples:

(216)   *The kyng took a laghtre, and wente his way.* (1412)
          'The king laughed and went on his way.'

(217)   *Now wyl I go wend my way With sore syeng and wel away.* (1450)
          'Now I will go wend my way With bitter song and well away.'

In the nineteenth century, expansions of this construction led to its use with verbs expressing the manner of motion, such as those expressing difficult or laborious motion as in (218) or a winding tortuous path as in (219).

(218)   *She started up, and fumbled her way down the dark stairs.* (1801)

(219)   *Mr. Bantam corkscrewed his way through the crowd.* (1837)

A further extension occurred at the end of the nineteenth century, when verbs expressing the noise associated with a motion began to occur, as shown in (220).

(220)   *There is a full stream that tumbles into the sea ... after singing its way down from the heights of Burrule.* (1890)

These observations do not exhaust the story of the *way*-construction (see Israel 1996 for the whole story), but we can pause here to draw some conclusions about this case and the case of *quedarse* + ADJECTIVE in Spanish. What we have observed in these examples is constructionalization – the creation of a new construction. Two aspects of this process are the fixing of parts of the construction, the verb *quedarse* in the first example and *way* in the second example, and the expansion of other parts of the construction. The expansion in the first example occurs when the category of adjectives that is used with *quedarse* expands and in the second construction when the set of verbs used in the construction expands. This later process is called *schematization* because it results in the construction covering more distinct lexical items, thereby creating a schematic category (Noël 2007). In both cases examined here, there are semantic constraints on the schematic category. Categories have degrees of schematicity. If the category is very broad in its semantic definition (verb of motion) it is highly schematic; but if it has fewer and more similar members (verb of winding motion) it is less schematic.

As mentioned earlier, researchers are just now beginning to investigate the question of how new constructions get started. Often it is difficult to find the actual starting point, but it is possible to find constructions in early stages of development and to follow that development. Corpus-based studies are particularly interesting in this regard because they can reveal the expanding and contracting environments in which constructions are used. As we see in the next section, it is also important to consider what other constructions are serving similar functions at any period in time.

8.3.2.   Layering and competition between constructions

In almost every example we have discussed in this chapter so far, the situation described includes more than one construction in competition for the expression of very similar functions. It is commonly the case that when a new construction arises by constructionalization or grammaticalization, it will only very gradually take over the functions of existing constructions. This leads to the very interesting synchronic situation in which there are two or more constructions that seem to do almost the same grammatical work. Hopper 1991 has named such situations *layering*. Layering of morphosyntactic constructions drives synchronic syntacticians absolutely crazy as they try to find semantic, pragmatic, or stylistic differences among very similar constructions.

A diachronic view is helpful here, especially if we understand the factors that are at play when one construction is taking over the functions of another.

Consider two constructions that are much discussed in the literature on English syntax. In (221) we see the ditransitives or double object construction (DOC) and in (222) a construction with a similar function, but one that uses a preposition for the recipient:

(221)   *She gave her brother a large dictionary.*

(222)   *She gave a large dictionary to her brother.*

In these sentences, *her brother* is the recipient or indirect object and *a large dictionary* is the patient or direct object. The two constructions represented by these sentences have a similar meaning, and in some cases can be used more or less interchangeably depending on discourse factors, but the DOC as in (221) can only be used with certain semantic classes of verbs, while the prepositional construction as in (222) has fewer restrictions on its use. For instance, both constructions can be used with verbs of communicated message as in (223) and (224), but when the verb also denotes the manner of speaking as in (225) and (226) the prepositional construction is preferred (Colleman and De Clerk 2011).

(223)   *John told Bill the news.*

(224)   *John told the news to Bill.*

(225)   **John whispered Bill the news.*

(226)   *John whispered the news to Bill.*

In terms of their development diachronically, the prepositional construction is a more recent development than the DOC. Old English had case marking on nouns and it had several double object constructions with different case markings, such as DATIVE + ACCUSATIVE, GENITIVE + ACCUSATIVE, or DATIVE + GENITIVE. Prepositions occurred in Old English, but they were much less frequently used than they are now. The preposition *to* in OE indicated a goal in a broad sense. So in OE we have recipients expressed with the Dative case, as in (227), or less frequently with the preposition *to* as in (228) (examples from Traugott 1972):

(227)   *þa   teð   hie brohton   sume þæm   cyninge*
         DEM+PL tooth+ACC/PL they bring+PAST/PL some DEM+DAT king+DAT
         'Those teeth, they brought some to the king'

(228)   *his suna   twegen mon   brohte   to þæm   cyninge*
         his son+ACC/PL two   he/one bring+PAST to DEM+DAT king+DAT
         'His two sons he brought to the king'

In the Middle English period, case marking on nouns was gradually lost, but the construction represented by (227) remained, with the recipient noun occurring closest to the verb. The prepositional construction continued to expand its usage and has come to be used with a wide range of verbs.

As mentioned before, in PDE the prepositional construction can be used with a wide range of verbs while the DOC is more restricted. But there is complete overlap in the sense that any verb that occurs in the DOC can also occur in the prepositional construction. Historically, what has been happening is that the set of verbs allowed in the DOC has gradually been contracting. As far as I know there are no detailed studies of how this has been happening through the entire period of the competition between these two constructions, but there is one study of the last 300 years that shows that some semantic classes of verbs that formerly occurred in the DOC no longer do (Colleman and De Clerk 2011). A case in point is the class of verbs that indicate manner of communication as in (229) and (230), which show that verbs such as *whisper* do not occur in the DOC currently. However, Colleman and De Clerk 2011 report examples with *whisper* in the DOC from the eighteenth century:

(229)   *At her departure she took occasion to whisper me her opinion of the widow, whom she called a pretty idiot.*   (Fielding 1751)

(230)   *I would grant neither, as something whispers me that it would be giving a sanction to adultery.*   (Goldsmith 1766)

Colleman and De Clerk also find examples of other verb classes that used to occur in the DOC but now require a preposition. For instance, now the DOC can be used for a benefactive object, as in (231), but only if the object is the intended recipient. However, as recently as the nineteenth century, the benefactive use of the DOC occurred even where the indirect object cannot be the recipient of the direct object:

(231)   *She found me a job. He baked me a cake.*

(232)   *Let a French woman nurse me when I am ill, let an English woman clean me my house and an Englishman write me my poetry!*   (Jean Ingelow 1882)

Nowadays we would say *clean my house for me, write my poetry for me*, so this is a usage that has been replaced by the prepositional construction.

How exactly does this replacement occur? With both constructions available for use with manner of communication verbs and benefactives where no object is received, it must have been the case that a trend in favor of the prepositional construction started and, as this trend strengthened, the cases of the DOC with these meanings became rarer and rarer. When a linguistic expression grows rare and thus unfamiliar, it can eventually be considered ungrammatical. The process is similar to analogical leveling in morphology: a more productive construction (regular *–ed* past tense) begins to be applied in more and more cases (giving *weeped* rather than *wept*). As with analogical leveling, high-frequency expressions resist change. For instance, certain formulaic expressions such as *give someone a call* or *give someone a nudge* retain the DOC and cannot be used with the prepositional construction: *?I gave a call to the doctor*. Others seem preferable with the DOC: *pay someone a visit, wish someone a good day*.

As might be expected, certain semantic classes of verbs remain in the DOC longer than others, as we see below.

The same trend is found in other Germanic languages according to the study by Barðdal (2007) of changes in the verb classes used with the DOC in Old Norse and Old Icelandic compared to the modern languages Icelandic, Norwegian, and Swedish. She finds that both the type and token frequency of the DOC have decreased between Old Norse-Old Icelandic to modern times. Barðdal argues that the verb classes used with the DOC in Icelandic (always considered a very conservative language) represent the original set for North Germanic, perhaps for Germanic as a whole. In all cases considered (including Modern Dutch), change is in the direction of loss of verb classes used with the DOC and expansion of the use of the prepositional construction.

An additional factor of interest here concerns the semantics of classes that continue to be used in the DOC and those that have been dropped. As Colleman and De Clerk point out, the constriction of the verb classes used with the DOC results in a semantically more coherent construction. These authors note that the constriction of the class of verbs found in the DOC results in the construction centering on the "recipient" and "addressee" meanings. Goldberg (2006) has noted that the most frequent items to occur in a construction represent the most basic aspects of its meaning. In the eighteenth century, according to the study by Colleman and De Clerk, far and away the most frequent verbs occurring in the DOC in English were *give*, *send* (the recipient sense), and *tell* (the addressee sense). Barðdal 2007 notes that in Old Norse-Old Icelandic 'give' and 'say' were the most frequently occurring verbs. Perhaps it is the case, then, that the verbs most distant semantically from these senses tend to be less used in this construction.

Colleman and De Clerk observe in addition that the semantic coherence of the construction allows for occasional extension. As they note, all the verb classes currently in use in the DOC were also in use in the eighteenth century, except the class that includes instruments of communication, such as *e-mail*, *fax*, *text*, and so on (*he faxed me the form*). The fact that these verbs, which reflect technological changes, can be accommodated by the DOC (as instances of the "addressee" sense) is further evidence that the perceived semantic coherence is real and fuels productivity.

Some general principles are derivable from this case as well as the others discussed in this chapter. When two constructions are serving very similar functions in a language it is often the case that one is older and the other is a more recent formation. Often the more recently created construction is gaining in productivity at the expense of the older construction, which will undergo a reduction in both type and token frequency. Also, the cases in which the older construction is retained are often high-frequency or formulaic expressions that are learned as whole formulae. As we have seen here, high-frequency expressions need not be relics, but can serve as the centers for productive semantic categories.

8.3.3.   How constructions are lost

In the case just discussed, competition between constructions has been going on for about a millennium. Based on this fact, we have no reason to expect the DOC to disappear from English or other Germanic languages any time soon. However, in some cases of competition and layering, one construction wins out over the other, leading to the loss of a construction. The case we discuss here also relates to changes from OE to PDE and also involves the loss of case marking in English.

As in other languages with case marking on nouns, OE had a number of constructions each involving different combinations of cases. We will not review all the types of constructions here but will focus on only two, the transitive construction as illustrated in (233) and the impersonal construction, as in (234).

(233)   *he*   *acwealde*   *þone dracan*
         3SM-NOM   kill-1/3 PAST   the-ACC dragon-ACC
         'He killed the dragon'

(234)   *him*   *ofhreow*   *þæs mannes*
         3SM-DAT   pity-3SG-PAST   this-GEN man- GEN
         to-him   pitied   because of the man
         'He pitied the man' or 'The man caused him pity'

The transitive construction uses a nominative case for the agent and accusative case for the patient. This is of course a very normal transitive construction. However, in OE there were other options as well. The example in (234) has the experiencer in the dative case and a source (for the situation described by the verb) in the genitive; it is called the impersonal construction by Trousdale 2008. What makes it impersonal is that there is no argument in the nominative and the verb inflection is third person singular, no matter what the person-number of the arguments.

Only certain verbs in OE were used in the impersonal construction. Allen 1995 lists *lystan* 'cause pleasure', *langian* 'cause longing', *ofþyncan* 'cause sorrow', *þyncan* 'seem, appear', *hreowan* 'regret, rue', *tweonian* 'cause doubt', *ofhreowan* 'pity'. Within that construction, the noun in the dative case is the one that experiences the emotion and the noun in the genitive is the cause of the emotion. The transitive construction was typically used with dynamic verbs whose object (in the accusative) is affected by the action of the verb. Trousdale argues that the transitive construction expanded to be used with more and more verbs, so that certain restrictions on it, e.g. that the nominative subject be an agent were gradually lost. Of course, at the same time, the case markings themselves were being lost except in pronouns, so speakers could easily interpret the first noun in the clause as the subject.

In the ME period we find verbs such as *rue* (spelled *rew*) with a nominative subject as in (235) from approximately 1325 (Trousdale 2008):

(235)   *We schold rew   þat sore.*
          'We should regret that sorely'

Also, the verb *think* has changed, but the first person singular with a dative subject was maintained up to the nineteenth century, as in this example, where *methinks* means 'it seems to me':

(236)   *Well, my honoured father, <u>methinks</u> you have carried your amusement at my expense to a sufficient length.* (1817)

Today, for the verbs that are still used, we treat the experiencer as the subject of the verb. Consider (237) and (238). Of course *think* has greatly expanded its use and usually has a clause as a complement, rather than a noun. Note particularly that *think* agrees with the subject now.

(237)   *If Yeltsin does not come to <u>rue</u> the price of his victory, he may <u>rue</u> the debts he has incurred.*

(238)   *My lawyer <u>thinks</u> it will go through pretty quickly.*

The verb *like* was used in OE in a construction with a dative experiencer and a nominative source. It has gradually changed to fit the dominant pattern as well, but in the sixteenth century the conservative pattern could be found, as in (239) where the experiencer(s) are expressed by *them* (Trousdale 2008).

(239)   *callinge for a pot of the best ale, sat down at the tables end: the lykor liked them so well, that they had pot vpon pot.* (1567)

Except for the occasional use of the archaic formula *methinks* or locutions such as *it seems to me*, the older constructions are gone from English. Even with *it seems to me*, note that a "dummy" subject has been inserted and a preposition is used rather than the case marking alone, so it is not the same construction at all. In fact, it has become almost categorical that English clauses have a subject which triggers verb agreement. Trousdale argues that this results from the development and expansion of the transitive construction, through which the first noun phrase in the clause is considered to be the subject. Trousdale likens this process to grammaticalization because the transitive construction has become more productive, being used with a wider range of subject types, and more general as it encodes a broader range of thematic relations. It is also less compositional in the sense that the original semantics of the transitive construction is no longer clear in many cases. As this case illustrates, the loss of a construction (the impersonal construction) is usually caused by the expansion of another construction that takes over the functions of the declining construction. The newer more general construction is more schematic, but it also lacks semantic coherence.

The loss of case marking and this expansion of the transitive construction, along with the prepositional construction discussed in the previous section, has dramatically changed English syntax over the centuries. The next two sections discuss other dramatic changes in the English language since the OE period.

8.4.   Word-order change: OV and VO languages

8.4.1.   Synchronic word-order correlations

In a large crosslinguistic study published in 1963, Joseph Greenberg reports on significant correlations among the ordering of syntactic elements, based on the order of subject (S), object (O), and verb (V). Based on his sample of thirty languages, Greenberg 1963 proposed that there were three types of languages according to the basic order of subject, verb, and object: VSO, SVO, and SOV. The absence in his sample of VOS, OVS, and OSV suggests a strong tendency for the S to precede the O. This tendency is usually explained by the preference for the topic to precede the comment and assumes a diachronic relationship between topic and subject, as exemplified above in Section 8.2.1. Later research revealed that VOS, OSV, and OVS languages also occur, though they are not common. The most common types are SVO and SOV. As SVO and VSO languages seem to have very similar characteristics, the typology was reduced to a two-way distinction between VO and OV by Lehmann 1973 and Vennemann 1975. The correlations that Greenberg found are shown in Table 8.1.

Before examining the table, consider certain important caveats: most languages allow alternate orders of S, O, and V. So when we say a language is of one type or another, we are talking about its most common or most basic word order (usually that in simple declarative clauses). Sometimes this is very difficult to determine, so some languages remain unclassified. Also, in natural discourse, it is not common for both S and O to be full noun phrases; rather it is more common for one or both to be pronouns or omitted entirely. So in a sense the classification based on S, O, and V is somewhat artificial. Reducing the typology to O and V reduces this problem somewhat. In any case, bear in mind that this typology is very important and revealing, but it does oversimplify to some extent. Table 8.2 exemplifies these correlations using the examples of French, which is a VO language, and Japanese, which is an OV language.

The intriguing question that was raised by these findings is why these correlations tend to hold across many unrelated languages and how word-order change

Table 8.1: *Word-order correlations*

VO (head-modifier)	OV (modifier-head)
Aux V	V Aux
V complement clause	complement clause V
Preposition N	N Postposition
N Genitive	Genitive N
N Adjective	Adjective N
N Relative Clause	Relative Clause N
Adjective Standard	Standard Adjective
Prefixing or mixed	Suffixing

Table 8.2: *Examples of word-order correlations from French and Japanese.*

French			Japanese		
(a)	*Jean a mangé* *une pomme*		*Taroo-ga* *ringo-o* *tabeta.*		
	John ate an apple		Taroo-SUBJ apple-OBJ ate		
(b)	*Jean peut* *parler* *anglais.*		*Taroo-wa* *Eigo-ga* *hanas-eru.*		
	John can speak English		Taroo English speak-can		
(c)	*avec un baton*		*boo-de*		
	with a stick		stick-with		
(d)	*la sœur* *de Jean*		*Taroo-no* *imooto*		
	the sister of John		Taroo-POSS sister		
(e)	*une* *fleur* *blanche*		*siroi* *hana*		
	a flower white		white flower		
(f)	*le garçon qui a frappé*		*inu-o* *butta* *otokonoko-wa*		
	the boy who hit		dog hit boy		
	le chien est mon frère		*watasi-no* *otooto-da*		
	the dog is my brother		me-POSS brother-is		
(g)	*plus grand* *que Jean*		*Taroo-yori ookii*		
	more big than John		Taroo-than big		

takes place when it does. As the second question may provide the explanation for the first, both of these questions have important diachronic implications.

First attempts to explain the word-order correlations rest on the observation that there is a parallelism in the ordering within constituents such that the head of a phrase is ordered the same with respect to its modifiers. Unfortunately, the term "head" is used in different ways in different theories, but here we will use the simple heuristic that the head is the element that gives its name to the phrase and thus determines the function of the phrase as a whole. Thus the verb is the head of the verb phrase, noun is the head of the noun phrase, the preposition the head of a prepositional phrase, the adjective the head of an adjective phrase, and so on. Vennemann 1975 proposed the Principle of Natural Serialization which says that constituents are ordered as follows:

(240)   head–modifier in VX languages
             modifier–head in XV languages

Hawkins 1979 proposes a similar principle of Cross-Category Harmony. The "principle" stated in (240), however, is nothing more than a restatement of the facts uncovered by Greenberg. Thus an explanation is still needed. Both Hawkins and Vennemann suggest that (240) represents an analogical organizing principle for grammars, but they both recognize that this principle is implemented only very gradually in languages undergoing word order change. It is by no means an absolute universal, as many languages exist which have ordering within constituents that are inconsistent with this principle. My own view is that the status of this principle is uncertain until we have examined carefully exactly how word orders change to become consistent with it. In the following we will examine how the ordering of constituents arises and search in this process for an explanation of the word-order correlations.

First it is necessary to refine Greenberg's findings. The sample of languages he used were chosen for "convenience" – meaning information about them was readily available to him. A problem with this sampling method is that the resulting sample can have biases, and in this case there were too many languages from Eurasia. Using a more representative sample of the world's languages, Dryer 1988 replicates most of Greenberg's findings with a major exception: Dryer finds no correlation between the order of noun and adjective and the order of verb and object. He finds instead that the order adjective-noun in OV languages is common in Eurasia, but the opposite order is common outside of Eurasia. Thus, in the following we will not consider the order of the noun and adjective.

8.4.2.   The diachronic source of word-order correlations

In this section we discuss a few examples that demonstrate that at least some of the word-order correlations in Table 8.1 are due to grammaticalization from existing constructions and derive their harmonic word order from their source. An obvious example is the order of the verb and auxiliary. Since the auxiliary was earlier a verb that took another verbal predicate as its object, auxiliaries follow the verb in OV languages and precede in VO languages (Givón 1984).

(241)   OV: (O) + V + V   VO: V + V + (O)
                              ↓   ↓
                          Aux   Aux

Then if the auxiliary goes on to become an affix, it will be a suffix in the OV language but a prefix in the VO language. The examples from Swahili illustrate the development in a VO language and those from Ute the development in an OV language. Examples are from Givón 1984.

(242)   Swahili: VO word order

(a)   *a-li-soma*   *kitabu*   *li* 'be'   > PAST
       he-PAST-read   book
       'he read a book'

(b)   *a-ta-soma*   *kitabu*   *taka* 'want'   > FUTURE
       he-FUT-read   book
       'he will read a book'

(c)   *a-me-soma*   *kitabu*   **mála* 'finish' > ANTERIOR
       he-ANT-read   book
       'he has read a book'

(243)   Ute: OV word order

  (a)   *wúukaxa*   *xa* 'have / be' > ANTERIOR
        work-ANT
  (b)   'he has worked'
        wúuka-vaa(ni)   **páa* 'go/pass' > FUTURE
        work-FUT
        'he will work'

While this is the general pattern, exceptions also occur. In Swahili there is a perfective from Proto-Bantu **gid* 'finish' which becomes a suffix. Presumably this results from the iconic ordering of the other verb and 'finish', with 'finish' occurring last (Heine and Reh 1984). The important point about this exception is that it obeys the general diachronic rule that elements do not change position when they grammaticalize and therefore their position is indicative of their source construction. In other words, we need search no farther for an explanation for why auxiliaries tend to precede the verb in VO languages and follow it in OV languages.

One of the strongest correlations that Greenberg found in his data is the correlation of prepositions with noun–genitive order and postpositions with genitive–noun order (see the analysis in Hawkins 1979). There is also a strong diachronic relation between adpositions and genitive constructions: genitive constructions give rise to new adpositions, and adpositions are often used to form genitive constructions. Let us consider the first case first.

It is common for genitive constructions to participate in the formation of new adpositions (Svorou 1994). In English, complex prepositions are constructed from a PREPOSITION + relational noun + *of* + NP. Of course, *of* + NP is a genitive or possessive. This gives rise to prepositional phrases such as those in (244). These are currently complex prepositions, but they can further evolve. For instance, *inside of the house* is now commonly *inside the house*.

(244)   English: VO
             in back of the house
             inside of the house
             in front of the house

Another comparable example from a VO language is (245) from Bari (Spagnolo 1933).

(245)   Bari: VO
             ŋa   sɪsɪ'da   ɪ   kɔmɔŋ   na   kadi?
             who   stays   in   front   of   house
             'who is staying in front of the house?'

In contrast, in OV languages such as Buriat and head-final languages such as Finnish, postpositions are formed from GENITIVE + relational noun + POST-POSITION constructions, as in (246) and (247):

(246)   Buriat:
          ger-ei   *xazuu-da*
          house-GEN   side-LOC
          'by the house; at the side of the house'

(247)   Finnish:
          poja-n   *kansa -ssa*   >   *poja-n*   *kanssa*
          boy-GEN   company-in   boy-GEN   with
          'with the boy'

Another source of correspondence between adpositions and genitives is that
genitive markers can derive from adpositions, as in the case of English *of*, which
came from *off*. Thus the correspondence between adposition and noun–genitive
order has a ready diachronic explanation and there is no need to invoke special
analogical principles.

Another diachronic source for correlations between verb–object order and
adposition order is found in serial verb constructions that give rise to adpositions.
If the language has the order VO, then when the verb is grammaticalized it will
become a preposition, as in the Yoruba examples in (248) where the verb *fi* 'take'
becomes an instrumental preposition; if the language has the order OV, then the
verb will become a postposition, as in the Ijo examples (249), where the verb *aki*
'take' becomes an instrumental postposition (Givón 1975).

(248)   Yoruba: VO > preposition

     (a) *mo*   *fi*   *àdá*   *gé*   *igi*
          I   took   machete   cut   tree
          'I cut the tree with a machete'
     (b) *mo*   *fi*   *gbòn*   *gé*   *igi*
          I   took   clever   cut   tree
          'I cut the tree cleverly'

(249)   Ijo: OV > postposition

     (a) *erí*   *ogidi*   *akį̇-nį̇*   *indi*   *pẹį-mį̇*
          he   machete   take-ASP   fish   cut-ASP
     (b) 'he cut a fish with a machete'
          áràų̇   *zu-ye*   *ákį̇*   *buru*   *teri-mí*
          she   basket   take   yam   cover-ASP
          'she covered a yam with a basket'

These examples illustrate the possibility of explaining certain of the prominent
word-order correlations through diachronic change – grammaticalization and the
creation of new constructions. Since the basis upon which these changes take
place are the existing patterns of the language, then new constructions have the
predicted order and the language remains consistent. However, when change is
occurring and new constructions are arising, gradual changes towards a new type
can be observed. In the next section we examine the reasons that a language
might undergo a major word-order shift.

8.5. Pragmatic reasons for changing the order of subject, verb, and object: drift in Indo-European languages

While there is no complete agreement about the dominant word order of Proto-Indo European, the ancient daughter languages (Sanskrit, Latin, Old English, Gothic) all have many characteristics of OV languages, such as the presence of suffixes for case as well as tense, aspect and modality, genitive-noun order, and the positioning of auxiliary-like elements after the verb. For these and other reasons, it is usually postulated that PIE was an OV language. Many of the modern Indo-European languages are VO (e.g. English and French), so a major shift in word order appears to have taken place. Indeed, this change may have already been underway in the ancient languages, as prepositions and some verbal prefixes are present in these languages. However, the major changes in Germanic and Romance languages have occurred in the last 1000 years.

The most insightful discussions of the changes that have taken place in English over the last 1000 years (many of them paralleled in other Germanic and also Romance languages) do not focus just on word-order change, but note that other changes have occurred as well and seek to find an integrative explanation of these changes. The famous early twentieth-century linguist Edward Sapir drew attention to some of these changes and the fact that they seem to proceed in the same direction over many generations. He reasoned that, if the variation that leads to change were random, then changes in different directions would cancel each other out. Instead, he noted a directionality to change and named this *drift*. The example he used was the loss of case marking in modern European languages (Sapir 1921). Subsequent researchers have drawn together several changes that appear to be related (Lakoff 1972; Vennemann 1975). Vennemann cites the following properties characterizing the older OV stage in Romance and Germanic languages vs. the more recent VO stage.

(250)	OV (Pre- Old English, Latin, etc.)	VO (Present Day English)
a.	case endings on nouns	no case-marking prepositions for indirect objects and possessives
b.	variable word order for topicalization	word order for grammatical relations (subject and object of the verb)
c.	no articles	definite and indefinite articles
d.	no obligatory pronouns	obligatory pronouns
e.	no periphrastic passive construction	periphrastic passive
f.	more synthetic	more analytic

I have already mentioned that Old English had case suffixes on nouns. Here is an example of the way nouns were inflected at that time:

(251)   *stān* 'stone'   Sg.   Pl.
       Nom./Acc.   *stān*   *stānas*
       Gen.   *stānes*   *stāna*
       Dat.   *stāne*   *stānum*

As for the word order, there was variation, but the following sequence of developments captures the major changes. Note that the position of the verb changes earlier in main clauses and only later in subordinate clauses. The change in the position of the verb was led by a class of verbs labeled here as "auxiliaries", but it includes the copula and modal verbs. This class of auxiliaries appears in the second position in the clause. Later all verbs took up this position.

(252)   Word order in different periods of English in main clauses (Hock 1986)

Early Runic inscriptions   S O MV Aux   MV = main verb
Later Runic inscriptions   S Aux O MV   Here the Aux refers to any reduced
and *Beowulf*   verb form: copula, modal, etc.
Later Old English   S V O   From Aux, second position
          generalized to all verbs

Example (253) from Beowulf shows the auxiliary in second position and the main verb at the end of the clause (Hock 1986).

(253)   *Bēowulfe*   *wearð*   *gūðrēð*   *gyfeþe*
               AUX   MAIN VERB
       Beowulf   was   glory-in-battle given
       'B was given glory in battle'

In later Old English all verbs appear in second position. As mentioned, this was a generalization of the construction applying to the "auxiliary" verbs. In (254) *witan* 'know' is the main verb.

(254)   *wē*   *witan*   *ōþer*   *igland*   *hēr*   *be*   *ēaston*
       we   know   another   island   here   by   east
       'We know another island east of here'

In subordinate clauses the order remains SOV. Both clauses of (255) show this more conservative order that reflects the earlier stage of OE, where the modal verb follows the main verb (an OV characteristic) (Hopper and Traugott 1993).

(255)   *nimþe*   *se*   *cyng*   *alyfan*   *wille,*   *þæt man*   *wergylde*   *alysan*   *mote*
       unless   the   king   allow   will   that one   ransom   pay   may
       'unless the king will allow one to pay ransom'

Modern German reflects a very similar situation: in main clauses the inflected verb or auxiliary occurs second in the clause, but in subordinate clauses, the inflected verb or auxiliary occurs at the end.

According to the theory presented in Vennemann 1975, changes (b)–(f) in (250) are related to the loss of case marking. Vennemann's idea is that managing the flow of old and new information in a language with case marking is easy because one can put the old (topical) noun first in the clause, without losing any information about argument structure. Indeed, most (but not all) SOV languages have case marking and can shift NPs around for pragmatic purposes. When the case suffixes begin to reduce phonologically in OE, then new ways of indicating the subject and object of the verb as well as old and new information must arise. Of course, we have said that OE had case markers, but examining a typical paradigm such as that in (251) shows that the nominative and accusative were often the same. Starting in OE, a long gradual process of fixing of word order got underway, the result of which was preverbal position for the subject and post-verbal for the object. This is basically the transitive construction discussed in Section 8.3.3, which, as we saw, generalized way beyond the canonical transitive verbs. Vennemann's point is that the fixing of word order and the absence of case marking make it difficult for the speakers to indicate old and new information. If the speaker wanted to put the topical NP first in the clause, the hearer might not know if it was the subject or the object, or might take it to be the subject. He proposes that the development of articles and a passive construction were responses to the pragmatic need to indicate the topicality of the NP while adhering to an SVO word order.

As we noted in Chapter 7, demonstratives develop into definite articles. Their development at this stage of English is a result of the increased use of demonstratives, possibly as a way of indicating that the referent of the NP is a known entity. Definite articles then fulfill the function of indicating old (known) referents from referents that are being newly introduced into the discourse. Indefinite articles (from *one* in English) serve the complementary function of indicating a referent that is new to the discourse. As mentioned in Chapter 7, many Indo-European languages have developed definite and indefinite articles, and this has happened as their basic word order changed from OV to VO.

Another development in English that seems to coincide with the change in word-order type is the grammaticalization of a passive construction. OE did not have a passive construction, though it had some constructions that were similar in some ways. With an auxiliary *beon* 'be' or *weorþan* 'be, become', the inflected participle of a verb indicated a resultative meaning (a past action leaving a resulting state) with no agent mentioned, as in these examples from Petré and Cuyckens 2009.

(256)   *þe cwyde, þe   awriten is on þere becc, þe   is ʒehaten "Actus apostolorum".*
        the saying, that written is in that book that is called   Actus apostolorum
        'The saying, that is written [and now present] in the book, that is called
        "Actus apostolorum"'. (c. 1025)

(257)   *Ac heora   bendas   sona   wurdon for-swelede.*
        but their   fetters:NOM.PL   immediately   were   away-burnt: NOM.PL
        'But their fetters immediately were burnt away [and now ashy].' (c. 1050)

As Petré and Cuyckens explain, three changes must occur for this resultative construction to become a passive: (i) the addition of an explicit agent marked by a preposition (such as *by*), (ii) the grammaticalization of the auxiliary with bleaching of its meaning, and (iii) the reanalysis of the participle as the main verb (instead of the auxiliary). These changes were completed in the ME period. Also in ME, this construction took on an important discourse function: it is often used where the passive's subject was also the subject of previous clauses in the discourse – in other words, where the subject is a continuing topic. Petré and Cuyckens note that in OE, OVS order could be used for this function, as in *me beswicode he* 'me betrayed he' but once SVO order was more or less fixed, the passive construction took over this function (see also Seoane 2006).

Another consequence of the loss of inflections, especially the loss of person–number agreement on verbs, which was present in OE, Latin, and other older Indo-European languages, is the increased use of personal pronouns. Indeed, Latin did not have third person pronouns, but used demonstratives instead and, as these increased in their use, the Romance languages developed third person pronouns for subject, object, and indirect object. In some languages, such as Spanish, the use of subject pronouns is still variable, but in others, such as French, it is obligatory. This drift then is also related to the loss of inflectional suffixes.

Finally, Sapir's drift also includes a general movement from highly inflectional or synthetic expression of grammatical categories and functions to more analytic (periphrastic) expression. As the grammaticalization process reaches its end and affixes are reduced phonologically and are highly bleached semantically, they begin to disappear. Before that happens, other constructions have developed to take their place: for instance, prepositions, articles, pronouns, and periphrastic passives. As these are newer constructions, they are not as grammaticalized as the older ones and therefore are more analytic. In addition, these new constructions follow the VO patterns with preposed auxiliaries and adpositions. There is a much lesser tendency for preposed grammaticalizing elements to become affixes than postposed elements. This tendency contributes to the maintenance of analytic structure in the evolving VO languages of Europe.

8.6.   Conclusion: the life cycle of constructions

In this chapter we have surveyed the types of changes that can occur in constructions, starting with how constructions are initially formed. We have seen two sources for new constructions: the fixing or syntacticization of discourse patterns, such as the fronting of a noun phrase, and the schematization of conventionalized word sequences, such as Spanish *quedarse* + ADJECTIVE, which started from very specific word combinations, such as *quedarse solo* 'to end up alone'. A third source for new constructions was discussed in Chapter 6 in the context of grammaticalization: a specific instance of a construction with a lexical item in it can grammaticalize into a new construction. A good example is the *be going to* future construction in English, which was earlier just a specific instance of a more general construction that involved a movement verb (*go*, *journey*, *come*...) and a purposive clause with an infinitive.

As newly developed constructions are used more they can change in various ways. The schematic slots in constructions can expand to take more and more lexical items. The more fixed slots can become even more fixed (e.g. the English passive earlier occurred with *be* and also *weorþan* 'to become' but now occurs only with *be*; the passive with *get* is a newer development). The elements in a construction can be reanalyzed in the sense that a clause-initial NP can be taken to be the subject of the clause even though previously it was not. Elements can be added, as when an agent phrase is added to a developing passive.

Constructions are lost from a language through competition with newer constructions. This process often takes a very long time so that competing constructions are common. The new construction is gaining in type and token frequency and the old construction is restricted to occurring with certain semantic classes of lexical items or in high-frequency phrases or discourse contexts.

The development of new constructions and their eventual replacement of older ones can lead to major changes in a language, as when a language is undergoing a change in its basic word order. Word-order shifts involving subject, object, and verb are long, gradual progressions in which pragmatic factors highly determine the constructions that arise. New constructions involving other consti-tuents (N-genitive, adposition-N) arise via grammaticalization from existing constituent orders and are thus consistent with them.

Suggested reading

A survey of the creation and change of many different construction types can be found in:

Harris, A.C. and Campbell, L., 1995. *Historical syntax in cross-linguistic perspective*, Cambridge: Cambridge University Press.

Questions for discussion

1. Go back over the examples in this chapter and identify cases where two or more constructions are in competition. What are the factors that determine which of the two competing constructions is favored to take over the functions of the other construction?
2. What factors that operate in grammaticalization also operate in the formation of new constructions?
3. Compare the two genitive constructions of English *the boy's bike* and *the leg of the table*. Which one is consistent with OV order and which with VO? Which one is older? How can you tell?

9 Lexical change: how languages get new words and how words change their meaning

9.1. Introduction

In this chapter we consider how the words of a language change. In previous chapters we have considered many changes that affect words. In Chapters 2 and 3 the discussion of sound change showed that the phonetic form of words can change, usually in a regular manner. In Chapters 4 and 5 we saw that the morphological composition of words can change as well. In Chapters 6 and 7 we saw that some words in specific constructions undergo grammaticalization and become grammatical morphemes. In Chapter 8 we saw that the particular constructions that words occur in can also change, which can affect the meaning of the words.

Here we consider additional types of change in words or the lexicon. First, we discuss the ways in which languages acquire new words in Section 9.2. Then we consider how words change their meanings, spreading this discussion over several sections: first in Section 9.3 we discuss the nature of the categories that constitute word meaning, and then we treat the mechanism by which words change their meaning over time. In Section 9.4 we discuss some general tendencies in lexical semantic change, and then in Section 9.5 we discuss the way words that are formed by derivational affixes lose their compositional meaning. Finally, Section 9.6 adds a few comments about how old words are lost from a language.

9.2. Where do new words come from?

9.2.1. Internal resources: compounding and derivation

All languages have means of creating new words from existing resources. As new artifacts and new concepts enter a culture, language users find ways of creating new words, including nouns, verbs, adjectives, and adverbs, to deal with these novel entities and ideas. Resources internal to the language are compounding (putting two words together to form a novel meaning) and various types of derivational morphology, usually involving an affix that produces a new word. These are all discussed in this section. Another source of new words is borrowing from other languages (Section 9.2.2). The study of the history of words, including where they come from and how they have changed, is *etymology*. Many English dictionaries include etymologies for words, but the most comprehensive source is *The Oxford English Dictionary*, which provides detailed histories of English words.

Languages differ as to how extensively they use compounding to create new words. Germanic languages are especially prolific in their use of compounds. In English there are compounds consisting of two nouns (*coffee cup, beauty sleep, TV show*), a verb and a noun (*drawstring, pull tab*), an adjective and a noun (*high chair, White House*), or a preposition and a noun (*overdose, in group*). In English a compound is distinguished from an ordinary phrase because the main accent is on the first word rather than the second one. Note that in English, compounds can either be written as one word or as two. How they are written seems to be rather arbitrary, which can be quite confusing! In addition, compounds can also be embedded in other compounds, so that they can become quite long. For example, *customer service* is a compound noun and it can appear in the compound *customer service representative*. In Dutch this is rendered as one word, *Klantenservicemedewerker* 'customer service representative' (*klanten* 'customers' + *service* 'service' + *medewerker* 'worker'), which produces quite a long word, though not by any means the longest word produced by compounding.

The meaning of a compound is not predictable from the words that go into it; rather the meaning is determined in the particular context in which the word is coined. For example, an *air conditioner* could do any number of things to air, but it has always been used in the context of cooling the air. A *lighthouse* could be any type of house having a light associated with it, but it happens to be a tower in or near water with a powerful light that serves as a reference point for ships at sea. Thus the meaning of compounds is conventional and language-specific.

As mentioned above, Germanic languages use compounds a great deal to create new words. Romance languages use them much less, but verb-noun compounds do exist, for example, Spanish *matasanos* (*mata* 'kills', *sanos* 'healthy people) 'quack doctor' and Italian *lavapiatti* (*lava* 'washes', *piatti* 'dishes') 'dishwasher'. In some languages, compounding of certain types becomes very productive to the point that one element of the compound actually becomes grammaticalized as a derivational morpheme. An example is the *–ly* suffix in English, which in Old English was *–lic*, derived from a word meaning 'body'. It created a compound with a noun and was very similar in use to PDE *like* as used in *dog-like*.

The other main resource that most languages have for creating new words is derivation, usually the addition of derivational affixes to existing stems or words, such as the English suffixes *–hood*, *–ness*, or *–ish* or prefixes *re–* or *un–*. Probably all languages have some derivational affixes. Many languages have affixes that can be added to a verb to mean 'one who does'; as these form nouns from verbs, they are one type of nominalization. Many languages have affixes that can be added to a verb to denote that someone causes the action of the verb (causative). These are just a few examples of the many types of derivational affixes or constructions that occur.

Words formed from derivational constructions can be more or less transparent in meaning. Presumably they start out as rather transparent, but over time they can change their meaning. We will discuss this process more in Section 9.5, but for now, consider the noun *business*, which was formed in Middle English with the meaning 'quality or state of being busy'. From there it took off in various directions, but it was not until the eighteenth century that it began to take on the use we would consider most central – that of trade or commerce and institutions doing trade. The changes in usage result in the loss of analyzability – that is, English speakers do not usually see this word as consisting of an adjective plus a suffix, even though both elements still exist in the language today. Related to this is the loss of a syllable, leaving the word with only two. Indeed, today *business* contrasts with another more transparent and analyzable formation, *busyness*.

Derivational constructions can be more or less productive, that is, more or less likely to be used to create new words. For example, the English suffix *–ness* is productively used to create nouns from adjectives as in these examples: *disinterestedness, waterproofness, standoffishness*. In these cases, we have *–ness* added to an already complex word – either a compound or one with other derivational affixes – and the meaning is quite transparent. Compare this flexibility of use to another suffix that creates an abstract noun from an adjective, *–th* as in *warmth, width, length*. This suffix is very limited in application and does not easily attach to new adjectives: *wrong, *wrongth; cool, *coolth*. As we saw in our discussion of inflection in Chapter 5, affixes can increase or decrease their productivity across time.

Another means of word formation present in many languages is reduplication, in which part or all of a word is repeated to express a different meaning. Reduplication occurs in many languages of the world and expresses a range of meanings that show significant commonalities even in unrelated languages. Reduplication can express the notions of plural in nouns (Mandarin *renren* 'everyone' from *ren* 'person') and repetition or iteration in verbs (Swahili *pigapiga* 'to strike repeatedly' from *piga* 'to strike'). It can also express intensity, for example Thai *díidii* 'to be extremely good' which is formed from *dii* 'to be good' or *wáanwăan* 'to be extremely sweet' from *wăan* 'to be sweet'.

Some languages allow nouns to become verbs and verbs to become nouns rather freely. English is one of those languages, as we can see in words such as *hammer*, which originally designated a tool but now can also be used to indicate the action done with the tool, or *walk*, which was earlier a verb, but can also be used as a noun to indicate a delimited time and path for the action of the verb (*he took a walk; our walks take us around the lake*). Note that in English the change takes place by adding the inflectional affixes for the new category and by simply using the stem in the context for the new category. This is called *zero conversion* since no derivational affixes are required. As with compounding, the meaning of the new noun or verb is not completely predictable; rather, the particular context in which it is used determines its meaning. For example, of all the things *dog* could mean as a verb ('pant like a dog', 'beg like a dog'), the verbal use means 'to track like a dog', presumably because of the common use of dogs for tracking game in the sixteenth century when it was first used.

This is by no means an exhaustive list of the ways that languages can acquire new words. A few other possibilities are: back-formations, such as when a part of a word like *burger* (from *hamburger* originally 'a person or thing from Hamburg') comes to be used on its own and in other combinations such as *cheeseburger* or *veggieburger*; clippings, or shortened version of longer words, such as *lab*, *tech*, *app*, *dis*. In languages that have writing systems, acronyms are the word-like pronunciations of the initial letters of a phrase, such as *radar* which came from *RAdio Detection And Ranging* or *laser* from *Light Amplification by Stimulated Emission of Radiation*. The other important source of new words – borrowing from other languages – is treated in the next section.

9.2.2.   Borrowing words from other languages

For most languages, a good source of new words can be another language. In particular, when cultures are in contact the exchange of artifacts or objects, for example food, is accompanied by the words for these items. The origin in other languages of common English words such as *spaghetti, chow mein, taco, sushi,* or *sauerkraut* are quite clear to most speakers, but English has been borrowing words for food for centuries, and many of them are now thought of as native words. Consider *orange, potato, tomato, squash, coffee,* and *tea. Orange* entered English around 1300, via Old French *orange,* which came from Italian *arancia,* originally *narancia,* which itself was an alteration of Arabic *naranj,* from Persian *narang,* from Sanskrit *naranga-s* 'orange tree'. Potatoes, tomatoes, and squash are all New World foods so, predictably, their names come from Native American languages. Spanish *patata,* attested from about 1560 came from a Carib language of Haiti and meant 'sweet potato'. Around 1590 the name was extended to the common white potato, from Peru. *Tomato* was first *tomate* (from about 1600) and it came from Spanish *tomate,* which was borrowed from Nahuatl *tomatl* 'a tomato', literally 'the swelling fruit' from *tomana* 'to swell'. *Squash* is attested in English from the 1640s as a shortening of Narraganset (Algonquian) *askutasquash,* literally 'the green things that may be eaten raw', from *askut* 'green, raw' + *asquash* 'eaten', in which the *–ash* is a plural affix as found in *succotash.*

Coffee and tea arrived in Europe via different routes from the East. The word *coffee* got into English around 1600, from Italian *caffè,* which was borrowed from Turkish *kahveh,* which in turn came from Arabic *qahwah* 'coffee'. The word for 'tea' has two major variants in the languages of Europe and the Middle East, one derived from Dutch *thee* and the other related to Portuguese *chá.* Thus English has *tea,* French *thé,* Spanish *té,* and German *Tee,* while Russian has *chai,* Persian *cha,* Greek *tsai,* Arabic *shay,* and Turkish *çay.* These different forms are the result of the use of tea entering the area through two different routes. The Dutch traders had their main contacts in Amoy in Fujian where the Min Nan languages were spoken, and in these areas the word for 'tea' was te^{55} (as in Chaozhou). The Portuguese traders traveled via Macao, where the Cantonese word for 'tea' was *cha*. Also those areas that got their 'tea' overland rather than from the Dutch use forms such as *chai* (Dahl 2013). The words discussed here are loanwords: they are words whose etymological source is a different language, but which are fully integrated into the borrowing language. It is easy enough to see that words for food travel along with the food itself. A similar scenario follows for other objects whose progress around the world one can trace in similar ways. For example, the Arabic word for 'book' *kitāb* using the tri-consonantal root *k-t-b* has travelled through Africa, finding its way into Swahili (Bantu) as *kitabu* and Hausa (Chadic) as *litaafi*, among other African languages. The word also travelled east and is found in Turkish (Turkic) as *kitap*, in Persian (Indo-European) as *ketâb*, and in Urdu (Indo-European) as *kitāb*. In fact, the use of this borrowed word is widespread in southern Asia and the Indian subcontinent.

Beyond names for objects new to the culture, other borrowings depend upon the type of contact, the extent of bilingualism, and community conventions. Many cases exist where words have been borrowed without the motivation of need – that is, words are borrowed even though the borrowing language already has a word for the object or concept. Poplack et al. 1988 studied a large corpus of English words used in French conversations in Ottawa and Hull in Canada, which are communities with extensive and active bilingualism. While some loanwords may have been motivated by lexical gaps (lack of name for an object or concept), there are also many loanwords such as *business*, *smart*, *bad luck*, *first*, *game*, or *party* which cannot be said to be motivated by linguistic need. Another important result of their study was that, even in this case of extensive bilingualism, the occurrence of loanwords in conversation constituted under 1% of all words used. So in this case, the use of loanwords is not a common practice. Rates of borrowing probably differ according to language and community, with some communities being more receptive to loanwords than others. Some languages do not provide good habitat for foreign words because their extensive morphology may not be adaptable to non-native words. Where borrowing does occur, it is nouns that are most often borrowed probably because of their high degree of lexical content and their lesser degree of integration into discourse than classes such as verbs and adjectives (Poplack et al. 1988). Grammaticalized words such as prepositions, pronouns, articles, and auxiliaries are rarely borrowed (Weinreich 1968; Poplack et al. 1988).

9.2.3.   Loanword adaptation

A true loanword (as opposed to just a nonce use of a non-native word) is integrated in the phonology, morphology, and syntax of the language. Phonological adaptation usually means substituting native phonemes for non-native ones, changing phonotactic patterns, and adjusting stress patterns.

The phonemes substituted in adapting loanwords are usually the closest ones possible – an /h/ for a velar fricative, as in English *junta* [huntə] for Spanish [xunta], or the particular /r/ sound as in English *rodeo* [ɹoudiou] for the Spanish word with a trilled [r]. Sometimes the substitution is more extreme, as when Sayula Popoluca (Mixe-Zoquean) borrows Spanish words with /r/ or /l/, sounds that are missing from this language. The substitution made is /n/, giving *kunuːʃ* 'cross' from Spanish *cruz*, or *muna* for Spanish *mula* 'mule' (L. Campbell 1999). In other cases, two native phonemes replace a single one in the loanword. The Norman French long front rounded vowel [yː] came into Middle English either as a back vowel [uː] or as a diphthong [ju], the latter in words such as *refuse* or *pure*. Finnish lacks /f/ so intervocalic /f/ was replaced by the sequence /hv/ as in *kahvi* 'coffee' from Swedish *kaffe* or Finnish *pihvi* 'beef' from the English (L. Campbell 1999).

Often the phonotactic patterns of loanwords have to be reworked if the borrowing language has a simpler structure than the donor language. Japanese, which accepts loanwords quite readily, does not have consonant clusters, so when borrowing English words, vowels are inserted to break up the consonant clusters. Also except for /n/, Japanese has no final consonants, so vowels must also be added to final consonants. Thus the English word *strike* is adapted to Japanese as *sutoraiku* and *printer* becomes *purintaa*. The adaptation of the word *Pepsi* as *Pecsi* in some dialects of Spanish (discussed in Chapter 3) is also due to phonotactics, but in this case it is interesting that a syllable-final /p/ does exist in some words in Spanish; it is just much rarer than syllable-final /k/.

The adaptation of stress patterns also depends a lot on the borrowing language. Since English has lexical stress, the stress pattern on borrowed words is usually maintained, at least for a while. But the English lexicon shows a tendency towards word-initial stress for nouns, so that French words with final stress may come into English with the stress preserved, but over time, the stress tends to migrate towards the initial syllable. The loanword *garage* is usually pronounced with final stress in American English but with initial stress in British English. Similarly, the French loanword *chauffeur* can be stressed on either syllable.

Languages that use tone rather than stress adapt words from languages with stress by reinterpreting the stressed syllable as carrying a high tone. In Yoruba (Niger-Congo) the stressed syllable of a loanword from English has a high tone and the final syllable (if unstressed) has a low tone: *paper* becomes *pépà* and *recorder* becomes *rikódà*. If the final vowel of the English word is stressed, then the Yoruba adaptation has a high followed by a low tone: *delay* becomes *dìléè* and *bar* becomes *báà* (Kenstowicz 2006).

Phonological adaptation can take place to varying degrees and loanwords may vary in their pronunciation, as the French loan in English, *chauffeur*, varies in its stress placement. *Garage* varies in its final consonant – some speakers use the French fricative [ʒ] and some use the more Anglicized affricate [dʒ]. Similarly, a word such as *niche*, also from French, can be pronounced [niʃ] or [nɪtʃ].

According to Poplack et al. 1988, there are two strong main determinants of the degree of phonological adaptation: the length of time the word has been in the language and the social integration of the word. What they mean by the latter is that the word is used by a large number of speakers in their corpus; in other words, the loanword is a common item in the language likely to be used by any speaker.

As might be expected, speakers adopting words from other languages cannot always identify the morphological structure of the word being borrowed. What often happens is that a morphologically complex word or phrase is treated as though it were simple. Then, of course, the borrowing language's morphology is imposed on the new word. Consider the borrowing of complex forms. During the 700 years in which Arabic speakers (the Moors) occupied parts of Spain, Spanish borrowed many nouns from Arabic. Very often they were borrowed with the definite article intact. Words such as *algodón* 'cotton', *alcalde* 'mayor', *almacén* 'warehouse', *almojada* 'pillow', and *alcoba* 'bedroom' date from this period and include the definite article *al* as part of the word. Note that English *cotton* also comes from Arabic *quṭn*, but without the article. These Spanish nouns all pluralize in the usual way – by adding *–s* or *–es* – though their Arabic plurals would have been quite different. Note also that borrowed nouns in languages such as Spanish and French must be assigned a gender. Poplack et al. note that speakers show a high degree of consistency in the assignment of gender to borrowed nouns in both Spanish and French. In Spanish, gender assignment is determined primarily by the phonological shape of the noun: nouns ending in *–a* are largely feminine, so *almojada* and *alcoba* are assigned to the feminine. In contrast, *alcalde*, *algodón*, and *almacén* are masculine. Adapting Spanish nouns into Arabic presents more challenges as Arabic forms plurals by internal changes. Spanish *recibo* 'receipt' is borrowed into Arabic as *resibo* with the plural *ruāseb*, Spanish *vapor* 'steamship' gives Arabic *bābor* with the plural *buāber* (L. Campbell 1999).

Adapting borrowed verbs into an inflectional language can also be difficult, though most languages have means of doing this. (But remember that the borrowing of verbs is much less frequent than the borrowing of nouns.) If the language has various means of inflecting verbs, loanwords will almost always follow the most productive pattern. Verbs such as *commence, continue, encounter, refuse,* and *retain* among many others came into Middle English from Norman French. They are all inflected with the regular *–ed* suffix. Some languages have special affixes for converting borrowed verbs into inflectable forms. For example, Kanuri (Nilo-Saharan) has two ways to inflect verbs. About 150 native verbs are inflected in a pattern that has many irregularities. All other verbs, including loanwords, are inflected by suffixing the verb *ŋin* 'to say' to a stem; then *ŋin* itself is inflected to provide a full set of tense/aspect and person/number forms. In fact a common strategy in many languages is to add an inflected auxiliary to an invariable verb form.

In Spanish the productive verb conjugation adds *–ar* to form a verb, but the conjugation leads to changes in the stress patterns and occasional vowel alternations. So most loanwords as well as verbs derived from nouns add an extra vowel and end in *–ear*, which allows the basic stem to remain unchanged. Among speakers of Mexican Spanish in the area where I live, the English verb *to leak* has come to be used as *liquear*. In the same community, the diminutive suffix *–ito*, *–ita* can be added to nouns to make them more Spanish-like, as when *trailer* is adapted as *treilita*.

Sometimes loanwords have an impact on the borrowing language beyond the expansion of the lexicon. New phonemes may enter a language in the loanwords, new stress patterns, new distributions of phonemes, and even some derivational morphology. Such cases generally require long-term high degrees of bilingualism in the community, or they occur in a language for which the change is minimal. For example, the English phoneme /ʒ/ arrived in English aboard French words such as *massage, garage, azure, rouge, regime*, or *camouflage*. Prior to this English did not have this voiced fricative, though it had the voiceless counterpart /ʃ/ as in *sheep*. It seems that click consonants in the Bantu language Zulu came from the neighboring Khoisan languages, and retroflex consonants in Hindi may have come from contact with Dravidian languages. We discuss these hypotheses further in Chapter 11. Japanese /p/ had weakened and become a fricative in word-initial position and following a vowel word-internally, but it remained as a geminate intervocalically. When Japanese adopted loan words from European languages, such as *pan* 'bread' from Portuguese, the /p/ was reintroduced in this position. In this case, since /p/ existed in a geminate version, the appearance of /p/ in initial position was a minimal change.

In the previous section it was observed that grammatical morphemes are rarely borrowed, yet English has a large number of derivational affixes that came through French from Latin: prefixes such as *pre–, re–, con–, anti–*, and suffixes such as *–ity, –tion, –al, –ence, –ism*, and so on. These affixes came into English not on their own but in a great influx of words that contained them: *president, remain, contain, antidote, university, nation, national, presence, criticism*, and so on. Their limited productivity and application to new words is due to the fact that they occur in a large number of words, and thus speakers are able to recognize them to some extent. However, most of them are less productive than the Germanic affixes that fill similar functions, such as *un–, –ness*, or *–ish*. More about derivational affixes and their impact on lexical change can be found in Section 9.5.

9.3.   How do words change their meaning?

Once a word gets into a language and starts being used by the speakers it often undergoes semantic change. There is an interesting tension between the need for words to be stable in their meaning so that language users understand each other and the tendency and need to adapt old words to new uses. In this section and the following one, we discuss the types of meaning change that have been identified in the literature. We have already considered rather thoroughly the types of semantic change that occur in grammaticalization, and in this chapter we see that many of the same types of change occur with individual words that are not grammaticalizing. We will consider the effect of context, metaphorical uses, inferences, metonymical uses, as well as broadening or generalization and narrowing of meaning.

There are two ways to go about studying changes in word meaning, though, for the most part, the two ways should be undertaken together. The first way asks, given a lexeme (word) L, what changes did the meaning of L undergo? This type of study is called *semasiology*. As an example, we might ask how it happened that the verb *starve*, which used to mean just 'to die' (OE *steorfan*), now means 'to suffer or perish from hunger' or how it happened that Spanish *caballero*, which earlier referred to a horseman or rider, now is used to mean 'gentleman'.

The second way of investigating change in lexical items and their meanings is to ask, given a concept C or meaning M, what changes occurred in the lexemes that express this meaning? This type of study is called *onomasiology*. In this approach we might ask how the way we talk about canines has changed. The earlier English noun *hound*, which was a general word for the species has in part been replaced by *dog*, of unknown origin. The native noun *hound* now designates a particular breed of dog. *Pup* and *puppy*, which were borrowed from French, have now replaced *whelp*, which used to designate the young of the species. As we will see, we have to take into account both the meaning of a word and the other words existing in the same domain.

Word meaning also has two aspects. There is of course the definition of a word – a statement of the defining features of the category the word designates. This is also called the *intension*. But in addition, to understand how meaning changes, we need to consider the range of entities or concepts the word may possibly refer to. These entities or concepts are the members of the category the word designates. This is called the *extension* or *reference* of the word.

9.3.1.   Prototype categories

As the previous paragraph assumes, words designate categories. For this reason, research on categories in both psychology and linguistics is relevant to the study of word meaning. This research has demonstrated that the categories human beings form have a prototype structure. This entails four characteristics (the following based on Rosch and Mervis 1975 and Geeraerts 1997):

a. Prototype categories exhibit degrees of typicality; not every member is equally representative of the category. Thus in the category *bird* some birds are more typical, such as sparrows or robins, while others are clearly more marginal, such as ostriches.The latter are more marginal because they do not fly, but also because they are quite a bit larger than most birds. Note that this property is predicated on the extension or reference of the category.

b. Not all members of a category share all features with other members. There may be central members that have all the relevant features, but there can also be members lacking in certain features. Thus while the ability to fly is an important feature of the category *bird*, there can be flightless birds. To be a member of a category, an entity must share features with some other member. As a result, prototypical categories exhibit a family resemblance structure, or more generally, their semantic structure takes the form of a radial set or chain of clustered and overlapping readings. Thus one might wonder how it is that hummingbirds and ostriches are in the same category; the answer is that they both share features with the more typical birds, sparrows and robins.

c. It is sometimes said that prototypical categories can be blurred at the edges. This is a consequence of the fact that such categories have marginal members, which in some cases might resemble members of other categories. While it is known that whales are mammals since they suckle their young, they somewhat blur the edges of the category 'mammal' because they resemble fish in many ways: they live in water and they have fins.

d. Finally, with respect to the defining features of prototypical categories, they cannot be a single set of criterial (necessary and sufficient) attributes. Rather the defining features are a set that occur in many members (but need not occur in all), and they do not necessarily distinguish one category from another. For birds, having wings, feathers, beaks, flying, laying eggs, and building nests are all important features, but there are birds that lack some of these features and are still birds. In addition, there are features, such as size, that are not criterial, but nonetheless determine the prototypicality of the members, making hummingbirds and ostriches less typical birds. The attributes that define the category emerge from the comparison of the members of the categories and their attributes. Attributes that belong to large numbers of members are strongly reinforced, while those that belong to few members are weakened.

9.3.2.   Mechanisms of semantic change

Given this view of the intension (definition) and extension (membership) of a category, then we can begin to see how words change their meaning. In the following we will cover the different mechanisms by which words change their meaning and discuss them within the prototype framework. The mechanisms of semasiological change we will discuss are: hyperbole, metaphor, metonymy, synecdoche, and inference. These lead to generalization and specialization which involve onomasiological change as words compete with one another. Changes in non-denotational meaning also occur; words take on connotations because of frequent contexts, both lexical and social. Semantic change always occurs in a particular discourse context, where the context helps to drive the interpretation in a certain direction.

One mechanism that gets semantic change rolling is *hyperbole* – using a word with a more exaggerated meaning than you might expect in the context. The interesting thing about this practice is that it eventually bleaches out the stronger meaning of the word just like over-use causes bleaching in grammaticalization. Consider the example of the use of the transitive verb *grab* in current American English. The OED defines *grab* as "To grasp or seize suddenly and eagerly; hence, to appropriate to oneself in a rapacious or unscrupulous manner". That's a pretty strong meaning. The examples in COHA up to the 1930s reflect this meaning, but starting about that time, some hyperbolic uses are recorded. For instance in the context of a dance, the announcer says *grab your partners*. Also around 1937 examples with food or drink show up: *grab a bite to eat, grab some supper, grab some coffee*. These uses do not seem to have much of the "suddenly and eagerly" or "unscrupulous" meaning. In 1936 there is also *I got to grab a streetcar and get home*, again, not expressing much more than 'get'.

Fast forward to 2012 and COCA provides many more examples of *grab* used to mean little more than 'get', as in these examples:

(258)   *Once you have the basics, grab a piece in today's look: all black*
         (about choosing a men's watch, COCA 2012)

(259)   *To copy the runway look you see here, grab a hot pink polish spiked with*
         confettilike particles   (translation: 'to look like a model, get this special
         nail polish', COCA 2012)

Both of these examples and many others from this period are imperatives. Using *grab* rather than *get* gives the imperative more force owing to the 'eagerly' sense that is part of the earlier meaning. As you can see, using *grab* this way could easily have the effect of changing its meaning entirely, so that it comes to mean simply 'get eagerly' or just 'get'.

Even more distant from the original physical grabbing are forays into other domains via *metaphor* by which a relational structure in one domain is transferred to another domain. Metaphor is often illustrated with nouns, as when body part terms such as *head* or *face* come to be used in domains other than the human body, as in *the face of a clock* or *the head of the class*. A verb denoting a physical action such as *grab*, which pictures a hand reaching out and seizing an object, can also be used metaphorically. Consider these two examples. In the first the object is a job, which one cannot grasp in one's hand, nor does one get it by grabbing, but rather by saying "I accept" or something similar. In the other the object is headlines, an interesting object since one cannot directly enter into the headlines, but rather one must perform in a certain way to be (passively) chosen for a headline.

(260)   *She'd wanted this job since she'd learned to count. She ought to grab it,*
         rather than wasting her talent by keeping the books for a few locals
         (COHA 2009)

(261)   *But no, you want to showboat all the time. . . you wanna take all the solos*
         and grab up all the headlines.   (COHA 2001)

The metaphorical extensions also have the effect of weakening the semantic features of the verb *grab*. In the case of hyperbole and metaphor, when speakers choose to use a word in a new context, they are adding possible contexts as members of the prototype category. These members do not share all the features of the earlier member – the one that includes 'seize eagerly, suddenly or unscrupulously'. The examples appear to preserve the 'eagerly' meaning but the other features of meaning are not reinforced as the category evolves.

Often metaphorical meaning changes create *polysemy*, or one or more separate (though perhaps related) meanings or senses for a single word. In the case of English *head*, there are multiple meanings coexisting: the head of an animal or human, the head of an organization or institution, the foam on a beer, or the image on the side of a coin, and many more. The extended uses of *head* do not seem to affect its original concrete meaning: it is still quite clear that *head* is used to refer to a human head or an animal head. Polysemy can lead to semantic change in a word's meaning if the earlier meanings are lost. An example where a metaphor once supplied the current common meaning and the previous meaning has been lost is Latin *perna* 'ham' which became Spanish *pierna* 'leg' but no longer means 'ham'; rather *jamón* is the word for 'ham'.

Metonymy occurs when a term for one concept is used for an associated concept; this process also results in polysemy. For example, the American English compound *White House* started out as the name of a certain house in Washington, DC, in which the President of the US lives and works. Very soon (in the 1830s), however, it came to be used with two other senses: the presidency (*he had his eye on the White House*) and the executive branch of the government (*information from the White House*). Since the earlier, concrete meaning of the compound is also used, the term is polysemous. In some cases of metonymic change, the earlier meanings are lost. Metonymy works because one conceptual entity conjures up a whole, more complex scene and can come to stand for that larger whole.

An example from French is the history of the word for 'office', *bureau*. Earlier, *bureau* indicted a piece of rough cloth (*bure*) placed on the table where one worked. It came to designate the table itself, then the room where the table was located, and finally the activities carried out in that room, each one a separate metonymic change (Robert 2008). Latin *penna* 'feather' came by metonymy to indicate a writing instrument because quills were used for writing. It continued to be used even when the instrument itself changed.

A more specific type of metonymy is *synecdoche*, in which a part of an entity comes to stand for the whole entity. Thus a *hired hand* is actually a full person, but mention of the *hand* (the relevant portion for working) gives access to the full person. *Boots on the ground* come with soldiers wearing them, so it is enough to say *boots* in this case.

Another type of semantic change that is often considered metonymic is change by the *conventionalization of inferences*, which we discussed earlier in connection with grammaticalization. There we saw that frequently made inferences can become part of the meaning of a word or construction. A good example comes from the conjunction *since*, which earlier meant 'after the time that'. In example

(262) *since* has only its temporal meaning, but in (263) the temporal meaning implies a causal meaning – that the drug is responsible for the cessation of sleepwalking. If such an inference occurs frequently, it can become part of the meaning of the word, so in (264) *since* indicates 'because' or 'reason why' and does not bear any temporal meaning.

(262)   *I think you'll all be surprised to know that <u>since</u> we saw Barbara last,*
          she made an amazing trip to China.   (COCA 1990)

(263)   *After 50 years of sleepwalking, he hasn't walked once <u>since</u> he started*
          taking the drug.   (COCA 1990)

(264)   *<u>Since</u> the hunters all have CB radios, they can warn each other before*
          he even gets close.   (COCA 1990)

Such changes are metonymic only in a very loose sense: the temporal meaning and the causal meaning are associated in some contexts. In (263) *since* invokes both meanings, but in (264) it does not. The extra meaning is added by inference because the listener is always trying to guess why the speaker is telling him/her this. Putting two propositions together in sequence leads the listener to infer that they are related, not just temporally, but also causally.

Many of these types of change occur when speakers choose to use words in novel ways. We can think of words as tools that help listeners activate certain areas of their knowledge base. Thus the speaker's and listener's encyclopedic knowledge (knowledge about the world) is used to interpret the words of a discourse. Novel uses occur in context, and it is the real world and discourse context that makes the assignment of a new meaning possible. The other words in the sentence or in the larger discourse help the listener assign the appropriate new meaning. The new context of use is categorized along with the more established contexts in which a word is used. When novel uses are repeated they become established as members of the category and may affect the semantic features that define the category.

9.3.3.   Change in non-denotational meaning ▬▬▬▬▬▬▬▬▬▬

Because context of use is so important in word interpretation, aspects of non-denotational meaning may also seep in from the context and affect the connotation of a word. In this section we will consider a few examples of the way use in context adds affect to particular words and constructions.

Consider first the example we discussed in the last section: the use of *grab* to mean 'get'. In the following example, *grab* brings along with it the sense that eating dinner will be brief, but also rather informal. In addition, the use of *grab* itself suggests informality in the conversational setting, as in this example:

(265)   *Listen, do you want to go <u>grab</u> some dinner at that little cafe we saw down*
          the street?   (COHA 2006)

When words and constructions are used differentially by people in different social classes, age groups, or gender groups, the words themselves become associated with these groups, and that becomes part of their affect or connotation.

Torres Cacoullos 2001 studied the distribution of two different verbs used in the progressive construction in Mexican Spanish and found that one of them was much more common in popular or colloquial speech than in formal speech. To form the progressive in Spanish, there are several auxiliary verbs that can be used along with the gerund form of the verb (with the *–ndo* suffix): these are *estar* 'to be located', *andar* 'to walk', *venir* 'to come', and *ir* 'to go'. Consider these two examples, first from educated speech in Mexico City and the second from the more popular speech community:

(266)   *Pero estás hablando de una forma de vida, Gordo.*
          'But you are (*estar*) talking about a way of life, Gordo.

(267)   *Ando buscando unas tijeras, porque se me rompió una uña.*
          'I am (*andar*) looking for some scissors, because I broke a nail.'

When Torres Cacoullos compared two different corpora of the Spanish of Mexico City – educated vs. popular speech – she found that *andar* + gerund was used four times more frequently in the popular speech corpus than in the educated speech corpus. In another corpus from a different city (Chihuahua, Mexico) she found that speakers with only a primary or secondary education used *andar* three times more often than speakers with a university education. In terms of semantics, *estar* and *andar* in the progressive are often interchangeable, but the choice between them is socially motivated. That is, along with the meaning of the *andar* progressive comes a mark of social identity.

The linguistic context can also have an effect on the connotation of a word. The verb *cause* has been studied in large corpora of English, and it is found that when the object of *cause* is a noun phrase, it almost always denotes something negative, such as *cause an accident, cause damage, cause a problem,* or *cause cancer* (Stubbs 2002). Dictionary definitions of *cause* do not mention this distribution, but the context adds what is called *semantic prosody* to the meaning of the *cause* + NP construction because phrases such as *it caused a resolution of the problem, cause a celebration* sound odd. Interestingly, when *cause* takes a verbal complement or when it is a noun, it is more neutral, as in *cause people to migrate* or *a cause for celebration*. A study of the diachronic development of this negative prosody shows that in Early Modern English, *cause* was as likely to occur with positive or neutral NPs as with negative ones, but the neutral ones far outnumbered the positive. This skewing towards neutral or negative NP collocates has been increasing over the years, leading to the current situation (Smith and Nordquist 2012).

Traditionally, the term *pejoration* has been used to describe semantic change that leads to a word taking on negative connotations and eventually changing its denotation as well. Most such changes probably take place via metonymy, so this may not be a separate type of change, but rather one influenced by the contexts of use. For example, *spinster* originally designated a person who spins and now means an older unmarried woman. *Villain* 'character with evil motives' was borrowed from French *villein* 'base or low-born rustic'. *Amateur* literally 'one who loves' in French came to mean one who pursues a topic out of love for it, but, in contrast to a professional, also takes on the related sense of a person not competent with respect to the topic. The opposite direction of change, *amelioration* also occurs. The Latin word *caballus* meant 'nag, workhorse' but in Spanish it is the general word for 'horse'. That is, the term was extended in use to refer to all horses: a case of generalization, as discussed in the next section.

9.3.4.   Onomasiological change: words in competition

When words generalize their meaning by being used in more and more contexts, they may encroach on the semantic territory of other words. Generalization of lexical meaning resembles generalization of grammatical meaning in the sense that specific features of meaning may be lost. We saw an example of incipient generalization with the English verb *grab*. Here is an example of a word that has undergone generalization twice: Latin *salārium* is derived from *sal* 'salt' and indicated a soldier's allotment of salt. From there it generalized to the soldier's wages in general (losing the association with salt) and eventually in Old French *salaire* to anyone's wages (losing the association with soldiers). It entered English with this meaning. Generalization also occurs when a brand name is extended to all products of a certain type. A good example is the use of the term *xerox* for a copy machine. This was the brand name for an early and very popular copy machine, and as other brands became available the name continued to be used. It has even become a verb (despite objections from Xerox's copyright department).

When words generalize their meaning, the number of members of the category increases – the word is extended. As this happens very often, some other word loses members of its category and has its definition narrowed. That is, in some cases narrowing of meaning is the result of onomasiological change. For example, according to the OED, the word *girl* referred to a child or young person of either sex into the fifteenth century, but by that time some uses had arisen that appeared to refer only to females, such as *gaye gerles* or *prety gyrle*. The word *boy*, first attested in the fourteenth century referred to a male servant, slave, assistant, or junior employee as well as a male person of low birth (OED). By the fifteenth century it could also be used to refer to a male child or youth, becoming the counterpart of *girl*, as seen in this sixteenth-century example.

(268)   *Whose child is that you beare so tenderly? Is it a boy or girle, I praie ye tell?* (OED)   (1594, R. Wilson *Coblers Prophesie* l.1080)

So the generalization of *boy* to any young male cut into the range of reference for *girl*, and, less than a century later, they had become a pair.

Another example concerns the world of canines. The inherited Germanic word for domesticated canines is *hound* (compare German *Hund* 'dog'). The word *dogge* (or some variant spelling) comes into use in the fourteenth century and refers to both sheep dogs and hunting dogs. *Hound* was used as a general word for canine until the fifteenth century, but as the use of *dog* spread and encompassed all types of dogs, *hound*, which was used for hunting dogs all along, became more restricted to hunting dogs, especially dogs that track their prey by scent.

Narrowing can also occur when a word becomes closely associated with a certain context and speakers are reluctant to use it outside of that context. Spanish *rezar* 'to pray' in Old Spanish meant 'recite'; but as reciting occurred primarily in a religious context, the verb became associated with praying, and other verbs such as *recitar* and *narrar* arose to indicate the more general idea of reciting.

9.4.   General tendencies in lexical semantic change

When we discussed grammaticalization, we saw that there were very clear directional paths of semantic change. In lexical change, directionality is much less clear, probably due to the very creative (and sometimes conscious) ways that speakers use words. However, there are a number of clear tendencies that apply across languages and some of them are the same as the tendencies that occur in semantic change in grammaticalization.

Metaphors generally move a meaning from a concrete domain to an abstract one, thus creating meaning change from more concrete to more abstract. Thus when spatial terms such as *high* and *low* are used for emotional states, a metaphor is involved and the resulting sense is more abstract. We have already noted many such examples, but it is important to realize that there are some changes that go in opposite directions. For example, when you use *shrimp* to mean 'small' referring to a small person you might think that you are moving from the concrete little sea creature to the more abstract domain of size. However, the actual etymology of *shrimp* goes in the opposite direction as it is derived from a Germanic verb attested in Middle High German, *schrimpen* 'to shrink up'; so a shrimp is a shrunken creature, or a small creature. So 'small' has always been a part of the meaning and is not derived metaphorically from the concrete use.

Three strong tendencies in inferencing have been identified by Elizabeth Traugott (1989). These three tendencies apply both in grammaticalization and in lexical change. These changes are all instances of increasing subjectification, in that they all emanate from the speaker's perspectives and attitudes. Here are the three tendencies with examples:

"Tendency 1: Meanings based in the external described situation > meanings based in the internal (evaluative/perceptual/cognitive) described situation" (Traugott 1989: 34). One example is the English verb *felan* 'to touch', an external act, which comes to mean *feel* 'to experience mentally or emotionally'. Another example would be the modern noun *creep* referring to a despicable person; from the external activity of creeping around (to steal something) to the internal character of such a person.

"Tendency II: Meanings based in the external or internal described situation > meanings based in the textual and metalinguistic situation" (Traugott 1989: 35). Thus when *since* 'after' comes to mean 'because' as illustrated in the examples above, it moves from the description of the external temporal sequence to indicating a textual (causal) relationship between the clauses. The verb *observe* has undergone a change of this type when it moves from meaning 'perceive' (an internal situation) to being a speech act verb, coding the metalinguistic situation by meaning 'state that.'

"Tendency III: Meanings tend to become increasingly based in the speaker's subjective belief state/attitude toward the proposition" (Traugott 1989: 35). One example is the connective *while* 'time that', which can mean 'during' (as a result of Tendency II) coming to indicate a concessive relation between two clauses, as illustrated here:

(269)   *We stayed in Paris a little while.*

(270)   *She slept while Harold worked on his manuscript.*

(271)   *While Pam didn't really need any help, she surely appreciated it.*

Another example of Tendency III is the change in the meaning of *very* from Old French *verai* 'true', which is a cognitive evaluation. Its use as a scalar (indicating topmost), as in *at the very height of her career*, gives a subjective evaluation. Its further use as an intensifier illustrates the same type of change.

As might be expected, certain specific semantic shifts show similar patterns across languages, that is, just as in grammaticalization certain semantic material tends to give rise to similar changes. For instance, the verb *grab* that we examined earlier is changing to mean something more like 'get', and this particular semantic change can be seen in other instances. For example, English *get* is from PIE root **ghend–* which meant 'seize, take', as found in the root of Latin *prehendere* 'seize'. Also English *have* comes from PIE **kap–* 'to grasp', a root also found in Latin *capere* 'seize'. Latin *habēre* 'have' comes from the PIE root **ghab(h)-ē* which meant 'hold'. Thus we can construct a common path of change:

(272)   grasp, seize   >   get, acquire   >   have, possess

The last stage of this change can also be illustrated with the American English childlike and nonstandard use of *got* to mean 'have' as in *Magic what people gots in dere bodies* (COCA 2002).

Another crosslinguistic example brought up by Zalizniak et al. 2012 is the use of a noun referring to a foreigner (though what nationality of foreigner varies across languages) to designate a cockroach. They cite the Russian word *prusak* from the meaning 'Prussian', the Czech word *šváb* 'Swabian', and Rhaeto-Romance *sclaf* 'Slavic', all being used to mean 'cockroach' in their respective languages. The crosslinguistic study of common paths of lexical semantic change is just beginning. Perhaps with more data about change in different languages, more tendencies in lexical semantic change can be identified.

9.5. Changes in derivationally related forms

Another type of semantic change in words, which has become the focus of some research attention recently, concerns how words formed by derivational morphology lose their compositional meanings and move away from the base word from which they were formed. Some English examples are *disease, dislocate,* or *business.* When a morphologically complex word is fully compositional in its meaning, the meaning of the whole can be predicted from the meaning of the morphemes in it. We assume that complex words start out as compositional and lose their compositionality gradually so that there are various degrees of lack of compositionality. Langacker 1987 also proposes that we consider the analyzability of a word, that is, the degree to which language users can identify the morphemes that compose the word. A word can lack compositionality but still be analyzable, as, for example, the verb *dislocate* where *dis–* is clearly discernible as is *locate*, but putting them together does not yield the current meaning of the word. In contrast, the word *disease*, consisting etymologically of *dis–* and *ease*, is neither compositional nor analyzable.

What makes a word retain or lose its compositionality? One factor is the frequency of use of the derived word. As we have mentioned before, a frequently used chunk is processed as a whole and therefore can have meaning assigned to the whole unit. One can compare words with the same affix, and it is likely that the ones that are more frequent will have a less compositional meaning. For example, English words with the prefix *pre–* differ in their compositionality. Words that are higher in frequency, such as *prediction* or *preface* have a much less compositional meaning than lower frequency words such as *predestine* or *predecease*. Note also the phonological differences: *pre–* in the higher frequency words is more reduced. Hay 2001 argues that it is not just the token frequency of the derived word that determines its loss of compositionality, but the relative frequency of that word compared to the base it was derived from. For example, *predecease* is derived from the base *decease*. In some cases a derived word is more frequent than its base; for instance, *inaudible, impatient,* and *immortal* are each more frequent than *audible, patient,* and *mortal* respectively. Hay predicts that such words will be less compositional than a derived word that is less frequent than its base, such as *unkind, invulnerable,* or *immodest.* Through various tests, Hay is able to show that this generalization holds.

While frequency is likely a factor, it cannot alone explain the meaning changes that occur. In fact, frequency itself may be the result of the semantic changes. Perhaps a more important factor is the contexts in which the derived word is used compared to its base. If a derived word is more frequent than its base, it is probably used in many contexts where the base is not used, and these contexts could be responsible for the loss of compositionality. Consider an informal study of a base and derived word that are both very high in frequency: *dirt* and *dirty.* The noun occurs 13,844 times in COCA and the adjective 12,975 times. The derived word is fairly analyzable and has some uses in which it is compositional, but in fact the two words are used in rather different contexts. *Dirt* occurs often in discussions of roads and in conjoined phrases such as *dirt and dust, dirt and oil, dirt and grease,* and *dirt and sawdust,* all indicating a rather concrete meaning for this noun. The adjective occurs in very different contexts, more metaphorical ones, such as *dirty words, dirty details, dirty looks, dirty messages, dirty work, dirty joke, dirty little secret,* and *dirty bomb,* none of which involves dirt in the sense of the noun examples.

Compare these results to those for a pair of words that are of lower frequency and more compositional: *legible* and *illegible.* The contexts in which these two words are used are very similar. Both are used with *handwriting, letters, notes, words,* and so on. The fact that they are used in similar contexts keeps them closely related semantically, and therefore *illegible* remains compositional. In contrast, *dirt* and *dirty* with so many non-overlapping contexts are likely to drift farther apart from one another, leading *dirty* to become less compositional.

These examples suggests that semantic change that leads to the loss of compositionality proceeds by the same mechanisms we discussed above – metaphor, metonymy, and so on – which lead to the use of the derived word in contexts where the base word is not found. A word's frequent use in certain contexts with certain senses is what drives the loss of its clear relation to its component morphemes or its growing autonomy from related words and morphemes.

Compounds undergo similar changes, which often leads to the loss of compositionality and analyzability. High frequency and semantic change also contribute to phonological change that obscures the component words. For example, the PDE word *lord* was in OE *hlāfweard* composed of *hlāf* 'loaf' and *weard* 'keeper'. In OE it had already reduced variably to *hlāford. Lady* was *hlǣfdige* 'loaf + kneader'. These compounds have reduced phonologically and changed their meaning as social structure changed. *Lady* has undergone considerable generalization and is no longer just the female counterpart of *lord.* Another compound from OE is *hūswīf* 'house + woman' or 'mistress of the household', which reduced to *hussy.* The meaning change that comes first is the generalization to women in general, and then a rude or playful form of address implying improper behavior. From this the further pejoration of the form occurred as the word has narrowed to mean only a woman displaying improper behavior.

9.6.   What happens to old words, morphemes, phrases?

When words become less frequent because a competing word is being used instead, they do not always disappear completely from the language. Rather, obsolete words or parts of them litter the lexicon and can be found in odd dusty corners, locked into other words or formulaic phrases. Infrequent, but still in use, is the phrase *kith and kin* which is just about the only place the old word *kith* (from *cuð* 'known') is found. It had a rather broad use in OE signifying kinsfolk or fellow countrymen but now is just a relic found in one phrase. Morphologically complex words can also be museums for the preservation of dead or dying words. Both *uncouth* and *inept* have stems that do not occur unprefixed except as back-formations from the prefixed words. Sometimes words are locked into contexts where they reflect an older meaning. For example, *tide* used to mean 'time' but many of its uses were overtaken by the word *time*, and *tide* has been left to designate the rise and fall of the sea, except in words such as *even-tide* or *Yule-tide* where it still means 'time'. In the proverb *time and tide wait for no man*, the original sense of *tide* was temporal – a season or a while; however, the more modern meaning of *tide*, designating the ebb and flow of the ocean, works just as well for the proverb's interpretation.

9.7.   Conclusion

Lexical change is characterized by a great diversity of sources for new words and thus seems less predictable than other types of change we have examined. Also there are various paths of change that words can take once they have entered the language. Despite this, we have seen in this chapter many themes from other chapters. First, some of the same mechanisms of semantic change that occur in grammaticalization occur in change of word meaning: metaphor, metonymy, inference, and generalization or bleaching. Second, as in morphosyntactic change, we can observe the competition among forms, whereby one word takes over contexts in which another word was formerly used, eventually ousting it completely or relegating it to a minor function. Third, we see here a role for frequency of use in that in meaning change, repetition is necessary for the connection between a word and a meaning to be established; further, more frequent uses can cause speakers to look for alternate means to express less frequent uses. Finally, we see again the very strong role of context in determining the meaning and use of particular lexical items.

Suggested reading

A book that explores the relation between grammaticalization and lexicalization is:

Brinton, L.J. and Traugott, E.C., 2005. *Lexicalization and language change*, Cambridge: Cambridge University Press.

A general textbook that has many good examples of loanwords in a large range of languages and also many examples of change in word meaning is:

Campbell, L., 1999. *Historical linguistics: an introduction*, Cambridge, MA: MIT Press, chapters 3 and 10.

Questions for discussion

1.   One source of new words is proper names that become common nouns. The word *mom* was originally used to address a female parent and was thus a proper noun. If you check COHA (Corpus of Historical American English) for the word *mom* you will find lots of examples of *mom* used as a common noun. Make a list of the grammatical characteristics that show it is now being used as a common noun.

2.   Explain what type of change has occurred in each of the following steps in the development of Dutch *winkel* (Geeraerts 1997):

   1. *winkel* meant 'corner' > 2. 'street corner' > 3. building situated on a street corner > 4. shop situated on a street corner > 5. shop

3.   Which of Traugott's tendencies are operating in the development of English *feel*, which meant 'touch' in Old English, to the uses we see in the following examples:
   i.   *Fulbright clapped Socrates on the shoulder. Maybe when he felt the rock-hard muscle of that upper arm he began to realize that he was in over his head.* (COHA 2000)
   ii.   *Karen reached out her hand to help the woman, whose palm felt hot and slightly swollen.* (COHA 1991)
   iii.   *Drift away. Feel every muscle in your body loosening up and freeing you to relax.* (COHA 2002)
   iv.   *I feel bad. I feel like I want to throw up.* (COHA 2001)
   v.   *No one's calling me. I feel neglected something fierce.* (COHA 2001)
   vi.   *By the tone of your voice, I feel you don't believe me.* (COHA 2001)

10 Comparison, reconstruction, and typology

10.1. Family relations among languages

Several times in earlier chapters we have compared forms in related languages as evidence that a change has taken place. For example, in Chapter 2, we noted that in Pre-Old English, an /n/ is lost before a fricative, and as evidence we cited a comparison of English *goose* to German *Gans*, English *tooth* to German *Zahn*, and English *five* to German *fünf*. The assumption behind this comparison is that if related languages are different from one another it is because a change has occurred in at least one of them. We are thus assuming that we have a way of knowing that two or more languages are related. And indeed we do. The comparative method is a way of examining the words of two or more languages and determining whether or not they are related and also the nature of the relation.

In this case, by "relation" we mean family relation, as opposed to areal relation, which just means two languages are spoken in geographically contiguous regions. Family relations derive from the common happenstance in which groups of speakers of a single language become separated from one another (usually geographically, by migration) and the language of each group undergoes different changes. At first, the two groups are said to speak different dialects, such as American or British English, because if they got back together they could understand each other. But after a certain time period, say 500 to 1000 years, enough changes would have accrued in both varieties that we have to recognize two different languages. This scenario played out in the territories colonized by the Romans, where Latin was spoken, at first alongside other indigenous languages (e.g. Celtic or Germanic languages), and then replaced or marginalized these languages. Then, for example, the Latin spoken in northern France changed such that it became different from that spoken in southern France. Latin spoken in France changed dramatically, differentiating itself from Latin spoken in Spain and Italy and so on until there are a group of related languages we designate Romance languages. The family relations are called *genetic* relations and more recently, and perhaps more appropriately, *genealogical relations*.

The study of the relations among languages began at the end of the eighteenth century when scholars of language began to note striking similarities among languages not previously thought to be related. In particular, Sir William Jones noted in an address to the Asiatic Society in 1786 a deep affinity between

Table 10.1: *Some corresponding words in Sanskrit, Greek, and Latin*

Sanskrit	Greek	Latin
nápāt 'descendant'	*anepsiōs* 'cousin'	*nepōs* 'grandson'
bhrátā 'brother'	*phrátēr* 'clansman'	*frāter* 'brother'
ád-mi 'I eat'	*édomai* 'I eat'	*edō* 'I eat'
dáśa 'ten'	*déka* 'ten'	*decem* 'ten'

Sanskrit, Greek, and Latin, and possibly also Gothic, Celtic, and Iranian. He noted for the first three a similarity in the roots of verbs and in the forms of grammar stronger "than could possibly have been produced by accident" (Jones 1788). What makes the similarities he noted surprising is that Sanskrit was the ancient language of the Hindus, spoken some 3000 years ago in what is now India, while Greek and Latin are ancient languages, used more than 2000 years ago in the area around the Mediterranean Sea. Table 10.1 shows some examples of the "affinities" Jones wrote about. Later scholars have established that these three languages, as well as Celtic, Slavic, Germanic, Persian, and a few other language groups, are all descendants of an earlier language, dubbed Proto-Indo-European (PIE). See the Appendix to this chapter for a list of Indo-European language families.

Jones' discovery stimulated a vast amount of work on the Indo-European languages and their relationship to one another. This scholarship laid the groundwork for the field of historical-comparative linguistics, which was well established by the end of the nineteenth century. In fact, this scholarship on the historical phonology and grammar of Indo-European languages and eventually other languages of the world led to the development in the twentieth century of the modern field of linguistics as practiced in the western world.

10.2.   The comparative method

The similarities illustrated in Table 10.1 are striking, but they do not by themselves demonstrate a genealogical relationship among these languages. The fact that there can be chance similarities among the words of different languages, or that one language can borrow words from another, means that strong criteria need to be set up to determine genealogical relationships. Thus if we compare the word for 'book' in the languages shown in Table 10.2, we might suspect a family relationship.

Of course, we would be wrong to think all these languages are closely related, even though they have similar words for 'book' and other concepts. These languages in fact belong to five different language families. The comparative method, which was developed in work on Indo-European languages and has been applied to many language groups around the world, helps to safeguard

Table 10.2: *Some corresponding words for 'book'*

Arabic	Swahili	Hausa	Urdu	Turkish	Persian
kitāb	*kitabu*	*litaafi*	*kitāb*	*kitap*	*ketâb*

against making unwarranted assumptions because of chance similarity or borrowing.

The comparative method is based on two properties of language change: the fact that, in most cases, the words of a language are rather stable and stay around for a long time, and second, the fact that most sound change is lexically regular (in that it affects all of the words of the language having the right phonetic conditions). These two properties mean that we can compare the words of two related languages and find that their phonological shape is not just similar, but that regular correspondences can be found among the phonemes of the languages being compared. It is the regular correspondences among the phonemes that rule out coincidental similarities and often similarities due to borrowing.

In applying the comparative method, one first constructs as long a list as possible of suspected cognates in the languages being compared. Cognates are pairs of words from different languages that share a common ancestor. Of course, if the researcher does not yet know whether the languages are related, cognates to compare must be selected on the basis of semantic and phonological similarity. The question of semantic similarity will be discussed further in Section 10.2.2, but for now we will work with an intuitive sense of semantic similarity (as most researchers do!).

At this point it is also important to try to distinguish words that are similar because the languages share a common ancestor and words that are similar because they have been borrowed. This is not always straightforward at the beginning, but as the process of comparison advances, loanwords can usually be identified. In addition, many researchers omit words that may be similar because of *sound symbolism*, that is, words whose sounds bear some relation to their meaning, such as words for sounds, such as *ah-choo* (for the sound of a sneeze).

To illustrate how the method of comparison works, some examples from known related languages, in this case Romance languages, will be used. The first step is to sort the (suspected) cognates into sets that share certain phonemes. For instance, in Table 10.3, consider words from four Romance languages that begin with /t/ and compare them to the words in 10.4 that begin with /d/.

Tables 10.3 and 10.4 lay out a pretty simple situation; in each of the four languages compared the selected cognates begin in comparable phonemes. These can be represented in correspondence sets, as follows:

(273)   It.   Sp.   Pt.   Fr.
    a.   *t–*   *t–*   *t–*   *t–*
    b.   *d–*   *d–*   *d–*   *d–*

Table 10.3: *Correspondence set with initial /t/ in four Romance languages*

Italian	Spanish	Portuguese	French	Gloss
tanto	*tanto*	*tanto*	*tant*	'so much'
torre	*torre*	*torre*	*tour*	'tower'
tu	*tú*	*tu*	*tu*	2nd sg. pronoun

Table 10.4: *Correspondence set with initial /d/ in four Romance languages*

Italian	Spanish	Portuguese	French	Gloss
duro	*duro*	*duro*	*dur*	'hard'
dama	*dama*	*dama*	*dame*	'lady'
dente	*diente*	*dente*	*dent*	'tooth'

It seems clear that the set in (273a) came from a **t* in the proto-language and the set in (273b) came from **d*. The reconstructed phonemes, or proto-phonemes, are written with a preceding asterisk, to indicate that they are reconstructed or hypothetical phonemes, rather than documented ones.

But our work is not actually finished yet. Because **t* and **d* are phonetically similar, we need to establish that they are separate phonemes in the proto-language. We do this in the same way we would in a synchronic phonemic analysis: we make sure that they contrast and are not in complementary distribution. So let us examine the cognates again. What we need to establish is that in at least one language the two correspondence sets contrast. As both these sets occur word-initially and before the vowels /a/, /o/, /e/, and /i/ as well as the glide /j/ (in *diente*), we can propose fairly confidently that these two sets contrast, and we can propose for the proto-language two proto-phonemes **t* and **d*.

Now consider a more complex correspondence set as shown in the words in Table 10.5, which also contain /t/ and /d/.

Table 10.5: *Correspondence sets with medial /t /, /d/, and Ø*

Italian	Spanish	Portuguese	French	Gloss
lato	*lado*	*lado*	*côté*	'side'
vita	*vida*	*vida*	*vie*	'life'
ruota	*rueda*	*roda*	*roue*	'wheel'

The first point to note is that the French word for 'side' does not appear to be a cognate, so it should be discarded. The remaining words give us the correspondence set:

(274)   –t–   –d–   –d–   –Ø–

This correspondence set is somewhat more complex, so we have a series of decisions to make. First, we note that there is phonetic similarity to the two sets already established but the phonemes in each language are different from one another; so this is clearly a distinct correspondence set. But the next question we need to answer is whether or not it represents a proto-phoneme distinct from *t and *d. We determine this in the same way we would for a synchronic phonemic analysis: we ask if this correspondence set contrasts with the ones established above. The answer is no. This set occurs only intervocalically, so it is in complementary distribution with both of the other sets.

So this set represents a variant of one of the proto-phonemes already set up: either *t or *d, but which one? There are two avenues for answering this question and both have to be investigated. First, we have to determine whether there are other medial correspondence sets involving dental stops. Indeed, there is one, and it is listed in Table 10.6. Second, we need to consider what sound changes would link the proto-phoneme to the attested forms and settle on the analysis that would provide the most plausible sound changes.

Table 10.6: *Medial correspondence set with /d/ and Ø*

Italian	Spanish	Portuguese	French	Gloss
sudare	*sudar*	*suar*	*suer*	'sweat, v.'
crudo	*crudo*	*cru*	*cru*	'raw'
nido	*nido*	*ninho*[1]	*nid* [ni]	'nest'
nudo	*nudo*	*nu*	*nu*	'nude'

[1]The Portuguese form may consist of *ni–* plus the diminutive suffix *–inho*.

The cognate forms in Table 10.6 yield the following correspondence set:

(275)   –d–   –d–   –Ø–   –Ø–

That is, where Italian has a medial /d/, Spanish also has /d/ and both Portuguese and French have Ø.

This medial correspondence set contrasts with the medial set in (274), even though for Spanish the medial sounds are the same. What matters for establishing contrast is a different outcome in at least one language. To do this, all four sets are repeated in Table 10.7.

Table 10.7: *Four correspondence sets compared*

Set number	Italian	Spanish	Portuguese	French
(273a)	*t–*	*t–*	*t–*	*t–*
(273b)	*d–*	*d–*	*d–*	*d–*
(274)	*–t–*	*–d–*	*–d–*	*–Ø–*
(275)	*–d–*	*–d–*	*–Ø–*	*–Ø–*

Comparing (274) and (275), we see differences in Italian and Portuguese. Set (275) is in complementary distribution with (273a) and (273b), just as (274) is. It is reasonable to suppose that the sets in (274) and (275) should be assigned to the proto-phonemes *t and *d, but which set goes with which proto-phoneme? We have two pieces of information we can use to make this decision. First, we have the contrast in Italian between /t/ and /d/ in the two sets. This suggests that set (274) belongs with *t and set (275) with *d. The second type of information we can use concerns what sound changes would be needed to derive each correspondence set. We should reconstruct the simplest and most natural sound changes, where the determination of naturalness is based on what is known generally about sound change in the languages of the world as laid out in Chapters 2 and 3. Let us consider the two different scenarios.

a.   If we propose that set (274) belongs with proto-phoneme *d, then in Italian the proposed sound change would devoice a medial stop. Assigning set (275) to *t means voicing in Italian and Spanish and deletion in Portuguese and French.

b.   If we propose to follow the evidence of Italian and assign set (274) to *t, then Italian stays the same, Spanish and Portuguese undergo medial voicing, and French has deletion. Assigning set (275) to *d means simply that Portuguese and French delete the /d/.

In terms of naturalness, the scenario in (a) is less plausible because medial devoicing is extremely rare while medial voicing is extremely common. In addition, scenario (a) requires *t to undergo more deletion than *d, while it is more likely that /d/ would delete than /t/. Thus we conclude that set (274) belongs to *t and set (275) belongs to *d.

To summarize this brief introduction to the comparative method, here are the steps we followed:

a.   We compiled a list of cognates in four languages based on both phonological and semantic similarity.

b.   We sorted the cognates into sets with phonetically similar sounds in similar positions.

c.   We extracted correspondence sets of phonemes.

d.   We compared phonetically similar correspondence sets looking for contrast or complementary distribution.

e.   On the basis of (d), we proposed relevant proto-phonemes for the proto-language.

f.   As a separate step, we proposed phonetic content for the proto-phonemes.

Using the traditional comparative method to establish a family relationship among languages, these steps need to be followed for a large number of the phonemes of the languages being compared. Only when it is clear that systematic correspondences exist for a large percentage of the sounds of the languages being compared can we say that a genealogical relationship has been established. In the next section, each of these steps is discussed in more detail, including the mention of problems and pitfalls that one encounters along the way.

10.2.1.   Cognate sets

How do you know which languages to compare? Usually comparison begins when a researcher notices similarities between two languages and wants to compare them more systematically. Greenberg 1970 compared word lists for a number of African languages and suggested some relationships that were later investigated by specialists in these languages using the comparative method. Many experts on language groups have hypotheses about the relations among the languages and can use the comparative method to test these hypotheses. If the hypotheses are successful, then it will be possible to work out the systematic correspondences among the languages.

Knowing which words are potential cognates is an important unsolved problem. While we know a lot about what makes words phonologically similar, our understanding of semantic similarity is much more primitive. Indeed, some researchers feel that lexical semantic change is quite unpredictable. This is unfortunate because, as the languages being compared are more distant from one another, the more difficult it becomes to find cognates. As languages are separated for longer periods of time, more of the vocabulary is replaced (by borrowing or other means) and more semantic and phonological change occurs, all of which make comparison more difficult. So if researchers feel that semantic change is a wildcard, they are more likely to make mistakes in identifying cognates. More recent research, such as that reported in Chapter 9, indicates that, while such change may be complex, there are strong tendencies that can be referred to in selecting cognates. What we saw in Chapter 9 is that metaphor and metonymy are very strong tendencies in lexical semantic change, often feeding into a tendency for meanings to move from the concrete to the abstract.

Empirical studies of semantic change in vocabulary can also help with establishing probable cognate meanings. As we saw when we discussed sound change, identifying similar sound changes in unrelated languages helps us define a notion of phonetic similarity. So identifying common semantic changes can help us establish plausible semantic similarities.

One such study uses synchronic polysemy to establish common paths of change, based on the assumption that synchronic polysemy indicates a change in the recent past, by which a word with one meaning added another meaning. Croft et al. 2009 take twenty-two basic concepts from the domain of celestial phenomena, natural substances, and landscape features and record any polysemy occurring with these terms in eighty-one languages from different families. From their results they construct a network showing degrees of relatedness of terms, based on the number of languages that exhibit the same polysemy. For example, the word for 'fire' is used for 'flame' in twelve languages and for 'firewood' in eleven languages – both instances of metonymy. 'Moon' is used for 'month' in fifty-four languages, but for 'mood' in only one. In this way, the probability of specific semantic relations can be gauged and applied to the selection of probable cognates. One such example concerns proposed cognates in Dravidian languages, where 'night' could be paired with 'darkness' or with 'charcoal'. The survey of eighty-one languages showed that the former polysemy is relatively common, supporting such a cognate pair, while the latter is not attested in the sample languages, making that pair much less probable. Empirical studies in other domains, such as the domain of body-part terms, also exist and can be used to establish semantically probable cognates.

Another source of empirical evidence about semantic change comes from the extensive work done on cognates in Indo-European languages. C. D. Buck's compilation, *A Dictionary of Selected Synonyms in the Principal Indo-European Languages*, shows at a glance the cognate and non-cognate words of a large number of Indo-European languages. From these lists, one can gain knowledge about the probability or at least the plausibility of certain semantic correspondences. For instance, in comparing the words for 'night' in IE languages, Buck finds that most are inherited and come from PIE *nokt(i)* with the straightforward meaning of 'night', but in Hittite this root occurs in forms meaning 'evening' or 'go to bed', as found also in the Croft et al. survey (2009). One Sanskrit word for 'night' relates to the Greek word for 'darkness', again reflecting the findings of Croft et al. Research of this nature on other languages, however, is only just beginning, and much more work needs to be done to aid in language comparison.

10.2.2.   The rate of lexical replacement

Cognate sets can be difficult to construct when many of the ancient words in one or more languages have been replaced by other words from various sources. Since lexical replacement is ongoing at all times, the greater the time depth of the relationship between languages, the fewer the cognates they will share. Some researchers have used this idea to work on ways in which vocabulary replacement can be used to gauge the degree of separation of languages, or the time depth of that separation. The method of *glottochronology* was developed to provide a way to calculate the number of years of separation between two languages based on the number of remaining cognate words. This method is intended to be applied to languages which have already been established as related by the comparative method, because it is important to know that the words being compared are true cognates. That is, it is only by extensive comparative work that we know that English *have* is related to Latin *capere* and not to Latin *habere*.

Another issue concerns the words to be compared, as some words are more prone to replacement than others. For this reason, one of the developers of this method, Morris Swadesh, came up with a list of concepts or entities the words for which are unlikely to be borrowed or easily replaced by semantic change in other words. There is both a 100-word list and a 200-word list. The words on the lists are words for concepts or entities that all human cultures would need to name: body-part terms, terms for natural substances, astronomical features or phenomena, and common verbal concepts. In addition to being basic in the sense of representing basic aspects of human experience, the concepts are ones that are likely to be frequently referred to in conversation. Both features make the words for such concepts less likely to be replaced.

Once it is established that two languages are related genealogically, then the words for the concepts on the Swadesh list can be compared and the number of cognates determined. For instance, if we were comparing English and Dutch, we would note that *bone* and *been*, *green* and *groen*, *sit* and *zitten* are cognates, but *tree* and *boom*, *bad* and *kwaad*, *walk* and *lopen* are not. To come up with an estimate of how long English and Dutch have been separated, we need to know how many cognates there are from the list, but we also need a constant – the rate of lexical replacement. This is where glottochronology runs into trouble. It has not been possible to establish a constant rate of lexical replacement that is applicable across languages. Several rates have been tested, but when applied to known situations, such as the separation of English from German, the results are off the mark. The problem is simply that lexical replacement is affected by a number of factors, and these are not present to the same extent across time and place. Some of these factors are social and cultural change, the size of populations, and contact with communities speaking other languages. The Northern Germanic language Icelandic has had a very low rate of lexical replacement over the last thousand years, probably because it is spoken on a remote island and has had a stable culture and population during that period. English words changed very quickly during the period in which the Normans occupied the British Isles, as many words from Norman French were adopted. These cultural and social factors make it difficult to find a constant rate of lexical replacement, limiting the usefulness of glottochronology.

10.2.3.   The phonological form of cognates

In our comparison for the four Romance languages in the tables above, the words were presented in their orthographic form with occasional reference to a phonetic form. Of course, we know that phonetic forms are more accurate for describing the synchronic state of a language, but in reconstruction sometimes orthographic forms are to be preferred, especially if the orthography represents an earlier phonetic or phonemic form. For example, the orthographic form of French *dent* makes it much more like the other three languages than its phonetic form [dɑ̃] would. Of course, the decision to use orthography has to be based on an understanding of how the orthography relates to the phonetic and phonemic form, but in most cases where there is divergence, the orthography was phonemic when originally established, so it does represent an earlier form of the language.

Also, if the language has several dialects, it makes sense to base comparison on the more conservative dialects, or the most conservative forms in the dialects. By the same token, if earlier stages of a language are attested, they may provide the appropriate forms for comparison. For instance, in a comparison aimed at reconstructing Proto-Germanic, it would make more sense to use Old English rather than Present Day English, or Old High German rather than Modern High German.

10.2.4.   When sound change is not regular

As we noted above, the comparative method is based on the regularity of sound change. If each word changed independently, there would be no way to find the systematic correspondences that are needed to establish genealogical relationships. But as we noted in Chapters 2 and 3, sound change is usually lexically regular, and that makes reconstruction possible. Nonetheless, there are cases in which sound changes are not lexically regular, that is, they affect only a portion of the lexicon, and such cases can throw a wrench in the workings of the comparative method.

Consider the forms compared in Table 10.6, repeated here:

Table 10.6: *Medial correspondence set with /d/ and Ø*

Italian	Spanish	Portuguese	French	Gloss
sudare	*sudar*	*suar*	*suer*	'sweat, v.'
crudo	*crudo*	*cru*	*cru*	'raw'
nido	*nido*	*ninho*	*nid* [ni]	'nest'
nudo	*nudo*	*nu*	*nu*	'nude'

The forms from Spanish were carefully chosen to show a systematic correspondence. Other cognates show a different correspondence, one in which the medial /d/ in Spanish has been lost, as shown in Table 10.8.

Compare the two correspondence sets from Table 10.6 and 10.8:

Table 10.8: *Medial correspondence set with /d/ and Ø*

Italian	Spanish	Portuguese	French	Gloss
credere	*creer*	–	*croire*	'to believe'
piede	*pie*	*pé*	*pied* [pje]	'foot'
udire	*oir*	*ouvir*	*ouie* ('hearing')	'to hear'

(276)   –d–   –d–   –Ø–   –Ø–

(277)   –d—   Ø—   Ø—   Ø–

The forms in Table 10.8 represent a correspondence set whose status must be determined by comparison with other sets. Does it contrast with the set shown in Table 10.6 or is it in complementary distribution? It is hard to tell with so few examples. Here it does appear that a following front vowel might condition deletion of /d/ in Spanish. The standard account, however, is that the medial /d/ in Spanish showed a lot of variation and deleted in some cases and was retained in others (Menéndez-Pidal 1968: 130). Perhaps a detailed study of all relevant words would yield an explanation for why some deleted and some retained the /d/, but for the purposes of comparative reconstruction, such a case presents a problem because it appears to represent a contrasting correspondence set, which would mean setting up a new proto-phoneme. The point of this case, then, is that the comparative method rests on the assumption of the regularity of sound change, and when sound change is not regular, many difficulties arise for the analyst.

10.2.5.   Proto-phonemes are abstract place-holders

The comparative method can tell us how many proto-phonemes there are, because we sort out contrasting vs. complementary correspondence sets, but in and of itself, it does not tell us anything about the phonetic content of the proto-phonemes. In the cases discussed in Section 10.2, the phonetic similarity of the phonemes in the daughter languages pointed clearly to *t and *d, but there are many cases where the phonetic content is much less clear. Consider the comparison of /r/ and /l/ in four Polynesian languages shown in Table 10.9 (Crowley 1997).

Table 10.9: *Cognates containing /r/ and /l/ in four Polynesian languages*

	Tongan	Samoan	Rarotongan	Hawaiian	Gloss
1	laho	laso	raʔo	laho	'scrotum'
2	lohu	lou	rou	lou	'fruit-picking pole'
3	ŋalu	ŋalu	ŋaru	nalu	'wave'
4	kalo	ʔalo	karo	ʔalo	'dodge'
5	oŋo	loŋo	roŋo	lono	'hear'
6	ua	lua	rua	lua	'two'
7	maa	mala	mara	mala	'fermented'
8	huu	ulu	uru	komo	'enter'

In examples 1–4 we have following correspondence set:

(278)   l   l   r   l

In examples 5–8 we have this set:

(279)   Ø   l   r   l

Because these two sets contrast in one language (Tongan) they have to be considered two distinct correspondence sets. Thus two proto-phonemes must be set up.

The phonetic content of these proto-phonemes is not immediately obvious, as /l/ predominates in both sets. A fair solution is to call them *l_1 and *l_2 unless there are good reasons to reconstruct the phonetic difference between them. Crowley entertains the idea that one could be /r/, but admits that the choice is 'fairly arbitrary'. He goes on to note that the loss of /r/ might be slightly more likely than the loss of /l/, so that set (279) could come from *r, with its loss in Tongan and set (278) from *l, which would have become /r/ in Rarotongan. Considering a wider range of Polynesian languages, Crowley finds more /l/ reflexes (outcomes) for set (278) than for set (279), also pointing to *l for (278) and *r for (279). The point, however, is that the reconstruction of the phonetic content is on much shakier ground than the reconstruction of the contrast between two proto-phonemes. Thus it is important to remember that these are two distinct steps in the process. It is also extremely important to remember that reconstruction of the phonetic content can range from highly motivated to highly speculative. For this reason, we must be very careful about using reconstructed changes as data when we consider what sound changes are more common than others. For example, this case could not be used to support the claim that changes of /l/ to /r/ are more common than changes of /r/ to /l/, or that deletion of /r/ is more common than deletion of /l/.

10.3.   Typological evidence: PIE obstruents

Extensive work on Indo-European languages using the comparative method yielded a reconstruction with three series of stops. The forms from four IE languages shown in Table 10.10 provide some of the evidence for this three-way contrast.

Table 10.10: *The three-stop series in initial position in four ancient IE languages (orthographic* c = /k/) (adapted from Trask 2007:119)

Series	Greek	Latin	Sanskrit	Old English	Gloss
1	patḗr	pater	pitā́	fæder	'father'
	treis	trēs	trayas	þrī	'three'
	(he)-katón	centum	śatám	hund	'hundred'
2	(no labials)				
	déka	decem	dáśa	téon	'ten'
	geúomai	gustus	dʒōs	céosan	'taste, test, choose'
3	phérō	ferō	bharāmì	beoru	'I carry'
	(é-)thēka	fēcī	(a-)dhām	dō	'do, put'
	kheúō	fu-n-d-ō	ho-tar	gēotan	'pour'

The first thing Table 10.10 shows is that comparing languages that are more distantly related than the Romance languages addressed in Section 10.2 is very difficult. However, all of the correspondences shown here are attested in many other cognates, so we are on pretty firm ground comparing the initial consonants in these words. The correspondence sets in series 1 are:

(280)   *p–*   *p–*   *p–*   *f–*
         t–   *t–*   *t–*   *þ–*
         k–   *k–*   *ś–*   *h–*

These are grouped together because they are all voiceless and they are all stops in Greek, Latin, and Sanskrit (except for the *ś–* which derived by palatalization before front vowels from *k–*; the front vowel then merged with *a*) and fricatives in Old English (representing Germanic).

Series 2 lacks a labial counterpart, though researchers searched for it intently. The correspondence sets of this series are:

(281)   *d–*   *d–*   *d–*   *t–*
         g–   *g–*   *dʒ–*   *k–*

In this series the initial consonants are voiced, except in Old English. Again, Sanskrit has palatalized the velar.

The third series contains voiceless aspirates in Greek, voiced aspirate (murmured) consonants in Sanskrit and voiced stops in Old English. Latin has a voiceless fricative, and there has also been an odd change in the place of articulation.

(282)   *ph–*   *f–*   *bh–*   *b–*
         th–   *f–*   *dh–*   *d–*
         kh–   *f–*   *h–*   *g–*

Given that these three series of stops all contrast in the daughter languages, we need to set up three contrastive series of proto-phonemes for PIE. As mentioned in the last section, deciding what their phonetic features might have been is a separate task. In previous sections, we used the naturalness of the sound changes that would be required by the reconstruction to decide what the phonetic features should be. In this case, when the early scholars proposed phonetic features for the proto-phonemes, not much was known about how other languages change or what types of stop series they might have, so the series of proto-phonemes that were proposed included a voiceless, a voiced, and a voiced aspirate series, following the Sanskrit situation (though our examples do not show it, a set of labial-velars, $*k^w$, $*g^w$, $*gh^w$ can also be reconstructed for PIE):

(283)   Traditional reconstruction of PIE stops:
         *p   *t   *k
               *d   *g
         *bh   *dh   *gh

This reconstruction has been more or less accepted since the early nineteenth century. Now that we know more about consonant systems in the languages of the world, several scholars have brought up the point that such a consonant system is very rare among today's languages, if one exists at all. Of course, it could be that a language that was spoken 6000 years ago might have a system of stops that is totally unknown today, but most historical linguists accept the working principle that reconstructed languages should conform to the properties found in in existing languages, otherwise, reconstruction would be too unconstrained. Now, we are not talking about languages that might have existed at the first emergence of human language 100,000 or 150,000 years ago. Such languages probably had not yet developed all the properties we see today. But reconstruction as practiced today does not extend back that far, so it is better to assume that our reconstructed languages have the same properties as existing languages.

Discussions of the phonetic properties of the PIE stops have not yielded good suggestions about how to reinterpret the third series, the voiced aspirate series, with some other phonetic type. Recently, however, some scholars have suggested a more thorough reorganization of the reconstruction, in which the three series are interpreted as comprising a voiceless stop, a voiceless glottalized (or ejective) stop, and a voiced stop, as shown in (284), which is based on Hopper 1973:

(284)   The "glottalic" reconstruction
          p   t   k
                t'   k'
          b   d   g

The voiceless stop series remains unchanged, but what was the voiced series in the older reconstruction of PIE is here considered glottalized and the reconstructed "voiced aspirates" are here considered plain voiced stops. A system such as this is very common in the languages of the world. As Hopper notes, the glottalized series could either be ejective or laryngealized.

The arguments Hopper presents for this reconstruction seem relatively strong. First, (284) is a crosslinguistically common type of system, confirmed by subsequent research on the languages of the world (Maddieson 1984). Second, the rarity or lack of a labial in the series that was earlier considered the voiced series is not explainable with the earlier reconstruction because voiced /b/ is not likely to be missing. It is common, however, for languages with ejectives to lack a labial ejective (Maddieson 1984). A third typological argument concerns the restricted distribution of the second series, which behave much as glottalized consonants do in other languages. This series of proto-phonemes are much rarer than the other series, and they do not occur at all in affixes.

Related to the last point is the reconstruction of PIE monosyllabic roots, which shows that the second series occurred with heavy restrictions: no root contained two consonants from this series. In the traditional reconstruction that would have meant that no root had two plain voiced stops, a very unusual restriction. In the "glottalic" reconstruction, the restriction is that no root have two ejective consonants. Such a restriction occurs in other languages that have ejective consonants, for example, in Hausa (Chadic), Yucatec Mayan, and Quechua (Hopper 1973).

Finally, a less compelling, but interesting, argument is that many scholars have placed the origin of the IE languages in the area of the Black Sea and the Cis-Caucasian Plain. The Caucasian languages spoken in this area today have glottalized stops. One Indo-European language, Armenian, today has glottalized stops as reflexes of the second series.

Of course, changing the reconstruction of the stop system of PIE means also altering the reconstructed sound changes that have been proposed for the daughter branches. The details of these changes have still to be worked out, but, as an example, we will consider the changes occurring in the Germanic branch under the two possible reconstructions.

Given the traditional proto-phonemes, the Germanic changes are characterized by what is referred to as the First Germanic Consonant Shift, or Grimm's Law. As you see in Table 10.10, the first series of stops became fricatives in Germanic, the second series became voiceless stops, and the third series became voiced stops (or fricatives, under certain circumstances). So from the traditional reconstruction, we would get the following changes:

(285)   PIE   Germanic
           p   t   k   >   f   þ   x (h)
                d   g   >   t   k
           bh   dh   gh   >   b   d   g

Given the revised, glottalic reconstruction, Germanic undergoes the following changes:

(286)   PIE   Germanic
           p   t   k   >   f   þ   x(h)
                t'   k'   >   t   k
           b   d   g   (unchanged)   b   d   g

Thus the First Germanic Consonant Shift is simplified and also more natural. The change of the voiceless stops to fricatives is the same in both scenarios. The results for the second series in the revised reconstruction are more natural than in the traditional one, because the glottalized stops simply lose the glottalic quality and become plain voiceless stops in the glottal reconstruction, while in the traditional one, the voiced stops must devoice, a change which is quite unusual. Also in the glottalic reconstruction, the third series, the voiced stops are unchanged, while in the traditional reconstruction, they lose their murmured quality.

More work needs to be done to compare these two competing solutions to the phonetic features present in the PIE proto-phonemes. The point of this section has been to illustrate how typological information – what we now know about the languages of the world – can be very helpful in reconstruction. Indeed, it becomes essential, if the goal of reconstruction is to recreate a language that we assume has the same properties as languages spoken today.

10.4.   Internal reconstruction

Reconstruction can also be done using data from a single language. As we have seen throughout this book, a language viewed synchronically contains a wealth of information about its history. Consider these examples.

If a language has different ways of inflecting nouns and verbs and some of them have more irregularities and stem changes, we can suppose that they represent an older pattern. For example, in English, to form the past tense we have the following means, depending upon the verb and the discourse situation:

Stem change:	*break, broke, broken*; *sing, sang, sung*; *bite, bit, bitten*
Suffix:	*talk, talked*; *play, played*; *rub, rubbed*
Periphrastic:	*did talk, did break, did bite*

Because we know a lot about how morphological systems change, we can confidently propose that the stem change means of expression is the oldest. There are two pieces of evidence for this: first, stem changes and the irregularities they involve take a long time to develop. The English strong verbs (the ones with the stem changes) are quite opaque and irregular today, indicating that they have undergone a long history of development. In contrast, the suffix system is quite regular and conditions stem changes in only a very few cases (such as *sleep, slept*). Second, we know that older constructions survive primarily in high-frequency forms, so the fact that the stem-change past tense in English is restricted to only about 150 verbs, which are mostly high frequency, indicates that it is the older system.

In grammaticalization we can also reconstruct earlier stages. If a future construction has a form in it similar to a movement verb, as the *go*-futures do in many languages, we are reconstructing the grammaticalization of the future construction by positing that it came from a movement construction. In addition, if there are competing constructions, we can work out which one developed earlier and which later by examining their formal properties, semantics, and the contexts in which they are used. For example, there are two genitive constructions in English, the *'s* and the *of* genitive.

(287)   *the street's name*   vs.   *the name of the street*

First we observe that the first is a clitic and the second a separate word – a preposition. Second, we note that one is postposed to the possessor and the other preposed to the possessor. These positions indicate different syntactic typologies, so, if we know anything about typological change in the language, that will help to identify which construction is older. Third, we examine the contexts of use of the two constructions. We note that for the most common types of possession – kinship terms and body parts – the first construction is preferred:

(288)   *John's mother, John's leg*   vs.   *?the mother of John, ?the leg of John*

This preference also indicates that the clitic construction is older than the prepositional one, since high-frequency contexts are more conservative and less likely to change.

A common type of internal reconstruction uses sound alternations in the morphological system to reconstruct an earlier stage. Such reconstructions are based on the assumption that morphological systems, especially inflectional ones, were regular earlier and that irregularities were introduced by sound changes. Using this assumption, data from a single language can be used to reconstruct these sound changes. Consider the Latin nouns in (289). While the nominative singular ends in *–s*, when the genitive is formed, the consonant in that position is *–r–*. Assuming that at one time the stem had only one form, we can reconstruct a sound change involving /s/ and /r/.

(289)   Latin

Nominative singular	Genitive singular	Gloss
genus	*generis*	'family, kind'
opus	*operis*	'work'
flōs	*flōris*	'flower'
corpus	*corporis*	'body'

The question of which consonant was the earlier one can be addressed by considering other paradigms in Latin. There are some that have /r/ throughout, such as *mulier, mulieris* 'woman', which would suggest that the stems in (289) originally ended in /s/ and underwent rhotacism. This is the correct reconstruction, but to do this successfully, one must know a great deal about the language, as there are also some nouns with medial /s/ throughout, such as *causa* 'cause', but these can be established as coming from a geminate /ss/ (Buck 1933).

Another interesting case of internal reconstruction concerns the Maori (Polynesian) passive forms we discussed in Chapter 4. The data from (46) are reproduced here as (290). You will recall that it appears as if the suffix added to the base form to make a passive has several different and unpredictable initial consonants. Also, note that all Maori words end in vowels. Assuming that at one time this system was completely regular, we need to find just one base form for each verb and only one form for the suffix. The only way to do this is to propose that the consonant that appears at the beginning of the passive suffix once belonged to the base form; thus the base forms ended in consonants: **awhit,* **mahuet, *hopuk, *arum,* and so on, and the suffix was *–ia.* The sound change that is involved deleted all final consonants, making it appear as if the consonant belongs to the passive suffix, and creating the irregularity of allomorphs of the passive, which can have different initial consonants.

(290)   Maori passives

Base form of verb	Passive	Gloss
awhi	*awhitia*	'embrace'
mahue	*mahuetia*	'leave'
mea	*meatia*	'say'
hopu	*hopukia*	'catch'
aru	*arumia*	'carry'
tohu	*tohuŋia*	'point out'
mau	*mauria*	'carry'
wero	*werohia*	'stab'
fao	*faofia*	'put in'

In this case, as in many others, comparative data can be used to support the internal data. The distantly related language, Bahasa Indonesian, has both vowels and consonants at the ends of verb roots, and some of them match the consonants in the passive suffix (Crowley 1997).

The most famous case of internal reconstruction is an application of this method to lexical roots in Proto-Indo-European. (This account is based on the very clear presentation in Trask 1995.) After extensive work using the comparative method during the nineteenth century, a large number of the roots of PIE had been reconstructed. Many of the IE languages show evidence of ablaut – vowel changes to signal grammatical meaning – as in found in Germanic verbs such as *break*, *broke* or *sit*, *sat*. Greek also has ablaut, as seen in the stem forms *leip–*, *–loip–*, and *–lip–*, all forms of 'to leave'. Because of these vowel changes, most of the roots of PIE are reconstructed with the vowel *e. A strong tendency in these reconstructed roots is a CVC structure, as seen in (291). (Consonants are shown in their traditional reconstruction.)

(291)   *bher–   'carry'   *dher–   'dark'
             *ker–   'horn'   *mel–   'soft'
             *ped–   'foot'   *sed–   'sit'

Another possible structure is CVC with the addition of a resonant, represented as *i*, *u*, *n*, *r*, or *l*.

(292)   *melg–   'milk'   *kers–   'run'
             *plek–   'plait'   *merg–   'boundary'

Also, some roots have an *s preceding the CVC structure.

(293)   *spek–   'observe'   *stel–   'put'

While these root structures are quite common, there are some exceptions. First, there are roots with only CV or VC structure:

(294)   *ed–   'eat'   *es   'be'
             *sē–   'sow'   *ghrē–   'grow, green'

Based on the ablaut patterns for these roots, many of them cannot be reconstructed with the usual vowel *e, but instead have *a or *o, and this vowel is often considered to be long.

(295)   *ag–   'lead'   *ank–   'bend'
             *stā–   'stand'   *snā–   'swim'
             *od–   'smell'   *op–   'work'
             *dō–   'give'   *gnō–   'know'

In 1879, when the famous linguist Ferdinand de Saussure was only twenty-one years old, and still a student, he proposed that the exceptions in (294) and (295) could be reconstructed as the regular CVC type if they had once had consonants in the required position that have subsequently deleted. He also proposed that the long vowels in the CV roots were the result of compensatory lengthening that occurred when the final consonant was deleted. The third part of his proposal was that the original *e vowels of the roots had changed to *a or *o by the consonants before they were lost. Thus, following the goals of internal reconstruction, he proposed a completely regular system of roots: *CeC (with the possibility of the added resonants). Saussure originally proposed that the lost consonants were resonants of some sort. As in comparative reconstruction, it is one step to propose the presence of a proto-phoneme, but yet another to determine its phonetic character.

Subsequent comparative work by many different researchers eventually established that there were three different proto-phonemes that have been lost. Rather than calling them "resonants", today researchers refer to them as "laryngeals", and thus Saussure's reconstruction is called the Laryngeal Theory. However, the phonetic character of these consonants is still uncertain. They are sometimes labeled as *h₁, which had no effect on the nearby vowel, *h₂, which lowered the vowel to *a, and *h₃, which rounded the vowel to *o. Some of the apparently exceptional roots in (294) and (295) are then reconstructed as follows (Trask 1995):

(296)   *h₁es–>   *es–   'be'   *dheh₁– >   *dhē   'put'
        *h₂eg– >   *ag–   'lead'   *steh₂–>   *sta–   'stand'
        *h₃ed– >   *od–   'smell' *deh₃–>   *dō–   'give'

Besides the regularization of the system of roots, these reconstructed consonants help to explain the patterns of ablaut in the different IE languages, a topic too complex to take up here.

For many years this clever reconstruction of the PIE roots attracted little attention, but the discovery of a previously unknown Indo-European language changed all that. At the end of the nineteenth century, a library of cuneiform inscriptions was excavated at Boğazköy in Turkey. The language of these inscriptions was called "Hittite" on the mistaken notion that they were associated with the Anatolian Empire mentioned in the Old Testament. These writings were deciphered by the Czech linguist Bedřich Hrozný, who argued in his

1917 book that Hittite was an Indo-European language. This language, which was called Nesili by the people who spoke it, was recorded fragmentarily from the nineteenth century BC and was spoken until 1100 BC on the Anatolian peninsula. In 1927 Jerzy Kuryłowicz pointed out that some Hittite words appeared to match Saussure's reconstruction, as they were written with a consonant in positions he had proposed. In the cuneiform syllabary the consonant symbols used are ones that represents velar fricatives. Consider these examples: the PIE root *plā– 'flat' would be *pleh₂– in Saussure's system and it appears in Hittite written as pal-ḫi-i-išɪ meaning 'broad' and the PIE word for 'bone' *os– shows up in Hittite as ḫastai. The reconstructed consonants were thus confirmed, which is a strong validation of the method of internal reconstruction.

As for their phonetic properties, there is still much controversy about these so-called laryngeal consonants. The consonant I have called *h₃ causes the preceding vowel to be back and rounded, and thus probably had those phonetic features itself. The one called *h₁ is thought by some to be a glottal stop, though Lehmann 1952 argues they were all fricatives. This consonant disappeared even in Hittite, so it was likely the weakest of the trio. Other ideas about their phonetic status include suggestions that the second and third were pharyngeal (Beekes 1995). Perhaps we will never know. The important point is that the method of internal reconstruction suggested that consonants had once existed and, indeed, evidence turned up to support that theory.

10.5.   Proposals for further genealogical relations

So far, the methods of comparative and internal reconstruction have been used to establish genealogical relations and propose reconstructions in a large number of language groups. Besides Indo-European, we have reconstructions of Dravidian languages (spoken in the Indian subcontinent), Sino-Tibetan (spoken throughout Asia), Uralic, Altaic, and other languages of Eurasia. Reconstruction has been done on Bantu languages in Africa, as well as other groups there. The Polynesian languages have been examined, as we saw in this chapter. In South America, the Quechuan languages have been compared, and in North America, several language families have been proposed – for instance, Algonquian, Athapaskan, Kiowa-Tanoan, Uto-Aztecan, and several more. However, genealogical relations remain to be discovered for a substantial number of languages still spoken in the world. There are many languages without known relatives, which are called *isolates*. The Basque language is one of the most famous isolates. Despite being spoken in the midst of several Indo-European languages for millennia, it has a structure and a lexicon that shows it is not related to any of the known languages of Europe. In addition, in some parts of the world – notably Papua New Guinea and South America – there are many languages yet to be classified. While there are comprehensive catalogs of the world's languages with affiliations listed, it is important to remember that some of these affiliations are based on strong evidence and others are much more speculative.

10.5.1.   Proto-Nostratic

Further work in language comparison is going in two directions: towards a greater time depth, that is, relating the families that have been reconstructed, and towards classifying languages so far lacking an affiliation. The first direction is a natural outcome of the application of the comparative method. Once we have a sufficient reconstruction of PIE, then it is time to look around for other proto-languages that might be related to this ancestral language. As early as 1903, Holger Pedersen proposed that IE might belong to a much larger family that included IE, Uralic (including Finnish, Hungarian, and Estonian), Altaic (including Turkish and Mongolian), Afro-Asiatic (including Semitic languages, Berber, Chadic, and other languages of North Africa), and Kartvelian (South Caucasian). Pedersen coined the term "Nostratic" from Latin *nostras* 'our countryman', but did not follow up on his proposal in any detail. During the 1960s a Russian linguist, V. M. Illich-Svitych, began comparing reconstructed proto-languages as suggested by Pedersen's Nostratic hypothesis. Following the comparative method on the proto-languages from the families just listed and adding another, Dravidian, he reconstructed a large number of Proto-Nostratic lexical items. Another Russian linguist, A. Dolgopolsky, worked independently on a similar project and then collaborated on the reconstruction. Now several historical linguists have contributed to the project, some proposing that other families such as Chukotko-Kamchatkan, Eskimo-Aleut, Sumerian, and even Nilo-Saharan and Niger-Congo might be related.

In spite of the fact that the usual methods of comparative reconstruction are used, and a large number of roots (more than 600) with the sound changes needed to explain them have been reconstructed, the Nostratic hypothesis is not yet fully accepted (Salmons and Joseph 1998). Besides the fact that historical linguists are generally slow to accept new proposals, there remains the fact that as we move farther back in time, both the phonological relations and the semantic ones become more tenuous. As mentioned in Section 10.2.2, the lack of a clear understanding of the possible ways in which words change their meaning makes identification of cognates in some cases a matter of speculation. Also, given that in some cases the qualities of the vowels cannot be reconstructed, sometimes only consonants appear firmly in reconstructed forms. Since there are a limited number of consonants in any language, the probability of a chance occurrence of a particular consonant in a word with a meaning similar to that of another language adds to the possibility for errors.

Still, the body of work is impressive and intriguing; it is certainly worth pursuing. Consider some of the reconstructed Proto-Nostratic forms, with the reconstructed forms used found in several proto-languages (Kaiser and Shevoroshkin 1988).

(297)   Proto-Nostratic   **k'olV   'round'
          Proto-Indo-European   *kʷel–   'round, revolve' (cf. English *wheel*)
          Proto-Afro-Asiatic   *k'(w)l   'round, revolve'
          Proto-Kartvelian   *kʷwer–/kʷal–   'round'
          Proto-Altaic   *kolV–   'mix, rotate'
          Proto-Uralic   *kola   'circle'
          Proto-Dravidian   *ku/ūl–   'round, whirl'

Besides a number of lexical roots with systematic correspondences such as these, correspondences have been found among grammatical morphemes, such as the word for 'who' and personal pronouns. Example (298) shows some proposed proto-cognates, also from Kaiser and Shevoroshkin 1988.

(298)   Proto-Nostratic *k̇o or *q̇o 'who'
          Proto-Indo-European *kʷo– 'who', *kʷi– 'what' (cf. English *wh–* words)
          Proto-Afroasiatic */k̇(w)/ and /k(w)/ 'who'
          Proto-Altaic *ka–, *xa–, or xo 'interrogative pronoun'
          Proto-Uralic *ko– or ku– 'who'

First singular personal pronouns are reconstructed for Proto-Nostratic as **mi* in the nominative and **minV* in oblique cases. Second person singular is **t'i* and/or **si* in the nominative; **t'inV* and/or **sinV* in the oblique cases. These are just a few examples to provide a taste of the interesting correspondences found.

Such reconstructions, if valid, take us far back in time in a way that excites the imagination. Estimates of when the language we represent by our reconstruction of PIE was spoken range from 6000 to 9000 years ago. The language we approximate with Proto-Nostratic is thought by some to have been used in the Fertile Crescent 12,000–20,000 years ago during the Mesolithic period (Renfrew 1991). There are several theories about which cultures these proto-language were associated with. Unfortunately, without the evidence of a written language, it is difficult to make the association of a language with a particular set of cultural artifacts. However, inferences about the social and material culture of groups of speakers can be made by determining what they have words for. This area of study is called *linguistic paleontology*. For example, PIE had words for 'wheel', 'ride, carry', and 'horse', indicating that wagons were used. Agricultural terms such as 'plowing' and 'milking' existed as well as words for 'cow', 'sheep', and 'goat', but not 'chicken' (Beekes 1995). These words give us an indication of what the culture was like, as do the words reconstructed for family relations and religion. Despite the knowledge that can result from such reconstructions, there are still several theories about what archeological remains correspond to the earliest speakers of Indo-European. It is even less certain who the speakers of Proto-Nostratic might have been. Notice that the time estimates given just above include vast ranges, emphasizing how difficult it is to pin down linguists' hypothetical proto-languages in either time or space.

10.5.2.   Multilateral comparison

Another approach to language comparison has been practiced with some success by Joseph H. Greenberg. Greenberg spent his life becoming acquainted with the languages of the world, keeping notebooks full of words and grammatical properties that he recorded as he sifted through material on a vast number of languages. Over time he used this material to address the question of the genealogical relationships among languages in different parts of the world. In his method he compares a large number of languages at one time. His idea is that one needs to find levels of similarity and also to find out which languages are not related. He argues that by just comparing two languages at a time you may come up with strange results, as, say, if one compares Swedish and Sicilian and concludes they are related and then compares Norwegian and Provençal and finds they are related – the larger picture is missed entirely, including the important detail that Swedish and Norwegian are very closely related. Thus Greenberg compares all the languages of an area. He does not establish sound correspondences, but rather groups languages as to how similar their cognates appear. He regards this as a necessary precursor to applying the comparative method, for how else will one know which languages to submit to comparison?

Using lists of basic vocabulary (such as found on the Swadesh list), he assembles possible cognates based on phonological and semantic similarity. To establish semantic similarity he uses translation equivalents into another language, such as English, asking, for example, what is the word for 'sun' in this language? He also uses widely attested one-step semantic change, such as 'sun' > 'day'; other more tenuous semantic relations are avoided. For phonological similarity, he relies upon widely attested sound changes. In both cases, the assumption is that linguistic change is very similar across languages. This is a theoretical point that Greenberg, in his other work, helped to establish (see Section 10.6). Note that the comparative method, as described in the first sections of this chapter, does not assume the universality of sound change, rather it assumes the regularity of sound change of whatever type.

Given lists of semantically and phonologically similar words, Greenberg applies a quantitative approach, counting which languages share the most cognates. He also applies a weighting system to the resemblances found, counting as less significant words that could be similar because of sound symbolism, and, of course, discarding words that could be similar because of borrowing. Besides lexical correspondences, Greenberg assigns great importance to morphological and morphophonemic similarities. If two languages have similar allomorphic alternations, such as Gothic –bindan, –band, –bundun, –bundans and Old English bindan, band, bundun, bunden 'bind', these are afforded importance. Even very irregular or suppletive relations such as English good, better, best and

German *gut, besser, beste* are highly significant, because, as we have seen, such high-frequency inflected forms tend to be very conservative, representing earlier stages of the languages. Other morphological criteria include the existence of a rare morphological process across languages, such as infixation, as a strong indicator of genealogical relationship, as Greenberg argues for Austroasiatic languages. The same morpheme combinations and similarity in grammatical morphemes such as pronouns are also considered to be strong indicators of a family relation.

Using this method Greenberg proposed a classification of the languages of Africa (Greenberg 1970), which has generally held up when the specific relations have been examined by specialists in those languages. In contrast, his 1987 classification of the languages of the Americas was met with strong protest (Greenberg 1987). This classification suggested a huge language family, which he called Amerind, stretching from Canada to the tip of South America. This family includes all Native American languages except the family of Eskimo-Aleut, spoken in the far northern reaches of the continent, and Na-Dené, which includes languages spoken in Alaska and Canada, but also in the American Southwest. His classification reflects what are probably migration patterns: Eskimo-Aleut people of the far north are the most recent arrivals in the Americas coming from Asia across the Bering Strait, and the Na-Dené people arrived before them. All other groups, who Greenberg argues are related, arrived much earlier.

The major outcry against Greenberg's proposal of a very large family, Amerind, is due to his using multilateral comparison rather than comparative reconstruction and also to the general trends among Americanists towards a very conservative approach to language classification (Croft 2005). Earlier research had suggested some high-level classification for North and Central America, as in an *Encyclopedia Britannica* article by Sapir in 1929, but by the 1980s, when Greenberg published *Language in the Americas*, researchers felt they should start with low-level classification among closely related languages and gradually work up to higher-level groups. People engaged in this program of research reacted strongly against Greenberg's very ambitious proposal of a very large family spanning two continents. As mentioned, some objections were based on his deviations from the traditional comparative method, and these Greenberg has successfully answered (see Croft's 2005 summary). Other objections were similar to those leveled at work on Nostratic – that distant relationships may be indistinguishable from chance similarities. It is up to the specialists in these languages to follow up on Greenberg's hypotheses. Greenberg's view is that the value of a set of hypotheses such as he has proposed is largely based on their ability to stimulate further fruitful research.

Soon after the publication of *Language in the Americas*, researchers in human genetics began to look for similar groupings of the indigenous peoples in terms of their genetic features. Several such groupings appear to support the idea that there were three waves of migration by humans into the Americas. One recent study using the whole genome of indigenous Americans from South America to Canada and Alaska also argues for three migrations (Reich et al. 2012). This work shows that the majority of the population descends from a single ancestral population which corresponds to Greenberg's Amerind. Two other groups – the Eskimo-Aleut and the Na-Dené – are distinct but share some of their genes with people from earlier migrations, as might be expected with people in contact with one another. In general, human genome profiles and linguistic affiliation show similar results on relatedness, as one might expect, based on the fact that, when groups of people change their locations on the globe, they bring both their genes and their language with them. Despite these intriguing attempts to correlate genes and language, as research has progressed, the picture has become more complicated, with different genetic studies turning up conflicting results. In addition, if a community of speakers shift to a new language – that is, the speakers abandon their heritage language and adopt the language of a nearby community – the relation between their genetic material and their language will be lost.

10.6.   Diachronic typology

As he worked to find similarities among the many languages of the world, Joseph Greenberg also became convinced that languages change in very much the same way whether they are related or not. Given this assumption, one can piece together extended paths of change based on data (sometimes just synchronic data) from different languages, related or unrelated. Greenberg took this approach in many works, including the essay "How Does a Language Acquire Gender Markers?", in which he traces the development of noun class markers from demonstratives, then shows how they become gender markers, and eventually disappear in the lexicon as generalized noun markers or just pieces of nouns (Greenberg 1978b). This approach, called "diachronic typology" has been presented here in various chapters, for example, Chapter 2, where Table 2.5 presents lenition paths for voiceless stops developed from examples from several languages. Grammaticalization paths, such as those discussed in Chapter 7, are also constructed on the basis of changes in different languages; sometimes each step on the path is represented by a different set of languages. Only languages with extended written histories exemplify the whole path; for that reason, in most cases comparing the parts of a path as shown in different languages is required to construct the whole path.

Diachronic typology gives us a way not just to describe recurrent changes, but also to explain these changes and explain how languages are alike and how they are different. We have seen how some mechanisms of change – such as the automation of production or the generalization of meaning – occur repeatedly in language change. Using these mechanisms, we can explain why we get certain crosslinguistic patterns. For example, if either noun argument in an ergative-absolutive system is zero-marked, it will be the absolutive, and the ergative will have an overt marker. We saw the reason for this in our discussion in Section 8.2.3, where we observed that the ergative construction developed out of a passive construction in which the agent had an overt marker. Indeed, in a passive construction, if the agent appears, it must be overtly marked in some way. The absolutive argument, on the other hand, tends to be zero-marked because it developed from an earlier subject argument. Similarly, in a nominative-accusative language, it is more common for the accusative to have an overt mark and the nominative to have zero-marking, because accusative markers develop from oblique markers, such as datives.

10.7.   Conclusion

In this chapter we have seen that there are several ways in which language change interacts with crosslinguistic comparison, and the comparisons can be used for different purposes. I have emphasized comparison for the purposes of determining linguistic genealogical relationships and for the reconstruction of hypothetical earlier languages because this type of comparison is the foundation for historical linguistics. What we saw for this type of comparison is that much progress has been made, but there is still much to be done in identifying family relationships, even for low-level relations in certain parts of the world. We have also seen that linguists are trying to push their methods so as to identify more distant relations by comparing proto-languages and by applying multilateral comparison. Such attempts can work in concert with research in archeology and in human genetics to piece together a picture of how our species populated the planet.

Questions for discussion

1. What are the consequences of incomplete lexical diffusion for the success of comparative reconstruction? What about "special reduction" such as that found in high-frequency phrases?
2. What role can morphology play in reconstruction?
3. Try a little internal reconstruction on some English present/past pairs that are quite distinct: *think/thought, bring/brought, teach/taught, catch/caught*. Your goal would be find a verb stem that can give both forms by regular sound changes. Bear in mind that the spelling *gh* represented a voiceless velar fricative. It is also fair to bring in other words and to look up earlier forms of these verbs in English. The vowel changes can possibly be attributed to the patterns found in other verbs.
4. Should linguists work on superfamilies such as Nostratic, or are the current methods too shaky to make this work worthwhile?

Suggested reading

Textbooks on historical linguistics go into more detail on the method of comparative reconstruction. I recommend:

Millar, R.McC., 2007. *Trask's historical linguistics*, 2nd edition, London: Hodder Arnold, Chapter 8.

A readable book on Indo-European, the language, and sociocultural context:

Beekes, R.S.P., 1995. *Comparative Indo-European linguistics: an introduction*, Amsterdam: John Benjamins.

For an evaluation of the Nostratic hypothesis from different points of view:

Salmons, J.C. and Joseph, B.D., 1998. *Nostratic: sifting the evidence*, Amsterdam and Philadelphia: John Benjamins.

The website *The Tower of Babel Project* has interactive maps of the proposed superfamilies, such as Nostratic: starling.rinet.ru

Appendix: The major branches of Indo-European

Indo-Iranian are languages spoken in various places in the Middle East and India, including on the Iranian side Persian or Farsi, Pashto, and Kurdish, preceded by the ancient languages Avestan and Old Persian. The large Indo-Aryan branch includes Hindi, Urdu, Punjabi, Gujarati, Nepali, and numerous other languages of India, including the ancient language Sanskrit.

Hittite is the extinct language of a group living in Anatolia from 1900 to 1100 BC.

Greek includes both ancient varieties and modern dialects.

Italic languages include Latin and the Romance languages (Italian, Spanish, French, Portuguese, Romanian) as well as languages spoken in Italy alongside Latin, e.g. Oscan and Umbrian.

Germanic is attested earliest in extensive texts in the extinct language Gothic, which represents the east branch of Germanic; west Germanic is represented by Dutch, English, German, and Frisian; north Germanic by Icelandic and the Scandinavian languages.

Slavic languages include the ancient language representing the southern branch, Old Church Slavonic, which is documented from the ninth century. Other south Slavic languages are Slovenian, Serbian, Croatian, Macedonian, and Bulgarian. Some of the west Slavic languages are Polish, Czech, Slovak, and major east Slavic languages are Russian, Belarusian, and Ukrainian.

Baltic languages are Latvian and Lithuanian and the extinct language Old Prussian. They are closely related to Slavic languages.

Celtic languages were once widespread in Europe, but were replaced by the expanding Romance and Germanic languages. Those still spoken are Welsh, Breton, Irish (Gaelic), and Scottish Gaelic. Cornish and Manx were on the verge of extinction but are now being revived. Old Irish is documented from 700 AD.

Albanian constitutes a branch of Indo-European on its own.

Armenian also constitutes a branch of Indo-European without close relatives. It has a unique alphabet, invented in the fifth century AD, and there are texts dating from that time.

Tocharian consists of two extinct languages documented in texts from the sixth to eighth centuries AD and discovered in the early twentieth century in the Tarim Basin in northwest China. Decipherment of these texts revealed two related languages classified as Indo-European.

11 Sources of language change: internal and external factors

In this final chapter, we take a look at the possible sources or causes of linguistic change. Of course, we have discussed the causes of change throughout the book, but in this chapter we address the issue of causes more directly and more generally. In broad outline, we consider factors internal to language as causes of change in contrast to external causes, in particular the influence of other languages. In this way, Section 11.1 on internal sources contrasts with Sections 11.2 and 11.3, which deal with situations of languages in contact. In Section 11.1 we will look briefly at some theoretical approaches that address issues of diachronic change, in particular Naturalness Theory in Section 11.1.2 and generative theories in Section 11.1.3. In Section 11.1.4 we consider briefly whether child language is a plausible source of linguistic change. After the sections on language contact, in Section 11.4 we consider the idea that language is a complex adaptive system, in which dynamic factors inherent in the speaker, listener, and context produce change.

11.1. Internal sources: language use

This section will first review the approach presented in the previous chapters, drawing together some common mechanisms and general patterns that have been identified across the different types of change. The approach taken here recognizes the role of language use in creating and propagating change and conforms to usage-based theory so we will call it the usage-based approach. Next, the discussion turns to other proposals, in particular that coming from Naturalness Theory, which proposes that language structures change to become more natural or less marked. Finally, we consider the generative approach, which hypothesizes that language change occurs in the language acquisition process.

11.1.1. The usage-based approach

In the preceding chapters on sound change, analogical change, grammaticalization, syntactic change, and lexical change we have been able to identify general patterns of change that show a broad directionality, strongly suggesting that language change is not random. The goal has been to focus on the cognitive mechanisms that operate during communicative events, as these mechanisms not only determine the directionality of change but also supply both the "why" and the "how" of change. It is my view that the validity of an explanation for a change rests heavily upon there being a proposed mechanism for the change that follows from the explanation.

The following is a list of the separate mechanisms discussed in previous chapters. These mechanisms are domain-general, meaning that they apply in other areas of human processing and cognition in addition to applying in language. As emphasized in previous chapters, these are mechanisms that are operative when language is being used.

1. **The automation of production**: As articulatory production is a neuromotor process, it is subject to the reduction and retiming that highly practiced behaviors achieve through repetition. Regular patterns of automation are a major source for sound change. More sporadic reduction in high-frequency material is an important process in grammaticalization of chunks of material. However, automation of production is not a theory of sound change. The particular direction that retiming and reduction take must be specified for an adequate theory. This specification will be based upon what is known about articulatory gestures and their interaction with one another, as well as the organization of gestures into syllables and words.

2. **The tendency to associate meaning directly with form**: In morphology this tendency has the effect of assigning a morphological function to alternations created by sound change. At the higher-chunked level of syntactic constructions, particular word combinations come to express particular meanings, determined by the pragmatic context (see "Semantic change by inference" below).

3. **Replacement of minor patterns with major ones**: Patterns with high type frequency tend to replace patterns with lower type frequency (except where particular instances have a high token frequency). Pattern productivity is evident in phonotactic change, where minor patterns are replaced by more robust patterns. In morphology, the "regular" patterns with high type frequency replace minor patterns. In syntactic constructions also, new patterns that become productive replace older patterns. The operative cognitive mechanism is the response to type frequency; use of a pattern with different items strengthens patterns and builds up a general category which can easily be extended to apply to novel items.

4. **Resistance to change by items with high token frequency**: Operating in concert with the extension of productive patterns, we find that high token frequency strengthens the mental representation of particular items and makes them resistant to change. This has been demonstrated in morphological change, where high-frequency irregular items tend not to change, and also in the competition between syntactic constructions, where older constructions live on with certain items and in certain contexts.

5. **Chunking**: At all levels of organization, the repetition of strings of elements leads to their forming chunks in cognitive representation. Chunks are stored and

accessed together. At the level of the word, phrase, or construction, they are assigned a meaning based on their contexts of use.

6. **Semantic generalization**: In grammaticalization and in lexical change there are many examples of semantic generalization by which a word or construction occurs in more and more contexts, as its meaning generalizes and loses specific features of meaning. Generalization does not necessarily act alone but rather can be the result of other mechanisms of semantic change such as metaphor and inference.

7. **Semantic change by inference**: Given the contexts in which words, phrases, and constructions are used, language users often make inferences that flesh out the meaning gleaned from what the speaker said. When the same inferences are repeated, they can become part of the meaning of the words, phrases, or constructions. Some inferences are more likely than others. It appears that human beings seem to want to know what others' intentions are, what caused what, what the speaker believes to be true.

These mechanisms are what determine the broad directionality of change that we have noted in the various domains. Sound change rarely adds in or expands gestures, because the mechanism behind it is neuromotor efficiency. Looser paratactic structures become tighter syntactic constructions because of the tendency towards chunking. The opposite trend of breaking chunks up, occurs occasionally (e.g. in folk etymology) but is by no means the main direction of change. Word meaning can become more specific, but usually because a competing word has become more general and is taking over some of the semantic territory of the other word.

Another general trend found across change of all types is that change is implemented gradually, and stages of change are characterized by variation between innovative and conservative forms.

11.1.2. Naturalness Theory and preference laws

As mentioned before, many approaches have been proposed to understand why languages change. A widely held idea is that languages change so as to become more "natural" or "unmarked". This Naturalness Theory has been developed in relation to syllable structure (by Vennemann 1988) and to morphology and morphophonology (by Dressler et al. 1987; Dressler 2003). Using information from typology, child language, and language change, linguistic phenomena are ranked for "naturalness" with respect to one another based on certain proposed preferences, such as a preference for iconicity and transparency in morphology, or a preference for weak segments in syllable-final position in phonology. Dressler 2003 cites two diachronic predictions from this theory.

First, the more natural a given phenomenon is on a given parameter, the more likely it is to resist change. Here it is important to note that the different parameters are at times in conflict with one another. That is, a natural phonological change, such as intervocalic voicing of fricatives, as in *loaf/loaves*, can create a less natural morphological situation in which one noun has two allomorphs.

Second, if there are two options for change and X → Y is more natural than Y → X on parameter Z, then the more natural change is more likely to occur than the reverse. Again, because a change on one parameter might create an unnatural phenomenon on a different parameter, languages never evolve to become perfectly natural. Rather, change creates only "local improvement".

For example, Dressler 2003 notes that the plural *oaf-s* is more iconic than the plural *loav-es* because the two units of meaning (noun + plural) correspond to constant units of form in *oaf-s* but not in *loaves*. The prediction, then, is that a change to *loafs* (as in *roofs* replacing earlier *rooves*) is more natural than a change of *oaves* replacing *oafs*. This prediction is very likely correct. However, as we saw in Section 5.3, for very high-frequency items, we do not expect "regularization". For instance, suppletive forms such as *am*, *is*, *are*, *was*, *were* which are of extreme high frequency can be thought of as "natural" because they allow the language user to access a single form rather than two forms that have to be joined together. Of course, this situation can also be handled in Naturalness Theory by adding a parameter of token frequency which interacts with the parameters of iconicity and transparency.

While the idea of competing parameters is very likely a necessary one for explaining language change (see Section 11.4), the problem with Naturalness Theory as practiced is that it is teleological. A teleological explanation is one that appeals to the goal or end result of the change, as if a language were trying to achieve a certain end state. Thus there is a certain circularity in the reasoning: we know that many languages have a lot of transparent morphology and perhaps that children acquire such morphology easily, therefore we assume that languages are trying to change their morphology to become more transparent. What is omitted here is the mechanism; the theory does not say "how" the change occurs. In fact, many of the preferences stated in Naturalness Theory could be re-worded so as to avoid teleology. Thus, as we noted in Chapter 5, to explain the change of *rooves* to *roofs*, we can appeal to the strength in memory of the regular plural construction due to its high type frequency and note that, when plurals are difficult to access, speakers tend to use the regular construction. There is no comparable mechanism for creating *oaves* instead of the regular *oafs*.

Note that in the previous example the teleological explanation did not cite a mechanism and did not involve the language user and his or her cognitive make-up. The circularity of teleology can be avoided by invoking a particular mechanism of change that provides a certain outcome, rather than by citing only the outcome.

Another related problem arises in identifying the competing parameters. In proposing preference laws for syllable-structure, Vennemann 1988: 1–2 explains how the theory can be tested:

The correctness of a preference law can be checked as follows. Every change in a language system is a local improvement, i.e. an improvement relative to a certain parameter. For instance, every syllable structure change is an improvement of syllable structure as defined by some preference law. If a change worsens syllable structure, it is not a syllable-structure change, by which I mean a change motivated by syllable structure, but a change on some other parameter which merely happens to affect syllable structure.

Though Vennemann states that preference theory can be tested in this way, in fact, the existence of a limitless set of multiple parameters means that the theory can never be falsified. If a change does not create a local improvement on one parameter, it does not disprove the preferences on that parameter, but merely points to a different parameter. Thus vowel deletion sometimes creates non-preferred syllable structure, as when English speakers delete the first vowel in *potato*, but vowel deletion is not motivated by syllable structure, but rather by "a preference for briefness", according to Vennemann.

This criticism does not disprove the syllable-structure tendencies that Vennemann proposes, but it does cast doubt on the explanatory value for diachrony of a theory based on preference laws. Vennemann does say, however, that ultimately the preference laws must themselves be explained by phonetic research, as they are observations based on crosslinguistic research. Thus he does not hold the preference laws to be the ultimate explanation, but rather a proposal for how diachrony and typology are related to one another.

11.1.3.   Generative theories of language change

Structuralist and generativist theories of language view the different components or domains of language – phonology, morphology, syntax, semantics – as separate, and the adult grammar as a closed system that can only undergo minor changes. Thus change occurs only when the grammar is initially being constructed by the child, and that change occurs because the child does not have direct access to the adult grammar, but must guess at its structure based on perhaps limited data and an innately given set of universal parameters. Andersen 1973 proposed a model for how change occurs, identifying the main acquisition mechanism as *abductive* reasoning, a type of reasoning described by Peirce (1965). In this model, the adults have constructed a grammar, which we can call Grammar 1, and, using this grammar, produce utterances in the language which children trying to construct their own grammars use as evidence. In addition, the child (in this theory) has access to certain innate universals of grammar which help to determine the grammar she constructs. Now the utterances of the adults, based on Grammar 1, do not always supply all the evidence needed to construct that grammar, so the child may construct a slightly different grammar, Grammar 2, based on the adult utterances and innate universals. The output of Grammar 2 will largely mirror the output of Grammar 1, but there may also be some differences, and these differences represent a change in the language. This type of change is called *abductive change* because it is based neither upon inductive nor deductive reasoning.

Consider the following three propositions, often used to illustrate types of reasoning:

(299)   The Law   (*All men are mortal*)
          The Case   (*Socrates is a man*)
          The Result   (*Socrates is mortal*)

In deductive reasoning, one works from the "law", applies it to a "case", and determines a "result" (for example, *all men are mortal, Socrates is a man, therefore Socrates is mortal*). In this type of reasoning, if the law and case are true, then the result must also be true. The other direction is inductive reasoning which examines the "result" and the "case" to come up with a "law" (*Socrates is mortal, Socrates is a man, therefore all men are mortal*). This type of reasoning can lead to errors if not enough cases and results are examined. The third type of reasoning is abductive: a "law" is applied to a "result" and the "case" is inferred (*all men are mortal, Socrates is mortal, therefore Socrates is a man*). This type of reasoning can also lead to errors – perhaps Socrates is some other type of mortal being rather than a man.

Despite the weakness of this type of reasoning – it could be called "guessing" – Peirce, Andersen, and many others believe that this type of reasoning is commonly used by human beings. Here is how it applies to a learner constructing a grammar: the result is the linguistic data the learner is exposed to; the laws are the innate universal capacities that come with being a human; and the case is the grammar. Largely because of ambiguities or incompleteness in the data to which the learner is exposed, the learner's guesses about the nature of the grammar that produces these data may differ from the actual adult grammar.

Even prior to Andersen's presentation of this theory of grammatical change, generative linguists had proposed that language change occurs in the first language acquisition process (Halle 1962). The evidence given for this proposal is that adults are not as good as children at learning languages. Thus it is proposed that the language acquisition device is only operative in young children. Children can construct a grammar from available data, but adults can only make minor adjustments to their grammars. As mentioned above, another property of generative grammars is that the grammar (in particular the syntax) is a closed and discrete system that is not affected by meaning, pragmatics, or language use. In fact, the syntax is considered "autonomous", meaning that it is independent of other components (semantics and pragmatics) and also usage. There is a distinction made between *competence*, which is the abstract knowledge of grammar, and *performance*, which is the output of grammar. It is the former that is of interest to the generative linguist, as performance is considered to be fraught with errors and dysfluencies that are of no interest. Let us see, then, how these assumptions affect the view of language change taken in this framework.

In the first full treatment of syntactic change within generative theory, Lightfoot 1979 treats, among other cases, the development of the English modal auxiliaries. The issue addressed is the fact that the modal auxiliaries (*will, shall, can, may, must, would, should, could,* and *might*) behaved in OE rather like verbs (though they already had some peculiarities), but in PDE they behave like modal auxiliaries. In a generative grammar, verbs and auxiliaries are quite different categories, so a change of one to the other is a major syntactic change. Since there are no gradient categories between verb and auxiliary, the change must have occurred abruptly in the grammar, as a reanalysis made by a generation of language learners.

We discussed this and related changes in Chapter 6 (Section 6.2 on *will*; Sections 6.8 and 6.9 on *can*) in the treatment of grammaticalization. There we noted that certain morphosyntactic changes and semantic changes were related to increases in frequency of use. In general, Chapters 6 and 7 treat grammaticalization as a whole cluster of related changes that affect form, meaning, and use. In the generative view, in contrast, the main change is the reanalysis by which certain verbs become auxiliaries, and the other changes are treated as independent developments that serve to trigger this change or are the results of this change.

Lightfoot indicates that prior to the reanalysis several changes took place. I will not review them all here, but just mention three. First, the verbs that would become modal auxiliaries (he calls them "pre-modals") ceased to take direct objects. The following is an OE example of *cunnen* 'can' with a direct object.

(300)   *Ge dweliað and ne cunnon halige gewritu.* (Gospel of Matthew xxii)
          'You are led into error and do not know the holy writing.'

Second, Lightfoot lists "increased opacity" of the past tense forms; by this he means that the distinction between the present and past forms did not signal tense, as we see today in the forms of *will/would, shall/should, may/might,* and *can/could.* Lightfoot claims that these two changes are independent of one another. Plank 1984 argues in rebuttal that both changes have a semantic basis. The pre-modals are used with direct objects when they have a certain meaning (in the case of *can* it is 'know'), and when they lose that meaning, they no longer occur with direct objects and their past forms are open to reinterpretation.

A third change leading up to reanalysis in Lightfoot's account is the development of *to* as an infinitive marker, which took place gradually, expanding into different constructions with different meanings. It is not extended into use with the pre-modals, however. I would argue that this is because they were already established in constructions without *to* and were used very frequently, making them resistant to change. Their high frequency is related to their semantic and pragmatic uses. Thus the three changes reviewed here are not independent, chance developments, but all follow from the grammaticalization of the pre-modals.

Lightfoot then claims that in the sixteenth century, rather abruptly, perhaps in one generation, the grammar was reanalyzed so that the pre-modals became modal auxiliaries and constituted a class separate from lexical verbs. From this followed several more changes, first, the inability of the old pre-modals to occur as infinitives, as in this example from 1520 from the OED:

(301)   *Dyscrecion to canne kepe peace on all partyes.*
          'Discretion to know how to keep the peace among all parties'

Second, the loss of –*ing* forms (example from 1513, Lightfoot 1979: 110):

(302)   *the potential mode signifyeth a thing as mayying or owing to be done*

Third, the loss of the ability of pre-modals to occur with other pre-modals (example from 1532; Lightfoot 1979: 110):

(303)   *I fear that the emperor will depart thence, before my letters shall may come unto your grace's hands*

Fourth, the non-occurrence of pre-modals in *have* + *en* constructions (from 1528; Lightfoot 1979: 110):

(304)   *if wee had mought conuenient come togyther, ye woulde rather have chosin to have harde y minde of mine owne mouthe.*

In Lightfoot's view these changes are purely syntactic: once these forms have been assigned to a new category, they are no longer available for these occurrences as infinitives, gerunds, or participles.

As Plank points out, however, these changes did not take place abruptly; rather, the non-finite forms of the pre-modals had been rare as far back as OE. Also, the changes did not take place at the same time for all the pre-modals. The reason is that these changes, like the loss of the ability to take a direct object, are not just syntactic changes, but relate to the loss of the lexical meaning of the pre-modals and therefore their use as main verbs. Indeed, the changes leading up to Lightfoot's reanalysis also took place gradually and at different rates for the different pre-modals. All of these characteristics are typical of grammaticalization: morphosyntactic and semantic changes, some of which are accompanied by increases in frequency of use in particular constructions and loss from other constructions, are all related. Trying to isolate the syntactic changes from other changes in distribution and meaning leads to a fragmented account in which many parts of the change go unexplained.

Roberts and Roussou 2003 address grammaticalization more specifically in their more recent account of change in a generative grammar. One issue they address is the directionality of grammaticalization, as they recognize that purely syntactic change does not have an inherent directionality predicted by their theory of minimalism. They propose that the grammar is simplified by the reanalyses that are made by language learners given that certain other changes have occurred in the language. For example, the change of a verb to a modal auxiliary produces simpler structures because what was earlier two clauses becomes one clause as the modal becomes part of the "functional structure" of the clause.

Roberts and Roussou also look for triggers or causes for syntactic change, and in the cases they examine, they propose that erosion of morphological contrasts is often the trigger. The trigger they propose for the change of English pre-modals to modal auxiliaries is different from what Lightfoot proposed. They propose that it is the loss of the infinitive suffix (by phonological reduction). In OE and variably in ME, infinitives ended in –*n*, which Roberts and Roussou propose was the indicator to the language learner that the pre-modal and the infinitive were in different clauses, as in *nat can we seen* 'not can we see', where the –*n* on *see* was the infinitive marker. Once this suffix had deleted, the learner would give such a sequence a mono-clausal interpretation, assigning the modal element to a functional category. As for the semantic bleaching of the pre-modal (see the discussion of *will* and *can* in Sections 6.2, 6.8, 6.9, and 6.11), Roberts and Roussou propose that this occurs when the pre-modal is assigned to the functional category (see below).

As another example of a trigger for syntactic reanalysis, consider the affixation of forms of the Romance auxiliary *haber* to the infinitive to form a future paradigm. As illustrated in Section 6.3 for Spanish, the affixation occurred gradually, first with a fixing of position of the auxiliary after the infinitive, then with the possibility of items intervening between the infinitive and the auxiliary, especially the clitic pronouns. We noted a variable stage as illustrated by the following example wherein the auxiliary appears as an affix on the first verb but is separated from the main verb in the second case.

(305)   *diesmará vuestro pan y vuestro vino. y dar lo ha a sus vasallos* (Mejia, fifteenth century)
'he will take a tenth of your bread and wine and he will give it to his vassals'

Roberts and Roussou propose that the reanalysis as affixation was blocked by the presence of the clitic pronouns between the infinitive and the auxiliary. Once these clitics no longer occurred in this position, affixation could proceed.

In these autonomous syntax accounts, syntactic change is always abrupt, though it might take place in several stages, and it is triggered by changes occurring external to the syntax. The learner is restricted to making choices between discrete options: Is it a verb or an auxiliary (a functional category)? Is it an auxiliary or an affix? One problem with this approach is that the way these changes are manifested in ongoing change and in the surviving documents, they appear to be gradual and characterized by lots of variation, as seen in (305), where the future gram is written suffixed on the first verb, but not on the second one. Also, as mentioned above, from a whole series of semantic, pragmatic, phonological, and morphosyntactic changes that seem to occur together in grammaticalization, the generative account is forced to choose one change as a trigger or cause and another as a reanalysis, rather than seeing the whole set of changes as related and occurring together.

Moreover, there are cases where no cause or trigger is apparent. In Section 6.8 we discussed the case of the development of a complementizer from a verb meaning 'to say' in some West African languages. In the following example (from Ewe) the gram *bé* is from the verb 'to say'.

(306)   *me-gblɔ   bé   me-wɔ-e*
          1s-say   that   1s-do-it
          'I said that I did it'

Roberts and Roussou discuss a similar case, which they treat as a reanalysis. However, in this case, they are not able to identify a cause or a trigger. The way grammaticalization has been treated here in Chapters 6 and 7, there is no need for a specific trigger for the process. Instead, usage patterns interact with cognitive representations (grammar) to expand contexts of use. Repetition leads to a number of other changes: phonetic reduction, semantic bleaching, entrenchment of structure, inference from contexts, and so on, all of which propel the grammaticalization process forward.

While all the issues brought up in Roberts and Roussou cannot be discussed here, my final comment concerns the treatment of semantic change in grammaticalization. The authors address semantic bleaching as a change that occurs when items are assigned to a functional position in the grammar, rather than a gradual change that occurs because of the way forms are used in context. They assume that there are certain universal (innate) functional categories a grammar can express, and in grammaticalization a lexical item enters one of these categories, shedding its lexical meaning and retaining only "logical content". Compare this account to the one developed in the grammaticalization literature in which it is shown that the particular use of a grammaticalizing construction in context affects the interpretation of its meaning and eventually leads to semantic and pragmatic change.

In general, then, the reason many functional and cognitive linguists do not adopt a generative point of view for diachrony and synchrony is the privileged position given to syntax in that framework, including the claim that syntax is autonomous from other aspects of language. The examples examined in the chapters of this book have shown that many factors work together to shape the morphosyntactic structure of a language over time. Our discussion of generative approaches to change also demonstrates that one's view of what grammar is and how it relates to instances of use will highly determine proposals about grammatical change. In the generative tradition, grammar is very abstract and consists of a fixed set of choices (verb or auxiliary, clitic or affix) that the learner must make which are not always directly reflected in usage. The alternative "usage-based" view would be that language users can cope with the many gradations and variations found in the usage data; each construction or gram has its own properties (phonological, morphosyntactic, pragmatic, and semantic) that can be learned from experience, and these properties can change over time. The language user's grammar is the cognitive representation of the experience that the user has had with language (Bybee 2006, 2010).

11.1.4. Language acquisition vs. language use as the locus of change

Throughout the preceding section, we reviewed claims that language change or reanalysis occurs during the first language acquisition process. Andersen's model of abductive change explicates how this might occur. However, through the course of this book, factors of language use, including patterns of usage, frequency or rarity of constructions, inference in context, etc. have been cited as important factors in change. Where did the idea come from that children change language, and how viable is it?

It is an assumption of generative theorists that human beings acquire or construct a grammar by an early age, and once it is constructed, it cannot undergo any significant change, even if a person's experience changes (Halle 1962). In a number of works, the influential linguist Roman Jakobson noted that the stages a child goes through in acquiring his or her language (especially the phonology) mirror to some extent certain universal preferences (Jakobson 1942). For instance, children often begin with only CV syllables, and all languages have CV syllables; then children gradually work up to more complex (or marked) structures, reflecting the frequency of occurrence of these structures in the languages of the world. If a generation of children fails to learn a certain complex structure, the language thereby is simplified. For those who believe that language change is simplification, the acquisition process is a plausible locus of change.

This view has not been adopted in this book because of the myriad problems with it (Croft 2000; Bybee 2010; Section 6.6). First, neither the order of acquisition nor the nature of children's productions reflects diachronic changes. For one thing, in child phonology some processes occur that are never found in adult phonology, such as consonant harmony by place of articulation. Certain kinds of pragmatic change, such as change by inference, are not attributable to children, as they only learn how to make appropriate inferences rather late in their development (Slobin 1997). Second, children are very good at acquiring the patterns of usage and variation that are in the language they experience; whatever early simplifications they might make are replaced by patterns found in the surrounding language (Roberts 1997; Díaz-Campos 2004; Chevrot et al. 2000). Third, children are not in a social position to impose their grammar on the adults around them; the direction of influence generally goes in the other direction, with young children adapting to the language of their peers and elders. As Labov 1982 points out, the youngest speakers to be agents of change are not toddlers, but adolescents and pre-adolescents; even among these speakers, however, innovation is usually lexical. Finally, if change occurred during acquisition and a whole generation of children reanalyzed their grammar, we would expect to find cases of abrupt change, but all our evidence shows clearly that language change is gradual.

For these reasons, focusing specifically on young children for the source of change has never been very productive. Instead, studies of variation and change in usage patterns, examining the role of frequency in promoting or resisting change, relating changes in meaning to changes in form, studying how change moves from one context to another in texts, all have provided a better handle on understanding language change. For these reasons, a usage-based approach has been adopted in this book. We return to this discussion in the final section of this chapter.

11.2.   External causes: language contact

Throughout this book the discussion has focused on the language users as the agents of innovation and change and has assumed that the input to the user is a single language. However, a vast number of language users in the world today, and presumably in the past, experience more than one language in their environment, as in many communities speakers use two or more languages. The question for a theory of language change is whether or not the presence of bilingual (or multilingual) speakers in a community can cause change in one or another of the languages used. We have already discussed lexical borrowing, which occurs fairly easily, even with minimal language contact – that is, contact in limited situations and a small number of speakers. The further question is whether more structural properties of language, such as properties of the phonetics/phonology, morphology or syntax can also be borrowed. Linguists have offered many different answers to this question, and we review some of their opinions in this section.

Any influence of language contact on language change beyond borrowing lexical items requires extensive bilingualism. Bilingual situations vary greatly, from cases in which the contact is temporary as speakers are shifting to the majority language (as when groups of immigrants enter a community), to cases of long-term bilingual communities (as have grown up in Canada, where in many places both French and English are used). Another social dimension is that often one language is used by a majority while the other is used by a minority of speakers, and the two groups may differ in their social prestige. Also the degree of bilingualism varies for speakers – some use both languages frequently while others use one language in most situations.

Most researchers distinguish cases of change by contact according to the agent of change: in one case, called *borrowing*, native speakers incorporate elements from another language into their native language. Borrowing thus describes lexical loans, for example. The other case, called *substratum interference*, occurs when the speakers' native language influences the phonology or grammar of the other language they are using.

It is common to find reports of substratum influence in explanations for change that otherwise seem mysterious, as well as for similarities among languages that are geographically adjacent. In fact, in earlier times historical linguists used substratum influence as an explanation of last resort, when no other explanation seemed apparent. Such references occurred even in cases where the substratum language was no longer spoken and in some cases where it could not even be identified! For this reason, it is important to have some strong criteria for identifying a change as due to language contact. Since most changes that are candidates for substratum interference are changes that follow the predominant directions we have identified in other chapters, there is often a choice between an explanation based on internal processes and one based on external influence. To get a good understanding of the extent to which language contact can result in change, it is necessary to study possible contact-induced changes in situations where ample documentation is available, as in cases of ongoing change.

Researchers have identified criteria that should be applied in cases of appeal to language contact as an explanation for a change. Here are some of these criteria (based on Thomason 2001 and Poplack and Levey 2010):

1. Poplack and Levey 2010 have shown that in some cases where change by contact has been presumed, there was always variation and no change has occurred. For example, it is often assumed that Canadian French is losing the subjunctive because of contact with English. While the subjunctive is in fact rarely used to express mood distinctions, this is true of most varieties of French. Thus it is important to establish that the proposed interference features were not present before contact.

2. Establish that sufficient bilingualism was present at the time the change occurred. Languages can be spoken in close proximity without their speakers being bilingual, so mere geographic proximity is not a sufficient criterion. Many studies, such as Heine and Kuteva 2005, simply assert that languages were in (close) contact without having or supplying information about the extent and nature of the contact. This weakens the argument that language contact triggered a change.

3. Compare the linguistic systems of the two languages involved and establish that the source language has the proposed interference features. Some researchers have proposed that grammatical change by contact usually occurs in cases in which the two languages are typologically similar (see Thomason and Kaufman 1988), so it is important to establish that change by interference would be possible.

4. Consider possible internal explanations and whether or not the change could have occurred without external influence. For example, German spoken in Pennsylvania (USA) has developed an immediate future using the verb *geh* 'to go'. As the surrounding majority language, English, has a *go*-future, this might be a case of borrowing. However, as Burridge 1995 and also Heine and Kuteva 2005 note, because *go*-futures are so common in the languages of the world, this could just as well be an internal development.

5. Compare the constructions in the two languages to determine if indeed they have the same properties. For example, Poplack and Levey discuss the case of "preposition stranding" in Canadian French, which has been attributed to English influence. Consider this example:

(307)   *Comme le gars que je sors <u>avec,</u> lui il parle – bien il est français.*
          Like   the guy that I go out with him he speaks – well he is   French
          'Like the guy I go out with, him, he speaks – well, he *is* French.'

The "stranding" of the preposition *avec* in this utterance is thought to be an English feature. However, a more detailed study reveals that monolingual (or non-contact) French also allows some prepositions to occur without their object following in some contexts. These turn out to be the very ones that are left bare in examples like (307). Poplack and Levey show that the use of this type of construction in Canadian French more resembles the way it is used in other varieties of French than it does preposition stranding of English, casting doubt on the idea that it is due to English influence.

6. Finally, as many researchers note, contact-induced change occurs in the bilingual individual and plausible cognitive mechanisms must be established for each type of change.

Careful studies that follow strict criteria can help us determine whether or not a contact-induced change has occurred. When careful sociolinguistic studies of putative contact-induced change are examined, Sankoff 2002 concludes that phonological change by interference occurs, but "Morphology and syntax are clearly the domains of linguistic structure least susceptible to the influence of contact, and this statistical generalization is not vitiated by a few exceptional cases". Instead, Sankoff finds that proposed contact-induced changes attributed to morphosyntax are more appropriately attributed to the pragmatic or semantic domains. Let us consider phonological change first and then come back to grammatical change and the pragmatic and semantic domains.

11.2.1.   Phonological changes due to contact

As mentioned above, it is useful to distinguish borrowing, by which speakers willingly take new words or phrases into their language, and interference, by which speakers unconsciously apply the linguistic habits of their native language to another language. In Chapter 9 we discussed lexical borrowing and noted that loanwords may be more or less adapted to the phonology of the borrowing language. That is, depending upon the proficiency of the speakers, a loanword may be pronounced either more or less like it is in the language from which it came. In cases where speakers are more proficient in the language of the loan, phonemes may be borrowed with the loanwords. For example, the phoneme /ʒ/ in English words such as French *beige* and *rouge* entered English via such words. Also the distribution of phonemes may be changed via loanwords. Middle English had [v] only as an intervocalic allophone of /f/, but

French borrowings such as *vase* and *vacation* established /v/ as a phoneme. The consonant cluster /sf/ is not native to English, but has arrived in this language via loans such as *sphere* and *sphinx*.

Phonological interference (also called "transfer" or "imposition") is the result of adults speaking a language which is not their native one. As we all know from practical experience, most second-language speakers have an "accent" – a set of phonological constraints or habits from their native language that show up in their pronunciation of a new language. When people migrate from one location to another, adults are forced to learn a new language, and their phonological habits affect how they produce the new language. In most cases, such interference is short lived because the children of the immigrants learn the new language as one of their native languages, so the language of the community is not changed. Such a situation is often seen in the US, where new immigrants speak with an accent, but their children are fully assimilated and perhaps do not even speak the native language of their parents.

In some situations, however, phonological interference is maintained over several generations and affects the conventional phonological character of a language or dialect. Sometimes the phonetic characteristics are largely rhythmic or intonational, but in other cases rather profound phonological traits survive. For example, the very special situation of European languages spoken in places colonized by Europeans set up conditions in which phonological interference could occur. In India, English has been spoken for a century, and the British made it an official language, as it still is. It is one of the languages of education. Most of the people using English in India and surrounding countries have another language as their native tongue. While there is much variation in how English is spoken, certain phonological tendencies are widespread. Rhythm and intonation differ from British and American varieties, with a lesser degree of lengthening of stressed syllables and reduction of unstressed syllables. The vowels [ɔː] and [ɑː] are usually merged and the diphthongs [ou] and [eɪ] are produced as monophthongs [oː] and [eː]. The alveolar consonants tend to be replaced by retroflexed consonants, and some other consonant contrasts are not made (Trudgill and Hannah 1994). These phonological traits are very likely due to the influence of the native languages of India.

Given that the only two ways contact can have an impact on phonology – through borrowing of lexical items and through interference from first-language phonology – phonological traits found in some areas of the world are not likely the result of contact. Now that we have information about many of the languages of the world, patterns of distribution of structural features in languages can be identified. Where such features cluster in geographic regions, linguistic areas can be proposed. But it is also necessary to weigh such areal clusters against the possibility that they occur by chance rather than because of language contact. For example, a survey by Crothers 1975 of the occurrence of front rounded vowels in the languages of the world revealed that such vowels seemed to cluster in certain regions. Of course, it is difficult to calculate whether such clusters might occur by chance. But in one area of the world where front rounded vowels occur in unrelated (or distantly related) families, northern Europe, we know a contact explanation is rather implausible. The language families in question – Germanic, Finnic, and Romance – all came by their front rounded vowels in very different and very likely independent means. In Germanic, front rounded vowels are the result of umlaut, or the fronting of stressed vowels conditioned by a palatal glide in the following syllable. In Finnish and related languages, front rounded vowels are due to the vowel harmony system. In French the high back vowel [u] fronted to [y] in Old French in an unconditioned change, perhaps similar to an ongoing change in some dialects of British and American English, where back rounded vowels are fronting. Given a completely different mechanism for each of these changes, claims that front rounded vowels are transmitted by contact are extremely implausible. Just because languages situated near one another on a map share some properties does not mean language contact is the source of these commonalities.

11.2.2.   Grammatical change

In multiple studies of contact-induced change in a long-term bilingual community, Silva-Corvalán has searched for examples of change in Spanish morphosyntax due to the dominance of English in bilingual communities in Los Angeles, California. Spanish was spoken there before English-speakers first arrived, but for a century or more English has been the dominant language. Spanish speakers shift to English, but a continuous influx of Spanish speakers keeps the communities bilingual. Conversations in this community, like many other bilingual communities, are characterized by regular *code-switching*, by which speakers move back and forth between languages as they converse. It is popularly believed that some convergent language, "Spanglish", arises from the practice of code-switching. However, after extensive analysis of the Spanish used in these communities, Silva-Corvalán 2008 concludes there is no convergence. Rather, each language retains its structural characteristics. Where there is apparent change, she concludes "that the transfer of features from one language to another does not involve syntax, but lexicon and pragmatics" (2008: 214–215) and this applies to the effects of English on Los Angeles Spanish as well as other situations of languages in contact.

Silva-Corvalán lists three types of possible grammatical change she has found in the Spanish of Los Angeles:

1. **Changes in frequency of an alternative construction**, which Silva-Corvalán takes to be the loss of some of the pragmatic constraints on their use. In the following example, it would be more common in native Spanish to position the subject after the verbs, as in (308b). In Spanish, this is a presentative construction and the NP that is being introduced comes after the verb. Silva-Corvalán finds that speakers of Los Angeles Spanish are more likely to use

(308a). She attributes this to the loss of the pragmatic conditions for the VS word order.

(308) a.   *Estaban peleando y entonces la policía llegó.* (bilinguals born in the US)
            'They were fighting and then the police came.'

      b.   *Estaban peleando y entonces llegó la policía.* (general Spanish)
            'They were fighting and then came the police.'

2. **Lexical borrowing of function words**, commonly conjunctions, subordinators, or prepositions. These items can be borrowed without any necessary syntactic adjustment. Another case of borrowing of function words occurred in northern dialects of Middle English. It is generally believed that the third person pronouns of English, *they*, *them*, *their*, were borrowed from the Scandinavian immigrants who populated the northern British Isles, as the inherited English third plural pronouns all began with /h/. Note that the borrowing of pronouns causes no further syntactic change and is indistinguishable from lexical borrowing, except that it is rare to find such high-frequency items replaced from outside.

3. **The creation of lexico-syntactic calques.** A calque is an expression that is formed by translating a corresponding expression from another language. Silva-Corvalán finds a few cases of change in the context of use of native elements due to their identification with an element in the other language. For example, English uses the adverb or particle *back* with certain verbs, such as *call back* or *go back* but no comparable uses of Spanish *atrás* 'back' occur among monolingual speakers. However, in Spanish spoken in California, and indeed more widely in the American Southwest, one finds *ir p'atrás* 'to go back' or *llamar p'atras* 'to call back' (where *p'* is the reduction of the preposition *para* meaning 'for, towards'). Another case is the extension of the use of Spanish *cómo* 'how' to be used more like English. In Spanish *cómo* is used to inquire about the manner in which a situation holds,

(309) a.   *¿Cómo te gusta el   café?*
            'How   do you   like coffee?'

      b.   *Me gusta cargado.*
            'I   like it strong.'

But now from Los Angeles bilinguals Silva-Corvalán finds *cómo* used to ask about the extent to which the situation holds, as in (310).

(310) a.   *Y tu carro que compraste,*   *¿cómo te   gusta?*
            lit. and your car that (you) bought, how   to-you pleases?

      b.   *Mi carro me encanta.*
            'I love my car.'

In general Spanish, the question in (310a) would simply be *¿te gusta?* 'do you like it?'.

Having searched thoroughly for syntactic influence of English on Spanish in this context, Silva-Corvalán 2008: 221 concludes that, despite long-term contact between these two languages, and extensive code-switching in the communities of contact, their grammars are not converging, but remaining separate. While there may be a few changes based on semantics, and in some cases changes in frequency of use due to the loss of pragmatic constraints, none of the borrowings she has discovered affects the syntax of the recipient language. Indeed, changes that are allowed are constrained by the structure of the affected language. Further evidence that the recipient language strongly resists change from external sources is the fact that borrowed lexical items that become established loanwords are fully integrated into the morphology, syntax, and often the phonology of the recipient language.

Another type of change that has been suggested to be induced by contact is called "grammatical replication" by Heine and Kuteva 2005 or "structural borrowing". This process is said to be based on the calquing process, since no phonological form is borrowed. Heine and Kuteva argue that a lexico-syntactic calque can enter into the grammaticalization process, creating a new grammatical category in a language due to contact. An example they give (see also Heine and Kuteva 2008) is the Slavic language Upper Sorbian of eastern Germany, which has been in contact with German for a millennium, developing definite articles due to contact with German. In Upper Sorbian, the gender-marked demonstrative *tóne, tene, tane* 'this, nom. sg.' has grammaticalized to a definite article *tón, te, ta*. Of course, this path of grammaticalization is crosslinguistically common, but most Slavic languages do not have definite articles. Heine and Kuteva propose that this development came about through a grammatical replication of the DEMONSTRATIVE + NOUN construction. Through contact with German, innovations in the patterns of use of demonstratives led to an expansion of contexts in which they occurred and their subsequent grammaticalization as determiners. Heine and Kuteva note that definite determiners in Upper Sorbian are not used in the same way as those in German, but they propose nonetheless that this development is due to contact.

Heine and Kuteva cite a number of cases in which a category occurring in a neighboring language appears via grammaticalization in a language that has not utilized the category before. They acknowledge that the exact mechanism by which this takes place needs more study. The best way to study such changes would use the sociolinguistic method that studies actual instances of language use by bilinguals documented in corpora. For many of the cases cited by Heine and Kuteva, documentation on the nature and extent of bilingualism is not available, so even though they can describe a number of potential cases of grammatical replication, there is a need for more detailed study of ongoing changes to reveal the processes involved. Since the cases they study involve crosslinguistically common paths of grammaticalization, it is difficult to say whether or not the described changes would have occurred even without contact with another language.

In many ways, the jury is still out on the nature and extent of change in grammar by language contact. What seems remarkable, in view of the many claims about contact-induced change, is how little of it we see in the close-contact situations that have been examined carefully, such as Los Angeles

Spanish and Canadian French (Poplack and Levey 2010). In fact, given how many bilingual and multilingual communities there are around the world, if convergence did occur, there should be much more evidence of it. But rather than finding convergence, we see that languages maintain their structure even when they incorporate foreign elements; they make the foreign element fit in instead of changing to accommodate the new element.

11.3.   Pidgin and creole languages

In certain extreme sociohistorical situations, new languages are created out of the resources available in a multilingual context. These are pidgin languages, which can further develop into creole languages. Pidgin languages develop in situations where speakers of multiple languages must communicate and the language adopted for this purpose is not native to a majority of speakers. Such languages developed in the past in situations where many groups come together for trade, and also in cases where slave or indentured workers speaking different languages were brought together in plantations. Pidgin languages use the lexicon from one language – often a European language used on the plantation – in a pared-down grammatical structure that does not seem to come directly from any language. The language that supplies most of the words of the pidgin is called the *lexifier* language and can also be referred to as the *superstrate*. The native language of the speakers involved in the pidginization process is referred to as the *substrate*. If a pidgin language continues to be used and expands to use in many different social situations, the system may become conventionalized and may eventually become the native language of some people. At that stage it is considered a creole language. During the period of European colonization of Asia, the Pacific, Africa, and the Caribbean, many pidgin and creole languages arose based on English, Spanish, Portuguese, and French. There are also pidgin and creole languages based on Arabic, Bantu, Hindi, Indonesian, and other non-European languages. The following subsections outline the stages of development for pidgin and creole languages, using primarily examples from the English-based pidgin, now a creole, Tok Pisin, one of the official languages of Papua New Guinea.

11.3.1.   Early pidgins

The first group of changes that occur in the creation of a pidgin language can be described as simplifications. Speakers do not have complete access to the source language, so many features of the language are lost in this imperfect transmission process. Also, the language may be used only in restricted situations. This stage is labeled "early pidgin" and has the characteristics listed below from Mühlhäusler 1986. Examples are Chinook Jargon, used by Native Americans in the Pacific Northwest, and Early Tok Pisin, used in Papua New Guinea and surrounding islands.

Early pidgins have no native speakers, very limited context of use (as for trade or on plantations), and as a result a very limited vocabulary. Word order is variable, and there is no consensus on how the language should be spoken. It is also often noted that the language is spoken at a slow and deliberate tempo. The grammar and phonology are simplified, and inflectional morphology and word-formation are nonexistent. Here are some examples from Tok Pisin; the source of lexemes is English and if English spelling is not used, the letters have their IPA value.

First, the phonology is simplified: there are no consonant clusters, stops replace fricatives and affricates, or fricatives replace affricates, the vowel system typically has only five vowels.

(311)   Early Tok Pisin *pelet* 'plate', *tarausis* 'trousers',
                              pis 'fish', *tesen* 'station', *sos* 'church' (Mühlhäusler 1986)

Second, the same word order is used for questions, commands, and statements.

(312)   Tok Pisin (SVO)   Gloss
           yu klinim pis   you are cleaning the fish
           yu klinim pis   are you cleaning the fish?
           yu klinim pis   clean the fish

Third, temporal reference is expressed with adverbs:

(313) a.   *Mi stap long Fiji wan faiv yia pipo.*   I was in Fiji fifteen years ago.
      b.   *Brata bilong mi baimbai dai.*   My brother will die.
           (New Caledonia 1880; Samoan Plantation Pidgin English, a predecessor to
           Tok Pisin; Mühlhäusler 1986; Romaine 1995)

Fourth, many utterances appear without any overt pronouns, as in the following example. Also, proper nouns or nouns are used instead of pronouns.

(314)   *Now got plenty money; no good work*
           'now I have lots of money so I do not need to work' (Early Tok Pisin, 1840)

The pronouns vary considerably in the forms used: 'I' appears as *me, my, I,* 'we' as *us, we, me, my, I.* There is no consistent marking of singular and plural.

Fifth, circumlocutions are commonly used to make new words, as in this Chinese Pidgin English example *big fellow quack quack makee go in water* 'goose' or Beach-la–Mar *coconut belong him grass not stop* 'he is bald'. (Beach-la-mar is an early pidgin giving rise to the Vanuatu creole Bislama, whose origin is very similar to that of Tok Pisin.)

11.3.2.   Stable pidgins

From these simple beginnings, a stable pidgin can develop as the language comes to be used more, and in a wider range of situations. Through use it becomes more conventionalized, and the vocabulary expands.

First, word order stabilizes and most pidgins settle on SVO word order. The following examples show how Kenya Pidgin Swahili rearranges the morphemes of Standard Swahili to produce an SVO word order.

(315)   Standard Swahili: *ni-tu- m-   piga*
                             I- fut-him-hit
                             'I will hit him'

        Kenya Pidgin Swahili: *mimi no-   piga yeye*
                                 I   aorist-hit   him
                                 'I hit him'

Second, pronouns stabilize, as shown with these examples from Samoan Plantation Pidgin (Mühlhäusler 1986). Note the introduction of a plural marker, *ol* (< *all*).

(316)

	Subject		Object	
	singular	plural	singular	plural
1	*mi*	*mi ol*	*(bilong) mi*	*(bilong) as*
2	*yu*	*yu ol*	*(bilong) yu*	*(bilong) yu ol*
3	*em, him, hi*	*emol, himol*	*(bilong) em*	*(bilong) dem*

Early Tok Pisin also grammaticalizes a plural marker in the pronoun system, *pela* (< *fellow*).

(317)

	singular	plural
1	*mi*	*mi-pela*
2	*yu*	*yu-pela*
3	*em*	*em ol*

Third, relations between clauses are not expressed directly by conjunctions, but rather by simple juxtaposition, with the relations being inferred. For example, concatenation can express the conditional conveyed in English by *if*, as in this early Tok Pisin example:

(318)   *patrol no longwe, very good, patrol longwe tumas, no very good*
         'if the patrol is not far away, that's good, if the patrol is far away that's bad'

The causative relation is expressed periphrastically, as in the following:

(319)   *yu mekim sam wara i boil*
         'Bring some water to a boil'

There are no relative clause markers; rather the words are strung together and the relative relationship is inferred, as in these examples:

(320) a.   *people stop along Sydney go look see picture*
            'People who visit Sydney go look at the picture.'
      b.   *that pigeon he been sing out my name, I plant him*
            'I killed the guy who ratted on me'

11.3.3. Expanded pidgins

At any point along the way, the pidgin can be converted into a creole when children begin to use it as their native language. However, if it has not creolized yet, the pidgin can continue to expand to be used in a still broader range of contexts, which causes the lexicon to continue to grow. As people use the language more, automation of production occurs, and the language is spoken at a faster tempo, leading to phonological reduction. The grammar grows as well, both through grammaticalization and the syntacticizing of discourse patterns into constructions. Some word formation affixes begin to develop. Consider these examples.

Romaine 1988 reports that phonological reduction creates consonant clusters in the speech of children using Tok Pisin:

(321)	*bilong*	>	*blo*	preposition
	yutupela	>	*yutra*	2nd plural
	mitupela	>	*mitla*	1st dual

The vocabulary expands by compounding and affixation, no longer by lengthy circumlocutions.

(322)	Compounds:	*waitgras*	'grey hair'
		lesman	'lazy man'
		meksave	'to inform'
	Suffixes:	*boilim*	'boil (trans.)'
		bagarapim	'mess up (trans)'
		droim	'draw (trans.)'

The development of affixes is gradual, as in these examples from Tok Pisin, which has developed a causative suffix probably out of the third person singular object pronoun *him* (Mühlhäusler 1986).

(323) a. –*im* makes stative intransitives into transitives (mid 1930s):

	slip	'to sleep'	*slipim*	'to make lie down'
	orait	'all right'	*oraitim*	'to mend, repair'
	pinis	'finished'	*pinisim*	'to finish'

b. –*im* is used to make adjectives into verbs (soon after):

bikim	'to make big, enlarge'
kolim	'to make cool'
sotim	'to shorten'
switim	'to make feel pleasant'
truim	'to make come true'
raunim	'to make round'
stretim	'to straighten'

c. –*im* on non-statives is used to form causatives (from early 1960s):

noisim	'to make noise'
sanapim	'to make stand up'
pundaunim	'to make fall down'
wokabautim	'to make walk'
pairapim	'to make belch'
gohetim	'to make advance'

d.   *–im* occurs on transitives to make causatives (1973):
      dokta i dringim sikman   'the doctor makes the patient drink'

The grammaticalization of tense and aspect markers takes place just as it does in all languages, by using lexical items and phrases in a construction with a main verb. In Tok Pisin we have the example of the adverbial phrase *by and by* becoming an intention and then future marker. It reduces phonologically to *bai* and stabilizes preverbally as in these examples from Romaine 1995.

(324)   *baimbai mi go*   'By and by I go'
          bai mi go   'I'll go'
          mi bai go   'I'll go'

The verb *pinis* 'finish' becomes a marker of anterior or completive aspect, as in these examples:

(325)   *tupela i pren pinis*   'The two are real friends'
          em i go maket pinis   'she has just gone to the market'

Also by grammaticalization, conjunctions and complementizers are developed, which allows the extensive use of subordinate clauses. The preposition *long* (< *belong*) generalized to express most of the prepositional functions ('to, of, for') and then further expanded to introduce purpose clauses and further to function as a complementizer, as in these Tok Pisin examples:

(326)   *long* (< *belong*) preposition 'to, of, for'

a.   *Yupela i go antap long ples.*   preposition
b.   'You (pl.) go up to the village.'
      No gat stori long tokim yu.   purpose
c.   'I don't have stories to tell you.'
      Ol i no save long ol i mekem singsing.   complementizer
      'They did not know that they had performed a festival.'

(327)   *olsem* (< *all the same*) becomes a conjunction 'thus' and then generalizes
          to introduce complement clauses:

a.   *Elizabeth i tok olsem "Yumi mas kisim ol samting pastaim".*
      'Elizabeth spoke thus: "We must get some things first."'
b.   *Na yupela i no save olsem em i matmat?*
      'And you (pl.) didn't know that it was a cemetery?'

(328)   The verb *se* (< *say*) becomes a complementizer (compare with Section 6.8).

a.   *Em i tok i se "Mi laik kam."*
      'He said: "I want to come." '
b.   *Em i tok se em i laik kam.*
      'He said that he'd like to come.'
c.   *Mi harem se papa plong yu i sik.*
      'I heard that your father was sick.'
      (Bislama, related to Tok Pisin)

A pidgin language that has developed to this degree has all the ingredients for use in a wide variety of situations.

11.3.4.   Creole languages

The previous discussion shows that a pidgin language which has expanded its domain of usage to many social situations, and which has an expanded lexicon and has begun the process of grammaticalization, begins to resemble languages evolving through more usual means. It is common at this stage and often even earlier for the language to be used as a first language by some speakers. In households where the common language is the pidgin, the children will grow up with that language as their "mother tongue". At this point, linguists designate the language a creole language, indicating that it now has native speakers, though it developed from a pidgin language.

As more and more creole languages have been described by linguists, it has become clear that they share some characteristics. For instance, it has been noted that most creoles have SVO word order. Some researchers have noted that pidgin and creole languages develop very similar tense and aspect markers (Bickerton 1975). Givón 1982 examines this hypothesis and shows that non-creole languages (such as Early Biblical Hebrew) also have many of the same tense and aspect categories. In fact, the proposed "creole prototype" for tense, aspect, and modality, such as progressive or habitual, a future (often from 'go'), and an anterior which becomes a perfective, are common grammaticalizations in all languages, as we have seen in Chapter 7. The fact that these categories emerge in creole languages has been taken by some to indicate that such categories are innate and belong to the human "bioprogram", which evolved as language evolved (Bickerton 1975, 1981). Under this theory, when children acquire a pidgin, thereby converting it into a creole, the tense and aspect categories are created as an expression of these innate universals. The problem with this theory is that the grammaticalization of markers for these notions begins while the language is a still a pidgin. It appears that these categories start to emerge as the pidgin is used in more situations and by more people. A study by Romaine (1995) of *baimbai* in Tok Pisin takes the reduction to *bai* and preverbal position for this gram to indicate grammaticalization. In a large database, Romaine shows that there is no difference in the rate of preposed *bai* in native vs. second language speakers of Tok Pisin. This finding indicates that the development from pidgin to creole is gradual, and that grammatical categories can develop even without acquisition by native speakers.

What makes creole languages seem similar in terms of grammar is that they first underwent an extreme simplification (as pidgin languages) and then began the process of grammaticalization. As we now know, grammaticalization is very similar crosslinguistically, and it is not surprising that the first categories to emerge are those that are very common in all languages. Still, there is controversy about whether or not creoles represent a distinguishable "type" of language. McWhorter 1998 has identified three features that together distinguish creole from non-creole ("regular") languages:

1.   little or no inflectional affixation;
2.   little or no use of tone to lexically contrast monosyllables or encode syntax;
3.   semantically regular derivational affixation.

The first two are features that, if present in the lexifier language, are highly likely to be lost in the pidginization process. We noted above that most inflections are lost, and tone of the type found in languages such as Chinese or Vietnamese would also not be maintained. Words formed by derivation are also not a part of the initial vocabulary of a pidgin. In addition, McWhorter notes, the first two are features of language that take a very long time to develop: grammaticalization carried through to affixation is a long process, and we saw in Section 3.6.1 that the development of tones on monosyllables, as in Vietnamese, is also a very long process. As for the third feature, we saw in Section 9.5 that the development of non-compositional meanings for derived words also takes some time and usage in context. Now of course there are many non-creole languages that do not have inflection and also many that do not have lexical tones, so these features are only minimally helpful in identifying the creole type. But all languages have some type of derivational morphology (even those with very little affixation) and it seems reasonable (though perhaps this has not been tested) that at least a few derivations are non-compositional in meaning, as English *awful* and *disease* are.

Thus the creole features that McWhorter identifies all reflect the sociohistorical conditions that created creoles – the fact that many of the features of the lexifier language were not carried into the pidgin and that many features have not yet had a chance to develop. In McWhorter 2001, he goes on to compare creoles to "regular" languages, noting the lack in creoles of complex phoneme inventories, specialized morphological systems for noun classification, such as gender systems and numeral classifiers, and complex morphophonemic alternations. Again, the explanation is that the changes that result in complex consonants (such as affricates, consonants with secondary features) and the morphological systems noted take time to develop.

Presumably, in the pidginization process the loss of inflection, gender categories, numeral classifiers, complex consonants, and vowel and tone systems occur because they are not strictly necessary for communication, at least not in the situations in which a pidgin is used. A question that arises is why languages have all this "baggage" anyway, if it is not used for speakers getting their point across to hearers? We have seen how many of the complexities of language develop as the cognitive processes used in communication affect speakers' utterances and listeners' interpretations. But still we can ask why do children take the trouble to learn all the niceties of their cultural language when they can communicate quite well without them? The reason is, in my opinion, that children are not just learning to communicate, but rather, under normal conditions, they are learning how to be a human being within a certain culture. They adopt facial expressions, gestures, and other movements as they find them in their culture. In order to become an adult within a culture, many of the complexities of the language must also be adopted. Language is an integral part of sociocultural identity, and if that means learning complex gender classifications or morphophonemic alternations, then these will be learned!

Pidgin and creole languages are fascinating because they allow us a rare view into the creation of language from, at least at first, minimal input. We see the interaction of language use with the emergence of grammar: as the number and type of situations in which the language is used expand, as speakers become more fluent and more structures are automated, phonological processes and grammaticalization processes begin to unfold and do the work of creating linguistic structure. As we have seen, the processes and mechanisms that apply in pidgin and creole languages are no different than those we have identified in other languages. A focus on the mechanisms of change rather than just the beginning and end stages, allows us to see language as a dynamic system, variable and changing, with grammar emerging rather than fixed. In this way it is like other complex adaptive systems.

11.4.   Language as a complex adaptive system

In a complex adaptive system or self-organizing system, structure evolves without any kind of "master plan" but only because the agents operating in the system have similar goals and are subject to similar mechanisms. John Holland 1995 writes that great cities, such as New York City, are complex adaptive systems. They provide all the goods, products, and services that residents need with only a minimal amount of central planning. Thus, consider ways of getting food: produce stands, delis, bakeries, supermarkets, restaurants; they are all there in plenty, yet there has never been any central plan to insure that food is available. Goods flow into and out of the city, restaurants come and go, yet the city in this regard and many others, despite diversity and change, maintains a short-term and long-term coherence. The system evolved and is maintained by "agents" – people who need food and people who supply food – who keep acting the same way. The consumer is regularly hungry and the supplier is always in need of income, and this is a happy co-existence. Changes in the system can occur: as sushi becomes more popular, more sushi restaurants open up and maybe a few pizzerias close down. But unless there is a major perturbation (e.g., a huge hurricane) the system buzzes on pretty consistently.

No one intended to create this great interconnected system; rather, it is a collective result of human actions which were directed at different goals – the goals of eating and earning a living. Another simpler example, from Keller 1994, concerns what happens when spectators gather to watch a street artist: they form a circle (not a square or a trapezoid). No one said "let's make a circle"; rather, each individual places him/herself at a good vantage point and the collective result is a circle. Keller calls this the action of the "invisible hand".

Many researchers have understood that language can also be viewed as a complex adaptive system, based on the particulars of the human capacity for language (from articulatory apparatus to social cognition). Lindblom et al. 1984 were among the first to explicitly model a typological phenomenon – the distribution of consonants and vowels in the languages of the world – as emergent from certain production and perception preferences. Hopper 1987 wrote about "emergent grammar", which also alludes to a system in which grammar is not fixed, but also changing and "becoming" from usage patterns. Further applications of complex adaptive system models to phonology are found in Cooper 1999 and de Boer 2000, and to the spread of a change in communities in Blythe and Croft 2012. While not explicitly citing complexity theory, Hawkins' (2004) "Performance-Grammar Correspondence Hypothesis" proposes that grammatical structures emerge from language use. This hypothesis says

> Grammars have conventionalized syntactic structure in proportion to their degree of preference in performance, as evidenced by patterns of selection in corpora and by ease of processing in psycholinguistic experiments.

Thus there seems to be a growing interest in considering language to be a complex adaptive system.

To summarize these various works and the model implicitly assumed in the chapters of this book, the way it works is this. No one intends to change language, but language users intend to communicate, and they use all the means at their disposal to do this. They are human and so their cognition and social awareness and goals come into play. As these are shared by language users, the same cognitive and social processes play out over usage events in all languages. Within a community, the accumulation of usage events as they are affected by production pressures, access of lexical and grammatical memories, productive use of these memories, and the necessary implications and inferences that go along with all communication create strong patterns across speakers and situations. In a positive feedback loop, these patterns affect cognitive or memory representations of language users and in this way affect future usage events. Thus languages are always changing but, in broad form, always staying the same.

Suggested reading

On pigin and creole languages:

Holm, J., 2000. *An introduction to pidgins and creole*, Cambridge: Cambridge University Press.

A general introduction to complex adaptive systems:

Holland, J.H., 1995. *Hidden order: how adaptation builds complexity*, Cambridge, MA: Perseus Books.

Questions for discussion

1. What sorts of change in language are easy for adults to make? Consider adaptations to new words, phrases, or constructions and changes in pronunciation.

2. From your personal experience with using a second language, or from knowing someone who uses two or more languages, consider under what circumstances full-fledged language changes might result from adults using two or more languages.

3. Consider a dynamic system such as waves in the ocean. If they are always changing, how is it that we can recognize them when we see them? How do they keep changing but always stay the same?

THE INTERNATIONAL PHONETIC ALPHABET (revised to 2005)

CONSONANTS (PULMONIC)

© 2005 IPA

	Bilabial	Labiodental	Dental	Alveolar	Postalveolar	Retroflex	Palatal	Velar	Uvular	Pharyngeal	Glottal
Plosive	p b			t d		ʈ ɖ	c ɟ	k ɡ	q ɢ		ʔ
Nasal	m	ɱ		n		ɳ	ɲ	ŋ	ɴ		
Trill	ʙ			r					ʀ		
Tap or Flap		ⱱ		ɾ		ɽ					
Fricative	ɸ β	f v	θ ð	s z	ʃ ʒ	ʂ ʐ	ç ʝ	x ɣ	χ ʁ	ħ ʕ	h ɦ
Lateral fricative				ɬ ɮ							
Approximant		ʋ		ɹ		ɻ	j	ɰ			
Lateral approximant				l		ɭ	ʎ	ʟ			

Where symbols appear in pairs, the one to the right represents a voiced consonant. Shaded areas denote articulations judged impossible.

CONSONANTS (NON-PULMONIC)

Clicks		Voiced implosives		Ejectives	
ʘ	Bilabial	ɓ	Bilabial	ʼ	Examples:
ǀ	Dental	ɗ	Dental/alveolar	pʼ	Bilabial
ǃ	(Post)alveolar	ʄ	Palatal	tʼ	Dental/alveolar
ǂ	Palatoalveolar	ɠ	Velar	kʼ	Velar
ǁ	Alveolar lateral	ʛ	Uvular	sʼ	Alveolar fricative

OTHER SYMBOLS

ʍ	Voiceless labial-velar fricative	ɕ ʑ	Alveolo-palatal fricatives
w	Voiced labial-velar approximant	ɺ	Voiced alveolar lateral flap
ɥ	Voiced labial-palatal approximant	ɧ	Simultaneous ʃ and x
ʜ	Voiceless epiglottal fricative		
ʢ	Voiced epiglottal fricative		Affricates and double articulations can be represented by two symbols joined by a tie bar if necessary.
ʡ	Epiglottal plosive		k͡p t͡s

VOWELS

Where symbols appear in pairs, the one to the right represents a rounded vowel.

SUPRASEGMENTALS

ˈ	Primary stress	ˌfoʊnəˈtɪʃən
ˌ	Secondary stress	
ː	Long	eː
ˑ	Half-long	eˑ
˘	Extra-short	ĕ
ǀ	Minor (foot) group	
ǁ	Major (intonation) group	
.	Syllable break	ɹi.ækt
‿	Linking (absence of a break)	

DIACRITICS

Diacritics may be placed above a symbol with a descender, e.g. ŋ̊

̥	Voiceless	n̥ d̥	̤	Breathy voiced	b̤ a̤	̪	Dental	t̪ d̪
̬	Voiced	s̬ t̬	̰	Creaky voiced	b̰ a̰	̺	Apical	t̺ d̺
ʰ	Aspirated	tʰ dʰ	̼	Linguolabial	t̼ d̼	̻	Laminal	t̻ d̻
̹	More rounded	ɔ̹	ʷ	Labialized	tʷ dʷ	̃	Nasalized	ẽ
̜	Less rounded	ɔ̜	ʲ	Palatalized	tʲ dʲ	ⁿ	Nasal release	dⁿ
̟	Advanced	u̟	ˠ	Velarized	tˠ dˠ	ˡ	Lateral release	dˡ
̠	Retracted	e̠	ˤ	Pharyngealized	tˤ dˤ	̚	No audible release	d̚
̈	Centralized	ë	̴	Velarized or pharyngealized	ɫ			
̽	Mid-centralized	x̽	̝	Raised	e̝	(ɹ̝ = voiced alveolar fricative)		
̩	Syllabic	n̩	̞	Lowered	e̞	(β̞ = voiced bilabial approximant)		
̯	Non-syllabic	e̯	̘	Advanced Tongue Root	e̘			
˞	Rhoticity	ɚ a˞	̙	Retracted Tongue Root	e̙			

TONES AND WORD ACCENTS

LEVEL			CONTOUR		
e̋ or ˥	Extra high		ě or ˇ	Rising	
é ˦	High		ê ˆ	Falling	
ē ˧	Mid		e᷄	High rising	
è ˨	Low		e᷅	Low rising	
ȅ ˩	Extra low		e᷈	Rising-falling	
ꜜ	Downstep		↗	Global rise	
ꜛ	Upstep		↘	Global fall	

IPA chart (from, http://www.langsci.ucl.ac.uk/ipa/ipachart.html, available under a Creative Commons Attribution-Sharealike 3.0 Unported License. Copyright © 2005 International Phonetic Association)

Glossary of terms used

ablaut: vowel alternations inherited from Proto-Indo-European, surviving into English in forms such as *rise, rose*; *sing, sang, sung*

absolutive case: the case that designates the subject of an intransitive verb or the object of a transitive verb; it contrasts with ergative case

accusative case: the case that designates the object of a transitive verb

adposition: a term covering both prepositions and postpositions

allomorph: a variant of a morpheme

allophone: a variant of a phoneme, usually conditioned by the phonetic context

alternation: a case in which a morpheme has more than one variant or allomorph

analogical extension: the introduction of an alternation into a paradigm through the creation of a new word with an alternation using the pattern of other words in the language

analogical leveling: the elimination of an alternation in a paradigm by the creation of a new word with a regular pattern lacking an alternation

analogy: the re-making of a form based on similarity to other existing forms in the language

analytic: morphological expression in which grammatical morphemes tend to appear as separate words

analyzability: said of a complex form whose parts are identifiable to users of the language

antepenultimate syllable: the third syllable from the end of a word

anterior: a grammatical morpheme or construction that indicates that the situation described by the verb is taken to be a past situation with current relevance; sometimes referred to as "perfect"

anticipatory assimilation or retiming: the production of an articulatory gesture that occurs early and thus affects segments preceding the one where the gesture originated

aspect: an inflectional category of verbs that makes distinctions concerning the temporal contours of the situation described by the verb stem; common aspectual distinctions are perfective/imperfective, progressive, habitual, completive, or iterative, among others

assimilation: a sound change by which one segment becomes more like a neighboring segment. Such sound changes can be described as the reorganization of the timing of gestures such that one gesture overlaps another.

atelic: the action of the verb has no natural completion point: *walk*

autonomy: a complex form becomes independent from the parts that compose it; related to the loss of analyzability and compositionality

auxiliary verb: a verb-like element that occurs only with a VP as its complement; being grammaticalized to some degree, it might lack some features of lexical verbs

bleaching: a meaning change in which specific features of meaning are lost

borrowing: adopting a word or other element or structure into a language due to contact with another language

calque: an expression formed by a literal translation of a corresponding expression from another language

carry over retiming: the extension of an articulatory gesture into a following segment; also called perseverative or progressive assimilation

chain shift: "A minimal chain shift is a change in the position of two phonemes in which one moves away from an original position that is then occupied by the other" (Labov 1994: 118). "An extended chain shift . . . is a combination of minimal chain shifts in which the entering element of one minimal chain shift replaces the leaving element of another" (Labov 1994: 119).

chunk: a sequence of words that are used together often enough to form a storage and processing unit; the basis of the formation of constructions

closed class: a class that does not readily admit new members as contrasted with an open or lexical class such as noun or verb

code-switching: the use of two (or more) languages by the same speaker within a single conversation, sometimes within a single clause or utterance

cognates: pairs of words from different languages that share a common ancestor, such as English *beam* and German *Baum* 'tree'

complementizer: a gram used to introduce or mark a subordinate clause that acts as an argument of the verb

compositionality: said of a complex form whose meaning is predictably derivable from the meaning of the parts

compounding: putting two words together to form a new word

construction: any form-meaning correspondence; in morphosyntax, a conventionalized pattern with some fixed elements and some schematic positions

creole language: a language that developed from a pidgin language when children acquired it as a first language

debuccalization: a sound change resulting from the loss of articulatory gestures made in the oral cavity

decategorialization: changes in grammaticalization by which nouns and verbs lose the properties of their lexical classes and become grammatical morphemes

degemination: a change by which a geminate consonant (a long consonant) loses its length and becomes the same duration as a simple consonant

deictic: words or grams whose meaning is based in the current speech situation such that reference changes according to changes in speech situation. Personal pronouns such as *I* and *you* change their referent according to who is speaking.

demarcative stress: stress of words reckoned from the beginning or the end of the word

demonstrative pronouns: a set of pronouns that indicate a referent by its location near or far from the speaker or addressee

discourse marker: an expression that provides pragmatic indications about how the utterance or parts of it are meant to be interpreted in the discourse context

dissimilation: a sound change by which one segment becomes less like another nearby segment

downdrift: in African languages, the tendency for the pitch of a high tone following a low to be lower than previous high tones in the utterance

downstep: a high tone lowered by downdrift, which remains lowered even though the preceding low tone has been deleted. The result is a sequence in which a high tone is followed by a lowered high tone, which in some cases is considered a mid tone.

drag chain: a chain shift that starts when one phoneme changes, leaving a gap in the phonetic space, which another phoneme moves in to occupy

drift: long-term change proceeding in a constant direction

epistemic: a modality that expresses the degree of confidence the speaker has in the proposition being asserted

ergative case: the case restricted to the agent of a transitive verb

etymology: the study of the history of words

excrescent consonant: a consonant that appears to be inserted in a string of sounds. Such a phenomenon is usually the result of retiming of gestures.

external change: change motivated by factors outside the language's structure per se

family resemblance: said of members of categories that share some but not all features with other members of the category

folk etymology: the erroneous analysis of the parts of words, assigning them meanings that were not etymologically present

fortition: a sound change resulting from the increase in magnitude or duration of an articulatory gesture

gemination: a change by which the duration of a consonant's articulation is increased

genealogical relation: the relationship of two or more languages due to their deriving from a common ancestor; earlier called a "genetic" relation

gram: grammatical morpheme

grammatical morpheme: a morpheme that is a member of a closed class; a "gram"

grammaticalization: the process by which a lexical item or phrase within a construction takes on grammatical meaning and form

grammaticization: an alternate term for grammaticalization

hyperbole: a figure of speech that is exaggerated in its meaning, e.g., *scared to death*

imperfective aspect: a grammatical morpheme or construction that indicates that the situation described by the verb is being viewed as ongoing at a reference point or over a period of time

indefinite article: a noun modifier that indicates that the noun's referent is new to the discourse context

inference: meaning that the listener draws from an utterance that was not explicitly stated. Frequent implications/inferences become part of the meaning or replace the old meaning: *since* 'after' > 'because'.

interference (substratum interference): change produced when speakers' native language influences the phonology or grammar of the other language they are using

internal change: change motivated by factors internal to the language's structure

intonation: the pattern of pitch changes that occurs across an utterance independently of the particular words or morphemes contained in the utterance

language contact: a situation in which the same speakers use two or more languages; change that occurs due to this situation

lenition: a sound change resulting from the reduction in magnitude or duration of an articulatory gesture that produces a consonant

leveling: the remaking of a morphological form in such a way as to eliminate an alternation; also called "analogical leveling"

lexical diffusion: the way a linguistic change progresses through the lexicon

lexical stress: a stress accent that does not occur in predictable positions and can be used to distinguish words

loanword: a word from one language that has been integrated and accepted into another language

ME: Middle English

metaphor: a figure of speech in which relational structure in one domain is transferred to another domain without changing the relational structure: *face of a clock*

metonymy: a figure of speech in which a term for one concept is used for an associated concept: *White House* for the executive branch of the government

morphologization: the process by which alternations created by a sound change move from being conditioned by phonetics to having an association with morphology

morphophonology: the study of or the phenomenon of phonological alternations conditioned by morphological or lexical categories

Neogrammarian Hypothesis: all sound change is regular and affects all the words of a language

nominative case: the case assigned to the subject of both transitive and intransitive verbs

OE: Old English

oblique cases: a cover term for cases other than the nominative, i.e. accusative, dative, instrumental, and so on

onomasiology: the study of what words express a particular meaning and how this may change over time

paradigm: the set of inflectionally related forms sharing the same stem

path of grammaticalization: the trajectory of semantic change that occurs in grammaticalization

penultimate syllable: the second syllable from the end of the word

perfect: see "anterior"

perfective aspect: a grammatical morpheme or construction that indicates that the situation described by the verb is being viewed as a completed whole; frequently used to narrate sequences of past events

perseverative assimilation: see "carry over retiming"

personal pronouns: a set of pronouns that distinguish the speaker, addressee, and other persons

PDE: Present Day English

phonotactic sequences: the permitted sequences of consonants and vowels in a language

pidgin language: a language that develops spontaneously in a situation where speakers of multiple languages must communicate but share no common language

phonologization: a change by which a phonetic feature previously predictable from universal patterns becomes a part of the phonology of a language, either by producing a language-specific allophone or becoming phonemically contrastive

polysemy: multiple distinct meanings for a word, phrase, or construction

postposition: a relational gram positioned after the noun phrase, corresponding to prepositions, which occur before the noun phrase

preposition: a relational gram in construction with a noun phrase and occurring before the noun phrase

productivity: the likelihood that a pattern or construction will apply to a novel item

progressive aspect: the situation described by the verb is ongoing at reference time

proposition: the semantic content expressed by a clause

push chain: a chain shift that begins when one phoneme changes so as to encroach on the phonetic space of another, causing the latter to also change by moving away from the encroaching phoneme

reconstruction: the process of comparing synchronic forms within or across related languages to hypothesize an earlier stage of the language or ancestors of the languages

reduction (phonetic): any phonetic change in which the magnitude or duration of a gesture is reduced

regularization: a change by which a formerly irregular (inflectional) form comes to be inflected by the regular rules or constructions

resultative: a grammatical category or construction that indicates that the situation described by the verb is being viewed as a past action with a resulting state

rhotacism: the change of an /s/ or /z/ to a sound with an /r/ quality

rhotic: describing an /r/ quality in a sound

root possibility: general enabling conditions exist, including internal ability and external conditions such as social conditions. Paraphraseable as "It is possible to . . ."

sandhi: alternations that take place when two words are used in sequence

schematic: the degree to which a position or slot within a construction allows a large number of lexical items to occur within it

semasiology: the study of the meanings of words and how these change over time

serial verb constructions: constructions available in some languages that allow two or more finite verbs to be joined together in a clause without any connecting particle

stress accent: one syllable per word that has special prominence expressed by some combination of pitch, intensity, and duration

subjectification: semantic or pragmatic change that leads to meanings increasingly situated in the speaker's beliefs

substratum interference: see "interference"

suppletion: an irregularity in inflectional paradigms created by the use of stems from etymologically different sources in the same paradigm, e.g., English *go*, *went*. In a purely synchronic sense the term is used for paradigms whose forms are so different that they could not be plausibly derived from one underlying form.

synecdoche: a figure of speech in which a term for a part is used for the whole or vice versa: e.g., *wheels* for 'car'

synthetic: a language type in which words have multiple inflectional affixes

telic: a lexical aspect in which the action of a verb has a natural end point: e.g., *throw*

tense: an inflectional category of the verb which places the situation described by the verb in time relative to the moment of speech or another established reference time

token frequency: a count of the number of times an item (e.g., phoneme, word, construction) appears in running text

tone language: a language in which pitch can be used to express lexical or morphological distinctions

tone spreading: a carry over or perseverative change by which the tone from one syllable spreads onto the next syllable

tonogenesis: the process by which contrastive tones arise in a language which previously did not have them

type frequency: the number of distinct lexical items that participate in a pattern; e.g., the number of lexical items that appear in the open slot(s) of a construction, or the number of words with a particular phoneme or phonotactic pattern

upgliding diphthong: a diphthong in which the last part has a higher tongue position than the first part

zero conversion: the change of the word class (e.g., from noun to verb or adjective or the reverse) without the addition of a derivational affix

References

Adelaar, W.F.H., 2004. *The languages of the Andes*, Cambridge: Cambridge University Press.

Allen, C., 1995. *Case marking and reanalysis: grammatical relations from Old to Early Modern English*, Oxford: Oxford University Press.

Allen, W.S., 1951. A study in the analysis of Hindi sentence-structure. *Acta Linguistica*, 6, pp. 68–86.

Andersen, H., 1973. Abductive and deductive change. *Language*, 49(4), pp. 765–793.

Anderson, S.R., 1977. The mechanisms by which languages become ergative. In C. Li (ed.) *Mechanisms of syntactic change*, Austin: University of Texas Press, pp. 317–363.

Anglade, J., 1921. *Grammaire de l'ancien provençal*, Paris: Klincksieck.

Ashby, W.J., 1981. The loss of the negative particle *ne* in French. *Language*, 57(3), pp. 674–687.

Ball, D., 2007. On ergativity and accusativity in Proto-Polynesian and Proto-Central Pacific. *Oceanic Linguistics* 46(1), pp. 128–153.

Barðdal, J., 2007. The semantic and lexical range of the ditransitive construction in the history of (North) Germanic. *Functions of Language*, 14(1), pp. 9–30.

Bateman, N., 2010. The change from labial to palatal as glide hardening. *Linguistic Typology*, 14(2/3), pp.167–211.

Beekes, R.S.P., 1995. *Comparative Indo-European linguistics: an introduction*, Amsterdam: John Benjamins.

Benveniste, É., 1968. Mutations of linguistic categories. In W.P. Lehmann and Y. Malkiel (eds.) *Directions for historical linguistics*, Austin and London: University of Texas Press, pp. 83–94.

Bergem, D. Van, 1995. *Acoustic and lexical vowel reduction*, Amsterdam: IFOTT.

Berman, R., 1985. The acquisition of Hebrew. In D. Slobin (ed.) *Crosslinguistic study of language acquisition*, Hillsdale, NJ: Lawrence Erlbaum, pp. 255–371.

Bickerton, D., 1975. *Dynamics of a creole system*, Cambridge: Cambridge University Press.

1981. *Roots of language*, Ann Arbor: Karoma.

Bisang, W., 2004. Grammaticalization without coevolution of form and meaning: the case of tense-aspect-modality in East and mainland Southeast Asia. In W. Bisang, N. Himmelmann, and B Wiemer (eds.) *What makes grammaticalization? A look from its fringes and its components*, Berlin: Mouton de Gruyter, pp. 109–138.

Blevins, J., 2004. *Evolutionary phonology: the emergence of sound patterns*, Cambridge: Cambridge University Press.

Blevins, J. and Garrett, A., 1998. The origins of consonant–vowel metathesis. *Language*, 74(3), pp. 508–556.

Bloomfield, L., 1933. *Language*, Chicago: Chicago University Press.

Blythe, R. and Croft, W., 2012. S-curves and the mechanisms of propagation in language change. *Language*, 88, pp. 269–304.

Boer, B. De, 2000. Self-organization in vowel systems. *Journal of Phonetics*, 28(4), pp. 441–465.

Bolinger, D., 1978. Intonation across languages. In J.H. Greenberg, C.A. Ferguson, and E.A. Moravcsik (eds.) *Universals of human language*, Vol. 2 *Phonology*, Stanford: Stanford University Press, pp. 471–524.

Brinton, L.J. and Traugott, E.C., 2005. *Lexicalization and language change*, Cambridge: Cambridge University Press.

Browman, C. and Goldstein, L., 1986. Towards an articulatory phonology. *Phonology Yearbook*, 3, pp. 219–252.

——— 1995. Gestural syllable position effects in American English. In F. Bell-Berti and L.J. Raphael (eds.) *Producing speech: contemporary issues*, Woodbury, NY: American Institute of Physics, pp. 19–34.

Brown, E.L., 2006. Velarization of labial, coda stops in Spanish: a frequency account. *Revista de lingüística teórica y aplicada*, 44(2), pp.47–56.

Brown, E.L. and Raymond, W.D., 2012. How discourse context shapes the lexicon: explaining the distribution of Spanish f- / h- words. *Diachronica*, 92(2), pp. 139–161.

Brown, G., 1972. *Phonological rules and dialect variation: A study of the phonology of Lumasaaba*, Cambridge: Cambridge University Press.

Buck, C.D., 1933. *Comparative grammar of Greek and Latin*, Chicago: University of Chicago Press.

Burridge, K., 1995. Evidence for grammaticalization in Pennsylvania German. In H. Andersen (ed.) *Historical linguistics 1993*, Amsterdam and Philadelphia: John Benjamins, pp. 59–75.

Bybee, J., 1985. *Morphology: a study of the relation between meaning and form*, Philadelphia: John Benjamins.

——— 2000a. Lexicalization of sound change and alternating environments. In M. Broe and J. Pierrehumbert (eds.) *Papers in laboratory phonology*, Vol. 5 *Acquisition and the lexicon*, Cambridge: Cambridge University Press, pp. 250–268.

——— 2000b. The phonology of the lexicon: evidence from lexical diffusion. In M. Barlow and S. Kemmer (eds.) *Usage-based models of language*, Stanford: CSLI Publications, pp. 65–85.

——— 2001. *Phonology and language use*, Cambridge: Cambridge University Press.

——— 2002. Word frequency and context of use in the lexical diffusion of phonetically-conditioned sound change. *Language Variation and Change*, 14, pp. 261–290.

——— 2003. Mechanisms of change in grammaticalization: the role of frequency. In B.D. Joseph and R.D. Janda (eds.) *The handbook of historical linguistics*. Oxford: Blackwell.

——— 2006. From usage to grammar: the mind's response to repetition. *Language*, 82, pp. 711–733.

2010. *Language, usage and cognition*, Cambridge: Cambridge University Press.

Bybee, J. and Brewer, M.A., 1980. Explanation in morphophonemics: changes in Provençal and Spanish preterite forms. *Lingua*, 52, pp. 201–242.

Bybee, J., Chakraborti, P., Jung, D., and Scheibman, J., 1998. Prosody and segmental effect: some paths of evolution for word stress. *Studies in Language*, 22(2), pp. 267–314.

Bybee, J. and Dahl, Ö., 1989. The creation of tense and aspect systems in the languages of the world. *Studies in Language*, 13(1), pp. 51–103.

Bybee, J. and Moder, C.L., 1983. Morphological classes as natural categories. *Language*, 59, pp. 251–270.

Bybee, J. and Pagliuca, W., 1987. The evolution of future meaning. In A. Giacalone Ramat, O. Carruba, and G. Bernini (eds.) *Papers from the 7th International Conference on Historical Linguistics*, Amsterdam and Philadelphia: John Benjamins, pp. 109–122.

Bybee, J., Pagliuca, W., and Perkins, R.D., 1991. Back to the future. In E.C. Traugott and B. Heine (eds.) *Approaches to grammaticalization*, Vol. 2. Amsterdam and Philadelphia: John Benjamins, pp. 17–58.

Bybee, J., Perkins, R.D., and Pagliuca, W., 1994. *The evolution of grammar: tense, aspect and modality in the languages of the world*, Chicago: University of Chicago Press.

Bybee, J. and Slobin, D.I., 1982. Rules and schemas in the development and use of the English past. *Language*, 58, pp. 265–289.

Campbell, A., 1959. *Old English Grammar*, Oxford: Oxford University Press.

Campbell, L., 1999. *Historical linguistics: an introduction*, Cambridge, MA: MIT Press.

Capell, A. and Layard, J., 1980. *Materials in Atchin, Malekula: grammar, vocabulary and texts*, Canberra: Australian National University.

Chevrot, J.-P., Beaud, L., and Varga, R., 2000. Developmental data on a French sociolinguistic variable: post-consonantal word-final /R/. *Language Variation and Change*, 12, pp. 295–319.

Chung, S., 1977. On the gradual nature of syntactic change. In C.N. Li (ed.) *Mechanisms of syntactic change*, Austin: University of Texas Press, pp. 3–55.

Coates, J., 1983. *The semantics of the modal auxiliary*, London: Croom Helm.

Colleman, T. and De Clerk, B., 2011. Constructional semantics on the move: on semantic specialization in the English double object construction. *Cognitive Linguistics*, 22(1), pp. 183–209.

Company Company, C., 2002. Grammaticalization and category weakness. In G. Diewald and I. Fischer (eds.) *New reflections on grammaticalization*, Amsterdam and Philadelphia: John Benjamins, pp. 201–215.

2006. Subjectification of verbs into discourse markers: semantic-pragmatic change only? In B. Cornillie and N. Delbecque (eds.) *Topics in subjectification and modalization*, Amsterdam: John Benjamins, pp. 97–121.

Comrie, B., 1976. *Aspect*, Cambridge: Cambridge University Press.

Cooper, D.L., 1999. *Linguistic attractors: the cognitive dynamics of language acquisition and change*, Amsterdam: John Benjamins.

Cristófaro-Silva, T. and Oliveira Guimarães, D., 2006. Patterns of lenition in Brazilian Portuguese. In C. Féry, R. van de Vijer, and F. Kügler (eds.) *Variation and*

Gradience in Phonetics and Phonology, Berlin and New York: Mouton de Gruyter, Vol. 1, pp. 25–35.

Croft, W., 2000. *Explaining language change*, Harlow, England: Longman Linguistic Library.

2005. Preface. In W. Croft (ed.), *Genetic linguistics: essays on theory and method by Joseph H. Greenberg*, Oxford: Oxford University Press, pp. 35–64.

Croft, W., Beckner, C., Sutton, L., Wilkins, J., Bhattacharya, T., and Hruschka, D., 2009. Quantifying semantic shift for reconstructing language families. Poster Presented at the Annual Meeting of the Linguistic Society of America.

Crothers, J., 1975. Areal features and natural phonology: the case of front rounded vowels. *Proceedings of the Second Annual Conference of the Berkeley Linguistic Society*, 2, pp.124–136.

Crowley, T., 1997. *An introduction to historical linguistics*, 3rd edition, Oxford: Oxford University Press.

Cyffer, N., 1998. *A sketch of Kanuri*, Cologne: Rüdiger Köppe Verlag.

Dahl, Ö., 1985. *Tense and aspect systems*, Oxford: Basil Blackwell.

2013. Tea. In M.S. Dryer and M. Haspelmath (eds.) *The world atlas of language structures online*. Leipzig: Max Planck Institute for Evolutionary Anthropology. (Available online at http://wals.info/chapter/138, accessed on 26 September 2014.)

Díaz-Campos, M., 2004. Acquisition of sociolinguistic variables in Spanish: Do children acquire individual lexical forms or variable rules? In T. Face (ed.) *Laboratory approaches to Spanish phonology*, Berlin: Mouton de Gruyter, pp. 221–236.

Dobson, E.J., 1957. *English pronunciation 1500–1700*, Oxford: Clarendon Press.

Dressler, W.U., 2003. Naturalness and morphological change. In B.D. Joseph and R.D. Janda (eds.) *The handbook of historical linguistics*, Oxford: Basil Blackwell, pp. 461–471.

Dressler, W.U., Mayerthaler, W., and Würzel, W., 1987. *Leitmotifs in natural morphology*, Amsterdam: John Benjamins.

Dryer, M., 1988. Object-verb order and adjective-noun order: dispelling a myth. *Lingua*, 74, pp.185–217.

Erman, B. and Warren, B., 2000. The Idiom Principle and the Open Choice Principle. *Text*, 20, pp. 29–62.

Fairbanks, G.H. and Stevick, E.W. 1958. *Spoken East Armenian*, New York: American Council of Learned Societies.

Fidelholtz, J., 1975. Word frequency and vowel reduction in English. *Chicago Linguistics Society*, 11, pp. 200–213.

Foley, J., 1977. *Foundations of theoretical phonology*, Cambridge: Cambridge University Press.

Foulkes, P. and Docherty, G., 2006. The social life of phonetics and phonology. *Journal of Phonetics*, 34(4), pp. 409–438.

Garrett, A., 1990. The origin of NP split ergativity. *Language* 66(2), pp. 261–296.

Geeraerts, D., 1997. *Diachronic prototype semantics: a contribution to historical lexicology*, Oxford: Clarendon Press.

Givón, T., 1971. Historical syntax and synchronic morphology: an archaeologist's field trip. *Chicago Linguistics Society*, 7, pp. 394–415.

1975. Serial verbs and syntactic change. In C.N. Li (ed.) *Word order and word order change*, Austin: University of Texas Press, pp. 47–112.

1976. Topic, pronoun and grammatical agreement. In C.N Li (ed.) *Subject and topic*, New York: Academic Press, pp. 149–188.

1979. *On understanding grammar*, New York: Academic Press.

1982. Tense-aspect-modality: the creole prototype and beyond. In P.J. Hopper (ed.) *Tense-aspect: between semantics and pragmatics*, Amsterdam: John Benjamins, pp. 115–163.

1984. *Syntax: a functional-typological introduction*, Amsterdam: John Benjamins.

Goldberg, A., 1995. *Constructions: a construction grammar approach to argument structure*, Chicago: University of Chicago Press.

2006. *Constructions at work: the nature of generalization in language*, Oxford: Oxford University Press.

Görlach, M., 1991. *Introduction to Early Modern English*, Cambridge: Cambridge University Press.

Greenberg, J., 1963. Some universals of grammar with particular reference to the order of meaningful elements. In J.H. Greenberg (ed.) *Universals of language*. Cambridge: MIT Press, pp. 73–113.

1966. *Language universals: with special reference to feature hierarchies*, The Hague: Mouton.

1970. *The languges of Africa*, Bloomington, IN: Indiana University Press.

1978a. Diachrony, synchrony and language universals. In J.H. Greenberg, C.A. Ferguson, and E.A. Moravcsik (eds.) *Universals of human language,* Vol. 1 *Method and theory*. Stanford: Stanford University Press, pp. 61–92.

1978b. How do languages acquire gender markers? In J.H. Greenberg, C.A. Ferguson, and E.A. Moravcsik (eds.) *Universals of human language*, Vol. 3. Stanford: Stanford University Press, pp. 47–82.

1987. *Language in the Americas*, Stanford: Stanford University Press.

Guion, S.G., 1998. The role of perception in the sound change of velar palatalization. *Phonetica*, 55, pp. 18–52.

Guy, G., 1980. Variation in the group and the individual: the case of final stop deletion. In W. Labov (ed.) *Locating language in time and space*, New York: Academic Press, 1–36.

Haiman, J., 1994. Ritualization and the development of language. In W. Pagliuca (ed.) *Perspectives on grammaticalization*, Amsterdam: John Benjamins, pp. 3–28.

Hajek, J., 1997. *Universals of sound change in nasalization*, Oxford and Boston: Blackwell.

Hale, K., 1973. Deep-surface canonical disparities in relation to analogy and change: an Australian example. In T. Sebeok (ed.) *Current trends in linguistics, 11: diachronic, areal and typological linguistics*, The Hague: Mouton, pp. 401–458.

Halle, M., 1962. Phonology in generative grammar. *Word*, 18, pp. 54–72.

Harlow, R., 2007. *Māori: a linguistic introduction*, Cambridge: Cambridge University Press.

Harris, A.C. and Campbell, L., 1995. *Historical syntax in cross-linguistic perspective*, Cambridge: Cambridge University Press.

Hawkins, J.A., 1979. Implicational universals as predictors of word order change. *Language*, 55(3), pp. 618–648.

2004. *Efficiency and complexity in grammars*, Oxford: Oxford University Press.

Hay, J., 2001. Lexical frequency in morphology: is everything relative? *Linguistics*, 39(6), pp. 1041–1070.

Hayes, L., 1992. Vietic and Viet-Muong: a new subgrouping in Mon-Khmer. *Mon Khmer Studies*, 21, pp. 211–228.

Heine, B., Claudi, U., and Hünnemeyer, F., 1991a. From cognition to grammar: evidence from African languages. In E. Traugott and B. Heine (eds.) *Approaches to grammaticalization*, Amsterdam and Philadelphia: John Benjamins, pp. 149–187.

Heine, B., Claudi, U., and Hünnemeyer, F., 1991b. *Grammaticalization: a conceptual framework*, Chicago: University of Chicago Press.

Heine, B. and Kuteva, T., 2002. *World lexicon of grammaticalization*, Cambridge: Cambridge University Press.

2005. *Language contact and grammatical change*, Cambridge: Cambridge University Press.

2008. Constraints on contact-induced linguistic change. *Journal of Language Contact*, 2(Thema 2), pp. 57–90.

Heine, B. and Reh, M., 1984. *Grammaticalization and reanalysis in African languages*, Hamburg: Helmut Buske Verlag.

Heine, B. and Song, K.-A., 2011. On the grammaticalization of personal pronouns. *Journal of Linguistics*, 47(3), pp. 587–630.

Henderson, J., 1996. *Phonology and grammar of Yele, Papua New Guinea*, Canberra: Australian National University.

Hock, H.H., 1986. *Principle of historical linguistics*, Berlin: Mouton de Gruyter.

2003. Analogical change. In B.D. Joseph and R.D. Janda (eds.) *The handbook of historical linguistics*, Oxford: Oxford University Press, pp. 441–460.

Hockett, C.F., 1958. *A course in modern linguistics*, New York: MacMillan.

Hoffman, C., 1963. *A grammar of the Margi language*, London: Oxford University Press.

Holland, J.H., 1995. *Hidden order: how adaptation builds complexity*, Cambridge, MA: Perseus Books.

Honeybone, P., 2001. Lenition inhibition in Liverpool English. *English Language and Linguistics*, 5(2), pp. 213–249.

Hopper, P.J., 1973. Glottalized and murmured occlusives in Indo-European. *Glossa*, 7(2), pp. 141–166.

1987. Emergent grammar. *Berkeley Linguistics Society*, 13, pp. 139–157.

1991. On some principles of grammaticization. In E.C. Traugott and B. Heine (eds.) *Approaches to grammaticalization*, Vol. 1. Amsterdam: John Benjamins, pp. 17–35.

1994. Phonogenesis. In W. Pagliuca (ed.) *Perspectives on grammaticalization*, Amsterdam: John Benjamins, pp. 29–45.

Hopper, P.J. and Traugott, E., 1993. *Grammaticalization*, 1st edition, Cambridge: Cambridge University Press.

Huback, A.P., 2011. Irregular plurals in Brazilian Portuguese: an exemplar model approach. *Language variation and change*, 23(2), pp. 245–256.

Hume, E., 2004. The indeterminacy/attestation model of metathesis. *Language*, 80(2), pp. 203–237.

Hyman, L., 1975. *Phonology: theory and analysis*, New York: Holt, Rinehart and Winston.

    1977. On the nature of linguistic stress. In L.M. Hyman (ed.) *Studies in stress and accent*. Southern California Occasional Papers in Linguistics, Los Angeles: University of Southern California, pp. 37–82.

    2007. Universals of tone rules: 30 years later. In T. Riad and C. Gussenhoven (eds.) *Tones and tunes: studies in word and sentence prosody*, Berlin: Mouton de Gruyter, pp. 1–34.

    2011. Tone: Is it different? In J. Goldsmith, J. Riggle, and A.C.L. Yu (eds.) *The handbook of phonological theory*, Oxford: Blackwell Publishers, pp. 197–239.

Hyman, L. and Moxley, J., 1996. The morpheme in phonological change: velar palatalization in Bantu. *Diachronica*, 13, pp. 259–282.

Hyman, L. and Tadadjeu, M., 1976. Floating tones in Mbam-Nkam. In L.M. Hyman (ed.) *Studies in Bantu tonology*, Southern California Occasional Papers in Linguistics, Los Angeles: University of Southern California, pp. 57–111.

Israel, M., 1996. The way constructions grow. In A.E. Goldberg (ed.) *Conceptual structure, discourse and language*, Stanford: CSLI Publications, pp. 217–230.

Jakobson, R., 1939. Signe zéro. In *Roman Jakobson, Selected Writings*, The Hague: Mouton, pp. 211–219.

    1942. *Child language, aphasia, and language universals*, The Hague: Mouton.

Jespersen, O., 1942. *A modern English grammar on historical principles, Part VI: Morphology*, London: George Allen and Unwin.

Jones, S.W., 1788. Third anniversary discourse, on the Hindus. *Asiatic Researches*, 1(422).

Kaiser, M. and Shevoroshkin, V., 1988. Nostratic. *Annual Review of Anthropology*, 17, pp. 309–329.

Keating, P., Cho, T., Fougeron, C., and Hsu, C.-S., 2003. Domain-initial articulatory strengthening in four languages. In J. Local, R. Ogden, and R. Temple (eds.) *Phonetic interpretation*, Papers in Laboratory Phonology 6, Cambridge: Cambridge University Press, pp. 143–161.

Keller, R., 1994. *On language change: the invisible hand in language*, London and New York: Routledge.

Kenstowicz, M., 2006. Tone loans: the adaptation of English loans into Yoruba. In John Mugane (ed.) *Selected proceedings of the 35th Annual Conference on African Linguistics*, Somerville, MA: Cascadila Proceedings Project, pp. 136–146.

Kent, R., 1945. *The sounds of Latin*, Baltimore, MD: The Linguistic Society of America.

Krishnamurti, B., 2003. *The Dravidian languages*, Cambridge: Cambridge University Press.

Kuryłowicz, J., 1947. La nature des procès dits analogiques. *Acta Linguistica*, 5, pp. 17–34.

Labov, W., 1972. *Sociolinguistic patterns*, Philadelphia: University of Pennsylvania Press.

1981. Resolving the neogrammarian controversy. *Language*, 57, pp. 267–308.

1982. Building on empirical foundations. In W.P. Lehmann and Y. Malkiel (eds.) *Perspective on historical linguistics*, Amsterdam: John Benjamins, pp. 17–92.

1994. *Principles of linguistic change,* Vol. 1 *Internal factors*, Oxford: Basil Blackwell.

2001. *Principles of linguistic change,* Vol. 2 *Social factors*, Oxford: Blackwell Publishers.

2010. *Principles of linguistic change: cognitive and cultural factors*, Chichester: Wiley-Blackwell.

Labov, W., Ash, S., and Boberg, C., 2006. *The atlas of North American English*, Berlin: Mouton de Gruyter.

Lakoff, R., 1972. Another look at drift. In R. Stockwell and R.S.K. Macaulay (eds.) *Linguistic change and generative theory*, Bloomington: Indiana University Press, pp. 172–198.

Lancelot, C. and Arnould, A., 1660. *Grammaire générale et raisonnée*, Paris: Pierre le Petit.

Langacker, R., 1987. *Foundations of cognitive grammar*, Stanford: Stanford University Press.

Lehmann, C., 1982. *Thoughts on grammaticalization: a programmatic sketch*, Cologne: Universität zu Köln, Institut für Sprachwissenschaft.

Lehmann, W., 1952. *Proto-Indo-European phonology*, Austin: University of Texas Press and Linguistic Society of America.

1973. A structural principle of language and its implications. *Language*, 49, pp. 47–66.

Lehmann, W.P., 1992. *Historical linguistics: an introduction*, 3rd edition, London and New York: Routledge.

Li, C.N. and Thompson, S.A., 1981. *Mandarin Chinese: a functional reference grammar*, Los Angeles: University of California Press.

Lichtenberk, F., 1991. On the gradualness of grammaticalization. In E.C. Traugott and B. Heine (eds.) *Approaches to grammaticalization*, Vol. 1, Amsterdam: John Benjamins, pp. 37–80.

Lightfoot, D., 1979. *Principles of diachronic syntax*, Cambridge: Cambridge University Press.

Liljencrants, J. and Lindblom, B., 1972. Numerical simulation of vowel quality systems: the role of perceptual contrast. *Language*, 48, pp. 839–862.

Lindblom, B., MacNeilage, P., and Studdert-Kennedy, M., 1984. Self-organizing processes and the explanation of phonological universals. In B. Butterworth, B. Comrie, and Ö. Dahl (eds.) *Explanations for language universals*, New York: Mouton, pp. 181–203.

Lord, C., 1976. Evidence for syntactic reanalysis: from verb to complementizer in Kwa. In S.B. Steever, C.A. Walker, and S.S. Mufwene (eds.) *Papers from the parasession on diachronic syntax*, Chicago: Chicago Linguistics Society, pp. 179–191.

1993. *Historical change in serial verb constructions*, Amsterdam and Philadelphia: John Benjamins.

MacWhinney, B., 1978. *The acquisition of morphophonology*, Monographs of the Society for Research in Child Development, 174, Vol. 43, nos. 1–2, Chicago: The University of Chicago Press.

Maddieson, I., 1984. *Patterns of sounds. With a chapter contributed by Sandra Ferrari Disner*, Cambridge: Cambridge University Press.

Mańczak, W., 1958. Tendances générales des changements analogiques. *Lingua*, 7, pp. 298–325, 387–420.

Marchese, L., 1986. *Tense/aspect and the development of auxiliaries in Kru languages*, Arlington, TX: Summer Institute of Linguistics.

Martinet, A., 1952. Function, structure and sound change. *Word*, 8, pp. 1–32.

Mattoso Camara, J., Jr., 1972. *The Portuguese language*, Chicago: University of Chicago Press.

McWhorter, J.H., 1998. Identifying the creole prototype: vindicating a typological class. *Language*, 74(4), pp. 788–818.

——— 2001. The world's simplest grammars are creole grammars. *Linguistic Typology*, 5 (2/3), pp. 125–166.

Meillet, P., 1912. L'évolution des formes grammaticales. *Scientia (Rivista di Scienza)*, 6 (vol.12), pp.130–148.

Menéndez-Pidal, R., 1968. *Manual de gramática histórica española*, Madrid: Espasa-Calpe.

Moore, S. and Knott, T.A., 1968. *The elements of Old English*, 10th edition, Ann Arbor: The George Wahr Publishing Co.

Moore, S. and Marckwardt, A.H., 1951. *Historical outlines of English sounds and inflections*, Ann Arbor: George Wahr Publishing Co.

Morin, Y.-C. and Kaye, J.D., 1982. The syntactic bases for French liaison. *Journal of Linguistics*, 18, pp. 291–330.

Mossé, F., 1952. *A handbook of Middle English. Translated by James A. Walker*, Baltimore, MD: The Johns Hopkins Press.

Mowrey, R. and Pagliuca, W., 1995. The reductive character of articulatory evolution. *Rivista di Linguistica*, 7(1), pp. 37–124.

Mühlhäusler, P., 1986. *Pidgin and creole linguistics*, Oxford and New York: Basil Blackwell.

Murray, R.W., 1982. Consonant developments in Pali. *Folia linguistica historica*, 3, pp.163–184.

Murray, R.W. and Vennemann, T., 1983. Sound change and syllable structure in Germanic phonology. *Language*, 59(3), pp. 514–528.

Neu, H., 1980. Ranking of constraints on /t,d/ deletion in American English: a statistical analysis. In W. Labov (ed.) *Locating language in time and space*, New York: Academic Press, pp. 37–54.

Newman, P., 1974. *The Kanakuru language*, Leeds: Institute of Modern English Studies, University of Leeds in association with The West African Linguistic Society.

——— 2000. *The Hausa language: an encyclopedic reference grammar*, New Haven and London: Yale University Press.

Noël, D., 2007. Diachronic construction grammar and grammaticalization theory. *Functions of Language*, 14(2), pp. 177–202.

Nyrop, K.R., 1914. *Grammaire historique de la langue française*, Copenhagen.

Ogura, M., Wang, W.S.-Y., and Cavalli-Sforza, L.L., 1991. The development of Middle English *i* in England: a study in dynamic dialectology. In P. Eckert (ed.) *New ways of analyzing sound change*, New York: Academic Press, pp. 63–106.

Ohala, J.J., 2003. Phonetics and historical phonology. In B. Joseph and R. Janda (eds.) *Handbook of historical linguistics*, Oxford: Blackwell Publishers, pp. 669–686.

O Siadhail, M., 1980. *Learning Irish*, Dublin: Dublin Institute for Advanced Studies.

Otsuka, Y., 2011. Neither accusative nor ergative: an alternative analysis of case in Eastern Polynesian. In C. Moyse-Faurie and J. Sabel (eds.) *Topics in Oceanic morphosyntax*, Berlin: Mouton de Gruyter, pp. 289–318.

Page, B.R., 1999. The Germanic Verscharfung and prosodic change. *Diachronica*, 16(2), pp. 297–334.

Patterson, J.L., 1992. *The development of sociolinguistic phonological variation patterns for (ing) in young children*, Dissertation, University of New Mexico.

Pawley, A. and Hodgetts Syder, F., 1983. Two puzzles for linguistic theory: nativelike selection and nativelike fluency. In J.C. Richards and R.W. Schmidt (eds.) *Language and communication*, London: Longmans, pp. 191–226.

Peirce, C.S., 1965. *Collected papers, ed. by Charles Hartshorn and Paul Weiss*, Cambridge, MA: Harvard University Press, Belknap.

Penny, R., 2002. *A history of the Spanish language*, 2nd edition, Cambridge: Cambridge University Press.

Perkins, R.D., 1989. Statistical techniques for determining language sample size. *Studies in Language*, 13(2), pp. 293–315.

Petré, P. and Cuyckens, H., 2009. Constructional change in Old and Middle English copular constructions and its impact on the lexicon. *Folia linguistica historica*, 30, pp. 311–365.

Phillips, B.S., 2006. *Word frequency and lexical diffusion*, New York: Palgrave.

Plank, F., 1984. The modals story retold. *Studies in Language*, 8(3), pp. 305–364.

Poplack, S., 2011. Grammaticalization and linguistic variation. In H. Narrog and B. Heine (eds.) *The Oxford handbook of grammaticalization*, Oxford: Oxford University Press, pp. 209–224.

Poplack, S. and Levey, S., 2010. Contact-induced grammatical change: a cautionary tale. In P. Auer and J.E. Schmidt (eds.) *Language and space: an international handbook of linguistic variation*. Berlin: Mouton de Gruyter, pp. 391–419.

Poplack, S., Sankoff, D., and Miller, C., 1988. The social correlates and linguistic processes of lexical borrowing and assimilation. *Linguistics*, 26, pp. 47–104.

Poppe, N.N., 1960. *Buriat grammar*, The Hague: Mouton.

Rand, M.K., Hikosaka, O., Miyachi, S., Lu, X., and Miyashita, K., 1998. Characteristics of a long-term procedural skill in the monkey. *Experimental Brain Research*, 118, pp. 293–297.

Raymond, W.D. and Brown, E.L., 2012. Are effects of word frequency effects of context of use? An analysis of initial fricative reduction in Spanish. In S.Th. Gries and D.S. Divjak (eds.) *Frequency effects in language*, Vol. 2 *Learning and processing*, Berlin: Mouton de Gruyter, pp. 35–52.

Recasens, D., 1999. Lingual coarticulation. In W.J. Hardcastle and N. Hewlett (eds.) *Coarticulation: theory, data and techniques*, Cambridge: Cambridge University Press, pp. 80–104.

Reich, D. et al., 2012. Reconstructing Native American population history. *Nature*, 488, pp. 370–374.

Renfrew, C., 1991. Before Babel: speculations on the origins of linguistic diversity. *Cambridge Archaeological Journal*, 1(1), pp. 3–23.

Rhodes, B.J., Bullock, D., Verwey, W.B., Averbeck, B.B., and Page, M.P.A., 2004. Learning and production of movement sequences: behavioral, neurophysiological, and modeling perspectives. *Human Movement Science*, 23, pp. 699–746.

Riddle, E.M., 1985. A historical perspective on the productivity of the suffixes *-ness* and *-ity*. In J. Fisiak (ed.) *Historical semantics, historical word-formation*, Trends in Linguistics, Studies and Monographs, The Hague: Mouton, pp. 435–461.

Robert, S., 2008. Words and their meanings. In M. Vanhove (ed.) *From polysemy to semantic change*, Studies in Language Companion Series, Amsterdam and Philadelphia: John Benjamins, pp. 55–92.

Roberts, I. and Roussou, A., 2003. *Syntactic change: a minimalist approach to grammaticalization*, Cambridge: Cambridge University Press.

Roberts, J., 1997. Acquisition of variable rules: a study of (t/d) deletion in preschool children. *Journal of Child Language*, 24, pp. 351–372.

Romaine, S., 1988. *Pidgin and creole languages*, London: Longman Linguistic Library.
        1995. The grammaticalization of irrealis in Tok Pisin. In J. Bybee and S. Fleischmann (eds.) *Modality in grammar and discourse*, Amsterdam: John Benjamins, pp. 389–427.

Rosch, E. and Mervis, C., 1975. Family resemblances: studies in the internal structure of categories. *Cognitive Psychology*, 8, pp. 382–439.

Rudes, B.A., 1980. On the nature of verbal suppletion. *Linguistics*, 18(7/8), pp. 665–676.

Ruhlen, M., 1978. Nasal vowels. In J.H. Greenberg, C.A. Ferguson, and E.A. Moravcsik (eds.) *Universals of human language,* Vol. 2 *Phonology*, Stanford: Stanford University Press, pp. 203–241.

Salmons, J.C. and Joseph, B.D., 1998. *Nostratic: sifting the evidence*, Amsterdam and Philadelphia: John Benjamins.

Samarin, W., 1967. *A grammar of Sango*, The Hague: Mouton.

Sankoff, G., 2002. Linguistic outcomes of language contact. In J.K. Chambers, P. Trudgill, and N. Shilling-Estes (eds.) *The handbook of language variation and change*, Oxford: Blackwell Publishers, pp. 638–668.

Sapir, E., 1921. *Language: an introduction to the study of speech*, New York: Harcourt, Brace.

Schachter, P. and Fromkin, V., 1968. A phonology of Akan: Akuapem, Asante and Fante. *UCLA Working Papers in Phonetics*, 9.

Schwenter, S.A. and Torres Cacoullos, R., 2008. Defaults and indeterminacy in temporal grammaticalization: the 'perfect' road to perfective. *Language Variation and Change*, 20(1), pp. 1–39.

Ségéral, P. and Scheer, T., 2008. Positional factors in lenition and fortition. In J.B. de Carvalho, T. Scheer, and P. Ségéral (eds.) *Lenition and fortition*, Studies in Generative Grammar, Berlin and New York: Mouton de Gruyter, pp. 131–172.

Seoane, E., 2006. Information structure and word order change: the passive as an information-rearranging strategy in the history of English. In A. van Kemenade and B. Los (eds.) *The handbook of the history of English*, Oxford: Basil Blackwell, pp. 360–391.

Silva-Corvalán, C., 2008. The limits of convergence in contact. *Journal of Language Contact*, 2(Thema 2), pp. 213–224.

Slobin, D.I., 1997. The origins of grammaticizable notions: beyond the individual mind. In D.I. Slobin (ed.) *The cross-linguistic study of language acquisition*, Mahwah, NJ: Lawrence Erlbaum, pp. 1–39.

Smith, K.A. and Nordquist, D., 2012. A critical and historical investigation into semantic prosody. *Journal of Historical Pragmatics*, 13(2), pp. 291–312.

Smoczynska, M., 1985. The acquisition of Polish. In D. Slobin (ed.) *Crosslinguistic study of language acquisition*, Hillsdale, NJ: Erlbaum, pp. 595–686.

Spagnolo, L.M., 1933. *Bari grammar*, Verona: Missioni Africane.

Stahlke, H., 1970. Serial verbs. *Studies in African Languages*, 1(1), pp. 60–99.

Stebbins, J.R., 2010. *Usage frequency and articulatory reduction in Vietnamese tonogenesis*, Dissertation, University of Colorado.

Stubbs, M., 2002. *Words and phrases: corpus studies of lexical semantics*, Oxford: Blackwell Publishers.

Sturtevant, E.H., 1947. *An introduction to linguistic science*, New Haven: Yale University Press.

Suwilai Premsritat, 2004. Register complex and tonogenesis in Khmu dialects. *Mon Khmer Studies*, 34, pp. 1–17.

Svorou, S., 1994. *The grammar of space*, Amsterdam: John Benjamins.

Tao, L., 2006. Classifier loss and frozen tone in spoken Beijing Mandarin: the yi+ge phono-syntactic conspiracy. *Linguistics*, 44(1), pp. 91–133.

Terrell, T., 1977. Constraints on the aspiration and deletion of final /s/ in Cuban and Puerto Rican Spanish. *The Bilingual Review*, 4, pp. 35–51.

Thomason, S.G., 2001. *Language contact: an introduction*, Washington, DC: Georgetown University Press.

Thomason, S.G. and Kaufman, T., 1988. *Language contact, creolization, and genetic linguistics*, Berkeley and Los Angeles: University of California Press.

Thurgood, G., 2002. Vietnamese and tonogenesis: revising the model and the analysis. *Diachronica*, 19(2), pp. 333–363.

   2007. Tonogenesis revisited: revising the model and the analysis. In J.G. Harris, S. Burusphat, and J.E. Harris (eds.) *Studies in Tai and southeast Asian linguistics*, Bangkok: Ek Phim Thai, pp. 263–291.

Thurneysen, R., 1956. *A grammar of Old Irish*, trans. D.A. Binchy and O. Bergin, Dublin: The Dublin Institute for Advanced Studies.

Tiersma, P., 1982. Local and general markedness. *Language*, 58, pp. 832–849.

Timberlake, A., 1978. Uniform and alternating environments in phonological change. *Folia Slavica*, 2, pp. 312–328.

Torres Cacoullos, R., 2000. *Grammaticization, synchronic variation, and language contact: a study of Spanish progressive -ndo constructions*, Amsterdam and Philadelphia: John Benjamins.

   2001. From lexical to grammatical to social meaning. *Language in Society*, 30, pp. 443–478.

Tranel, B., 1981. *Concreteness in generative phonology: evidence from French*, Berkeley: University of California Press.

Trask, R.L., 1995. *Historical linguistics*, London: Arnold Van Bergem.

Traugott, E.C., 1972. *A history of English syntax*, New York: Holt, Rinehart and Winston.

1989. On the rise of epistemic meaning: an example of subjectification in semantic change. *Language*, 65, pp.31–55.

Traugott, E.C. and Dasher, R.B., 2002. *Regularity in semantic change*, Cambridge: Cambridge University Press.

Travis, C.E. and Silveira, A., 2009. The role of frequency in first-person plural variation in Brazilian Portuguese: *nós* vs. *a gente*. *Studies in Hispanic and Lusophone Linguistics*, 2(2), pp.347–376.

Trousdale, G., 2008. Words and constructions in grammaticalization: the end of the English impersonal construction. In Susan M. Fitzmaurice and Donka Minkova (eds.) *Studies in the History of the English Language*, Berlin and New York: Mouton de Gruyter, pp. 301–326.

Trudgill, P. and Hannah, J., 1994. *International English: a guide to the varieties of standard English*, New York and London: Edward Arnold.

Underhill, R., 1976. *Turkish grammar*, Cambridge: Cambridge University Press.

Vafaeian, G., 2010. *Breaking paradigms: a typological study of nominal and adjectival suppletion*, Stockholm: University of Stockholm.

Vennemann, T., 1972. Rule inversion. *Lingua*, 29, pp. 209–242.

1975. An explanation of drift. In C.N. Li (ed.) *Word order and word order change*, Austin: University of Texas Press, pp. 269–305.

1988. *Preference laws for syllable structure and the explanation of sound change*, Berlin: Mouton de Gruyter.

Veselinova, L., 2003. *Suppletion in verb paradigms: bits and pieces of a puzzle*, Stockholm: Stockholm University.

Watkins, C., 1962. *Indo-European origins of the Celtic verb I: the sigmatic aorist*, Dublin: The Dublin Institute for Advanced Studies.

Weinreich, U., 1968. *Languages in contact: findings and problems*, The Hague: Mouton.

Welmers, W.E., 1973. *African language structures*, Berkeley and Los Angeles: University of California Press.

Wiedenhof, J., 1995. *Meaning and syntax in spoken Mandarin*, Leiden: Cnws Publications.

Wilbur, T.H., 1977. Introduction. In T.H. Wilbur (ed.) *The Lautgesetz-controversy: a documentation (1885–86)*, Amsterdam: John Benjamins, pp. 9–91.

Wilson, D.V., 2009. From 'remaining' to 'becoming' in Spanish: the role of prefabs in the development of the construction *quedar(se)* + ADJECTIVE. In R. Corrigan, E. Moravcsik, H. Ouali, and K. Wheatley (eds.) *Formulaic language*, Typological studies in language, Amsterdam: John Benjamins, pp. 273–295.

Zalizniak, A.A., Bulakh, M., Ganenkov, D., Gruntov, I., Maisak, T., and, Maxim, R., 2012. The catalog of semantic shifts as a database for lexical semantic typology. *Linguistics*, 50(3), pp. 633–669.

Zendejas, E.H., 1995. *Palabras, estratos y representaciones: temas de fonología léxica en zoque*, Mexico City: Colegio de Mexico.

Language Index

Language name is followed in parentheses by the name of the region where it is spoken.

Languages

Language families, subgroupings, and proto-languages

Subject index